Providence
Lost

Providence
Lost

Genevieve Lloyd

Harvard University Press
Cambridge, Massachusetts
London, England · 2008

Credits appear on the continuation of the copyright page, p. 371.

Library of Congress Cataloging-in-Publication Data
Lloyd, Genevieve.
   Providence lost / Genevieve Lloyd.
      p.   cm.
   Includes bibliographical references and index.
   ISBN 978-0-674-03153-1 (alk. paper)
   1. Providence and government of God.   I. Title.
   BD541.L56 2008
   214'.8—dc22   2008023693

Contents

Introduction   *1*

1   Euripides, Philosopher of the Stage   *14*

2   The World of Men and Gods   *57*

3   Agreeing with Nature: Fate and
Providence in Stoic Ethics   *90*

4   Augustine: Divine Justice and
the "Ordering" of Evil   *129*

5   The Philosopher and the Princess: Descartes
and the Philosophical Life   *160*

6   Living with Necessity: Spinoza and
the Philosophical Life   *192*

7   Designer Worlds   *235*

8   Providence as Progress   *279*

9   Providence Lost   *302*

Notes   *333*

Acknowledgments   *345*

Further Reading   *347*

Index   *361*

Providence
Lost

Introduction

The history of providence belongs in the history of the interactions and the crossovers between philosophy and religion in
Western thought. The rationale for this book is the belief that the
largely neglected history of providence can help us understand
much that can be puzzling in our contemporary ways of thinking
about freedom, necessity, and responsibility. Providence may now
be largely "lost" from our secular consciousness; but it continues
to exert an influence on our thought and on our lives. My intention is not to argue for a revival of providence—either by reassert-
ing the importance of religion or by attempting to develop an alternative secular version of providence. The guiding conviction
informing the book is simply that a better understanding of this
largely forgotten strand in the history of Western thought can
throw some light on the functioning—and increasingly the mal-
functioning—of familiar ideas of free will, autonomy, and responsibility that we now so readily take as defining our modernity.

At the heart of the book is a study of the contrasts between
two rival early modern approaches to the nature of human freedom—Descartes's account of the will as the locus of freedom,
and Spinoza's rival treatment of freedom as involving the capacity
to shape a life in accordance with the recognition of necessity.
Central to those differing versions of freedom are very different
stances toward the idea of providence. To understand those differences, and how they bear on our contemporary ways of think-

ing, we need to understand also the continuities that connect them with the earlier history of providence.

It is undeniable that early modern philosophy represented in many ways a radical break with the past. This is true not least of the revaluations the philosophers of the Enlightenment offered of the intellectual and political authority of religion. The continuities that nonetheless tied Enlightenment philosophy closely to ancient thought, however, have received rather less consideration in contemporary commentary. Our distant cultural and intellectual origins can seem strange and alien to "us now." Yet Bernard Williams has suggested in his study of ancient Greek ethics and culture, *Shame and Necessity,* that we are now in an ethical condition that lies not only beyond Christianity, but also beyond its Kantian and Hegelian legacies. Williams has argued that in important ways—now that the intervening assumptions of modernity are falling away—we can see some striking affinities between the mentality of the ancient Greeks and our own. "We are in our ethical situation," he says, "more like human beings in antiquity than any Western people have been in the meantime."[1]

This book explores some of the ramifications of those intervening assumptions of modernity that we have inherited—often in distorted forms—from the philosophy of the Enlightenment. The idea of individual autonomy—which is now central to our understanding of human freedom and responsibility—owes much to Descartes's treatment of the human will as akin to—though greatly more limited than—the will of God. The idea of a meaningful balance between good and evil—and between competing goods or values—owes much to Leibniz's idea of a harmony inherent in the rational structure of the world. Our modern idea of progress has been strongly influenced by Kantian and Hegelian ideas of human history as purposive. I will try to show that these familiar ideas were, in their context in early modern philosophy, conceptually dependent on ideas of providence that have now largely receded—both from professional philosophy and from our "ordinary" consciousness.

By bringing the missing idea of providence into focus, we can hope to see more clearly some of the tensions in the functioning of those more familiar ideas. We can also regain some understanding of the lost continuities that tied early modern philosophy to its ancient sources. Bernard Williams was not directly concerned with the history of providence. But it is in the spirit of his call for a reconnection with the thought of the ancient Greeks that this book explores the ways in which the history of the idea of providence—in its strange connections with ancient ideas of fate and necessity, as well as ideas of purpose and design—can illuminate some of what is otherwise confusing in our contemporary "ethical situation."

The book's subject matter highlights the continuities between the writings of Enlightenment philosophers and older philosophical writing; and it highlights also the crossovers between philosophy and religion in both ancient and early modern philosophy. I have also attempted in the writing of it to give prominence, where appropriate, to another set of neglected continuities and crossovers—between philosophical writing and literature. Ideas of providence have strong emotional and imaginative force—whether in their evocation of a loving God or through the wonder elicited by ancient visions of a cosmos structured in accordance with necessary order. The intellectual content of providence has a rich history; but to fully understand it we must take into account its constant interplay with imagination and emotion.

I have given the imaginative and emotional dimensions of ideas of providence a central place in the structure and the writing strategies of this book. I have tried, wherever possible, to engage seriously with the play of imagination, and with the workings of emotion, in the philosophical writings addressed. To understand providence as it operates in specific texts is to enter into particular ways in which human minds have tried to accommodate themselves to their presence in the world—and to the thought of their absence from it. This engagement involves seeing more in the conceptual shifts with regard to providence than a succession of competing definitions of a unitary idea. Often, it is not a matter of adjudicating the adequacy of competing theories of providence. For providence changes according to the clusters it forms at different times with other concepts—freedom and necessity; chance and contingency; ideas of good and evil, of justice and injustice, of responsibility, deserts, and punishment. As those clusters shift and re-form, the emotional resonances of providence also change. Understanding the history of providence thus involves engaging with the emotions the idea evokes, and the writing strategies that philosophers have used to engage and educate those emotions. It involves taking seriously the literary dimensions of philosophical writing.

It is common for contemporary philosophers to resist talk of such rapprochements between reason, emotion, and imagination. It was not always thus. The philosophers discussed in this book not only offered theories about emotion; they also engaged directly with the emotional dimensions of thought. They thought emotionally—not in the sense that they allowed subjective feelings to dominate their reasoning processes, but in that they took seriously the affective dimensions of reason. Nor were they concerned, as contemporary philosophers often are, to make any sharp distinction between the "theoretical" and the "practical" or "rhetorical" aspects of their writing. In articulating ideas of the good life, they wrote in ways designed to engage the imagination and emotions, no less than the intellects, of their readers. It is particularly appropriate, then, that in studying them we try to engage with those literary dimensions of their writing, no less than with its argumentative content.

In taking into account these emotional and imaginative aspects of the crossovers between philosophy and religion, the approach to intellectual history in this book has some affinities with Charles Taylor's rich study of the emergence of modern "secularity" in *A Secular Age*. The secular, in the sense in which Taylor addresses it, is not to be understood at the level of religious belief or disbelief. It is rather to be understood through exploring a set of "new conditions of belief." It consists, he says, in "a new shape to the experience which prompts to and is defined by belief; in a new context in which all search and questioning about the moral and spiritual must proceed."[2] There is a distinction here between the intellectual content of beliefs and an imagined background against which both religious belief and unbelief unfold. Taylor elucidates this frame of secularity by drawing on the idea of a "social imaginary."[3] Our modern social imaginary in his sense is the way we collectively imagine the societies we inhabit and sustain. A social imaginary here contrasts with an explicit intellectual scheme or set of theories, although it may be penetrated by, and eventually transformed under the impact of, new theories.

Taylor's narrative of the emergence of the modern "secular" age unfolds as a succession of changing social imaginaries. He describes the transition from an "enchanted" view of the world—as a cosmos rich in correspondences and similitudes—to the idea of an ordered universe, susceptible of scientific explanation; and associated transitions in which our modern public sphere, for example, is imagined as a common space of shared communication across differences. His narrative emphasizes the role of imagination in the transformation of a religious consciousness, centered on transcendence, into a humanism centered on immanence. But these processes, as he shows, cannot be understood as a simple process of the "subtraction" of inadequate beliefs under the impact of more sophisticated theories. The processes can involve changes, for example, in the ways in which time is collectively imagined. They can also involve shifts in emotional resonances—as in the transition from an imagined world full of unpredictable, demonic forces to one in which the self is "buffered" by a sense of confidence in its own powers of control.

There are points of connection between Taylor's illuminating narrative of the emergence of the "secular age" and my study of changing ideas of providence. I argue that the formation of the controlling, autonomous self of modernity—which we now so readily take for granted—was conceptually dependent on changing ideas of providence. Put in Taylor's terms, my thesis is that the "loss" of providence from our contemporary social imaginary brings with it a new precariousness in the "buffered" self of modernity.

Providence Lost tracks a succession of shifts in the history of ideas of providence—from the thought of the ancient Greeks, through Augustine, to the crucial divide between Cartesian and Spinozist approaches to freedom; then on through eighteenth-century philosophy to the loss of providence in contemporary thought patterns. Where better to start that story than with Euripides—the ancient master of dramatic representation of the conflict-ridden intersections of passions, piety, and philosophy? I begin with a study of Euripides against the background of Heraclitus's famous doctrine of a cosmic justice in the interplay and transformation of opposites. I focus on the philosophical dimensions of the dramas—especially Euripides' anticipation of later Stoic ideas of a single moral universe of gods and men.

The metaphor of the "cosmic city" is an important element in early ideas of providence. But other themes also set the scene for the ethical force that will come to be carried by ideas of providence. I address Euripides' treatment of the intersections of necessity and contingency, and of death and life, in *Alcestis;* the moral dilemmas of acting under conditions of uncertainty, in *Helen, Electra,* and *Orestes;* the ambivalences of piety, and the transformation of emotions into their opposites, in the *Bacchae.*

There are intimations throughout Euripides' dramas of a sense of cosmic order that transcends the vagaries of the gods—an order to which they too must answer. It is an idea that finds fuller expression in later Stoic philosophy, where the old Heraclitean themes of the transformation of opposites are developed into more explicit ideas of the cosmic city as a unified world of gods and men. The Stoics drew also on related themes from other sources. In Chapter 2 I explore some of them: Plato's interweaving of design, chance, and necessity, in the remarkable tale of the origins of the world that is embedded in his *Timaeus;* and old mythological stories of the transformations of Zeus.

The Stoics take much further than Plato did the idea of the cosmos as not merely intelligible, but itself suffused with reason. In Stoic thought, purpose and necessity are even more closely connected than they were for Plato: Zeus comes to be identified both with the idea of a guiding intelligence and with the force of necessity. In the concluding sections of Chapter 2 I present the tensions in that Stoic version of providence, as brought out in Cicero's dialogue *On the Nature of the Gods.* Here Cicero has the ideas of an imagined Stoic ridiculed by an imagined Epicurean antagonist. For the Epicureans, human lives are governed neither by divine purpose nor by necessity. The Epicureans were concerned, no less than the Stoics, to affirm the independence of human beings from the whims and caprices of the gods. But whereas the Stoics grounded their accounts of responsibility by bringing gods and men together in a shared cosmic city, the Epicureans insisted that the gods were entirely removed from, and indifferent to, human affairs. That liberation from what the Epicureans saw as the constraints of a superstitious belief in the interventions of the gods was for them the key to human freedom and well-being.

Cicero presents the rival Stoic and Epicurean views of human responsibility with eloquence and humor. Later we will see some of the complexities of that debate reenacted in the seventeenth and eighteenth centuries, in the thought of Spinoza and Hume. Yet other strands in the early history of ideas of providence, however, must first be brought into the picture. In Chapter 3 I examine more closely some of the ways in which the Stoics were able to find ethical force in the understanding of necessity. Their ideal of detachment, and the associated ideal of living in agreement with necessity, can be difficult for us now to grasp. But Stoic ethical ideals, I try to show, did not involve a bleak endurance of what cannot be changed. The idea was rather to cultivate a joyful "appropriation" of the natures of things; and the content of that idea of appropriation was closely connected with ideas of providence. In the context of Stoic ideas of things as "appropriated" to the cosmos, Stoic "detachment" is realized in attaining a smooth flow of life. In examining them in works of Seneca, Epictetus, and Marcus Aurelius, I highlight the bearing of these ideals on Stoic detachment in the face of the ultimate necessity—death.

Chapter 4 is the final piece of stage setting for understanding the place of providence in early modern philosophical approaches to freedom, necessity, and responsibility. Here I turn to Augustine's role in establishing the connections between providence and emerging ideas of free will. Augustine represents a turning point in the history of ideas of providence. Here the preconditions fall into place for a close association between providence and ideas of a divine will, construed as radically opposed to necessity. Two things happen in the thought of Augustine that will prove crucial for later developments. First, there is a transition to the idea of the will as locus of freedom: Augustine sets the scene for Descartes's later modeling of human free will on divine transcendence of necessity. Second, providence comes to figure in the resolution of an increasingly explicit "problem" for religious believers: how to explain the existence of evil. Here the ancient idea of a cosmic justice, played out in the antagonism of opposites, takes a new twist: providence becomes the "right" ordering of evils by a divine will. Providence is invoked in reconciling divine freedom and justice with the suffering of innocent human beings. In this respect, Augustine sets the scene for Leibniz's later preoccupation with the role of God in the ordering of the "best of all possible worlds."

Chapters 5 and 6, on Descartes and Spinoza, are the core of the book. Here we see providence play a central role in the conceptual division between two ways of thinking about human freedom—Descartes's approach, centered on free will, and Spinoza's, centered on the rejection of the will in favor of the recognition and acceptance of necessity. It was to be Descartes's approach that prevailed; his treatment of the will had a profound and lasting influence on modern ways of thinking about freedom and necessity. As I will argue more fully at the end of the book, however, Spinoza's alternative can open up a rich alternative approach that has continuities with ancient Stoic thought—the idea of freedom as the shaping of necessity.

The alternative accounts of freedom offered by Descartes and Spinoza involve different approaches to the nature and operation of human passions. In offering rival philosophical accounts of the passions, they were also concerned to offer alternative "remedies" for their destructive power—alternative practical recommendations for dealing with the passions and for integrating what is positive about them into a well-lived life. The differences of Descartes and Spinoza in relation to providence are part of that broader practical agenda that connects both thinkers with older philosophical concerns over how to live and die well. Their rival theories of emotion and, more generally, about the relation between minds and bodies point forward to the more "theoretical" concerns of more recent philosophy. But it is no less true that both thinkers are continuing those older traditions of practical philosophy. To highlight those practical concerns which tie these seventeenth-century philosophers to their philosophical past, I have organized the discussion of their treatments of providence and the passions in Chapters 5 and 6 around some key aspects of their own lives that illuminate their philosophical differences.

Chapter 5 discusses Descartes's efforts to develop a remedy for the passions in the context of his moving correspondence with his friend Princess Elisabeth of Bohemia, who was at the time living in exile with her family at The Hague. My discussion centers on some of the unresolved problems that emerge in the course of Descartes's attempts to develop, with Elisabeth, a shared "method" for remedying the passions—problems that Elisabeth sees as arising from difficulties in Descartes's understanding of embodiment, especially in relation to the asymmetries of sexual difference. In Chapter 6 I explore Spinoza's very different approach to the remedy of the passions and related differences in his treatment of freedom as residing in the acceptance of necessity—an ideal that echoes some aspects of Stoic appropriation of necessity. By way of illustration, I discuss Spinoza's treatment of freedom in relation to his response to a crucial formative event in his own life—his expulsion from the Amsterdam synagogue, and his subsequent resolve to shape his life around the recognition of necessity. I also discuss Spinoza's rejection of prevailing ideas of providence—and more generally his treatment of the relations between the divine and the human—in the context of his exchange of letters with his friend the English scientist Henry Oldenburg.

Chapters 7 and 8 continue the narrative of ideas of providence through eighteenth-century philosophy. Chapter 7 focuses on Leibniz's treatment of providence as expressed in the exercise of a loving, all-powerful divine will, guided by infinite wisdom; on the critique of the "optimism" implicit in that idea, offered by Voltaire in *Candide;* and on Hume's rejection of "design" in the *Dialogues concerning Natural Religion.* As is often the case in the history of philosophy, the symbolic force of Spinoza's philosophy came to diverge considerably from what its author had in mind.

Leibniz, in restoring a creative role for divine will, was reacting against what he saw as the bleak godlessness associated with Spinozism. His own philosophy, in turn, was to be later simplified and satirized by Voltaire in his critique of the facile optimism associated with the claim that human beings live in the best of all possible worlds. Leibniz's version of providence, I argue, involves an ingenious synthesis of earlier ideas; but it is in the end a flawed synthesis—even if its nuances are not presented altogether fairly in Voltaire's caricature. The chapter concludes with a discussion of Hume's entertaining critique of ideas of design and providence in the *Dialogues concerning Natural Religion* in the context of his broader treatment of the rational basis of belief.

Chapter 8 completes my study of the transformations of providence in the history of Western thought. Here we see providence incorporated into the idea of progress. We see Kant, in his *Political Essays,* draw on Rousseau's imaginative tale of the development of the human species to offer a temporalized version of providence. Kant casts providence as the unfolding of Nature's purpose in human history. In the philosophy of Hegel, we see providence disappear even more completely into the grand unfolding of Nature into Absolute Spirit.

Throughout this narrative of shifts and transformations in ideas of providence, I try to show how providence has played in varied ways a central role in conceptual formations that continue to sustain and inform our emotional lives. Providence has now largely retreated from philosophical and political thought into the domain of theological reflection and popular religious belief. In my final chapter, "Providence Lost," I bring the preceding historical studies to bear on some of our contemporary attitudes toward freedom, necessity, and responsibility. Much of our thinking about these issues continues to be influenced by the powerful legacy of Descartes's doctrine of free will. But we have largely lost the frame of providence, which once made that Cartesian ideal of autonomy emotionally viable. I argue in conclusion that by reconnecting through Spinoza with largely forgotten ancient links between ideas of providence and necessity, we can see some of the limitations in our modern preoccupation with the idea of the autonomous human will. In closing, *Providence Lost* comes full circle back to Euripides, offering a reading of his late drama, *Iphigenia at Aulis,* highlighting the theme of acceptance of necessity, and relating it to contemporary challenges arising from living in conditions of uncertainty.

This book does not offer by any means a complete history of providence. In selecting authors and themes for discussion, I have emphasized points of connection between philosophy and religion, and between philosophy and literature. I have also tried to keep in view the contrasts between Descartes and Spinoza that form the structural core of the book, and their bearing on our own ways of thinking about freedom and necessity. Some selections have been guided also by a preference for close engagement with texts within which significant movements of thought are accessible, and in which the interaction between philosophical argumentation and literary strategies can be readily seen.

Those self-imposed constraints have meant that some aspects of the rich and complex history of providence have been set aside or given relatively cursory treatment. Much more could be said, for example, about developments that occurred within Christian theology, especially during the Middle Ages and Renaissance. My discussions of modern philosophy do not explore the ramifications of Nietzsche's famous announcement of the death of God. Nor have I directly addressed the relevance of older ideas of natural design to contemporary controversies about evolution and creationism. The place of providence in the changing relations of science and religion, and in the processes of secularization, are among the other themes that a complete history might address.

I believe that the narrative I present of the changing concep-

tual configurations of providence, fate, fortune, freedom, and necessity is nonetheless a true story, and one that can illuminate our
own times. In the history of philosophy, there is never just one
true story to be told, or any one story that can capture the whole
truth. But I hope that this one captures some of the truth about
movements of thought that underlie what Hegel, in the introduction to his *Lectures on the History of Philosophy,* called "the Becoming
of ourselves."

I Euripides, Philosopher of the Stage

There are rare authors whose work acquires the status of an enactment of the culture in which they were formed. Shakespeare was one such, using the resources of the theater to integrate received philosophical thought with themes that captured the emotional and imaginative preoccupations of his contemporaries. A much older model for that extraordinary achievement in the transmission and transformation of culture appears in the plays of Euripides, produced in the fifth century BCE. Euripides was a contemporary of Socrates and of Thucydides, and his life overlapped with Plato's. By that time, the thought of the earliest Greek philosophers had converged with the retelling of Homeric legends and mythology to form a rich repository of historical narrative, legend, and myth—an oral history and literary culture that were reenacted and transformed in theatrical festivals for the edification and delight of the people of Athens.

Cosmic Justice: The Worlds of Gods and Men

Popular though he was, Euripides was also known even in his own times as the philosopher of the stage. His plays abound in philosophical themes. Some of these had already been explored by other Greek tragedians. The unfolding of fate in human lives, the ironies of unexpected outcomes, the epistemological riddles of ambiguous oracles—these themes were already familiar to his audiences, not only from myth, but from the plays of his predecessor Aeschylus and his contemporary and rival, Sophocles. Euripides went further, though, in integrating philosophical reflection on fate and necessity, chance and contingency, with the critique of the accepted wisdom of folklore and legend on the role of the gods in human life.

Euripides' plays are not an apologia for philosophy as opposed to the superstitions of religion. They do, though, enact multi-voiced critical reflections on religious belief and practice and explore the philosophical complexities of human action—the interaction between the inexorability of fate and the apparent chaos of human emotion—in new depth. Dramatic depictions of dire situations—of fallible and fragile characters confronting suffering and death—are often to be found in Greek tragedy. So too are the ironies of the unforeseen outcome that fulfills the oracle in ways that could not have been anticipated. Euripides continues to exploit the theatrical possibilities of those familiar twists and turns of fate. Parents unknowingly kill their children; children unknowingly kill their parents. Sometimes they are rescued from the expected tragic outcome by clever twists of plot; sometimes by the intervention of the gods. Even so, Euripides' presentation of human motivation and responsibility reveals new depths of complexity—especially in the predicament of human action under conditions of uncertainty. The gods can intervene for human good, but they are just as likely to do so for human harm; and even an act decreed by the gods for our good can unpredictably become evil in the doing of it.

The fluctuations of human fortune—the oppositions and the transformations between good and evil—had long been familiar themes in Greek philosophy and drama. The idea of a cosmic justice that balances out opposing forces—a moral order implicit in the world itself—goes back at least to the sixth century BCE, when Anaximander talked of opposites as "making amends" and "paying the penalty" to one another for their "aggression," according to "the ordering of time." It was Heraclitus who, in the same century, gave the most powerful expression to the idea of a cosmic justice. The sun, he said, "will not transgress his measures." If he does, the Furies—the administrators of justice—will find him out.[1]

In the elusive and eloquent fragments of Heraclitus we can already find many of the themes that will be reworked by the Stoics, and through them profoundly influence modern thought: the idea of a cosmic conflict that can be interpreted in terms of justice or fate; the interconnections between death and life; the idea of mind as imbuing the cosmos; and of a dynamic balance between good and evil. In these tantalizing ancient fragments, we can see already the idea of a world containing order that does not depend on the will of any orderer—of mind immanent in the cosmos itself, without reference to a creator. Heraclitus, in his famous metaphor of fire, gives powerful expression to the alternation and transformation of opposing forces: "The ordering, the same for all, no god or man has made, but it ever was and will be: fire ever-living, kindled in measures and in measures going out."[2]

We cannot read these luminous fragments now without being struck by their power—by their capacity to engage emotion, imagination, and intellect all at once. They speak to us from an ancient past where the poetic has not yet separated out from the philosophical; where the dark mood of irony readily associates with the coolness of philosophical detachment. The poignancy of existence is expressed in ambiguous metaphors that can be read in both directions. The "fairest order of the world" is nonetheless "a heap of random sweepings"; but it is no less true that the apparently random in fact conforms to exquisite order: "lifetime" is "a child at play," moving pieces in a game. "Kingship belongs to the child."[3] The metaphor can be taken as expressing a chilling lack of purpose: the universe is governed not by the wisdom of maturity but as if by an irresponsible child, idly moving counters in an inconsequential game. Yet if the analogy seems to detract from the supposed wisdom of divine planning, it can also—at least to a modern ear—lend to the world an engaging aura of childlike playfulness. The emotional resonances can shift from awe at a relentless divine justice to the delight and wonder of play.

It is such imaginative and emotional ambiguities as these that leap out at us when we read the dramas of Euripides. That he was at least acquainted with the thought of Heraclitus is suggested by an early fable recorded by Diogenes Laertius. Euripides is said to have given Socrates a copy of Heraclitus's book and asked him what he thought of it. Socrates allegedly replied, "What I understand is good; and I think that what I don't understand is good too—but it would take a Delian diver to get to the bottom of it."[4] We do not know how far Euripides himself dived into the Delian depths of Heraclitus; but whether or not he is consciously reworking them, Heraclitean themes of fate and necessity—of the inextricability of purpose and chance and of the dynamic transformation of opposites—often surface in his tragedies.

To a modern reader, the plays may well seem even more philosophically sophisticated than they in fact were—so often have they been mined by later philosophers as sources of illustrations and quotations that are now familiar. The playwright's contemporary audiences too would have found in the plays rich reworkings of themes and concepts familiar from earlier philosophy and legend. Euripides was nonetheless not simply representing familiar attitudes toward the gods and toward human predicaments; he was challenging and transforming them.

In *The Women of Troy,* Euripides puts into the mouth of Hecabe an extraordinary prayer: "Zeus, whoever thou art, upholding the earth, throned above the earth, whether human intelligence or natural law, mysterious and unknown, I praise thee: for thou movest on a noiseless path and guidest all human affairs to their just end!" In response Menelaus says, "That's a strange prayer. What does it mean?"⁵ Menelaus, as later critics have commented, has good cause for astonishment at this prayer: it was of a new kind, and Zeus would never have heard its like. God is presented as an unknown power, manifesting itself equally in the laws of nature and as human intelligence. Such a God, whether construed as the laws of nature or as the laws of thought, is something beyond the gods of Greek legends. Euripides' audiences are called upon to judge, from that larger perspective, the deeds not only of human beings, but also of the familiar gods, and the strange and tragic outcomes of the intersection of the two domains.

In thus offering up for judgment both human beings and the gods, the tragedies of Euripides look forward to the Stoics; however, the plays also look back to the elusive fragments of Heraclitus. It is only with the Stoics that we see the full development of the idea of the world as redolent of thought—of Logos, as rational principle, but Heraclitus already had the idea of the human mind and the cosmos as sharing a common structure. The Stoics will develop the idea of a cosmic order that transcends the whims of the gods into the idea of the cosmic city, common to gods and men. As the ideal of cosmopolitanism, it will become an important thread in later Western philosophy. It is Euripides' skepticism about his contemporaries' piety vis-à-vis the will of the gods that makes possible that continuity which we can now see as linking modern thought back to Heraclitus.

Ambivalence about the gods of Greek legend did not originate with Euripides. He did, however, give voice to the tensions between prevailing religious belief and practice and the more austere ideas of cosmic justice that formed the link between his audiences and those ancient Heraclitean ideas. Those tensions are not resolved in the plays. Euripides offers no definitive rejection of conventional religion, though the succession of plays does track a growing skepticism. Speeches criticizing the foibles and cruelties of the gods in their supposed interventions in human affairs are often counterbalanced by more conventionally pious choruses.

Euripides anticipates not only many of the themes of later philosophy but also many of its strategies. He will often set up two proponents in an exchange of ideas and arguments—a distancing technique that shows the influence of the Sophists and mirrors some aspects of Plato's later reconstructions of Socratic dialogue. These debates—where audience members are required to distance themselves from the immediacy of the emotions presented—go beyond the cathartic depiction of strong emotion. The exchanges engage the audience in reflection on how human beings can best respond to external misfortune, to the force of their own passions, and to the understanding of their own mortality.

It is not only in these more consciously reflective moments, however, that Euripides shows himself to be a philosophical dramatist. The unfolding action of the plays is also informed by his reflections on the dilemmas of human action—on vengeance, on justice, and on the fear of death; and on the role of the gods in the understanding and resolution of those dilemmas. Judging human passion and action is never straightforward in these plays. Human action is for Euripides complex; and a large part of that complexity comes from our being so often forced to act under conditions of uncertainty. Let us now look more closely at how he deals with these intersecting themes of uncertainty and necessity as they manifest themselves in the intersecting worlds of gods and men.

Alcestis: Death-in-Life

The imagining of a reversal of roles between gods and human beings runs through Euripides' plays. In his early play *Alcestis,* first performed in 438 BCE, the axis around which those reversals move is the theme of human mortality—the great difference between human life and the lives of the gods; the inexorable necessity to which mortal lives are subject. The confrontation with mortality is the most powerful way in which Euripides' characters come to an understanding of necessity. On the face of it, mortality makes human life subject to necessity in a way that has no equivalent in the lives of the gods; the fear of death makes human beings vulnerable to the will of those gods and anxious to accommodate their whims and their jealousies. It is striking, though, that we also find in Euripides' plays a preoccupation with a different way of responding to the fact of human mortality: rather than seek to avoid death and misfortune by placating the gods, human beings can find liberation in the acceptance of necessity.

Cicero translated from Euripides a powerful passage on the theme of acquiescence to the necessity of mortality—a fragment of a Euripides play *Hypsípíle,* which has not survived:

> Never was man born but to toil and pain.
> He burieth children, getteth him new babes.
> And dies himself: yet men are grieved hereat,
> When dust to dust they bear! Needs must it be
> That death like corn-shocks garners lives of men,
> That this man be, that be no more. Now why
> Mourn what all must by nature's law pass through?
> There is no horror in the inevitable.[6]

The passage was celebrated in antiquity. Chrysippus, the founder of the Stoic school, was said to have admired its lofty tone and to have recognized Stoic doctrine in it. Carneades, the skeptic, was more dubious about whether such language was likely to console human beings for the cruelty of death. Modern readers may well share Carneades' skepticism on the point. Why should we find comfort in the mere recognition of necessity? Why should the fact that death comes to all make the horror any more bearable in our own case? In his early play *Alcestis,* Euripides himself explores the issue and, by retelling a familiar story in which the ordinary conditions of mortality and grief are suspended, challenges his audience to reflect on those conditions.

A Bitter Reprieve

What is set in abeyance in *Alcestis* is not the necessity of mortality as such, but rather the necessity of death's happening here-now-to-me—the necessity of a human being's individual life span. The different layers of fear of death are nonetheless interconnected in ways that are exposed in the play. If we are reluctant to die now, when will we be ready and willing? This is one of the challenges posed for the central character, Admetus.

Admetus's predicament arises from a series of prior reversals of the roles of gods and men, which frame the action of the play. The god Apollo has been forced to live as a mere mortal—in servitude to Admetus—as punishment for the ways in which he has rebelled against the right order of things. Apollo's rebellion itself arose from the issue of human mortality at another level. Zeus struck Asclepius, Apollo's son, with a thunderbolt, for violating the distinction between men and the gods by raising the dead to life through the art of medicine. The theme of failure to live in accordance with the necessities of mortal existence—and the related issue of due deference to the distinction between gods and men with regard to mortality—run through the whole play. It is for his failure to respect that distinction that Apollo was condemned to servitude; he challenged Zeus by taking vengeance on the Cyclopes, who had forged for Zeus the thunderbolt that brought death to Asclepius. It is as a reward for the kindness and courtesy that his mortal master Admetus has shown him that Apollo has now once more breached the order of things by granting Admetus a respite from the ordinary conditions of human mortality. Although

he must, like all mortals, eventually die, Admetus is offered a reprieve from the immediacy of death: he can postpone the appointed time of his death—provided he can find someone willing
to die in his place.

The aging parents of Admetus decline his request; but his wife
Alcestis agrees. The unfolding of the paradoxes of grief, and of
the ways in which life can be transformed into death and vice ver-
sa—the poignancy of death-in-life and of life-in-death—lie at the
heart of this richly reflective drama. Admetus's deliverance from
his appointed time for death turns out to be a bitter gift: a life
spent grieving for the loss of a noble wife is not a life worth living.
The reprieve is also a condemnation; but this is not the worst of
it. Admetus's predicament has greater complexities and will reveal deeper levels of the intersections of death and life. "I rescued
him from death by tricking the Fates," boasts Apollo in the prologue.[7] Still, the god must confront resentful Death again when
the latter arrives to take Alcestis to the underworld. Has Apollo
come, Death asks, to cheat him again of his promised prey? "Was
it not enough that you prevented the death of Admetus, tripping
up the Fates by cunning trickery?" (*Alcestis,* line 33). In the end
Death will be deprived of Alcestis—not by the trickery of Apollo,
but through the efforts of the boisterous, self-invited guest Heracles, who has arrived, seeking hospitality in the midst of his legendary labors. This victory, as Heracles is well aware, is not a permanent one; it does, however, achieve a welcome restoration to
matters as they stood before the "trickery" of Apollo—a return to
ordinary conditions of mortality.

Admetus's tussles with death present many twists and turns. In
apparently outwitting fate, Apollo has challenged the power of
necessity. Death, it seems, has—at any rate for a while—come under human control; it has become a matter for negotiation and
consent. Yet even in delaying the necessity of death, Admetus
finds no remedy for the rawness of grief. Indeed, in agreeing to

the suspension of the normal, Admetus has brought on himself a new and insidious form of grief. To suspend what is normal in death is also to suspend what is normal in grief.

"Time will heal you," Alcestis tries to assure Admetus. "One who is dead is nothing" (*Alcestis,* line 381). Admetus's acceptance of the healing power of time depends, however, on his prior acceptance of the idea of necessary order. Once that is suspended, things take on a terrifying contingency. The impending death of Alcestis is something that happens not in accordance with the necessary order, but rather under the conditions of the suspension of that order. There can be no comfort here in the thought of a healing passage of time. If Admetus had died, says the maidservant, he would be gone, but since he has escaped death, he "lives with such grief as he shall never forget." His predicament is not just that he has avoided his own death only to be stricken with grief for Alcestis. He has survived into a distinctive kind of grief for which there can be no healing. Admetus's leftover life is not just a sad life but, as the chorus leader says, "a life that is no life at all" (*Alcestis,* line 242).

Admetus remains mortal. Apollo's intervention has brought no gift of immortality. He has only a reprieve, and one that has come at enormous cost: the loss of the sense of necessity that makes death bearable to mortals. Admetus, a mortal, respected Apollo's status as a god by not taking advantage of his servitude; the master treated his servant with the courtesy due to a god. In exchange Apollo arranges Admetus's reprieve from mortality. It is a reciprocation of kindness played out on the border separating gods and men. However, ambiguities obscure that border, along with the nature of Apollo's gift.

Alcestis's death is untimely—and not just in the straightforward sense of her dying young. She is now to die at a time that is not her own *necessary* time to die. The perception of a terrible contingency opens up with her impending death: death unaccompanied by necessity—death that has not come at the appointed time. Apollo's intervention has deprived both Admetus and Alcestis of the possibility of dying at their *right* time. Admetus is left with a grief that time cannot heal, because he is not grieving for someone who has—as others do—died at her necessary time. He is left to live a "life which is no life at all" because he has himself been deprived of the possibility of dying at his own necessary time.

What exactly is it to die at one's appointed time—or to be deprived of the possibility of doing so? What is supposed to determine the necessary time for an individual to die? Against the background of the story of Apollo and Asclepius, Euripides confronts his contemporary audience with the darker side of the developing art of medicine—the changes it wreaks in human expectations. To know about new ways of avoiding death is to live with increased uncertainty. Euripides offers a multivoiced exploration of the issue, in which it quickly becomes apparent that Admetus's predicament goes beyond the consideration of medicine's attempts to push back the bounds of necessity. It also involves the clash of expectations between the generations. The issue of the right time to die comes into clearer focus in the angry recrimination scene between Admetus and his father Pheres, who has come to take part in Alcestis's funerary rites and to offer condolences to his son. The exchange is both sad and funny. Admetus is convinced that the sacrifice he asked of his father was appropriate: old age, he thinks is the *right* time to die; it is appropriate, then, that his aging parents should be willing to die in his stead. For Pheres that expectation amounts to moral cowardice on his son's part.

Pheres, as Admetus sees it, has had his prime of life; old men should be willing to let go. He mocks the common reluctance of the old to die—their readiness to forget, once death approaches, how burdensome they find old age. From Pheres' point of view it is Admetus who is guilty of refusing to accept the appointed time to die. "What injustice have I done you? Of what am I robbing you? Do not die on my behalf, and I shall not die on yours. You enjoy looking on the light. Do you think your father does not? Truly I regard the time below as long and life as short but sweet for all that. At all events you have shamelessly striven to avoid death, and you live beyond your fated day by killing *her*" (*Alcestis*, lines 685–696). For Pheres, it is not he but Admetus that is the coward. Admetus has agreed to have a woman die in his place. Will it stop there? Perhaps, he sarcastically suggests, Admetus has cleverly found out a way never to die, by persuading a succession of wives in turn to die on his behalf.

Pheres and Admetus berate one another for cowardice in the face of death. No clear winner emerges in their poignant debate. "What?" demands Admetus. "Is death the same thing for a man in his prime as for an old man?" To this Pheres responds, "We must live with a single life, not with two" (*Alcestis*, lines 685–711). Of course, it is not as simple as that. The ties that bind us to others mean that we do live more than one life, die more than one death. "I envy the unmarried and childless among mortals," Admetus cries in a later speech. "For they have but a single soul, and to feel its pains is only a moderate burden. But diseases of children and wives snatched by death from their marriage beds are unendurable to see when one can live unwed and childless all one's days" (*Alcestis*, lines 880–888).

The issue of what it might be to die at one's necessary time remains unresolved; but what Admetus has lost thanks to Apollo's gift becomes clearer through the efforts of Heracles to make good that loss for Admetus and Alcestis. It is the rowdy, unbidden guest, whose inappropriate behavior disrupts the grieving household, that effects the restoration of the ordinary conditions of mortality and grief. The meeting between Heracles and Death goes on offstage. We do not know whether it is a Herculean struggle to the death, or another negotiated arrangement, that delivers Alcestis from the underworld. Yet the ambiguity is appropriate. For it is not the brute strength of Heracles that is most crucial in his dealings with death. Euripides, in exploring his central theme of the crossover between life and death, has given this familiar figure of strength a more complex role to play.

Death, Contingency, and Hospitality

One of the strangest and most frequently discussed scenes in *Alcestis* is Admetus's initial deception of Heracles and his remarkable hospitality toward that obtrusive guest. Admetus allows him to believe that Alcestis is still alive, although the household is in fact preparing her funerary rites. It is a puzzling deception—to the household, to Heracles when he later discovers it, and no doubt to the audience. Yet it is perhaps nothing other than the familiar inconsistent behavior of the newly bereaved. Faced with the sudden shock of loss, Admetus does what many have done since and no doubt before: he acts as if nothing has happened. The exchange that follows is a representation of prevaricating double meanings; yet it also captures something of the underlying truth about the intersection of life and death, which is the central theme of the play:

> Heracles: Surely your wife Alcestis has not died?
> Admetus: There is a double tale to tell of her.
> Heracles: Do you mean that she has died or is still alive?
> Admetus: She is and is no more. It is a grief to me.
> Heracles: I'm still no wiser: you speak in riddles.
> Admetus: Do you not know what doom she is fated to suffer?
> Heracles: I know: she promised to die for you.
> Admetus: How can she be still truly alive once she had promised that?
> Heracles: O do not mourn your wife beforehand! Put it off till the day!

Admetus: Someone who is doomed to die is dead, has died and
is no more.

Heracles: Existence and non-existence are deemed to be
separate things.

Admetus: You have your views on this, Heracles, and I have
mine. (*Alcestis,* lines 518–529)

Heracles resists the fusion of death and life—resists, with a robust
common sense, the intrusion of death into life. Unbeknownst to
Heracles, though, Alcestis is indeed—literally and categorically—
already dead. For Heracles the distinction between life and death
is a sharp one. Death should not intrude on life; existence and
nonexistence are "separate things." In the strange half-life that
Admetus has entered, however, the two cannot be separated. Even
before Alcestis is dead, her arranged, bartered death casts its
shadow over the time between Admetus's deliverance and the exacting of the price for it. Asked by the chorus leader whether the
queen yet lives or has died, the maidservant replies: "You might
call her both living and dead" (*Alcestis,* line 142). The same description could be given of Admetus both before and after the death of
Alcestis. It is not only the content of Heracles' speech on existence and nonexistence that contrasts sharply with this half-life
of Admetus. Heracles' eruption onto the scene of grief—the very
unexpectedness of his noisy presence—gives dramatic expression
to the immediacy, the unexpectedness of death. Admetus accepts
his disruptive arrival; and it is this apparently inappropriate hospitality toward the uninvited guest that begins Admetus's return
to the ordinary possibilities and necessities associated with grief.

The theme of hospitality, which runs through Euripides' plays—
is here linked to the theme of mortality. The outrageously drunken
Heracles has a strong sense, not only of the abstract inescapability
of death-in-general, but of death's imminent reality. "Come here
so that you may be made wiser," he shouts to the frustrated, griev-

ing servant who is trying to follow Admetus's orders that the un-
wanted guest be made welcome. "Do you know the nature of our
mortal life? I think not. How could you? But listen to me. Death
is a debt all mortals must pay, and no man knows for certain
whether he will still be living on the morrow. The outcome of our
fortune is hid from our eyes, and it lies beyond the scope of any
teaching or craft. So now that you have learned this from me,
cheer your heart, drink, regard this day's life as yours but all else as
Fortune's!" The advice of the drunken Heracles is, "Being mortal,
we ought to think mortal thoughts" (*Alcestis,* lines 780–800).

It is a speech in the spirit of what we have come to associate
with later Epicurean doctrine: pleasure in the passing moment is
grounded in the necessity and finality of death. Heracles founds
his exuberant pleasures on the sharp separation of life and death.
Yet it is Heracles who takes on the struggle with Death that will
accomplish Alcestis's return from the underworld. There may
seem to be a contradiction here—between the acceptance and the
resistance. As Heracles himself knows full well, however, the outcome of his struggle with Death is, again, not an ultimate victory
for Alcestis, but rather a return to the ordinary conditions of mortality. Heracles' triumph yields a restoration of the conditions under which his own attitude toward death can once more be viable
for Admetus and Alcestis. They will again be able to experience
the conjunction between an understanding of the inevitability of
death and uncertainty about the time of its coming; and in that
conjunction they will experience anew the normal pleasures of
being alive.

The necessity for us all to die remains unassailable, despite the
return of Alcestis. Still, Heracles has restored the ordinary conditions of mortality, of grief and of joy. The return of Alcestis is a
fable of loss—the satisfaction onstage of the hopeless longings of
mortal grief. Admetus has been given—in a dramatic realization

of the fantasy of every grieving mortal—the joy of regaining his lost love. But he has also been restored to ordinary possibilities of future grief—and to the necessity of his own future death.

It is Admetus's hospitality—his determination that Heracles should be welcomed rather than sent away—that makes possible the intervention which will restore the ordinary conditions of mortality. It is because Admetus, in the midst of grief, is open to the unexpected—ready to welcome the uninvited guest—that his fortunes are reversed. Heracles' struggle with Death complements and parallels, in the structure of the play, the gift of Apollo that sets the frame of the drama. It is through his hospitality that Admetus receives the bitter gift of the reprieve from death; and it is through hospitality that his fortunes are again restored.

Hospitality, here, is not just kindness; it is a deeper expression of openness to the unexpected. It is an aspect of the ancient ideal of hospitality that can easily go unnoticed by modern readers. The connections between hospitality and openness to the unexpected—to contingency—are accentuated in the poet Ted Hughes's version of *Alcestis*.[8] Hughes's *Alcestis* occupies an interesting space, somewhere between translation and adaptation—an informed reading that stays close to the spirit of the text, while nonetheless expanding and enriching its emotional and imaginative possibilities for modern readers. Hughes embellishes the hospitality theme and its connections with mortality. In his version the chorus calls for the acceptance of whatever happens—for the acceptance of misfortune itself

> Generously, as a guest,
> As a welcome, noble guest
>
> Chorus 2:
> There is a mystery in it.

Something is always being delivered
Out of the unknown. Often
Out of the impossible—
The hour's every moment, like a spring source,
Divulges something new.
A thought out of the heart.
A strange hand knocking at the door.[9]

Hughes's variations on Euripides' text bring out important conceptual connections that link hospitality, contingency, and mortality. That aspect of the ancient ideal of hospitality has been
revived in some of the later works of Jacques Derrida, especially in
The Politics of Friendship. Derrida talks of the conceptual instability
at the heart of the "perhaps"—a thought located at the crossroads
of chance and necessity. To expose oneself to the contingency of
the "perhaps" is, for Derrida, to "address oneself to the possible";
but the very uniqueness of the contingent event brings with it
the inevitable recognition of unrepeatability and hence of necessity. This openness to the unexpected is also at the heart of
what Derrida calls true—unconditional—hospitality. It opens up
to someone who is neither expected nor invited—to the arrival of
something new, unidentifiable, and unforeseen. True hospitality—
"hospitality itself"—is, Derrida suggests, a hospitality of *visitation,*
rather than *invitation.*[10]

Hospitality, thus understood, is bound up with the recognition
of contingency. Death is itself contingent in that way; even when
anticipated it comes unexpectedly. Yet Death is also necessary. "If
it be not now," as Hamlet says, "yet it will come." It is this conjunction of necessity and contingency that is captured in the "ordinary" experience of mortality evoked in *Alcestis.* The contingency
of the unexpected can seem to be at odds with the idea of a *necessary* time to die, which also runs through the play. Yet it is in the

very recognition of the contingency of the time of our death that we most truly accept necessity. That at any rate is the message of Heracles: it is by fully knowing that death is necessary that we can best live with the contingency of its coming, without seeking forlorn reprieves.

Alcestis addresses a striking though familiar failure of rational comprehension—the capacity to understand the universality of death-in-general while failing to grasp its particularity in our own case. A similar incomprehension is wonderfully described by Tolstoy in the story of the death of Ivan Ilyich. The dying Ilyich reflects with sad irony that the syllogism he learned as a boy in his logic text—"Caius is a man, men are mortal, therefore Caius is mortal"—has seemed to him all his life to be true, as applied to Caius, but certainly not in relation to himself. That Caius—man in the abstract—was mortal, was perfectly correct; but he was not Caius, nor man in the abstract: "he had always been a creature quite, quite different from all others." In short, "Caius was certainly mortal, and it was right for him to die; but for me, Little Vanya, Ivan Ilyich, with all my thoughts and emotions—it's a different matter altogether. It cannot be that I ought to die. That would be too terrible."[11]

George Eliot narrates a similar poignant moment in the consciousness of Casaubon in *Middlemarch*. "Here was a man who now for the first time found himself looking into the eyes of death— who was passing through one of those rare moments of experience when we feel the truth of a commonplace, which is as different from what we call knowing it, as the vision of waters upon the earth is different from the delirious vision of the water which cannot be had to cool the burning tongue. When the commonplace 'We must all die' transforms itself suddenly into the acute consciousness 'I must die—and soon,' then death grapples us, and his fingers are cruel; afterwards, he may come to fold us in his arms as our mother did, and our last moment of dim earthly discerning may be like the first. To Mr Casaubon now, it was as if he suddenly found himself on the dark river-brink and heard the plash of the oncoming oar, not discerning the forms, but expecting the summons."[12]

The contingency of its timing in the here and now is the other face of the necessity of death. Alcestis's agreed-upon death is anticipated as something incapable of being changed. Yet so long as it has not actually happened, it carries within it the possibility of not happening at all. Again, Ted Hughes has accentuated the conceptual point by replacing an ambiguity with a determinate meaning. The Loeb version has the chorus say of Alcestis's impending death: "Her fate is plain, my friends, all too plain, but still let us pray to the gods: the gods' power is supreme" (*Alcestis,* lines 218–219). It is not altogether clear whether they are called to pray for divine intervention or simply to offer pious acknowledgment of the power of the gods over human life and death. In Hughes's version the praying becomes a simple acknowledgment of possibility, a reminder of our incomplete knowledge.

> The powers of the creation are the powers
> Of every atom in it, and all these atoms
> Are slaves to laws of which we are ignorant.
> Anything can happen.
> We must pray.
> . . .
> We must pray and stare into the darkness
> For that spark.
> Without hope.
> Without expectation.
> Only confident
> That anything can happen.[13]

Prayer becomes not a plea for intervention but rather just the acknowledgment of a possibility that is already there—an acknowledgment that can yield nonetheless a brief respite from bleakness.

Semblance and Resemblance

Before Alcestis is finally restored to him, Admetus has one more
trial to undergo—exposure to the vulnerability that attends re-
semblances of the real. Before being returned to normal conditions of grief and mortality, Admetus must struggle for truth. The
veiled woman before him resembles his lost wife; and the resemblance is a source of anguish. "Woman, whoever you are, know
that in shape you are like Alcestis and resemble her in appearance.
What agony! Take this woman out of my sight, by the gods, do not
slay again one who is dead! For when I see her I think I see my
wife. She makes my heart pound, and tears stream from my eyes.
Oh luckless me! It is but now that I taste the full bitterness of this
grief!" The chorus responds that Fate cannot be called kind, but
that "one must endure what the god gives, whatever it is" (*Alcestis*,
lines 1061–1071).

Admetus must first fully experience the truth of his loss before
he can have the joy of Alcestis's restoration. In experiencing the
reality of grief—in accepting the fullness of his loss—he is restored
to the ordinary conditions of mortal life. He can have Alcestis
back only when he knows that he can indeed really lose her. We
lose the dead over and over; and what restoration or reconnection
may be possible can come only out of the experience and acceptance of their loss. Yet there are false forms of restoration; and the
disappointment that follows their exposure as delusions must first
be endured.

Admetus's struggle with the truth of loss has a grotesque twist to it; and again Hughes's adaptation accentuates it with a further twist of the poet's own. Admetus tells Alcestis that after she dies he will have a skilled craftsman make an image of her to be laid out in his bed. "I shall fall into its arms, and as I embrace it and call your name I shall imagine, though I have her not, that I hold my dear wife in my arms, a cold pleasure, to be sure, but thus I shall lighten my soul's heaviness. And perhaps you will cheer me by visiting me in dreams. For even in sleep it is pleasant to see loved ones for however long we are permitted" (*Alcestis,* lines 348– 356). In Hughes's version, the construction of the image is not a clear intention but a rejected fantasy:

> What shall I do,
> Have some sculptor make a model of you?
> Stretch out with it, on our bed,
> Call it Alcestis, whisper to it?
> Tell it all I would have told you?
> Embrace it—horrible!—stroke it!
> Knowing it can never be you,
> Horrible![14]

The thought that he might dream of Alcestis is also a source of horror rather than of comfort:

> To dream you have come back
> Alive, happy, full of love as ever—
> Then to wake up![15]

The action of *Alcestis* unfolds in the borderland between the worlds of gods and of men; and there both necessity and death retain an ambiguous status—not clearly on either side of the border between the divine and the human. Toward the end of the play the chorus is given a lyrical celebration of Necessity as a goddess. Yet her implacability makes her a goddess with a difference: "Of that goddess alone," says the chorus, "there are no altars, no statues to approach, and to sacrifice she pays no heed. Do not, I pray you, Lady, come with greater force than heretofore in my life. For whatever Zeus ordains, with your help he brings it to fulfillment. Even the iron of the Chalybes you overcome with your violence, and there is no pity in your unrelenting heart" (*Alcestis,* lines 973–983).

What of Death? His special character is even more marked than that of Necessity; for he is neither god nor mortal. "You know my character," he says to Apollo. "Yes," Apollo responds, "hateful to mortals and rejected by the gods" (*Alcestis,* lines 62–63). In his brief appearance, Euripides' Death is a petulant figure. He is resentful of being cheated, but not unreasonable—an officeholder, with an eye to his own satisfaction in a job well done. "I too, you must know, get pleasure from my office" (*Alcestis,* line 53). He carries out the task at hand—not so much a demonic force as an unimaginative hangman, going about his business. He can even engage in a little political discussion about his egalitarian approach. The deal Apollo wants to do with him on Admetus's behalf, Death sneers, is "to the advantage of the rich," who can buy themselves a little extra time (*Alcestis,* line 58).

The persona of Death is one of Hughes's most striking embellishments of the text. In his version Death is a "roaring" character—more balanced with the figure of the drunken Heracles. He does not claim to be a god; but he does present himself as an awesome force—"the magnet of the cosmos."

> What you call death
> Is simply my natural power,
> The pull of my gravity. And life
> Is a brief weightlessness—an aberration
> From the status quo—which is me.[16]

Our life rests on a "nod of permission" from this power of Death.

> As if I dozed off and dreamed a little.
> I take a dream—and Admetos calls it his life.[17]

This is embellishment. Yet in its evocation of the power of death Hughes's version is true to Euripides' presentation of the relentless necessity that confronts fragile human life. The inexorability of this Death balances the implacability of the goddess Necessity. In both cases, Euripides challenges the conventional pieties. An implacable necessity in things transcends the power of human beings to control their destinies; but although the gods are immortal, there is little point in human beings' looking to them for protection. They too, as Euripides will go on to show in his later plays, are subject to necessity.

"All for Nothing": Truth, Illusion, and Action in *Helen, Electra,* and *Orestes*

Much of the tragedy in ancient Greek drama arises from the necessity for human beings to act under conditions of uncertainty, especially in the lack of knowledge of the future. To remedy that lack, the characters typically resort to oracles or prophecy; but the ambiguities of their deliverances are themselves the stuff of tragedy. Euripides, however, takes further the dilemmas in the relations between gods and men. Not only are the guiding voices of the gods tragically difficult to interpret; the gods also often deceive us for ends of their own—in reaction to their own rivalries and jealousies, to which human well-being is sadly incidental.

The gods, moreover, are subject to their own irrational intermissions. Even in an authenticated communication from the gods, as Orestes warns his sister in *Electra,* some demon might speak. The gods do not always make just or even rational responses to human needs; divine commands may be "wild and rash," and the discord in the ranks of the gods themselves can increase human vulnerability. Not only can the gods send false appearances to mislead us; in still more complex ways human action can be affected by men's interactions with the gods: even wise and honest advice from the gods may turn into folly when human beings act on it. The complexity of human action is such that the nature of what we do can be transformed in the doing.

Helen, first produced in 412 BCE, draws on an old legend according to which it was not the real Helen whose abduction from Menelaus by Paris started the Trojan War. The goddess Hera, so the story went, had sent a phantom Helen to accompany Paris to Troy, while the real Helen remained in Egypt. Euripides takes up this legend in a moving, though often comical, exploration of the vagaries of truth and appearance, trust and deception, as well as of less easily articulated issues about the bearing of knowledge on action. Our lack of knowledge of the future, it transpires, is not the only source of the uncertainty we must live with. The prophetess Theonoe is gifted with foreknowledge; but that does not release her from normal human perplexities about how best to act. The limitations of prophecy as a guide to action seem here to have more to do with the complexity of truth itself than with the problems posed by human incapacity to interpret cryptic oracles. "Many things plainly said may be false," the chorus warns. "Yes, and conversely they may be true," Helen replies.[18] Even what is real can deceive us; and those who speak honestly of what is real may find that reality not accepted.

The challenge Euripides has his characters face in *Helen* is not just that of avoiding credulity, but that of knowing how to engage with the truth; and here trust in the gods can lead them astray. Prophets can be dubious guides. They are worthless liars, the old servant tells Menelaus. The friendship of the gods is the best prophecy a man can have, the chorus leader agrees in response

(*Helen,* lines 744–760). Yet the friendship of the gods—both with human beings and with one another—is part and parcel of changing fortunes in the world of gods and men. The providence of the gods, even when they do wish us well, does not allow us to escape from chance. The real issue is not how to please or follow the gods; nor is it to accept our lot as the mysterious providence of the gods, who know what is for the best. It is rather to learn how best to live with uncertainty.

In Euripides' retelling of the legend, Menelaus—washed up in Egypt after being shipwrecked on his voyage from Troy with the phantom Helen, whom he has left waiting in a cave—now encounters, to his astonishment, the real Helen. "In seeing me, aren't you convinced you see your wife?" she asks. "You look like her," Menelaus responds, "but certainty eludes me. . . . My trouble is this: I have another wife." "That was an image. I never went to Troy," Helen assures him. It was from "the upper air" that the other Helen came—she is a "god-fashioned bride" (*Helen,* lines 576–585).

Disoriented though Menelaus clearly is by the discovery of the real Helen, it is only for a short time that he has to deal with the coexistence of the two versions. The phantom has the grace to return to the place from which she has come, once the real Helen claims him. The facsimile has "swept out of sight into the sky's recesses, vanished into the heavens," a servant reports (*Helen,* lines 605–606). The coherence of the real in Menelaus's world is quickly reestablished; but another source of disorientation is at work in this moving interplay of truth and illusion. Menelaus and his soldiers must not only find their way back to present reality; they must also learn to live with the knowledge that the long, arduous war they fought was all for nothing more than the beautiful illusion.

"Was this woman not the author of all our trials in Troy?" the servant asks Menelaus. "No, not this one," Menelaus replies, "the gods had deceived us. We had in our embrace a baleful image made of cloud." The servant responds in bewilderment: "What do you mean? Do you mean we toiled in vain for a cloud?" (*Helen,* lines 703–706). The phantom Helen becomes an emblem for the futility of war. In a poem based on the Euripides story, by the Greek poet Seferis, Menelaus and Helen reflect on the sad truth that the pitiful Trojans and the unlucky Greeks alike have suffered for nothing. Menelaus reflects that Priam and his people perished for nothing; the Greeks have sacked a city for nothing.[19]

Euripides' story of that war fought for nothing becomes a symbol for the elusiveness of a more general ideal—that of living in accordance with the truth, of shaping human action to the necessities that govern human existence. How are we to live in accordance with truth in a shifting world where all that seems most real is liable to disappear into thin air? The belief that human lives are governed by necessity continues to be invoked throughout the play. "It can't be helped," says Menelaus, reciting the story of his "miserable woes." The chorus chimes in, "It was some wise man who said it, not I: nothing has more power than cruel necessity" (*Helen,* lines 510–514). But the apparent necessities belong in an uncertain world whose cruelty is just as liable to derive from the duplicity of the gods as from anything real. Where the apparent limits of the real and the possible are constantly open to revision, it is not a fatalistic acceptance of the inevitable that is needed. Uncertainty demands not passivity but good judgment. Nor is the practical wisdom required inconsistent with a calculated disregard for the truth. Menelaus and the restored Helen face a dangerous predicament. Theoclymenus, the son of the Egyptian king, Proteus, is determined to have Helen for his wife. A "wise man does not undertake the impossible," the shrewd Helen advises Menelaus (*Helen,* lines 811–813). To escape, the threatened couple must instead develop a dishonest "clever ruse."

One of the ironies in the drama that now unfolds is the role played by Theonoe, sister of Theoclymenus, in the deception through which Menelaus and Helen will make their escape. Although Theonoe knows the future, she must nonetheless exercise her own judgment about whether she should inform her brother of the plot that will deprive him of his intended bride. The ironies of the gap between foreknowledge and practical wisdom are brought out in Helen's attempt to persuade Theonoe to conceal her knowledge of the intended escape. Theonoe, Helen argues, must take into account much about the past in reaching her decision about how to act—her father's wishes, debts contracted between him and the gods, the duty of returning what belongs to another—as well as pity for the present condition of the couple. "If you are a prophet and believe in the gods but yet corrupt your father's justice by doing your unjust brother a favor, it is a disgrace that you know from the gods the present and the future but not what is just" (*Helen,* lines 920–923).

The ambiguities of chance and the elusiveness of truth are interconnected themes throughout *Helen.* Euripides presents the changeability of the gods as part of the general changeability of human fortunes; divine providence does not save us from chance; wisdom does not lie in learning how to please the gods in order to escape misfortune. Nor is wisdom served by simply accepting misfortune as the mysterious will of the gods, who know what is for our good. True wisdom lies in the delicate art of learning to live with both necessity and chance.

The chorus sings:

> What mortal can search out and tell
> what is god, what is not god,
>   and what lies between?
> The farthest bourne is reached by him who sees that what
>   the gods send

veers first this way, then that,
   and once more this way,
with outcomes wavering and unexpected.
(*Helen,* lines 1137–1142)

Whatever the ultimate truth of things may be, human action requires a capacity for careful judgment in the midst of uncertainty.
Judgment is needed—including the capacity to know when to accept something as inevitable, and when to continue trying to
change it. In the final sections of the play, Theoclymenus argues
with the "second servant," who has brought the news of Theonoe's betrayal, about how he should respond. For Theoclymenus,
his sister is "vile" and deserves death; for the morally righteous
servant, she is "god-fearing"; her behavior was "a noble piece of
treachery," a "righteous act." It is the servant who is allowed to
claim the high moral ground:

Theoclymenus: Who has a claim to what is mine?
Second Servant: The man who received her from her father.
Theoclymenus: But chance gave her to me.
Second Servant: And fate took her away.
Theoclymenus: You should not act as judge in what belongs to
   me.
Second Servant: Yes, if I am in the right. (*Helen,* lines
   1634–1637)

If chance is finally overcome here, it is only through the making
of something meaningful out of the apparently random—only
through the telling of a coherent narrative; and such narratives,
like the play itself, remain open-ended. The interaction of rival
voices is always subject to interpretation and reinterpretation
by an attentive, critical audience. The chorus has the final word,

which we will see repeated almost exactly at the end of the *Bacchae:*
"What heaven sends has many shapes, and many things the gods
accomplish against our expectation. What men look for is not
brought to pass, but a god finds a way to achieve the unexpected.
Such was the outcome of this story" (*Helen,* lines 1688–1692).

Euripides' exploration of the complexities of human action under conditions of uncertainty—and of the ways in which they are
affected by the intersection of the divine and human realms—goes
still further in his retelling, in *Electra* and in *Orestes,* of another famous story of the aftermath of the Trojan War—Clytemnestra's
murder of her husband Agamemnon and her murder in revenge
by their children. Before Agamemnon returned from Troy, the
story goes, Electra, the daughter of Agamemnon and Clytemnestra, arranged for her brother Orestes to be sent away from Argos, for fear that he would be murdered by Clytemnestra's lover
Aegisthus. When Orestes reaches manhood, the Delphic oracle
commands him to return to Argos and avenge his father's death
by killing Clytemnestra and Aegisthus. Having arrived in Argos in
disguise, Orestes makes himself known to Electra, and the two
collaborate in the murders. In consequence of the crime of mur-
dering his mother, Orestes is then pursued by the Furies.

Even without attention to the complicating role of the gods,
this saga of revenge clearly provides rich possibilities for the exploration of human agency. Aeschylus and Sophocles both wrote
versions of the story. *Electra,* produced about 430 BCE, is the first
of Euripides' plays on the theme. Here he focuses on the moral
uncertainties that arise at the points of intersection between the
divine and human realms. A tension is set up between following
the will of the gods and taking responsibility for one's own actions. Much of human deliberation goes on at the nexus between
the two. Electra and Orestes are presented as fumbling, indecisive
characters—uncertain about the basis for their actions. Although

Orestes has the authority of the oracle to support him, he fears that the act of vengeance they contemplate might nonetheless be overly rash. Orestes seems able to trust neither the utterances of the oracle nor the voice of his own reason. What is most disturbing in Euripides' presentation of Orestes' vacillation, and of the sorry outcome of the murder of Clytemnestra, is not the thought that the divine justice of which Orestes is to be the instrument might be arbitrary; it is rather that the act of carrying out divine justice might itself be shameful in human terms—that moral unity between the divine and human realms might not be possible.

As the instrument of divine justice, Orestes is performing a noble deed, in bringing the vengeance of the gods on his mother for her murder of Agamemnon. Yet his murder of his own mother is rightly seen as shameful. The dramatic tension stems from the painful conflict in the relations between gods and human beings. The possibility opens up that the two realms are incommensurable—perhaps that the conflicts between these moral imperatives associated with being human are unresolvable. The simple view of the problem is that the same act is susceptible of different descriptions—good insofar as it is seen as carrying out divine justice, bad insofar as it is described as matricide. From this point of view, the dilemma might be resolved by deciding between different competing principles, each demanding different actions. But for Orestes it is more complex: his one act splinters. As Castor observes, when the two Dioscuri appear shining in the night sky to comment on Orestes' deed, the god, though wise, has given a response that is unwise. The treatment Clytemnestra received was just, but Orestes' act was not justified (*Electra*, line 1243).

More is going on here than an expression of ambivalence in human attitudes toward the gods. It is not simply that we do not know whether or not to trust their wisdom. Another level of uncertainty exists in the way the judgment of the gods is translated

into human action. What is just in the eyes of the gods can become unjust in the human enactment of it. Human responsibility
is not mitigated by the fact that we act in obedience to the gods.
Euripides here presents a fractured moral universe. From the perspective of the later Stoics—whose thought he can in many ways
be seen as anticipating—it is possible to interpret the dilemmas of
these characters as expressing a longing for a "common world of
gods and men"; for a way of living with both chance and necessity
that is not vulnerable to either the vagaries of the gods or the unsettling fracturing of human action along the fault lines between
the two worlds.

Euripides returned to the story of the sibling-matricides in one
of his last plays, *Orestes,* first produced in 408 BCE. In this version,
Orestes and Electra seem even more enfeebled; the act of divinely
commanded revenge is even more distanced from the status of
the "noble deed." Commentators have remarked on the anachro-
nism of Euripides' placing their predicament in the context of a
possible appeal to the courts—to a rule of law, which would be familiar to his audience but not available to his characters. Orestes
and Electra seem stranded between different worlds. Orestes rails
against the court's finding that he and Electra must die—shifting
constantly between the acceptance of his sentence, as a necessity
that must be endured, and a search for further schemes and plots
that might save him. Electra seems never even to contemplate
acceptance. They have confidence neither in the justice of the
court's verdict nor in older ideals associated with the will of the
gods.

Here again, no one authorial voice predominates; rather, the
action is presented from multiple perspectives; and what moral
certainty seems possible is liable to shift dramatically as the meaning of an action unfolds. What seems good can become evil as
soon as completed. All that is ultimately certain is the endless reversals of human fortune.

And, ah, you race of mortals, full of tears, trouble-laden,
see how fate
defeats your expectations!
Different woes come by turns to different men
over the length of days,
and beyond our power to reckon
is the whole course of human life.[20]

In *Orestes* the role of the gods reaches the point of parody. The gods have become entertaining theatrical devices, cleverly exploited to move the plot along and get characters on- and offstage. Their machinations carry no moral authority. The play endorses no vision of the right ordering of relations between gods and men. It is in the *Bacchae,* first performed posthumously, probably in 405 BCE, that Euripides offers his richest and most balanced presentation of the complexities of human action in the intersecting worlds of gods and men.

The *Bacchae*

Heraclitean themes make frequent appearances in Euripides' plays—especially in relation to the unity of—or transformations between—opposites: death and life, chance and necessity, truth and illusion, justice and injustice. In the *Bacchae,* though, we see the strongest connections between Euripides' reworking of ancient legends and myths and the themes of Heraclitus. It is a play of dynamic transformations, in which a poetic Heraclitean vision of the interplay of opposites finds expression in a masterly exploitation of the resources of drama. The play encompasses extraordinary transitions of mood, in which comical enactments of the familiar foibles of both gods and men can veer in an instant toward intense horror and violence. It is a play too of extraordinary philosophical depth, packed with wise observation of the inner logic of emotion, which allows gentleness to turn with breathtaking suddenness to cruelty; love into hate and back again to love; the frenzy of vengeance to calm acceptance of what cannot be changed. The *Bacchae* offers a fresh perspective on many of the themes that Euripides has addressed in his earlier plays—a glorious summation, not only of his own preoccupations as a dramatist but of the rich cultural memory he shares with his audiences.

At the center of the shifting moral and emotional landscape of the play is the theme of overlapping and conflicting spheres of action and decision of gods and men, which runs through so much Greek tragedy. In a familiar theme from Greek legend, the divine makes its appearance in the human world in the arrival of a stranger. Draped in a fawn skin and carrying a fennel wand, the god Dionysus comes to Thebes in the guise of a youth with long, flowing hair and an ivy crown. The scene of the action is redolent of ancient legends about divinities entering the human world; here, in the midst of a fire started by a lightning flash, Dionysus was prematurely delivered from the womb of his mother Semele—the daughter of Cadmus, founder of Thebes. As the youthful stranger reminds the audience in the prologue, Zeus was the father of Dionysus, yet his divine origin has not been accepted in Thebes. The god has taken his revenge by driving all the women of the city raving to the mountains, where they have now joined with other female followers to honor him in frenzied revelry; this development has outraged the current ruler of Thebes, Cadmus's grandson Pentheus.

For us, it can only be comical to see the antics of the Bacchae cast as piety; it was comical also to Euripides' audiences. The scenes in which the blind seer Teiresias and the aging Cadmus plan their journey to "toss their old grey beards" with the dancing women in the mountains—meanwhile discussing whether it would perhaps be more prudent to travel by carriage—are hilarious. Yet in the exchange between the two old men Euripides offers a sharp insight both into what is distinctive about the cult of Dionysus and into the obedience to custom—into the observance of what is fitting and appropriate in human conduct. "No," says Teiresias, "it would not become a wise man to look down on the traditions we have received from our fathers, old as time itself: no argument will overthrow them, whatever subtleties have been invented by deep thinkers. Will someone say that in preparing to dance with my head crowned with ivy, I show no respect for my old age? No, for the god has not distinguished old from young where dancing is concerned: he wants to receive joint honor from everyone and to be magnified by all without exception."[21]

The graybeards, sagely deliberating as they set out to toss their beards with exultant abandon, are clearly figures of fun; but they are just as clearly meant to elicit from the audience an admiration for their openness to the new—for their capacity to recognize and honor the gift of spontaneity. They represent a conjunction of respect for custom and delight in the unexpected. It is a delicate balance, which captures something of the subtlety of Euripides' attitude to religion. What matters more than the rightness or wrongness of belief is the attitude toward "custom"; and that should be neither a rigid conformity to convention, excluding openness to the unexpected, nor a dogmatic repudiation of all that "the gods" represent. "We are a pair of grayheads," Teiresias acknowledges in the face of Pentheus's frustration, "but still we must dance" (*Bacchae*, lines 323–324).

Dionysus—as Teiresias stresses in his speech of admonition to Pentheus about his disregard for the god—represents the place of madness in human life. That madness can take several forms: we can experience it in prophecy, in the release associated with wine, and in the horrors of war. In all its forms it relates to things that lie within our nature—things that we ignore at our peril. The problem with Pentheus is that he seeks power and control but lacks any attentive understanding of the natures over which he would exert his power. Pentheus distrusts and disdains the madness associated with Dionysus; that is what makes him—in Teiresias's prophetic diagnosis—himself "mad and most painfully so," in a way that no drug can cure (*Bacchae,* lines 326–327).

Euripides presents Cadmus and Teiresias as objects of good-humored derision; but the unfolding of Dionysus's vengeance on Pentheus will show them to be wiser than he, the initially more dignified younger man, who scorns the misplaced "piety" of their attempts to honor the god. Pentheus lacks both the understanding of necessity and openness to contingency. He has closed himself off both from the necessities of his nature and from the contingency of the unexpected. There is no medicine that can heal such a disease. Pentheus has cut himself off from his own sources of healing; and the remainder of the play will show the horrific revenge taken by the god he has denied.

The *Bacchae* has at times been read as Euripides' recantation of his own stance of skepticism toward the gods. Here again, though, no single stance toward the gods is endorsed in the play. The audience can of course see that what happens on the mountain is no ordinary abandonment to the irrational. This is no ordinary harmless, joyous honoring of a god; what unfolds is rather part of a chillingly calculated act of vengeance on the part of the disgruntled Dionysus. The behavior of the god is no less open than human behavior to criticism. We find no endorsement here either of piety or of its rejection; at stake is a different kind of wisdom.

The sorry tale of Pentheus is not a fable of disrespect toward the gods. It is a fable rather about the lack of understanding of our own nature. If folly is at issue here, it resides in an excess of human confidence—an excess of moral certainty. Pentheus is confident that he knows how his subjects should behave—that he knows what counts as folly. The figures of Cadmus and Teiresias in their fawn skins, carrying their fennel wands, elicit in him not good-natured amusement but rage at their "pernicious performances"—at their lack of decency. Were it not for their age, he rages, they should be in prison along with the crazy females. Teiresias berates Pentheus for this inappropriate show of power— for thinking that "kingly rule is the most powerful force in human life"; for mistaking "unsound" ideas for wisdom (*Bacchae,* line 310).

It is Pentheus himself whose ideas are in disarray, Cadmus insists. "At the moment you are all in the air: you are clever, but your cleverness amounts to nothing." Euripides then reveals another, more disconcerting, aspect to Cadmus's advice to his overzealous grandson, one that takes us back to Euripides' concern with the complexities of truth in relation to human action. "Even if this god does not exist, as you maintain, you should say that he does and tell a wholesome lie: thus Semele will be thought to have given birth to a god and your whole family will win honour" (*Bacchae,* lines 353–356). The pragmatic Cadmus sees Pentheus's zealous insistence on proclaiming the truth—on loudly repudiating error and folly—as manifesting a lack of good sense. Pentheus responds with a show of force, by ordering that Teiresias's place of augury be smashed with crowbars. The ruler's fury is to be wreaked also on the "effeminate foreigner" who has taught the old men their madness; he is to be brought in chains to be stoned to death. "You are now quite deranged," comments Teiresias. Pentheus's moral confidence—his certainty about where madness lies—is itself a form of madness, more dangerous than the folly of dressing up in a fawn skin or carrying a fennel wand. "Cleverness is not wisdom," says the chorus, "nor is it wise to think thoughts not mortal. Our life is short: this being so a man who pursues great things may miss what lies to hand. To live thus is to be, in my judgment, a madman and a fool" (*Bacchae,* lines 394–401).

Dionysus is the god not only of wine but of the theater; and the long-haired stranger delights in mocking Pentheus with semblances. When Pentheus tries to imprison him, the god deludes him into tying up an imaginary bull, while Dionysus sits by, qui-

etly watching. Pentheus then suffers the illusion that the building
is on fire, and tries to quench the imaginary flames with water—
all "for nothing." Made to fight a phantom figure, he reduces the
stables to rubble before dropping his sword in exhaustion. All this
is but the prelude to the horrors that ensue when the god leads
the deluded Pentheus off to the mountain—supposedly to observe the women at their orgies—where he will be torn to pieces
by his own frenzied mother, Cadmus's daughter Agave.

In the pathetic confusion of the once proud and confident Pentheus, no clear distinction remains between the disguises he as-
sumes, for his own reasons, and real madness. Still deliberating
with some appearance of clarity about what he should wear and
about whether he should make the trip at all, Pentheus is nevertheless descending, pathetically, into fatal confusion. "Well, any
course is better than having the bacchants treat me with contempt," he assures himself as he gives apparently judicious consideration to Dionysus's ruse of disguising him. "I myself shall
deliberate about what seems best" (Bacchae, lines 842–843). But
Pentheus's capacity for deliberating at all is clearly disintegrating
under the delusions induced by the god. The disguise suggested as
a ploy by the playful god of theater will also be the instrument of
madness, cruelly exploited by the vengeful god.

The messenger's report on the horrors that ensue, and the chorus's lyrical accompanying songs about the transformations enacted on the mountain, powerfully evoke the metamorphosis of
reason into madness and the sad return from madness to truth.
Emotions undergo a transformation on the mountain—from
harmless delights to violence; from playfulness to frenzy. In the
report given to Pentheus by the herdsman who has observed the
women at their revels, the scene is one of peaceful festivity—"a
marvel of ordered calm to look at"—women young and old gar-
landed with flowers, draped in fawn skins and suckling young

wild animals (*Bacchae,* line 692). The tranquil scene changes utterly. As the women sense the presence of the hidden ambushers, they transform themselves immediately from hunted to hunters. They tear the herdsman's cattle to pieces and, rampaging on to the villages, destroy everything in their path with a power that resists all counterattack. In the end it is not fear of the vengeful god that dominates the perception of any who are not themselves crazed. "So, master," the herdsman concludes, "receive this god into the city, whoever he is. For apart from his other greatness, they report this, I am told, that he gave to mortals the vine that puts an end to pain. If there is no wine, there is no Aphrodite or any other pleasure for mortals." The chorus leader chimes in, "I hesitate to speak frankly to the ruler, but speak I shall: there is no god greater than Dionysus" (*Bacchae,* lines 774–777).

Euripides captures the transformations of mood in skillfully nested accounts. The herdsman's report captures a dramatic shift from the harmony of the women with the animals to the barbarity of a marauding horde. In a parallel motif, the messenger who returns to Thebes to report the fate of Pentheus describes the sudden reversal of Pentheus's position—from prurient observer to hunted prey. But before Pentheus's downfall is recounted, there is a poetic interlude on the motif of transformation from hunted to hunter in the chorus's wonderful description of the fawn at play:

> Shall I ever in the
> > nightlong dances
> move my white feet
> in ecstasy? Shall I toss
> my head to the dewy heaven
> like a fawn that plays
> amid green meadow delights
> when she has escaped the dread huntsmen,

> eluding their guard
> and leaping their fine-spun nets?
> (*Bacchae*, lines 862–869)

In its evocation of the positive pleasure that resides in the mere cessation of pain—of a sensuous immediacy in the release from danger—the fawn passage anticipates some aspects of later Epicurean doctrines. Cicero will later sum up the Epicurean position as follows: "Quite generally the removal of pain causes pleasure to take its place. Hence Epicurus did not accept the existence of anything in between pleasure and pain. What some people regarded as in between—the complete absence of pain—was not only pleasure but also the greatest pleasure. For anyone aware of his own condition must either have pleasure or pain. Epicurus, moreover, supposes that complete absence of pain marks the limit of the greatest pleasure, so that thereafter pleasure can be varied and differentiated but not increased and expanded."[22] We can discern a darker side to the fawn's transition from pain to pleasure in the *Bacchae*—another transformation, which Euripides seems to see as no less immediate than that from distress in the face of danger to the sensuous awareness of safety. The sense of release from danger gives way immediately to the celebration of a different pleasure. The sweetness of escape is immediately transformed into the sweetness of revenge:

> What good is cleverness? Is there
>   any god-given privilege
> nobler in the sight of men
> than to hold one's hand in triumph
> over the heads of foes?
> What is noble is always loved.
> (*Bacchae*, lines 877–881)

There is something mysterious about this metamorphosis of emotion. The fawn, after all, is in no position to take vengeance on its predators. Once again, the passage has resonances with older Heraclitean ideas of the interactions and transformations between opposites. Without the fierceness of the fawn hunt, Dionysus and his companions cannot disport themselves in fawn skins; and the lack of reverence toward the god who represents playfulness and oblivion is part of a dark play of opposing forces. The fable of the transformation of the Bacchae repeats old cosmic struggles. The downfall of the pathetic Pentheus is part of a bigger picture than the individual tragedy unfolding on the mountain; the Euripidean transitions in emotion reenact Heraclitean conflicts and transformations. Dionysus pursues Pentheus, while the chorus cries:

> On, you swift hounds of madness, on to
>   the mountain,
> where Cadmus's daughters keep their assembly!
> Set them in frenzy
> against him who in womanish dress
> spies in madness upon the maenads!
> (*Bacchae*, lines 977–981)

Euripides has brilliantly exploited his sources, and his dramatic resources, to bring together emotions and attitudes not normally associated. The ideal of respect for the gods—rather than taking the form of pious restraint—here manifests itself as an openness to spontaneity. Again, the issue of respect or disrespect toward custom lies at the heart of the issue. Pentheus, in the words of the chorus, has set out "with maddened heart and crazed wits, thinking to master by force what cannot be mastered" (*Bacchae*, lines 999–1001); but the reality is that in his demented state Pentheus

has neither the spontaneity of madness nor the wisdom of restraint associated with respect for custom.

The increasingly dazed Pentheus is led off, supposedly to observe the women at their revels. The horrific reversals—from observer to observed, from figure of authority to animal prey—are
vividly recounted to Cadmus by the messenger. The ill-fated Pentheus seeks to climb a pine tree to get a better view of the women. Dionysus uses his suprahuman strength to draw the topmost
branches of the pine down to earth. After setting Pentheus on it,
the god returns the tree to its upright position, so that Pentheus is
now plainly visible to the distant women. The observer becomes
vulnerable to observation, and the stampeding horde is relentlessly drawn to him. Pentheus's crazed mother, Agave, tears him
apart, under the illusion that she is sacrificing a young lion cub.
"Are you joyous?" the chorus asks. "Exultant," she responds,

> since with this catch I have accomplished
> great deeds, great and plain to see!
> (*Bacchae,* lines 1198–1199)

To Cadmus is left the sad task of drawing his daughter out of
her delusions and bringing her to knowledge of the truth. In the
remarkable passage in which Cadmus gently leads the deranged
mother to a recognition of what she has done, Euripides amplifies
his earlier explorations of the confusion of moral agency that can
result from the interaction of gods and men. He has her first look
at the sky, which she sees as "brighter than before and clearer." As
she gazes at it, Agave slowly becomes aware of a change in her
mind too; her thoughts are becoming clearer. Cadmus urges her
to now look at the head she holds in her hands: "Look at it, get
surer knowledge" (*Bacchae,* lines 1263–1281). Here is a powerful
enactment of the tragedy that resides in gaining a clear understanding of what we have done in a state of confusion. Responsi-

bility is not removed by the knowledge that the gods can intrude on what we do. There is no escape into blaming Dionysus for a mother's having slaughtered her son. Cadmus's need to pass judgment on the god as well as on his own household is not lessened by that recognition. The god has reacted too harshly to the contempt shown him. The poignant exchange between Cadmus and Dionysus captures the interplay between necessity and responsibility. "Gods ought not to be like mortals in their tempers," Cadmus chides. "Long ago, Zeus my father ordained this," Dionysus responds (*Bacchae,* lines 1348–1349).

Justice and vengeance—along with fate and responsibility—are inextricably woven together in this exchange. Cadmus rebukes Dionysus in the name of a higher standard that ought to govern the actions of the gods; Dionysus exonerates himself by appealing to a fate ordained by Zeus. The drama of human and divine madness has run its course. Cadmus and Agave sadly face their separate exiles. The play ends with the refrain celebrating openness to the unexpected, already familiar from the end of *Helen:* "What heaven sends has many shapes, and many things the gods accomplish against our expectations. What men look for is not brought to pass, but a god finds a way to achieve the unexpected. Such was the outcome of this story" (*Bacchae,* lines 1388–1392).

Because of corruptions in the text of the concluding passages of the *Bacchae,* we cannot know what, if any, was Euripides' final judgment on the role of the gods. Some have seen in the conclusion of the *Bacchae* a recantation of his earlier skeptical stance. In any case, the play remains multivoiced. Dionysus may see himself as having done no more than exact rightful vengeance; he may see himself as the vehicle of the just deliverances of fate, having been "treated with contempt, though a god." The final judgment is not allowed to rest there, however. Cadmus has his say against the excess of the gods, while acknowledging the wisdom nonetheless of observing the force of custom in paying them respect. A certain kind of reverence toward the gods is desirable, even if the gods do not deserve it—even, perhaps, if there are no gods. This right attitude is no longer about religion as such; it is about custom, and about the insights embodied by custom and legend: to ignore the gods is to neglect our own complex natures.

Where in all this is providence? If we think of it as the idea of divine concern and provision for human needs, the most obvious location for it is among the gods whose wisdom and goodwill is subjected to skeptical challenge throughout the dramas. But we can also see in these plays the elements of a different way of thinking of providence—in the idea of a higher necessary order to which the gods themselves should conform. The sense of an ethical force residing in necessity is not clearly articulated in the struggles of these characters. Neither free will nor the acceptance of necessity can be distinguished with sufficient clarity to allow for a clear opposition here between alternative ethical ideals. Throughout the *Bacchae,* however—and more generally throughout Euripides' plays, of which it is in many ways a summation— intimations are offered of a sense of cosmic justice that transcends the vagaries of the Greek gods; of a justice to which they too must be subject. It is an idea that will find fuller expression in later Stoic philosophy, which will draw on the Heraclitean vision of a transformation of opposites to articulate a more explicit idea of a cosmic justice that yields a unified world of gods and men—a unity of cosmic and human nature. Only with that transition will it be safe to ignore the gods.

2   The World of Men and Gods

Plato notoriously distrusted literary representations as distortions of truth. In book 10 of his *Republic* he has the poets exiled from his ideal state. He was no lover of the theater. Just as notoriously, though, he appropriated literary strategies into his own philosophical writing. His reconstructions of the figure of Socrates in his dialogues draw on dramatic techniques that the early Greek dramatists had used to explore ethical dilemmas. In the *Timaeus* he brings the dialogue form together with narrative strategies in a remarkable and at times bizarre synthesis of literature and philosophy.[1]

Plato's *Timaeus:* A Tale of Design and Necessity

As a work of philosophy, the *Timaeus* must rate as one of the strangest ever produced. It is a tale of origins—of how the world came into existence and human beings were fashioned within it. Although it is constructed as a fictional narrative, the story claims not only to be a true account of "becomings," but also to ground judgments about how human beings should live, and about how their political life should be organized. Audacious, exuberant, and beautiful, it remains an anomaly among the works of Plato. Contemporary philosophers can readily admire other dialogues for their subtle argumentation on questions still recognized as philosophical; the *Timaeus* can at first seem to belong in the genre of fantasy rather than serious philosophy. Yet here it is: dazzling storytelling, unapologetically combined with the argumentative procedures of philosophy, in a narrative that presents design and necessity as so little at odds that they can complement—even require—each other's existence.

The dating of the *Timaeus* in relation to Plato's other dialogues remains contentious. It has often been seen as one of Plato's final works. Yet its subject—the nature of the well-governed city—relates so closely to the political masterpiece of Plato's middle period, the *Republic,* that some commentators have wanted to reassign it, along with its companion piece, the *Critias,* to that earlier period. Whatever the *Timaeus's* chronological relation to the *Republic,* it is clear that the dialogue is meant to remind us of his political utopia. The action of Timaeus's story takes place between a fictional "yesterday"—in which Plato has had Socrates explore his own views on political organization—and a "tomorrow" in which Critias will return to those political themes; but the promised revisiting of the themes of the *Republic* will remain unfulfilled. What remains—for our edification and mystification—is the putative founding of the utopian Republic: the story of the world's beginnings. It is a creation story that continues to haunt us with its outrageous self-confidence and its wild beauty.

The frame of the dialogue is complex and subtle. Plato, with consummate literary skill, positions Timaeus's story within careful nestings of cultural allusions and rhetorical strategies. Having listened to Socrates, his interlocutors are now to entertain him in turn with "a feast of discourse" that will demonstrate their mastery of the art of philosophy—"the greatest gift the gods have given men"; but the exercise is to be no light entertainment. The performers, Socrates assures them, are better fitted "by nature and education" than the poets to take part in both politics and philosophy. They will demonstrate their skills by continuing the intellectual exercise he has begun: starting from the imagined ideal citizens he has already created, Socrates' companions will now put them to work at performing some imagined noble action (*Timaeus* 19e–20c).

The performance that ensues, however, takes a significant turn: Timaeus and Critias add an element that Socrates has not requested. The story they intend to tell is not of a nonexistent utopia; it is purportedly set in the ancient past of Athens. This is a clever move on Plato's part. Socrates' art of philosophy—which Plato has honored throughout his dialogues—will receive cultural legitimation through association with the collective enactment of ancient stories. His followers will be cast in the roles of competing performers and storytellers, seeking the approval of Socrates in a way reminiscent of that in which ancient drama festivals were presented to judges. At the same time, the political content of the story also gains legitimation: rather than being set as an imaginary utopia in a possible future, Socrates' ideal state will be set in the real past. But of course it is a past so distant that its reconstruction must be an exercise of imagination—of storytelling.

Timaeus's imagined long-lost Athens is depicted as contemporary with the mythical city of Atlantis; the "noble acts" that Critias is expected to sketch eventually will be the deeds performed by the ancient Athenians in their war against the aggressive citizens of Atlantis, at a time before both cities were destroyed by an earthquake and flood. The storytelling itself is also positioned as a performance of noble deeds—as an exercise in reasoned imagining that, being at once politics and philosophy, will surpass the previous efforts of both the Sophists and the poets.

Critias tells Socrates that the tale which he and Timaeus will jointly tell is, though strange, certainly true. It has, he says, been attested by the wise leader Solon, who told it to Critias's grandfather, who passed it on to him. The story will be, as Socrates requested, a story of action—a story of war; but it also incorporates reflection on the activity of storytelling itself—the recitation of poems and the delivery of speeches at the festival known in their boyhood as the Registration of Youth. The story supposedly told there is in turn one from an older past—a tale allegedly brought by Solon from Egypt. Critias says it might have made Solon as famous a poet as Homer or Hesiod, if only Solon had not become distracted.

What they will tell, then, is a story of ancient Athens, transmitted via Egypt—a story of a past so ancient it has been lost to the Athenians themselves. The political organization of the ancient city corresponds remarkably, Critias claims, to Socrates' version of the ideal state. Plato pushes the artifice further: the political ideals of the Republic are grounded not only in the ancient past of Athens but beyond that, in the rational principles governing the organization of the world itself. This first part of the story will be told by Timaeus, because of his interest in astronomy. Critias will then, in the "tomorrow" of the dialogue, tell that part of the story which relates more directly to the political organization of ancient Athens and the war in which its citizens took part.

The frame of the story thus provides a nesting of performances and of the judging of performances: Socrates' anticipated judgment of the promised performances of Timaeus and Critias; the youth festival at which Critias claims first to have heard the story; and Solon's alleged recitation in Egypt of stories of ancient Athens—which the Egyptians are said to have regarded as simplistic genealogies, "no better than the tales of children" (*Timaeus* 23b). At the root of it all is the story itself—the story told by the Egyptians in response to Solon's inadequate performance; the very story that will now be told to Socrates.

The carefully constructed framework allows the narration of the story to be self-reflective; the telling of the story encourages reflection on the Socratic art of philosophy—on the appropriation of literary strategies to philosophical ends. The dialogue is as much about the notion of design in philosophical narration as it is about the design of the world. The theme of necessity—of its part in the origins of the world, of its relations with design—runs through the story. So too, at another level, does the notion Timaeus calls probability, which he sees as the appropriate mode of evaluation for truth seeking of the kind enacted in Socratic method.

The story—both in its content and in the accompanying reflection on its production—explores the interrelation of design, chance, and necessity. The layer of methodological reflection links the storytelling to the consideration of copies and representation, which is part of the story of origins. It links it also to the related consideration of the connection between knowledge and opinion, which Plato has had Socrates explore in other dialogues. The whole process is an exercise in constructing fictions in the service of truth seeking; and the truth of the story must be judged accordingly. We should not have expectations, Timaeus warns, that are inappropriate—either to the nature of the exercise or to our own natures. "Enough, if we adduce probabilities as likely as any others, for we must remember that I who am the speaker, and you who are the judges, are only mortal men, and we ought to accept the tale which is probable and inquire no further" (*Timaeus* 29d).

It is possible to discern three layers to Timaeus's tale of origins; and at each of them design and necessity are interrelated. At the first level, we find "an intelligible pattern, which is always the same"; at the next, the imitation of the pattern, which is generated and visible; and at the third, the strange notion of the "receiving principle" or "receptacle"—the "nurse" of all generation. The creation of the world is the combined work of Necessity and Mind. The story goes that Mind, the ruling power, "persuaded" Necessity to bring the greater part of created things to perfection. "And thus and after this manner in the beginning, through necessity made subject to reason, this universe was created." Still, Necessity is never entirely subject to Mind. Generation involves causes that are endowed with mind—the "workers of things fair and good"—and other causes, deprived of intelligence, that produce "chance effects," without order or design (*Timaeus* 46e–47e). God acts in accordance with the guiding principle of producing the best as far as possible; but he uses different levels of causes as his "ministers" (*Timaeus* 68e).

Mind may be the "ruling power"; but in this complex structure it does not of itself determine what will happen. Necessity may be amenable to Reason, but Reason does not have the power to override it. As Leibniz will later observe in his own version of the production of the best of all possible worlds, to "persuade" is not thereby to "necessitate." In the world of the *Timaeus,* the convergence between chance and necessity can seem strange to modern minds, accustomed to associate necessity with the nonrandom, and chance with the random. Purpose operates in this world, but it has no power to override necessity; design is limited by spontaneous or irrational movements, associated with "unpersuaded" necessity.

The idea of Necessity (*Ananke*) as a pervasive feature of the world runs through Greek mythology and earlier Greek philosophy. Roberto Calasso, in *The Marriage of Cadmus and Harmony,* traces it through a succession of images of an imprisoning net or girdle—a set of bonds with which human beings must struggle. "According to Parmenides, being itself is trapped by the 'bonds of powerful Ananke's net.' And in the Platonic vision of things, we find an immense light, 'bound to the sky and embracing its whole circumference, the way hempen ropes are bound around the hulls of galleys.'"[2] In the view of the world presented in the *Timaeus*, necessity is a constant presence—never entirely "persuaded" by reason, but also never constituting the entire story.

Necessity, chance, and design are interwoven in an intricate dance throughout the *Timaeus* narrative. It is in the treatment of the third layer of the origins of becoming—the "receptacle"—that the interaction of chance and design comes most clearly into view. Plato has Timaeus liken the "receptacle" to a mother—a receiving principle that is not to be termed earth or air or fire or water, or any of their compounds. Rather, it is "an invisible and formless being which receives all things and in some mysterious way partakes of the intelligible, and is most incomprehensible." This originary receptacle is not entirely passive in relation to the forms it receives. Being "full of powers" that are neither similar nor "equally balanced," it was "never in any part in a state of equipoise" but "swaying unevenly hither and thither." Shaken by these unequal powers, the originary elements are "carried continually, some one way, some another," as grain is "shaken and winnowed by fans and other instruments used in the shaking of corn." The "receiving vessel" thus moves "like a winnowing machine," scattering the elements (*Timaeus* 51b–52e).

Is that a model of design, chance, or necessity? Plato seems not to mind that the issue is never resolved. Metaphors of nurturance, of caring for things, unite the apparently opposed concepts. "Now there is only one way of taking care of things, and this is to give to each the food and motion which are natural to it. And the motions which are naturally akin to the divine principles within us are the thoughts and revolutions of the universe" (*Timaeus* 90d). The notion of providence—of the adapting of things to their natures—allows Plato to move between what might otherwise be disparate accounts of the world and of human behavior within that world. Providence is a central concept in the content of the story. It is also methodologically crucial; determining what will and will not be included, it guides the construction of the narrative. As the story proceeds through the generation of the human body and its members, and of the human soul, Timaeus reminds his listeners that the whole narration is a story of how things must have come to be—"for what reason and by what providence of the gods; and holding fast to probability, we must pursue our way" (*Ti-*

maeus 44d). Providence is here the other side of the coin to Timaeus's version of "probability." It is what allows the story to carry its own force of necessity: this is how things must have been; this is how "we must pursue our way"—in the "strange and unwonted inquiry" that is to "bring us to the haven of probability" (*Timaeus* 48d).

The old Greek gods occupy an interesting position in the *Timaeus*. They are encompassed in the wider story of the providence of the creator, the "great Artificer." The gods have beginnings, although they will not be "liable to the fate of death" (*Timaeus* 41b). Here Zeus, along with the other gods, is a lesser being—a creation of the great Artificer. The gods do play a mediating role in the creation of human beings. The creator, having made a beginning, sowing the seed of the divine in mortal beings, hands over the rest of their fashioning to the gods. A place is made in the story for the old ideas of divination; but they too are firmly circumscribed. No longer an authoritative source of knowledge, the art of divination has been given by God as an accompaniment "not to the wisdom but to the foolishness of man." Prophetic truth and inspiration are attained not when people are awake and "in their wits," but only when they are asleep or demented (*Timaeus* 71e). Their interpretation demands that we have our wits about us. Divination is accommodated into the life of reason; but it has no authority independent of it.

Timaeus's "language of probability" delivers conclusions that may look fanciful, to say the least. From knowing that the world is fashioned like "the fairest and most perfect of intelligible beings," we are to conclude that it is "one visible animal comprehending within itself all other animals of a kindred nature." Timaeus's world is not only permeated with reason; it came into being as a "living creature truly endowed with soul and intelligence by the providence of God" (*Timaeus* 30c–30d). This world-creature has no need of sensory organs—for there is nothing outside itself to be perceived—or, indeed, of any organs at all, because it is entirely self-sufficient. Its only movement is a circular one, requiring no legs or feet. Soul is at its center, but in such a way that it is diffused throughout the whole, providing also its exterior environment. "And he made the universe a circle moving in a circle, one and solitary, yet by reason of its excellence able to converse with itself, and needing no other friendship or acquaintance" (*Timaeus* 34b).

We will see this idea of the world as a unified animal ridiculed later by Cicero in his work *On the Nature of the Gods;* and still later by Hume in his *Dialogues concerning Natural Religion,* which was modeled on that work. Timaeus's conclusions can indeed seem arbitrary and bizarre. Yet his reasoning is designed to appeal to intellect, imagination, and emotion all at once. It relies on a sense of fittingness—of "this is how it must all have been"—which cannot be readily separated out into a level of pure logic and the attendant layers of imagination or emotion that embellish it. It appeals to the soul as a dynamic unity. What we have here is no mere dressing up of something that could—without loss of persuasiveness—be presented as bare logical argument.

Similar observations can be made of the central concept of providence that plays such an important role in both the content and the form of Timaeus's tale. We misunderstand how that idea operates if we think it can be readily captured in the logical idea of God as a "first cause." This caveat may make us less inclined to see the ethical implications of the worldview in *Timaeus* as springing without prior grounding out of a purely factual description of the world. The descriptions themselves are already suffused with imagination and emotion. This is philosophy as literature, no less than it is literature at the service of philosophy.

The way the arguments work can be seen in the central place Timaeus gives to the idea of proportion. It is manifested, for example, in the relations between the "prime" elements out of which the world is fashioned. Water and air are placed between fire and earth and stand in constant proportion to each other. "As fire is to air, so air is to water, and as air is to water, so is water to earth." This version of proportion is not just a matter of satisfying a mathematical formula—though Plato does have Timaeus include some detailed calculations. What drives his use of it is a literary exercise in imagining—though one that is never divorced from philosophical reasoning. The arrangement of the elements is described in terms of a "spirit of friendship," which allows the world to be "reconciled to itself" (*Timaeus* 32b–c). It is because emotion and imagination are already there in the description of the world that Timaeus can draw out the implications of harmony as an ethical ideal.

Central to the strategy of argumentation is the notion of providence, which is at work in every layer of the grounding description. Providence here works together with another central concept—the concept of imitation or copying; together they carry the weight of the argumentation. This is not to deny the rational force of the arguments. It is simply to insist on the importance of the guiding principle of what is fitting. Timaeus, in insisting that this is how the story "must" proceed, is not seeking to blind his audience to the invalidity of his logical moves. He is simply insisting that his listeners enter into the spirit of the inquiry he is conducting—that they respect the canons of this "art" rather than judge his performance in accordance with inappropriate expectations. "This is how we must pursue our way." What Wittgenstein would later call "the hardness of the logical *must*" is here carried by the shared sense of fittingness that binds the audience to the storyteller.

Thus there emerges an ethical ideal of living our lives in accordance with the truth of a world of which we are part. "God invented and gave us sight to the end that we might behold the courses of intelligence in the heavens, and apply them to the

courses of our own intelligence which are akin to them, the un-
perturbed to the perturbed; and that we, learning them and par-
taking of the natural truth of reason, might imitate the absolutely
unerring courses of God and regulate our own vagaries" (*Timaeus*
47c). Providence—as the idea of things being cared for, provided
for—is crucial to this ethical layer of the work. There is, as Timaeus says, "only one way of taking care of things"—by giving to
each thing what is natural to it, and within that frame, each man is
to renew in himself the "harmonies and revolutions of the universe," so that having assimilated them, "he may attain to the best
life which the gods have set before mankind, both for the present
and the future" (*Timaeus* 90c–90d).

Timaeus, having finished the part of the story for "today," hands
the sequel over to Critias, who will continue it in the fictional tomorrow. His part of the story promises to meet Socrates' specifi-
cation that it will put his ideal citizens into action in noble deeds
of war. The promise, however, remains unfulfilled in the dialogue
that bears Critias's name. Critias takes us through the preliminar-
ies to a point where Zeus is about to address the assembled gods:
he will tell them how he proposes to humble the warriors of Atlantis at the hands of the Greeks. Before the story of noble deeds
can proceed, Zeus's speech breaks off in midsentence: "And when
he had called them together he spake as follows."[3] Zeus falls silent.
When we see him reappear, in Stoic thought, it will be as part of a
very different configuration with concepts of necessity and providence.

Stoic Providence: The Transformation of Zeus

He was a force to be reckoned with, by gods and men. Violence
and power struggles surrounded the origins of Zeus and continued to mark his supremacy among the Greek gods. His father was
Cronus, the youngest of the Titans, who had wrested power from

their father Uranus. The stories of struggles for supremacy went back further than that too—stories of rebellion and of revenge for rebellion; of fathers castrated by sons, and of sons swallowed by angry, threatened fathers. Uranus had thrown his sons, the Cyclopes, into Tartarus; the Titans released them and awarded the sovereignty of earth to Cronus, who then used his newfound power to confine the Cyclopes all over again.

After Cronus married his sister Rhea, their dying father, Uranus, prophesied that one of Cronus's own sons would dethrone him. So, every year, Cronus swallowed the children Rhea bore him—until the rhythm was broken by the emergence of his newborn son Zeus. Rhea hid the infant, but Cronus pursued him across the skies. In response, Zeus turned himself into a serpent, and his nurses into bears. It was the first in a long history of self-transformations that etch the exploits of Zeus, his spectacular flights and pursuits, permanently on the cosmos. A god of cosmic proportions, Zeus's status as Lord of the Universe was not easily ignored: his doings were writ large in the constellations of the night sky.

The supremacy of Zeus was forged in rebellion and maintained in ongoing vengeance—commemorated in tales of swallowing and regurgitation. Cronus was forced by Zeus to disgorge his older brothers and sisters, along with the stone Cronus had been given to swallow in place of Zeus. He then led them all in a war against the Titans, in the course of which the Cyclopes were once again liberated from Tartarus. In gratitude they gave Zeus the weapon that would be forever associated with him—the thunderbolt, mark of his supremacy in the heavens. Even so, powerful and supreme though he undoubtedly was, the fearful sagas of gorging and disgorging continued. He swallowed the Titaness Metis— whom he had pursued across the sky, after it was prophesied that she would bear him a son who would depose him. His raging headache then made him let out a howl of rage that echoed

through the cosmos until other gods broke his skull open. Thus
was born the warrior-goddess Athena, who, famously, sprang fully
armed from her father's head—a fitting origin for the goddess of
wisdom.

Conflict and lust marked the exploits of Zeus. His powerful
desires, combined with his remarkable capacity for self-transfor-
mation, made him a scheming and rapacious lover. When his twin
sister, Hera, rejected his courtship, he cunningly took the disguise
of a poignant, bedraggled cuckoo, which she obligingly warmed
at her breast; then Zeus assumed his true form and raped Hera,
to shame her into marrying him. Their ensuing marital conflicts
were also engraved on the night skies, along with Zeus's other am-
orous adventures. Hera led a revolt of the gods: the rebels bound
Zeus while he slept with his thunderbolt out of reach. In revenge,
Zeus hung her from the sky with golden bracelets on her wrists.

From Zeus's loves sprang other gods—Hermes, Apollo, Artemis,
Dionysus—whose relations with mortals were to bring many fortunes and misfortunes on the human race. Zeus's part in the lives
of mortals went deeper, though, than the common vagaries of
human dealings with the gods. It is in his relations with Necessity,
Chance, and Fortune that his legendary power most strongly per-
meates human affairs. The legendary power of Zeus could not
prevail against Necessity. But he did order the movement of the
heavenly bodies; and through the Fates—of whom he claimed to
be the leader, and at times even the father—he could interfere in
human affairs. Through his complex relationship with the Fates,
with Necessity, Chance, and Fortune, a new set of transformations
entered the Zeus narrative at the nexus between myth and philosophy.

Stories of Zeus were interwoven with philosophical reflection
in early Greek thought. Robert Graves, in his compilation and
study of the Greek myths, describes the formation of the "artificial" deity Tyche, allegedly the daughter of Zeus, to whom he gave

the power to decide the fortunes of individual mortals. Tyche, at least in Graves's account, was "artificial" in that she was a product not of legend but of philosophy—an imaginative construct designed under the guidance of philosophical definition. Tyche was altogether irresponsible in the awarding of good or bad fortune; she is represented as running about juggling with a ball, exemplifying the uncertainty of chance—sometimes up, sometimes down. The counterweight to her fickleness is given by the philosophers to the ancient goddess known as Nemesis. If it happens that a mortal arrogantly boasts of Tyche's favor—neither sacrificing a part of them to the gods nor using them to alleviate the poverty of his fellow-citizens—Nemesis intervenes to humble him.

This idea of Nemesis as exerting a moral control over Tyche is a redefinition—a philosophical twist to the persona of Nemesis; however, the links between Zeus and Nemesis had a long prior tradition. Zeus is supposed to have pursued Nemesis—the nymph-goddess of death-in-life, also known as Leda—over the earth and through the sea. Though she constantly changed her shape, he violated her by taking the form of a swan; and from the egg she laid came Helen, whose beauty profoundly influenced human fortunes through the devastating Trojan War. That older Nemesis was already associated with the wheel of Fortune whose turning reflected the solar year. Graves suggests that her Latin counterpart was Fortuna (that is, Vortumna, "she who turns the year about"). When the wheel had turned half-circle, the sacred king—raised to the summit of his fortune—had to die; but when it had come full circle, he returned to avenge himself on the rival who had supplanted him. The cycles of devouring and being devoured, of supplanting and vengeance, link the myths of Zeus—the great supplanter—to older nature cycles.

The metamorphoses of Zeus in Greek mythology were many and marvelous. With the entry of the philosophers into the business of reshaping myths in accordance with philosophical analysis, though, his transformations entered a new phase. His place in philosophical thought is most strikingly articulated in the famous "Hymn to Zeus," written by the Stoic philosopher and poet Cleanthes, who succeeded Zeno as the head of the Stoic school in 262 BCE. Whereas for Plato Zeus was a part of the whole, created by the "great craftsman," he becomes for Cleanthes the creator of mortals, the omnipotent ruler of the cosmos: "Prime mover of nature, who with your law steers all things, hail to you." The hymn goes on, "All this cosmos, as it spins around the earth, obeys you, whichever way you lead, and willingly submits to your sway."[4]

Zeus's thunderbolt was previously the symbol of a dominant being whose will must be reckoned with by gods and men; but it now becomes something more. The "double-edged fiery ever-living thunderbolt," which Zeus holds at the ready in his "unvanquished hands," now becomes the symbol of the universal law that governs gods, men, and the whole cosmos. With it all the works of nature are accomplished.[5]

Modern commentators have pointed out that the god to whom the hymn is addressed is at once the Zeus of popular religion, the ordering fire god of Heraclitus, and the Stoic providential deity. The Stoics believed that reason pervaded the cosmos; and for Cleanthes Zeus's thunderbolt directs this "universal reason," which "runs through all things and intermingles with the lights of heaven both great and small." This reason that governs the cosmos is not only a locus of universal power; it is also a benign, loving force for good.[6]

Zeus, in the persona Cleanthes gives him, knows how to make crooked things straight and to order that which is in disorder. By bringing all things together into the unity of universal reason, he acts as a restorative force—as an antidote to evil. Zeus loves things that are otherwise unloved. "For you have so welded into one all

things good and bad that they all share in a single everlasting reason." This "bountiful Zeus of the dark clouds and gleaming thunderbolts" is a source of protection for mankind against its own
"pitiful incompetence." The hymn ends on an exultant note: "For
neither men nor gods have any greater privilege than this: to sing
forever in righteousness of the universal law."[7]

The Stoic transformation of Zeus is not a simple matter of extending to him the status of creator that Plato had given to the
"Great Craftsman." Cleanthes, along with the other Stoics, has a
different view from that developed in the *Timaeus* of the relationship between the creator and the world he produces. Like Plato,
they see the world as having the unity of a creature—as if it were a
single vast organism. But where Plato's craftsman-God works on
a preexisting material, which then takes on its own life, the Stoics
see God as identical with the cosmos—at the same time, Heraclitean fire and divine providence. It is difficult to separate out here
what came from Heraclitus and what was original to the Stoics;
for the Stoics are themselves among the most important sources
of interpretation of Heraclitus. The Heraclitean elements, in any
case, coexist with more Platonic teleological themes.

Along with the view of the cosmos as a unified living creature,
the Stoics took from the *Timaeus* the idea of a fittingness in the
adaptation of things to one another and to the whole. They developed much further than Plato did the idea that the cosmos is not
merely intelligible, but itself suffused with reason. Not only can it
be rationally understood; it is itself a rational being, the corporeal
form of Mind or Logos. This makes for a distinctive version of the
idea of the world as providentially ordered. Providential order is
now immanent in the world itself, not imposed from outside by
an independently existing "master craftsman."

The Stoic world, like the world of the *Timaeus,* is permeated
with purpose. For the Stoics, however, providential purpose can

be seen as another way of describing the course of nature itself. In that respect, the Stoic version of providence can be seen as the convergence of the Platonic model and the Aristotelian model that was opposed to it. According to the *Timaeus* account, the cosmos was produced by a maker whose purpose was to make it as good as it could be, given the limitations of the material with which he had to work. In the Aristotelian account, by contrast, nature works for ends or goals, but this activity is immanent in the natural world, rather than chosen or imposed on it by an external agent. For the Stoics, God is the maker of the world; and he made it to be as good as possible. Yet this God is at the same time immanent in—indeed identified with—the world.

The closeness of Stoic identification of providence with the natural course of events is clearer in the accounts of providence offered by Cleanthes' predecessor Zeno, and by his successor Chrysippus, than it is in Cleanthes' own invocation of the loving solicitude of Zeus. The Greek anthologist Stobaeus attributes to Zeno in *On Nature* the view that Fate is "the force which moves matter in the same respect and in the same way" and that "it makes no difference to call this Providence and Nature."[8] Cleanthes, by contrast, allowed for some distinction between providence and fate; for him, not everything that is fated happens in accordance with providence. His "Hymn to Zeus" makes it clear that the acts of the wicked, as a class of events, come about without the aid of Zeus, though he does absorb them into the ordered whole in which the disorderly becomes ordered. "You love things unloved. For you have so welded into one all things good and bad that they all share in a single everlasting reason."

Chrysippus, who succeeded Cleanthes as head of the Stoic school, sided with Zeno; he treated providence and fate as identical and made an even closer identification than his predecessors had between god and the material world. In his work *On Providence*

Chrysippus presents providence as working through the necessary chain of determining causes in the natural world. Fate is the continuous causal chain of all existing things. It was Chrysippus who articulated the strongest version of this Stoic idea of fate as inexorable necessity, saying, "Fate is a certain natural everlasting ordering of the whole: one set of things follows on and succeeds another, and the interconnection is inviolable."⁹

The traditional picture of fate, expressed in ancient Greek drama, was that of a preordaining of certain crucial events in human life—the return of a hero, victory or defeat in war, a sacrifice, the time and circumstances of an individual death. Outcomes could be predetermined without the details' being fixed: how they would come to pass was not preestablished. Chrysippus was committed to a stronger version of fate, according to which every detail of the world process is determined—the origins of human actions no less than their outcomes. Cicero later commented, in his work *On Divination,* that the Stoic version of fate is the fate not of superstition but of physics—an "everlasting cause of things—why past things happened, why present things are now happening, and why future things will be."¹⁰ This view may sound like a relentless determinism that leaves no scope for human freedom or responsibility; but for the Stoics it was a natural development of the idea of the world as a unified rational being, which they had inherited from Plato.

Alexander of Aphrodisias, a commentator of the second century CE, emphasized in his work *On Fate* the connection the Stoics saw between universal determinism and the idea of the unity of the world: "Since the world is a unity which includes all existing things in itself and is governed by a living, rational, intelligent nature, the government of existing things which it possesses is an everlasting one proceeding in a sequence and ordering." He attributes to the Stoics the view that "the very fate, nature and rationale in accordance with which the all is governed is god. It is present in all things which exist and happen, and in this way uses the proper nature of all existing things for the government of all."[11] In this Stoic emphasis on fate as immanent providence, the transformation of Zeus is complete. The Greek historian and biographer Plutarch, writing in the second century CE, reported that Chrysippus had ended up believing "that no state or process is to the slightest degree other than in accordance with the rationale of Zeus, which he says is identical to fate."[12]

Zeus was not the only god appropriated by the Stoic philosophers; but he came to be identified as the primary cosmic force, whose several aspects could also be subsumed under other names. The dazzling richness of the Stoics' version of God—and their appropriation and adaptation of the old themes of the supremacy of Zeus in Greek mythology—are emphasized in a number of later commentaries. Diogenes Laertius, describing the Stoic philosophy early in the third century CE, reported that the Stoics' idea of God as pervading all things allowed them to call him by many descriptions according to his powers. "For they call him Zeus [Dia] as the cause . . . of all things, Zen in so far as he is responsible for, or pervades, life . . . Athena because his commanding-faculty stretches into the aether, Hera because it stretches into the air." It was, however, as Zeus, Diogenes Laertius says, that this god-cosmos was honored as "the creator of the whole and, as it were, the father of all."[13]

In the first century BCE, Cicero, in *On the Nature of the Gods*—of which we shall hear more shortly—talks about the variety of ways in which the Stoics described the unified cosmos, yet he stresses that all-pervasive reason lies at the center of the Stoic idea of God. Chrysippus, he says, "musters an enormous mob of unknown gods," for "divine power resides in reason, and in the soul and mind of the universe," as well as in the whole series of individual gods, along with "water, earth, air, the sun, moon and stars, and the all-embracing unity of things; and even those human beings who have attained immortality."[14]

Perhaps the most powerful of all descriptions of the transformation of Zeus—and of his power to absorb not only all other deities but all the elements and force of the universe—was offered by the Epicurean Philodemus, also writing in the first century BCE. He attributes to Chrysippus the view that Zeus is the "Reason which administers all things and the Soul of the All, and that all things by participation therein are in various ways alive, even the stones." For the Stoics, he observed, there are no male or female gods, just as cities or virtues are not really male or female; but Stoic philosophers have tried to accommodate their doctrines to "what is in Homer and Hesiod and Euripides and the other poets."[15] Zeus's power to subsume all is here linked with the power Chrysippus attributed to the Stoic philosophy of absorbing all that had gone before it. The power of Zeus has now been completely encompassed in the Stoic providence.

This transformation of the lustful and vengeful Zeus into the benign orderer of the cosmos may seem paradoxical; but if Zeus is identified with Stoic providential intelligence, it is no less true that he comes to be identified with the force of necessity that is manifested in whatever happens in the world—something that may at first sight seem very different. Design and necessity now become even more closely connected. In later thought concerning purpose and necessity, the idea of providence will again diverge, to align itself with the idea of a God-creator who transcends the natural world. So close has that association—between the idea of providence and the belief in a transcendent creator—now become, that it may seem surprising that providence could ever have been seen as existing independently of a transcendent divine will, unrestrained by necessity. The Stoic understanding of providence as closely connected with the inexorable necessities of the natural world, as we shall see, persisted in a strand of modern thought associated especially with the philosophy of Spinoza.

The Rotund and the Self-Absorbed:
Cicero on the Nature of the Gods

The Stoic transformation of Zeus was not the only change wrought in the gods of Greek mythology under the influence of the philosophers. The Epicureans, from a very different perspective, also challenged the notion of divine intervention in human affairs. For the Stoics the conjunction of design and necessity provided a bulwark against fear and vulnerability in a world subject to chance. As their principal philosophical opponents, the Epicureans rejected both beliefs—seeing the world instead as pervaded by neither necessity nor purpose. From the perspective of the Stoics, that could only be a bleak world; but the Epicureans found an exhilarating sense of freedom in the rejection of cosmic design and necessity. Indeed, their philosophy was largely driven by the desire to offer release from the debilitating effects of fear, which they saw as resting on false beliefs about human nature and about the nature of the world. The belief in an immaterial soul, they thought, left human beings vulnerable to fear of a perilous afterlife; and the false belief that the world is governed by relentless necessity, from the Epicurean perspective, gives rise to a sense of helplessness and passivity.

The Epicurean vision of a world liberated from design and necessity found beautiful expression in Lucretius's poem *De Rerum Natura,* written in the first century BCE. The world of Epicurean physics, as Lucretius saw it, was a world free of designing gods—safe from "haughty overlords." Without the gods' participation, Nature itself becomes the "free autonomous agent of everything." In this liberated world, human beings acquire a new autonomy; but the gods too gain their freedom from the onerous and irksome responsibilities of providing for human well-being. "For I appeal to the holy hearts of the gods, in their tranquil peace, leading their life of calm serenity. Who is capable of ruling the totality of the measureless, of holding in his hands and controlling the mighty reins of its depths? Who could turn all those heavens at the same time? Who could warm all those bountiful earths with celestial fires? or be present everywhere at all times to darken the earth with clouds, to shake the calm sky with thunder, to despatch thunderbolts (often rocking his own abodes with them!) and to withdraw to the wilds and furiously hurl his weapon?" The gods can be left to enjoy their tranquil lives, released from the furious hurling of cosmic weapons that in any case, Lucretius wryly observes, often miss the guilty and wipe out the innocent.[16]

Lucretius, with his skepticism about the role of the gods, can be read as mocking the Stoics' version of Zeus as well as the designer-god of the *Timaeus:* the burden of teleology is too weighty even for the most powerful of the gods. That burden has been placed on the gods unnecessarily; the idea that everything exists or happens for a purpose is a product of distorted reasoning. The fallacy can be seen clearly, Lucretius suggests, in perverse teleological reasoning about the human body, its senses and organs. "For nothing has been engendered in our body in order that we might be able to use it. It is the fact of its being engendered that creates its use. Seeing did not exist before the lights of its eyes were engendered, nor was there pleading with words before the tongue was created." Where things exist in advance of their use, it cannot be claimed that they came into being for the sake of their use. It is quite different with artifacts—the paradigm of design. The practice of resting the tired body, Lucretius goes on, is presumably much more ancient than the spreading out of soft beds; and the quenching of thirst came into being before cups. "Hence it is credible that these were desired for the sake of their use, for they were invented as a result of life's experiences."[17]

Like the Stoics, the Epicureans wanted to free human beings of the fears and superstitions associated with the need to placate temperamental deities; but their strategies for achieving this shared aim could not have been more different. Whereas the Stoics strove to bring gods and human beings together in a common world governed by rational design and necessity, the Epicureans were happy to have the gods retreat to an untroubled serenity, beyond human importunings and flattery. It is absurd, Lucretius argues, to think that the gods could ever have wished to create a wonderful world for the sake of humankind. What novelty could have tempted such tranquil beings to desire such a change in their lifestyle? In any case, what harm could it possibly have done us never to have been born? "Did our life lie in darkness and misery until the world's beginning dawned? Although anyone who has been born must wish to remain in life so long as the caresses of pleasure hold him there, if someone has never really tasted the passion for life and has never been an individual, what harm does it do him not to have been created?"[18]

As the Epicureans saw it, rejection of belief in providence should make life not harder, but easier, to bear. With the retreat of the designing gods, the "caresses of pleasure" can be more readily enjoyed. Yet it is not only design but also necessity that is driven from this Epicurean world. Freed from the relentless demands of fate—the illusory "overlord of everything," as Epicurus describes it in the *Letter to Menoecus*—human life will attain to a sense of responsibility that is not available under the reign of necessity. Necessity, Epicurus says, is "accountable to no one"; and fortune is "an unstable thing to watch." It is important to find what depends on ourselves, apart from any intruding overlord. If we are to be able to hold ourselves responsible for what we do, we must first free ourselves from belief in necessity, no less than from belief in interfering gods. "For it would be better to follow the mythology about gods than be a slave to the 'fate' of the natural philosophers: the former at least hints at the hope of begging the gods off by means of worship, whereas the latter involves an inexorable necessity."[19]

Epicurus and his followers avoid what they see as the harsh necessity of the Stoic cosmos through appeal to an intriguing and controversial concept—the "swerving" of the atoms of which the world is composed. As Lucretius describes it, the "decrees of fate" are intermittently broken—at no fixed points of space or time—by unpredictable swerves of atoms. These random "swervings" introduce an element of indeterminacy into the world. Epicurean physics thus leaves some scope for human free will. The Epicurean soul is no less material than the rest of the world; but the atoms that compose it are more fluid, less dense, than those which make up material bodies. Human volition, as a movement in this material soul, can influence other events—at any rate where a "swerving" has left an opening of indeterminacy between alternative possibilities. Still, the knowledge that our free will rests on random cosmic "swervings" may hold terrors of its own. Critics of the Epicureans questioned whether knowing that our escape from necessity depends entirely on chance offers any real reassurance.

From an Epicurean perspective, the Stoic is imprisoned by necessity. From a Stoic perspective, the Epicurean lives in a world empty of purpose; and such freedom as he has can be no true freedom, for it is subject to the vagaries of chance. The competing strengths—and absurdities—of the two perspectives are wittily observed in the dialogue *On the Nature of the Gods,* also written in the first century BCE, by the great Roman orator, statesman, and scholar Cicero. Cicero wrote the work, as he says in the prologue, in search of relief from the "dejection of spirit" he suffered following a "heavy and crushing blow" dealt by fortune. That event was the death of his daughter, in 45 BCE. Cicero's motives, though, went beyond dealing with personal grief: "I was languishing in idle retirement, and the state of public affairs was such that an autocratic form of government had become inevitable. In these circumstances, in the first place, I thought that to expound philosophy to my fellow countrymen was actually my duty in the interests of the commonwealth, since in my judgement it would greatly contribute to the honour and glory of the state to have thoughts so important and so lofty enshrined in Latin literature also" (*Nature of the Gods* 1.4.7–9).

The dialogue is set at the house of the narrator's friend Gaius Cotta, who himself participates in the argument as the "suave" exponent of the philosophical approach of the Academicians. This was the school that evolved from Plato's Academy; the Academicians were questioning, skeptical, skilled in the strategies of argument, doggedly opposed to dogmatism. As narrator, Cicero brings the three main philosophical schools of ancient Greece—Stoic, Epicurean, and Academic—into interaction through Roman characters in a Roman context. His own intellectual affinities are with the Academicians; but the spirit of open-ended inquiry is reflected not only in the content of Cotta's contribution, but also in the form of the dialogue as a whole. Cotta argues against the Epicurean attack on Stoicism offered by Velleius; but also against Balbus's defense of Stoicism against Velleius. In keeping with the spirit of the Academicians—and with Cicero's own skills as an orator—we are left with the understanding that no one speaker has had the final word; that the exchange of arguments is to be imagined as continuing beyond the confines of the work.

The debate is opened by Velleius, the confident and prolix Epicurean. As is customary with Epicureans, the narrator observes, Velleius is "afraid of nothing so much as lest he should appear to have doubts about anything." One would suppose he had himself "just come down from the assembly of the gods." Velleius ridicules the origins of Stoic theology in the designer-god of the *Timaeus*—a "baseless figment of the imagination," along with "that old hag of a fortune teller, the *Pronoia,* which we may render 'Providence'"

(*Nature of the Gods* 1.8.18). He is particularly scathing about the reverence for "rotund" gods, which the Stoics have taken over from the celebration of the sphere in *Timaeus*. Velleius mockingly suggests that the sphere is not conducive to mental stability; he would prefer a cylinder, a cube, a cone, or a pyramid. Infatuated with the sphere, the Stoics have assigned a bizarre mode of existence to their deity: "Why, he is in a state of rotation, spinning round with a velocity that surpasses all powers of conception. But what room there can be in such an existence for steadfastness of mind and for happiness, I cannot see. Also, why should a condition that is painful in the human body, if even the smallest part of it is affected, be supposed to be painless in the deity?" (*Nature of the Gods* 1.10.24).

Velleius confidently dismisses the all-pervading world-soul, as conceived by the Stoics, as belonging with "the dreams of madmen" rather than with "the considered opinions of philosophers" (*Nature of the Gods* 1.15–16.42). And what a "bondage of irksome and laborious business" it is to inflict on a god this endless maintenance of the world and guarding of the interests and lives of men (*Nature of the Gods* 1.20.52). As for Stoic doctrine of necessity or fate, it is "a belief for old women, and ignorant old women at that." Velleius asserts: "Epicurus has set us free from superstitious terrors and delivered us out of captivity, so that we have no fear of beings who, we know, create no trouble for themselves and seek to cause none to others" (*Nature of the Gods* 1.20.56). The gods can be left to themselves.

Velleius's version of Stoic theology is of course presented from the perspective of a hostile Epicurean critic. Cicero now subjects Velleius's speech to critique by a supposedly detached Academician, the "suave" Cotta. Velleius, Cotta argues, may have thought he was doing the gods a service by removing them from the arduous and absurd responsibilities of the Stoic gods; but the version of the gods he is left with presents its own anthropomorphic absurdities. The fault, according to Cotta's analysis, lies in precisely that Epicurean confidence—the lack of skepticism—which makes Velleius so dogmatic in his rejection of Stoic providence: "How delightful it would be, Velleius, if when you did not know a thing you would admit your ignorance, instead of uttering this drivel, which must make even your own gorge rise with disgust!" (*Nature of the Gods* 1.30.84). Having rejected the ridiculous spherical god of the Stoics, the Epicureans have reinvented the gods in the form of pleasure-seeking humans. In releasing the gods from the burden of caring for humans, the Epicureans have rendered those divinities idle. "This language not merely robs the gods of the movements and activities suitable to the divine nature, but also tends to make men slothful, if even god cannot be happy when actively employed" (*Nature of the Gods* 1.37.102).

An Epicurean god, Cotta mocks, would have to be "occupied for all eternity in reflecting: 'What a good time I am having! How happy I am!'. . . . Now how can there be any excellence in a being so engrossed in the delights of his own pleasure that he always has been, is, and will continue to be entirely idle and inactive?" (*Nature of the Gods* 1.40.114–116). Moreover, it seems that such a god could not elicit piety in human beings, since god and men could have nothing in common. The real upshot of Velleius's treatment of the gods, Cotta concludes, is that the gods in fact do not exist. Epicurus, though professing to retain the gods, has removed them so far from concern with human beings that he has actually abolished them.

So far, Cicero has offered his readers a hostile Epicurean account of Stoic theology, and a skeptical Academician riposte, exposing in turn the inadequacy of the Epicurean gods. Balbus, the Stoic spokesman, expresses a wish that Cotta should now use his eloquence to present a version of the gods that he regards as true, rather than merely use his skill at argumentation to abolish false ones. True to the spirit of his school, however, Cotta insists that he finds it easier to say what he does not think than what he does. It falls to Balbus, then, to provide the positive account of the Stoic version of the gods; and to Cotta once again to respond from the skeptical standpoint of the Academician.

The version of Stoicism that Balbus offers in response to Velleius differs in important ways from the account of the purposeful cosmos articulated by the earlier Greek Stoics. Balbus's providence is not immanent in the world; it is attributed to a plurality of creator-gods whose identities are differentiated from the cosmos. "Providence," he says, is used elliptically here for "the providence of the gods." These gods are not subjected to a superior craftsman-God on the Platonic model. Nor is this the providence of an all-powerful Zeus who has absorbed the other gods into himself. The ancient Stoic version of Zeus, as we have seen, radiated forth the plurality of the gods as different aspects of a single universal reason that pervaded the cosmos. Balbus's gods, by contrast, seem to conform very much to conventional religious belief in a plurality of deities; the gods expect reverence in exchange for their benevolent concern with the needs of humankind.

Balbus presents his departures from the beliefs of the Greek Stoics as stylistic embellishments, rather than substantial differences. His defense of the Stoic view of the cosmos aims for a "fuller and more flowing style" than that found in the brief syllogisms of the ancient Greeks. He wants a "flowing stream of eloquence," which will sweep aside the captious objections of his critics (*Nature of the Gods* 2.7.20). His rhetorical eloquence, however, is not always matched by the quality of his reasoning. He argues that since nothing is superior to the world—and nothing is superior to reason and wisdom either—we should expect that the world should possess reason and wisdom. The world must be endowed with wisdom, "for if it were not, man, although a part of the world, being possessed of reason would necessarily be of higher worth than the world as a whole" (*Nature of the Gods* 2.12.32).

Hence, he concludes, the world is an intelligent, and indeed also a wise being. It is not an argument for the unity of the cosmos that was endorsed by the ancient Stoics, though Balbus claims to be expounding Zeno's ideas in concluding that this "world mind" not merely is "craftsmanlike" but must be construed as itself a craftsman, which can be correctly designated as "prudence" or "providence." "And this providence is chiefly directed and concentrated on three objects, namely to secure for the world, first, the structure best fitted for survival; next, absolute completeness; but chiefly, consummate beauty and embellishment of every kind" (*Nature of the Gods* 2.22–23.58).

From all this it follows, Balbus claims, that the Stoic gods must be very different from the "insubstantial, do-nothing" gods of the Epicureans. "On the contrary, they are endowed with supreme beauty of form, they are situated in the purest regions of the sky, and they so control their motions and courses as to seem to be conspiring together to preserve and to protect the universe" (*Nature of the Gods* 2.23.60). Velleius was unjustified, then, in presenting the Stoic providence "in the guise of an old hag of a fortune-teller." For the Stoics do not imagine providence to be a "kind of special deity who rules and governs the universe." Rather, "providence," in Balbus's account of Stoic beliefs, is "as a matter of fact an elliptical expression. . . . When we speak of the world as governed by providence, you must understand the words 'of the gods' and must conceive that the full and complete statement would be 'the world is governed by the providence of the gods'" (*Nature of the Gods* 2.29.73–74).

Balbus has departed significantly from the ancient Greek Stoics. That modification now allows him to appeal to conventional piety, to bolster his argument in defense of Stoic providence. "If mankind possesses intelligence, faith, virtue and concord," he asks, "whence can these things have flowed down upon the earth if not from the powers above? Also since we possess wisdom, reason and

prudence, the gods must needs possess them too in greater perfection, and not possess them merely but also exercise them upon
matters of the greatest magnitude and value; but nothing is of
greater magnitude and value than the universe; it follows therefore that the universe is governed by the wisdom and providence
of the gods" (*Nature of the Gods* 2.31.81).

The interweaving of design and necessity, which was such a
striking feature of the early Greek versions of providence, here
seems to have unraveled. Providence, rather than being identified
with necessary purpose—immanent in the cosmos—becomes the
benevolent wills of a multiplicity of revered gods who govern the
world. The alignment between providence and necessity is broken. Indeed, later in his speech Balbus aligns necessity with
chance—opposing both to the design or purpose evident in the
universe. Just as works of art require an appeal to design, he argues, so too must the world that contains them. It cannot be the
product of "chance or necessity of some sort" but must rather be
a product of "divine reason and intelligence" (*Nature of the Gods*
2.35.88). "Can any sane person believe that all this array of stars
and this vast celestial adornment could have been created out of
atoms rushing to and fro fortuitously and at random? or could any
other being devoid of intelligence and reason have created them?
not merely did their creation postulate intelligence, but it is impossible to understand their nature without intelligence of a high
order" (*Nature of the Gods* 2.44.115).

Although Balbus's attack on chance is directed at Epicurean
doctrine, his version of the "providence of the gods"—manifesting
design rather than necessity—puts a new twist on the Stoic idea of
providence. The world reveals design and purpose; but what is
more, everything else in the world is made for the sake of those
living things endowed with reason and thus able to appreciate design and purpose; things are made for the sake of gods and men.
Here we have a new version of the cosmic city: "the world of gods

and men" is now the world that belongs to them, rather than the world they are privileged to inhabit. For the Greek Stoics the cosmic city resulted from bringing both gods and men under a common universal law of reason, which structures the cosmos as a whole. For Cicero's Balbus it is the exclusive society of those beings distinguished by reason for whose sake the rest of the universe has been designed. "For the world is as it were the common dwelling-place of gods and men, or the city that belongs to both; for they alone have the use of reason and live by justice and by law. As therefore Athens and Sparta must be deemed to have been founded for the sake of the Athenians and the Spartans, and all the things contained in those cities are rightly said to belong to those peoples, so whatever things are contained in all the world must be deemed to belong to the gods and to men" (*Nature of the Gods* 2.62.154).

Providence is no longer identified with the necessity that governs all, but with the direction of nonhuman things toward the end of meeting human needs. It is "the providence of the gods" that sees to it that those human needs are benignly met. Balbus's defense of Stoicism is explicitly a defense of piety. The skills in argument and eloquence that Cotta has learned at the Academy should, Balbus complains, be exercised not in "arguing both *pro* and *contra*," but in defense of the gods. "For the habit of arguing in support of atheism, whether it be done from conviction or in pretence, is a wicked and an impious practice" (*Nature of the Gods* 2.67.168).

Not surprisingly, the skeptical Cotta is unimpressed by the quality of Balbus's arguments. He ironically suggests that, if it follows from the excellence of the world that the world is rational, then it should also be concluded that the world is literate, that it is an orator, a mathematician, a musician, a philosopher. And if the world cannot give birth to rational beings without itself being rational, should we not conclude that it is not only a living being and wise but also that it is a harpist and a flute player? (*Nature of the Gods* 3.8–9.23). Cotta also repudiates Balbus's apparent assumption that reason is an unqualified good and hence to be regarded as a benevolent gift of the gods. "The divine bestowal of reason upon man is not in itself an act of beneficence, like the bequest of an estate; for what other gift could the gods have given to men in preference if their intention had been to do them harm? and from what seeds could injustice, intemperance and cowardice spring, if these vices had not a basis in reason?" (*Nature of the Gods* 3.28.71). "If the gods gave man reason, they gave him malice, for malice is the crafty and covert planning of harm; and likewise also the gods gave him trickery and crime and all the other wickednesses, none of which can be either planned or executed without reasoning" (*Nature of the Gods* 3.30.75).

Cotta concludes that Stoic providence deserves censure rather than praise, for bestowing reason on those who would undoubtedly use it wrongly and for evil. When we see the misfortunes that afflict human beings, we can conclude that "either providence does not know its own powers, or it does not regard human affairs, or it lacks power of judgement to discern what is the best" (*Nature of the Gods* 3.39.92–93).

Cicero himself, despite his identification with the Academicians, was not unsympathetic to the spirit of Stoic thought—at any rate in its more austere form. In other works, he defended doctrines of necessity—in particular of the fatalism that he saw as underlying the practice of divination; Cicero had himself after all held the office of augur. At the end of the dialogue *On the Nature of the Gods,* he allows himself, in the persona of the narrator, to give a qualified endorsement to the Stoics: Balbus's evocations of providence have "approximated more nearly to a semblance of the truth," than Cotta's suave skepticism (*Nature of the Gods,* 3.40.104).

The meanings of providence shift throughout these early texts. Providence as it appears in the *Timaeus* has overtones of what we now most readily associate with the idea: as Timaeus says, a "way of taking care of things," a provision of what is needed. Yet although providence has those clear associations with design and purpose, it is also evident that Plato does not see it as at odds with necessity. The connections between providence and necessity become more pronounced in the Stoic transformation of Zeus into a strong version of fate as the necessity for all that happens. In Cicero's dialogue, as we have seen, providence appears in various guises. According to which character is speaking, it can be presented as Pronoia—"that old hag of a fortune teller"; as universal cosmic necessity; or in the nurturing, "providing" manifestation of a multiplicity of benign gods. Yet a pattern is emerging.

The version of Stoic providence that Cicero has Balbus express, and allows Cotta to ridicule, has already moved some distance from the purer, more austere version envisioned by the ancient Greek Stoics. The "flow of eloquence," which Balbus suggests will enhance the pithier Greek arguments, brings with it doctrinal accretions. Balbus's providence is the responsibility of a plurality of purposeful gods, rather than the power of universal rational law. The older version—immanent providence—will persist in the continuing Stoic ideal of living in accordance with necessity. The plurality of benevolent gods, demanding to be honored and placated, will cease to be relevant to the development of that Stoic ideal. Balbus's version of the providence of purposeful gods, floating free of the necessities of the cosmos, will have a very different future: it will be absorbed as an element in later Christian versions of providence as a unified, omnipotent divine will.

3   Agreeing with Nature

Fate and Providence in Stoic Ethics

To live like a Stoic—as we now imagine that—is not a cheering prospect. The Stoics are best known for their reputed endurance—for the capacity to suffer with fortitude misfortunes that cannot be changed. The common understanding of their ethical theory is not particularly enlightening. They are best known as the principal ancient exponents of the ideal of living in accordance with our "natures"—if only we could decide what those are. Both strands in the stereotype of the Stoic have some truth. But the stereotypes fail to capture the magnetism of the Stoics' way of thinking about necessity. They leave it mysterious how Stoicism could elicit a joyful acquiescence, rather than a dour acceptance; and how necessity could be for them associated with—rather than at odds with—a sense of purpose.

The Ethical Force of Necessity

The vague cliché—"following nature"—does not do justice to the richness of Stoic ethical theory. It is often overlooked, for example, that the Stoics' version of nature is closely connected with the origins of modern ideas of cosmopolitanism. What is natural to human beings is, for the Stoics, what pertains to us—not by virtue of our belonging to any particular polis, but by virtue of our being citizens of the world. This transcendence of self-interest and provincialism is one of the great legacies from their remarkable idea that we inhabit a cosmic city—"the world of gods and men."

To understand how the Stoics could have found joy in the thought of necessity—and how they could have made living in accordance with it the core of a sustaining ethical ideal—we must first try to understand their distinctive conjunction of necessity and purpose. It was the Stoic version of providence that allowed the convergence of the two. In the thought of the early Greek Stoics, providence was not an expression of a freely operating divine will—except insofar as that idea could itself be identified with the necessary order of the cosmos, otherwise known as Zeus.

According to the account of Chrysippus's view offered by the commentator Calcidius in the fourth century CE, it was God's will that allowed providence and fate to be mutually identified. "For providence will be God's will, and furthermore his will is the series of causes. In virtue of being his will it is providence. In virtue of also being the series of causes it gets the additional name 'fate.'"[1] Providence, fate, and divine will are here inseparable. The Stoics may well have tried to infuse their view of the cosmos as ordered by necessity with the emotional residue of older reverence for the gods. The awareness of necessity also carried for them an emotional force of its own, however, capable of usurping the piety directed toward the traditional gods. What can we now make of this magnetism they found in necessity?

It is important to note, first, that the emotional force that Necessity carried for the Stoics was not primarily a matter of the rational content of the idea. It is the cognitive process of apprehending necessity—the recognition of the mind's own appropriate object—that carries the emotional punch. For the Stoics, reason rests on—or, as some of them would say, "supervenes" on—a base of what they call impulse. It is at the level of impulse that the mind's understanding of necessity becomes an affective engagement. Impulse is here closely connected with another crucial Stoic concept, which they call *oekeinosis*—"appropriation" or "familiarization." Under the influence of impulse, animals move toward what properly belongs to them. In this process of "appropriation," they make themselves at ease with what is to their benefit. Appropriation functions for the Stoics as both a description of the behavior of particular animals and as a feature of the cosmos as a whole. Animals are said to appropriate what is "proper" to them; but nature is also said to appropriate animals, thereby ensuring that they do indeed accept what is appropriate to them.

Stoic appropriation thus depends on Stoic ideas of providence. The movement within the concept of appropriation—the shifts of subject between particular animals and nature as a whole—are outlined in Diogenes Laertius's summary of Chrysippus's views on impulse and self-preservation: "They [the Stoics] say that an animal has self-preservation as the object of its first impulse, since nature from the beginning appropriates it, as Chrysippus says in his *On Ends,* Book I. . . . The first thing appropriate to every animal, he says, is its own constitution and the consciousness of this. For nature was not likely either to alienate the animal itself, or to make it and then neither alienate nor appropriate it. So it remains to say that in constituting the animal, nature appropriated it to itself. This is why the animal rejects what is harmful and accepts what is appropriate."[2] What the animal experiences as impulse, is at the same time the benevolent providential management of its nature within the world as a whole. "Appropriation" is in this context a recognition suffused with affection. At the level of the individual, it is a recognition of—and movement toward—what is fitting or suitable to it; but this movement of impulse is also a manifestation of a cosmic appropriation of the individual.

The Roman Stoic Seneca illustrated the idea of impulse, and its implications for Stoic ethics, by describing it as the effort to do what nature demands—even at the cost of pain and struggle. The baby struggles to stand, despite the frustration of falls. "A tortoise on its back feels no pain, but desire for the natural state makes it restless, and it does not stop struggling and shaking itself until it stands on its feet." In human life, he continues, there are stages, each of which can display its own kind of consciousness of the human being's changing constitution. "Each period of life has its own constitution, one for the baby, and another for the boy, another for the youth, and another for the old man. They are all related appropriately to that constitution in which they exist."[3] Fate and providence are equally, and inseparably, involved in this interplay between impulse and appropriation. Another early commentator, the Platonist Nemesius, attributed to Chrysippus and other Stoics the view that "every generated being has something given to it by fate: water has being cool as its gift, and each kind of plant has bearing a certain fruit; stones and fire have downward and upward movement respectively; so too animals, as their gift, have assent and impulse."[4]

The Stoics saw human reason as part of this structure of appropriation, "supervening" on human impulse to shape or craft the nonrational. As rational beings, we appropriate impulse, recognizing with affection our own natures. This basic connection between reason and impulse underpins the joyful recognition of necessities that is the core of Stoic ethics. All this gives a distinctive concreteness to the Stoic version of detachment; necessity is embedded in the unpredictable vicissitudes of life. The mind can give form to impulses, but it is limited by surrounding circumstances; things that are not of themselves impossible can be made so by circumstances external to them. The Stoic sage may in later periods of thought have been pilloried for his detachment from everyday realities, but the original ideal involved recognizing his insertion in a chain of concrete causes that bound him to the cosmos as a whole.

How then could Stoic ethics reconcile the all-important recognition of necessity with human freedom? Their Epicurean critics saw the Stoics as unable to accommodate free will to a thoroughly determinist physics. Freedom was for the Stoics an ideal to be attained, though, rather than a preexisting fact; it represented the achievement of a good life, rather than a precondition of it. Rather than trying, as the Epicureans did, to allow room for free will in the midst of interlinked determining causes, the Stoics saw freedom as a capacity for accommodating our lives to necessity. The concepts of impulse and appropriation are central to this ideal. So too is another concept—reservation. Stoic reservation saves us from being disappointed by what happens in our lives. While bearing some resemblance to modern concepts of detachment and acceptance, it differs from both; it can be seen as a tactical withholding of engagement. Although impulse may seem to us to be opposed to detachment, Stoic reservation shapes and complements impulse.

Stoic impulse—with or without reservation—belongs with necessity. In the transformation of Stoic impulse in the long history of the modern concept of the autonomous will, these connections are lost. The will, whether divine or human, is seen as opposed to necessity. With Stoic impulse recast as the will, necessity has little scope for being ethically significant. The mediating role of the concept of providence allowed the Stoics to see freedom and necessity as interconnected. In the older versions of Stoic ethics, these connections are explicitly grounded in Stoic cosmology and especially in the idea of the cosmic city—the world of common necessities governing gods and men.

Fate and providence—linked by their common identification with cosmic necessity—provide the context for human beings to cultivate the joyful appropriation of the necessities that govern their lives. Because we belong within the totality of a cosmic city, imbued with reason, our efforts to find coherence and consistency in our own lives are grounded in the order of the cosmos. To live in agreement with our own natures is at the same time to live in agreement with other human beings and with the world as a whole. Without the conceptual connections with fate and providence, our adapting to necessities would be a joyless endurance; but within the shared habitation of a cosmic city, the pursuit of our own needs and desires can be readily accommodated to, as well as restrained by, concern with a shared human good. "The Stoics hold," Cicero reports in *On Ends,* "that the world is governed by divine will; it is as if it were a city and state shared by men and gods, and each one of us is a part of this world. From this it is a natural consequence that we prefer the common advantage to our own."[5]

Stoic reservation—the source of happiness and virtue—depends on these interconnections with providence and necessity. The wise Stoic learns to detach himself from "indifferents." This important concept cuts across the distinction between things that are "in accordance with nature" and things that are not. Health, strength, the possession of well-functioning sense organs—such things are "in accordance with nature"; ill health, by contrast, is not in accordance with nature. Health and strength are nonetheless "indifferents" in relation to the attaining of happiness. This concept marks a crucial difference between Stoic and Aristotelian ethics. For the Stoics, happiness does not depend at all on good fortune; it does not require that we be given lives in which the preponderance of things accords with our nature. The ideal is rather to attain to a well-shaped life; and that involves remaining detached from things that are "indifferent" while appropriating the things that are in accordance with our nature.

The point is not that we should avoid the "indifferents"—or that we should refuse the pleasures they bring. They may be "preferred" or "selected" as part of the well-shaped life; but they are not its core. Conversely, the presence of things not in accordance with nature—such as ill health—is not an obstacle to the well-shaped life. The relation between impulse and the sense of necessity is, again, crucial to this aspect of Stoic ethics. In one of its most striking formulations, Epictetus says that "Chrysippus was right to say: 'As long as the future is uncertain to me I always hold to those things which are better adapted to obtaining the things in accordance with nature; for god himself has made me disposed to select these. But if I actually knew that I was fated now to be ill, I would even have an impulse to be ill. For my foot too, if it had intelligence, would have an impulse to get muddy.'"[6]

The acceptance of necessity—far from being incompatible with freedom—was required for it. In the possibility of adapting our impulses to necessity lies the key to freedom. In a notorious Stoic metaphor Zeno and Chrysippus invoked a relentless necessity, which nonetheless is transformed, through acceptance, into a noble ideal. "When a dog is tied to a cart, if it wants to follow it is pulled and follows, making its spontaneous act coincide with necessity, but if it does not want to follow it will be compelled in any case. So it is with men too: even if they do not want to, they will be compelled in any case to follow what is destined." A similar thought is attributed by Epictetus to Cleanthes: "Lead me, Zeus and Destiny, wherever you have ordained for me. For I shall follow unflinching. But if I become bad and am unwilling, I shall follow none the less."[7]

The idea is of a chain of necessary causes flowing through human beings, as through all else. In the wise man the acceptance of necessity lends a grace and smoothness of movement that is lacking in the rough actions of the unwise. Freedom and virtue reside in this smooth flow of life, rather than in any exemption from the chain of causes. In a summary of Chrysippus given by Gellius: "If our minds' initial natural make-up is a healthy and beneficial one, all that external force exerted upon them as a result of fate slides over them fairly smoothly and without obstruction."[8]

Rather than being exempt from fate, human action is "co-fated."

Whether we embrace it or resist it, fate will have its way. Again, the capacity to embrace fate, which was so crucial to Stoic ethics, depends on being able to think of fate as providential—as encompassing our good—rather than as being imposed from the outside and exhibiting no respect for what is natural to us. As the commentators A. A. Long and D. N. Sedley sum it up, for the Stoics, "morality belongs first and foremost to the entire cosmic plan. It is from there that it filters down to individual human lives. . . . Far from conflicting with morality, fate *is* the moral structure of the world."[9]

Metaphors of smoothness—of a gracious free flow of life—recur throughout the history of Stoic ethical ideals. The feelings they regard as good—the "well-reasoned" feelings, which they allow into the core of the wise life—are described in metaphors drawn from the quality of bodily movement. The Stoics, says Diogenes Laertius, say that "there are three good feelings: joy, watchfulness, wishing. Joy, they say, is the opposite of pleasure, consisting in well-reasoned swelling (elation); and watchfulness is the opposite of fear, consisting in well-reasoned shrinking. For the wise man will not be afraid at all, but he will be watchful. They say that wishing is the opposite of appetite, consisting in well-reasoned stretching [desire]."[10]

Zeno, Cleanthes, and Chrysippus all accepted the definition of happiness as "a good flow of life"—an ideal inseparably bound up with the idea of "living in agreement" (with nature). Early Stoic formulations of this ideal draw readily from cosmology. Diogenes Laertius attributes to Chrysippus the identification of the good flow of life with agreement with the universal law, which is the Stoic transformation of the idea of Zeus: "Therefore, living in agreement with nature comes to be the end, which is in accordance with the nature of oneself and that of the whole, engaging in no activity wont to be forbidden by the universal law, which is the right reason pervading everything and identical to Zeus, who is this director of the administration of existing things. And the virtue of the happy man and his good flow of life are just this: always doing everything on the basis of the concordance of each man's guardian spirit with the will of the administrator of the whole."[11]

Living thus in accordance with nature is within human power; it is the wise man's "proper function." In the thought of the later Stoics, the ideal becomes less tightly tied to cosmology. The identification of proper function becomes part of a more earthly concern with describing the features of the well-lived life—the character of the good human being—in particular civil contexts. But the underpinning of providence, and the implicit ideals that make us citizens of the world rather than just of any particular polis, persist. So too, as we shall see, does the ideal of conforming our lives to necessity.

Seneca on the Good Life: A Smooth Flow

A life that flows smoothly, regardless of what obstacles it encounters, tranquillity in the midst of misfortune—it is a lot to ask. Yet according to the Stoics, it is within the reach of the wise. Giving advice on how it could be achieved lay at the heart of Roman Stoicism. The innumerable discourses, epistles, and dialogues of the Stoics on the formation of the wise man agree on three stages of moral development. Seneca summed them up in a series of epistles written between 63 and 65 CE to his friend Lucilius, who was at the time procurator in Sicily. The stages, Seneca tells Lucilius, are devoted to, first, "your assessment of the value of each thing"; second, "your adopting a controlled and balanced impulse towards them"; and third, "the achievement of an agreement between your impulse and your action so that you are consistent with yourself in all these matters."[12]

Order and consistency—as we might expect—are central to

Seneca's version of virtue, which he outlines in these letters to Lucilius—all written in the last few years of his life, after his retirement from public life. Virtue, he says, is "nothing other than the mind disposed in a certain way." It is revealed especially in orderliness—in a man's "seemliness, consistency, the mutual harmony of all his actions, and his great capacity to surmount everything." That is what allows us to perceive "that happy life which flows on smoothly, complete in its own self-mastery."[13]

Seneca puts his own stamp on the old Stoic ideals and gives a new twist to the metaphor of a smooth flow, for which he seems to have had a special fondness. He uses the metaphor in describing his preferred writing style, as well as in presenting his ideals for the good life as a whole; and the two uses reinforce each other. In the fortieth of his epistles, "On the Proper Style for a Philosophical Discourse," he urges on Lucilius a philosophical style that avoids excessive force—like a stream flowing unceasingly, which, however, never becomes a torrent. A stammering slowness will, Seneca warns, distract the listener. The challenge is to avoid a "heedless" flow, in favor of one that is both restrained and effortless. Later, in letter 46, he expresses delight that Lucilius, in a new book he has sent him, has found such a style: "I found that there was no burst of force, but an even flow."[14]

In the fortieth letter, Seneca criticizes both the "rapid" style—which "sweeps down without a break like a snow squall"—and the slow "dripping out" of words. In Homer, he notes, the rapid style is assigned to the younger speaker, whereas "from the old man eloquence flows gently, sweeter than honey." Seneca uses similar metaphors of liquid flow to express more general ideals of intellectual character—to capture aspects of the well-developed soul. "The wise man's life spreads out to him over as large a surface as does all eternity to a god," he says in the fifty-third letter.

The metaphor of flow to express ideals of intellectual character is not in itself new; we have already seen that the ancient Greek

Stoics made use of it. And in the *Theaetetus,* Plato had his character Theodorus use a similar metaphor to describe to Socrates the intellectual qualities of the youth Theaetetus. "This boy approaches his studies in a smooth, sure, effective way, and with great good temper; it reminds one of the quiet flow of a stream of oil."[15] The analogy takes on an additional force in Seneca's writing. In the absence of Plato's commitment to the immateriality of the soul, the idea of a soul that flows freely can now become almost literal. Seneca says in the fiftieth epistle that the soul is pliable and more yielding than any liquid. "For what else is the soul than air in a certain state?"

The most revealing aspects of Seneca's talk of smooth flow, however, are found in his observations about what distinguishes the wise man's sense of the flow of time. If a smooth temporal flow is to be desired in a writing style, it is greatly more to be desired in the style in which we live. In this case it is of course more difficult to sum up the content of the metaphor, but it is clear that Seneca thinks that the wise man has a distinctive sense of the flow of time. The ideal of a continuous flow of life is not consistent with a succession of false starts. He warns Lucilius in the thirty-second letter that we should not be always starting afresh, as if our lives were not yet already under way. To understand Seneca's point we need to move away from thinking of our lives in terms of a linear progression. The parts of a life, he suggests, fall rather into a series of concentric circles of diminishing size—from the span of our whole life down through the periods of our youth and adulthood to the span of a year, a month, a day. With that in mind, we should think of each day, he says in the twelfth epistle, "as if it closed the series, as if it rounded out and completed our existence."

To live our lives as a succession of beginnings is to be vulnerable to fortune and chance. The "real good," Seneca insists in the twenty-third epistle, comes from having a contempt for the "gifts of chance"; it comes from having "an even and calm way of living, which treads but one path." Continuing the metaphors of motion, he observes that to be always leaping from one purpose to another is not really even to leap, but to be "carried over by a sort of hazard"—to be wavering and unstable rather than to control ourselves and our affairs by a "guiding purpose." True to the Stoic belief that the wisdom of the sage is a rare achievement, Seneca observes that only a few can claim to live thus; the rest of us do not "proceed," but are merely swept along, like objects afloat in a river. "And of these objects, some are held back by sluggish waters and are transported gently; others are torn along by a more violent current; some, which are nearest the bank, are left there as the current slackens; and others are carried out to sea by the onrush of the stream." To avoid these hazards of fortune—to "proceed," rather than being simply swept along, we must "decide what we wish, and abide by the decision."

Steadiness of purpose is the key to achieving the ideal smoothness; but it must be complemented by insight into our nature as temporal beings, and here our attitude to death is crucial. To live as if life were always just beginning is to have our lives always "incomplete," he says at the end of the twenty-third letter. "A man cannot stand prepared for the approach of death if he has just begun to live." Rather than living as if we are always planning our lives anew, we must aim to have already lived long enough. We can then hope to avoid the plight of those who only begin to live when it is time for them to leave off living. Some men indeed, Seneca warns, have left off living before they have begun.

Throughout Seneca's reflections on the good life, a motif of meditation on the flow of water recurs. Rather than shifting in different directions according to the wind, the mind intent on wisdom will aim to stay where it is—tossing up and down in the sea, but not changing position. It becomes clear in the thirty-fifth letter that the completely wise man—the rare Stoic sage—will not even be subject to this kind of motion. Like a boat tossing aim-lessly in the sea, the mind whose goals are shifting fails to attain stability in the midst of changing fortunes. Such fixity in the face of events is one of the more exalted—and also perhaps one of the least appealing—of Stoic goals. At one point, in the twentieth letter, Seneca quotes with approval the definition of wisdom as "always desiring the same things, and always refusing the same things." His descriptions of poignant longing for a smoothly flow-ing life, however, are more appealing than the austere single-mindedness he recommends as the remedy; and his reflections on temporal flow have a transforming power that can stand indepen-dently of his sterner ideals.

Despite the value he places on fixity of purpose, Seneca gives moving expression to human awareness of the vagaries, of the passage, of time—to the sense of mystification at our powerless-ness to hold back its "headlong flight" or even to match our sense of the rate of its passage to real duration. "I seem to have lost you but a moment ago," he says, reflecting, in the forty-ninth letter, on Lucilius's absence. "For what is not 'but a moment ago' when one begins to use the memory?" It was, he reflects, but a moment ago that he sat, as a lad, learning philosophy; but a moment ago that he began to plead in the courts, a moment ago that he lost the desire to plead, but a moment ago that he lost the ability. "Infinitely swift is the flight of time, as those see more clearly who are looking backwards. For when we are intent on the present, we do not no-tice it, so gentle is the passage of time's headlong flight. Do you ask the reason for this? All past time is in the same place; it all presents the same aspect to us, it lies together. Everything slips into the same abyss."

Accompanying and complementing Seneca's recommendations for fixity of purpose is an alternative strategy for achieving the much-desired smooth flow of life. We cannot slow the passage of time; but we can, it seems, adjust our powers of anticipation. This involves not only adapting our desires, so that we are no longer thwarted by their being unfulfilled, but also reimagining our lives in relation to the flow of time. As he says in the twelfth letter, rather than thinking of our lives as at their beginning, we are to think of them as if they are approaching their end; we are to think of the time that remains as "rounding out" or "completing" a life.

Seneca's geometric image of the concentric circles, in the twelfth letter, serves effectively to make the point. We might think of the circle of our whole life as coinciding with the circle of today, rather than encompassing it. That may well of course turn out to be false; we may have a reasonable expectation that our lives will continue beyond the present day. The point is that we never really know how many such circles are encompassed within the circle of our whole life. Despite that lack of foreknowledge, we can, he thinks, attain the kind of flow in which the good life consists. For our capacity to do this depends on how the mind stretches itself out—on the imaginative wholeness or incompleteness of the life, rather than on its actual duration. A long life might nonetheless be experienced as a constantly thwarted life—a life of uneven flow; whereas a life that is short in duration might be experienced as a completed, smooth flow of time.

For Seneca, the dread of future misfortune is in general a disruption of this desired even passage of life, for it draws our thought away from the present. Yet the specific fear of death occasions particular disruption. He acknowledges that it is difficult to rid ourselves of this fear. Echoing ancient Stoic notions of impulse, he remarks that a fearless contempt of death is something that must be learned. Death, he says in the thirty-sixth letter, is not something toward which we move with a voluntary instinct, as we do toward the preservation of life. Even so, how we think of death—the ultimate necessity—is crucial to whether we achieve the desired fullness of life. It is possible, even usual, he says in the forty-ninth letter, for a man who has lived long to have lived too

little. If we cease trying to escape from death, we can hope that
life may cease escaping from us.

The idea of a smoothly flowing life is Seneca's version of the
Stoic ideal of appropriating necessity. The wise man, he insists in
the fifty-fourth letter, does nothing unwillingly. "He escapes necessity because he wills to do what necessity is about to force upon
him." This transformation of necessity into freedom echoes the
ancient Stoic image of the dog graciously following the cart to
which it is chained. We also find deliberate echoes here of Epicurus, whom Seneca frequently quotes with approval in his letters
to Lucilius. His reflections on death echo Epicurus's observations
on the unusual status of death as an event—on the paradoxical
character of a change that consists in the loss of the subject that
changes; on the irrationality of fearing the event that brings an
end to all possibility of fear; and on the symmetry of the time after death and the time before birth. "Would you not say," Seneca
asks Lucilius in the fifty-fourth letter, "that one was the greatest
of fools who believed that a lamp was worse off when it was extinguished than before it was lighted? We mortals also are lighted
and extinguished; the period of suffering comes in between, but
on either side there is a deep peace. For, unless I am very much
mistaken, my dear Lucilius, we go astray in thinking that death
only follows, when in reality it has both preceded us and will in
turn follow us. Whatever condition existed before our birth, is
death. For what does it matter whether you do not begin at all, or
whether you leave off, inasmuch as the result of both these states
is non-existence?"

In urging us to reflect on death, Seneca suggests in the twenty-
sixth letter, Epicurus is bidding us to think about freedom: "He
who has learned to die has unlearned slavery; he is above any external power, or, at any rate, he is beyond it." True to the Stoic origins of his thought—even where he is quoting Epicurus—Seneca

links this freedom with the acceptance of necessity. "There is only one chain which binds us to life, and that is the love of life. The chain may not be cast off, but it may be rubbed away, so that, when necessity shall demand, nothing may retard or hinder us from being ready to do at once that which at some time we are bound to do."

Seneca, however, brings together these borrowings from earlier thinkers with his own reflections on temporal flow to say something new. He urges Lucilius to confront not only the necessity of his death as an event in the future, but also the reality of death as a process unfolding in the present. Wisdom, he says in the twenty-fourth letter, resides in knowing that we are dying daily. For we are mistaken when we look forward to death; its major portion has already passed. Dying is a lifelong process, and each day is shared between ourselves and death. "It is not the last drop that empties the water-clock, but all that which previously has flowed out; similarly, the final hour when we cease to exist does not of itself bring death; it merely completes the death-process. We reach death at that moment; but we have been a long time on the way."

By shifting focus from the final drop in the bucket to the whole flow, Seneca tries to put the final stage in a more positive light: death is not sharply separated from the process of life. In the fourth letter, on "the terrors of death," he comments: "No evil is great which is the last evil of all. Death arrives; it would be a thing to dread, if it could remain with you. But death must either not come at all, or else must come and pass away."

The dread of death is for Seneca always intimately linked with the failure to engage properly with the process of life. This dread, he says in the twenty-second letter, always reflects an incompleteness—a lack of wholeness, a disruption—in our approach to living; and we are vulnerable to such disruptions at all stages of our life. "Take anyone off his guard—young, old or middle aged; you will find that all are equally afraid of death, and equally ignorant of life." It is in ridding ourselves of the fear of death that we find ourselves most free.

Some of Seneca's observations on death have for us—and perhaps they did even for him—the ring of clichés: the warnings against spoiling our enjoyment of the present by the anticipation of future trouble; against allowing our souls to "drown" in "petty anxieties," as he puts it in the twenty-fourth letter. But his stress on completeness or wholeness—integrated with his recurring theme of the smooth flow of life—makes for a distinctive blend of Epicurean and Stoic insights that goes beyond those clichés. "You know what I mean by a good man?" he asks in the thirty-fourth letter. "One who is complete, finished—whom no constraint or need can render bad."

Seneca has made it clear in the thirty-second letter, however, that the completeness arises from pleasure: "It is true; the enemy is indeed pressing upon you; you should therefore increase your speed and escape away and reach a safe position, remembering continually what a noble thing it is to round out your life before death comes, and then await in peace the remaining portion of your time, claiming nothing for yourself, since you are in possession of the happy life; for such a life is not made happier for being longer. O when shall you see the time when you shall know that time means nothing to you, when you shall be peaceful and calm, careless of the morrow, because you are enjoying your life to the full?" Seneca's wise man, as this letter stresses, has "at length passed beyond all necessities—he has won his honourable discharge and is free—who still lives after his life has been completed." In the sixty-first letter, Seneca tells Lucilius of his own efforts to live in accordance with this ideal of completeness: "I am endeavouring to live every day as if it were a complete life." Approaching his final farewells, he assures his friend, "To have lived long enough depends neither on our years nor upon our days, but upon our minds. I have lived, my dear friend, Lucilius, long enough. I have had my fill; I await death."

The acceptance of necessity is crucial to Seneca's ideal of the well-flowing life. The ideal is grounded in his commitment to the Stoic doctrine of an interconnected sequence integrating human beings into the cosmos as a whole. He addresses this theme, with explicit reference to providence, in an earlier work, *On Providence,* which is also addressed to his friend Lucilius.

On Providence was written during a troubled period in Seneca's own life—probably during the early years of his exile, after a scandal arising from an alleged sexual relationship with Caligula's sister. Anticipating the imagery of flowing water, which will recur throughout his later letters to Lucilius, he assures his friend that no evil can befall a good man; for opposites cannot mingle. "Just as the countless rivers, the vast fall of rain from the sky, and the huge volumes of mineral springs do not change the taste of the sea, do not even modify it, so the assaults of adversity do not weaken the spirit of a brave man. It always maintains its poise, and it gives its own colour to everything that happens; for it is mightier than all external things." Not only is this desired poise consistent with bad fortune; it depends on being tested by adversity. "Justly may they be termed unhappy who are dulled by an excess of good fortune, who rest, as it were, in dead calm on a quiet sea; whatever happens will come as a change."[16]

In both *On Providence* and the letters to Lucilius, it is clear that for Seneca, as for the ancient Stoics, the confidence of the wise man that evil will not affect him does not rest on trust in a divine will that is not subject to necessity; his confidence rests rather on the acceptance of fate. Seneca, unlike his Stoic predecessors, treats God as both producing and obeying the decrees of fate. Seneca observes in *On Providence,* "Fate guides us, and it was settled at the first hour of our birth what length of time remains for each. Cause is linked with cause, and all public and private issues are directed by a long sequence of events. . . . What, then, is the part of a good man? To offer himself to Fate. It is a great consolation that it is together with the universe we are swept along; whatever it is that has ordained us so to live, so to die, by the same necessity it binds us also to the gods. One unchangeable course bears along the affairs of gods and men alike. Although the great creator and ruler of the universe himself wrote the decrees of Fate, yet he follows them."[17] It is not obvious that he can have it both ways, treating the "great creator" as both the author of fate and a being subject to it. But it is clear that he sees the concatenation of necessities, the chain of interconnected causes, as ultimately underlying the smooth flow of the virtuous life.

Seneca wrote longingly to Lucilius of his hope that his death would be the peaceful letting-go of a life already rounded out and complete. "Is there any better end to it all," he reflects in the twenty-sixth letter, "than to glide off to one's proper haven, when nature slips the cable? Not that there is anything painful in a shock and a sudden departure from existence; it is merely because this other way of departure is easy,—a gradual withdrawal." Sad to say, he was not to have his preferred way of dying.

In keeping with his ideals, Seneca appropriated the necessity of a life of exile that was imposed on him, finding in it—as he says in a letter of consolation to his mother, Helvia—the joys of a retirement he might have freely chosen: "So this is how you must think of me—happy and cheerful as if in the best of circumstances. For they are best, since my mind without any preoccupation is free for its own tasks."[18] His letters to Lucilius record his hopes that in his final years his life had at last reached calm waters—that his sufferings had entered the abyss of the past. Seneca was to die by his own hand, but not of his own will—condemned to suicide for his alleged part in a plot against Nero. He had hoped to have "passed beyond all necessities"—to have entered reflectively on the final encompassing, on a gradual letting-go. Instead he had to appropriate the final necessity of a more violent departure.

The Slave and the Emperor: Epictetus and Marcus Aurelius

The name was probably an expression of literal truth: Epictetus was the "acquired" one—a slave; and the experience of slavery was a constant reference point in his philosophical thinking. Epictetus was a Phrygian. His life covers roughly the period from 55 to 135 CE. He was owned for some time by Epaphroditus, himself a former slave who became an administrator for the Roman emperor Nero. It was during his years as a slave that Epictetus attended the lectures of the Stoic teacher Musonius Rufus, whose thoughts are reflected in Epictetus's own teaching. Epictetus eventually gained his freedom and was teaching philosophy in Rome by the time the emperor Domitian exiled him, along with other philosophers, in 89 or 92 CE. Epictetus continued to teach, at a school he described as a "healing place for sick souls."

Visitors at the Fair

It is through the records of his devoted student Arrian (Flavius Arrianus) that we know the work of Epictetus. The *Discourses,* and the condensation of their contents—the *Encheiridion* or *Manual*—are lively reconstructions of Epictetus's own passionate advice on how to live. This is a practical Stoicism—intended to instruct the young in a way of life, rather than to leave a body of written doctrine for debate among the philosophers. Epictetus frequently stresses that philosophy can itself become a barrier to the good life if it is pursued as a skilled performance, motivated by a desire to impress, or allowed to ossify into a doctrinal system, rather than practiced as a way of living. The history of Stoicism offers more subtle expositions of Stoic doctrine but none that present more vividly the lineaments of a life lived in accordance with its principles.

Arrian shows how Epictetus drew together different strands in Stoic thought to yield a formula for living that is challenging without being altogether impractical. The elements are acknowledged as coming from earlier sources; but the cast of mind Epictetus brings to them is distinctive. This is in some ways a purer, more austere Stoicism than that of Seneca. Whereas Seneca is happy to draw on Epicurus to complement his Stoic sources, Epictetus invokes the acerbic, uncompromising teachings of the Cynics, whom he obviously admires, even if he finds their antics an unrealistic model for his students. His teachings hold in an energizing tension elements that can pull in different directions: an intense sense of freedom anchored in his own experience of slavery; a detachment that resonates with the Cynics' sardonic castigation of human folly; and an intense piety toward the gods, which he retains from his Phrygian religious background.

The recurring themes of the *Discourses* are familiar from the earlier Stoics: the acceptance of necessity; the idea of providence; the interrelated distinctions between what is and is not external or "indifferent"; ideas about "proper functions," and about human life as unfolding in a cosmic city common to gods and men. But the central ideas are differently clustered and the emphasis falls differently. The theme of necessity is still strongly present, but it is now subsidiary to the purposes of gods and men. Necessity is here understood primarily as what lies outside human control and is hence "external" to our moral purpose. It is not the understanding of necessity as such that carries ethical weight for Epictetus; it is rather purity of "moral purpose"; and that in turn rests on the conviction that a cosmic providence exists. The gods have released humankind from accountability for the things they have not put under human control, leaving us to answer only for what does properly belong to us—"the proper use of impressions."

For Epictetus the inward moral purpose, as distinct from anything external to it, is what is important in life, and that purpose is also the benchmark of freedom. Epictetus presents freedom as the antithesis of slavery; but his version of freedom—because of its essential inwardness—is as accessible to the slave as it is to the master. "He is free for whom all things happen according to his moral purpose, and whom none can restrain."[19] "My leg you will fetter, but my moral purpose not even Zeus himself has power to overcome" (*Discourses* 1.1.25). The life of freedom, however, is no power struggle between human beings and the gods. In a moving evocation of the shared freedom of gods and men, which will echo through later adaptations of Stoicism—especially in Descartes's account of the autonomous will—Epictetus imagines himself in conversation with Zeus: "'Epictetus, had it been possible I should have made both this paltry body and this small estate of thine free and unhampered. But as it is—let it not escape thee—this body is not thine own, but only clay cunningly compounded. Yet since I could not give thee this, we have given thee a certain portion of ourself, this faculty of choice and refusal, of desire and aversion, or, in a word, the faculty which makes use of external impressions; if thou carest for this and place all that thou hast therein, thou shalt never be thwarted, never hampered, shalt not groan, shalt not blame, shalt not flatter any man. What then? Are these things small in thy sight?' 'Far be it from me!' 'Art thou, then, content with them?' 'I pray the gods I may be'" (*Discourses* 1.1.10–13).

Knowledge of the distinction between what is and is not ours—between what does and what does not lie within the scope of our moral purpose—is for Epictetus the key to contentment. Even so, despite the obvious resonances with later doctrines of the freedom of the will, this is not an affirmation of human exemption from the necessities that govern the rest of the world. Epictetus retains from earlier Stoicism the ideal of adapting human desires to necessity. He instructs his students that if they wish for serenity, they must learn to "desire each thing exactly as it happens" (*Discourses* 1.12.16). They are to study how to live "not in order to change the constitution of things—for this is neither vouchsafed us nor is it better that it should be—but in order that, things about us being as they are and as their nature is, we may, for our own part, keep our wills in harmony with what happens" (*Discourses* 1.12.17–18).

Epictetus constantly insists that all that is under our control is "the proper use of impressions." To take upon ourselves things for which we are not responsible is to make trouble for ourselves. This alignment of freedom with the acceptance of necessity can seem so at odds with modern ideas of autonomy that it is easy to overlook that Stoicism was, in its ancient settings, not so much a system of self-abnegation as a philosophy of contentment. The ideal of being "conformable to nature" may sound austere, but it involves an ease of being—a lack of discomfort with either our own presence or the presence of others—that allows both solitude and sociability to become a source of joy. "But you are impatient and peevish, and if you are alone, you call it a solitude, but if you are in the company of men, you call them schemers and brigands, and you find fault even with your own parents and children and brothers and neighbours. But you ought, when staying alone, to call that peace and freedom, and to look upon yourself as like the gods; and when you are in the company of many, you ought not call that a mob, nor a tumult, nor a disgusting thing, but a feast and a festival, and so accept all things contentedly" (*Discourses* 1.12.20–21).

Epictetus's descriptions of Stoic joy often resonate with older pieties whose naiveties had already come into question in the dramas of Euripides. Epictetus asks: "What else can I, a lame old man, do but sing hymns to God? If indeed, I were a nightingale, I should be singing as a nightingale; if a swan, as a swan. But as it is, I am a rational being, therefore I must be singing hymns of praise to God. This is my task; I do it, and will not desert this post, as long as it may be given me to fill it; and I exhort you to join me in this same song" (*Discourses* 1.16.20–21). It is piety; but the piety is now suffused with a philosophical understanding of humanity as part of a necessary cosmic order—and with the perception of an ethical power as residing in that necessity. Epictetus is praising not blind obedience to the gods, but rather the sense of responsibility that comes from knowing that we are at the mercy of no one—whether divine or human—if only we can hold firm in our "moral purpose," which is the right use of external impressions.

Epictetus's elaboration of this theme of the right use of impressions yields a rather clearer account of the interconnections between truth and freedom than earlier Stoics had provided. The mind's assent to whatever comes before it distinctly provides a model for its yielding to necessity; but that assent is at the same time a model of inner freedom. Just as no one can make us assent to what is false, the mind is free also from hindrance or restraint when it comes to the choice of what we really want. In relation to both truth and desire, the joyful assent of the mind becomes the enactment of its recognition of what belongs to it and of a readiness to let go of what does not.

In Epictetus's reworking of Stoic themes, the life of the Stoic becomes a celebration of the truth of the cosmos. Adapting an old comparison dating back to Pythagoras, he compares perceptions of the good life to the situation of spectators at a fair. Some are concerned solely with the buying and selling of cattle; only a handful go to see and study the fair—"how it is conducted and why, and who [is] promoting it, and for what purpose. So it is also in this 'fair' of the world in which we live; some persons, like cattle, are interested in nothing but their fodder; for to all of you that concern yourselves with property and lands and slaves and one office or another, all this is nothing but fodder! And few in number are the men who attend the fair because they are fond of the spectacle." These rare lovers of the spectacle of life itself come with one purpose only—"to study well the 'fair' of life before they leave it." The crowd often derides them, just as at the fair the merchants and hagglers laugh at the mere spectators. "Yes, and if the cattle themselves had any comprehension like ours of what was going on, they too would laugh at those who had wonder and admiration for anything but their fodder" (*Discourses* 2.14.24–29).

The Call of the Captain

The power—and the limitations—of Epictetus's practical philosophy are most evident in his reflections on the least easily escapable of human emotions—the fear of death. Like other Stoics before him, he insists that death is no evil—that the evil it brings lies not in death itself but in the anxious anticipation of it. True freedom lies in release from that crippling apprehension. Resorting again to metaphors of slavery, Epictetus compares the false freedom of eluding imminent death to the temporary freedom of a runaway slave. The runaway slave gains only a respite from fear of his master, which will resume once the slave is recaptured; whereas the truly emancipated slave gains freedom not only from the master, but from what made him terrifying. So too with the fear of death. "For what is a 'master'? One man is not the master of another man, but death and life and pleasure and hardship are his masters. So bring Caesar to me, if he be *without* these things and you shall see how steadfast I am. But when he comes *with* them, thundering and lightening, and I am afraid of them, what else have I done but recognized my master, like the runaway slave? But so long as I have, as it were, only a respite from these threats, I too am acting like a runaway slave who is a spectator in a theatre; I bathe, I drink, I sing, but I do it all in fear and misery. But if I emancipate myself from my masters, that is, from those things which render masters terrifying, what further trouble do I have, what master any more?" (*Discourses* 1.29.60–63).

Death, Epictetus observes, is seen as "the epitome of all the ills that befall man"; but we should see that epitome not in death itself but in the fear of death (*Discourses* 3.26.38–39). Death itself is in truth the harbor of all human beings, and their refuge. In the grip of fear of death we reverse the proper relations between caution and confidence; it is perverse, he thinks, to be cautious rather than confident about the things that lie beyond our control, beyond the limits of our moral purpose. We should instead be both cautious and confident—"confident in regard to those things that lie outside the province of the moral purpose, and cautious in regard to those things that lie within the province of the moral purpose" (*Discourses* 2.1.40).

Epictetus cites with approval Socrates' dismissal of death as a "bugbear"—a fear based on childish ignorance. "Turn it about and learn what it is; see, it does not bite" (*Discourses* 2.1.17). His attempted demystification of the bugbear has a number of strands, some of which seem more effective than others. Body and spirit, he reasons, must at some time be separated. Why be grieved that it should happen now; for after all, if it is not now, it will be later. It is a common Stoic observation on death, reiterated by Shakespeare's Hamlet. Yet as mentioned earlier it is not obvious why the inevitability of death at some time should reconcile us to its coming now; or why it is not reasonable to prefer death in old age—the agreeable, natural slipping of the anchor, as Seneca described it—to the wrench of early death. Epictetus can concede, consistently with his Stoicism, that death in old age may be a "preferred indifferent"—one it is rational to prefer as long as the time of our death remains uncertain; yet it is also evident that he believes that a deeper necessity requires our acquiescence in dying, whenever it comes. To attain to this purer Stoicism, we must not merely accept the fact of early death if it comes; we must also learn to detach ourselves from all the things of which early death would deprive us.

This cultivation of detachment offers much that is unappealing. We are to withdraw our attachment from externals—from "indifferents"—so that we become ourselves indifferent. We are urged to become acquiescent in the loss of that to which we were not in any case deeply attached. Other strands in Epictetus's treatment of death are, however, more amiable. He urges us, for example, to accept our own deaths in a spirit of generosity—making way for others, who have an equal right to participate in the ongoing festival of life. When the festival has come to an end, rather than wanting to go on with the holiday, we should "depart as a grateful and reverent spectator departs," while others arrive. "Yet others must be born, even as you were born, and once born they must have land, and houses and provisions. But if the first-comers do not move along, what is left for those who follow after? Why are you insatiate? Why never satisfied? Why do you crowd the world?" It is only discourteous guests who complain when the time for departure has come. "God has no need of a fault-finding spectator. He needs those who join in the holiday and the dance, that they may applaud rather, and glorify, and sing hymns of praise about the festival" (*Discourses* 4.1.106–109). The pleasures—and also the duties—of living are, of their nature, temporary. Shall I, then, be no more?—No, you will not be, but something else will be, something different from that of which the universe now has need. And this is but reasonable, for you came into being, not when *you* wanted, but when the universe had need of you" (*Discourses* 3.24.94–95).

The two grounds Epictetus has offered for accepting death— detachment from life's pleasures, and a generous readiness to make way for others to participate in the delights we have ourselves experienced—may seem to be in tension. But Epictetus sees them as belonging together; both rest on an understanding of our place in the universe. In the lack of a sustaining belief in such a necessary larger whole, Stoic detachment can seem like a withdrawal of attachment from life itself—from our very selves. For Epictetus, however, this detachment shapes and expresses self-knowledge. "If you regard yourself as a man and as a part of some whole, on account of that whole it is fitting for you now to be sick, and now to make a voyage and run risks, and now to be in want, and on occasion to die before your time. Why then are you vexed? Do you not know that as the foot, if detached, will no longer be a foot, so you too, if detached, will no longer be a man?" (*Discourses* 2.5.25–26).

Epictetus's version of detachment depends not only on recognizing the vaster wholes of which human beings are themselves part, but also on recognizing what is and what is not part of ourselves. Thus understood, the cultivation of detachment introduces a kind of playfulness. We should live, he advises, in the spirit of Socrates—playing the game of life as we would play with a ball. "And at that place and time what was the ball that he was playing with? Imprisonment, exile, drinking poison, being deprived of wife, leaving children orphans. These were the things with which he was playing, but none the less he played and handled the ball in good form. So ought we also to act, exhibiting the ball player's carefulness about the game, but the same indifference about the object played with, as being a mere ball. For a man ought by all means to strive to show his skill in regard to some of the external materials, yet without making the material a part of himself, but merely lavishing his skill in regard to it, whatever it may be" (*Discourses* 2.5.21–22).

Within this context of cautious and confident playfulness Epictetus articulates his version of the Stoic's indifference to death. He quotes with approval Chrysippus's dictum that once the necessity of things becomes evident to us, we appropriate them. In the frame of Epictetus's distinctions, the acceptance of death becomes the fullest expression of confidence in the things that are not ours to control. "If you always bear in mind what is your own and what is another's, you will never be disturbed" (*Discourses* 2.6.9). The core of the strategy is to refrain from the exercise of judgment, which is the real locus of misfortune. "Let a man but transfer his judgement to matters that lie within the province of the moral purpose, and I guarantee that he will be steadfast, whatever be the state of things about him" (*Discourses* 3.3.19).

The Stoic finds comfort both in being part of a larger whole and in knowing that some things are beyond our own "moral purpose"—comfort in knowing that whatever happens to us is framed by the cosmos, but also that the order of the universe will not be upset when we die (*Discourses* 3.10.15). In the chapter "On the Calling of a Cynic," he endorses the Cynic's disdaining of bodily comfort. The Stoic, in Epictetus's view, has a broader, framing concern with his place in the cosmos. "My paltry body is nothing to me; the parts of it are nothing to me. Death? Let it come when it will, whether it be the death of the whole or some part. Exile? And to what place can anyone thrust me out? Outside the universe he cannot. But wherever I go, there are sun, moon, stars, dreams, omens, my converse with gods" (*Discourses* 3.22.22–23). This reassuring picture of our place in the cosmos rests firmly on the belief that the whole of nature is endowed with providential purpose. That is what allows our individual deaths to be seen as a ripening for the harvest—no more a misfortune than the maturing of heads of grain. The wise live in a proper relationship with the universe, one grounded in understanding of their own providential place within it. "To reach out for the impossible is slavish and foolish; it is acting like a stranger in the universe, one who is fighting against God with the only weapons at his command, his own judgements" (*Discourses* 3.24.21).

All this can sound like a reversion to pious trust in the will of the gods. Yet discernible, again, is a distinctively Stoic cast to the piety. Underlying the pious reverence for divine purpose is the sense of necessity, which keeps Stoic providence from descending into superstition. There is a further softening of the apparent harshness of the Stoic ideal in Epictetus's elaboration of the old theme of "proper functions." Our responsibility for what happens in the whole is limited. Each of us, having played his part, must then be content to leave to others the part they have to play. We are to live our lives as if we were on a voyage. Certain things lie within our control—the choice of helmsman and sailors, of the day, the moment. "Then a storm comes down upon us. Very well, what further concern have I? For my part has been fulfilled. The business belongs to someone else, that is, the helmsman. But, more than that, the ship goes down. What, then, have I to do? What I can; that is the only thing I do; I drown without fear, neither shrieking nor crying out against God, but recognizing that what is born must also perish. For I am not eternal but a man; a part of the whole, as an hour is part of a day. I must come on as the hour and like an hour pass away. What difference, then, is it to me how I pass away, whether by drowning or by a fever? For by something of the sort I must needs pass away" (*Discourses* 2.5.11–14).

Epictetus seeks to present his Stoicism in a gentler light by distancing himself from what he sees as the harsher strictures of the Cynics. The aim of the philosopher, in the eyes of the Stoic, is to "bring his own will into harmony with what happens, so that neither anything that happens happens against our will, nor anything that fails to happen fails to happen when we wish it to happen." The Stoic's version of acceptance allows him nonetheless to fulfill his civic duties honorably, while maintaining "both the natural and the acquired relationships, those namely of son, father, brother, citizen, wife, neighbour, fellow-traveller, ruler, and subject" (*Discourses* 2.14.8–9).

Epictetus sees himself as offering, in contrast to the Cynics, a realistic practical philosophy—one whose content is attuned to the realities of the lives of the students who come to his "school for sick souls." A constant undercurrent of joy runs through what Arrian has captured of his lively, ironic speaking style; in the imagery—at times exuberant, at times restful—of scenes of sun and sea, of children at play, of festivals and fairs. Yet there remains something disturbing about this Stoicism. The harsher ideals of the true Cynic, which Epictetus sets aside, seem nonetheless to retain an appeal for him. The stricter asceticism of the Cynics persists at least as an ideal. For most of us, Epictetus says in the *Encheiridion,* the goal should be to behave in life as we would at a banquet—taking what is offered to us, but not impolitely grasping at food as it passes. So should we act toward children, wife, office, wealth, so that some day we will be worthy of the banquet of the gods. The higher ideal remains—not taking these offerings at all. We would then be worthy not only of sharing the banquet of the gods but of sharing their rule. "For it was by so doing that Diogenes and Heracleitus, and men like them, were deservedly divine and deservedly so called" (*Encheiridion,* sec. 15).

For himself, though, Epictetus will settle for something less than the lofty achievement of the Cynics. "What is it, then, you wish to be doing when death finds you? I for my part should wish it to be some work that befits a man, something beneficent, that promotes the common welfare, or is noble. But if I cannot be found doing such great things as these, I should like at least to be engaged upon that which is free from hindrance, that which is given me to do, and that is correcting myself as I strive to perfect the faculty which deals with the external impressions, labouring to achieve calm, while yet giving to each of my human relationships its due" (*Discourses* 4.10.11–13).

Notwithstanding his sensitive observations about human pleasure, Epictetus remains committed to the doctrine that the good life requires detachment from all affections that leave us vulnerable to what we cannot control. In a moving analysis of the predicament of Euripides' Medea, he locates the real tragedy in her deep attachment to things that lie outside her control. Medea has taken revenge on her unfaithful husband by killing their children. Epictetus leaves no doubt that we are witnessing "the outbursting of a soul of great force" (*Discourses* 2.17.21). But this is also a deluded soul, which has failed to realize that we can gain the power to do what we wish neither by finding it outside ourselves nor by rearranging things. "Give up wanting to keep your husband, and nothing of what you want fails to happen" (*Discourses* 2.17.22). If we give our desires to health, they will come to grief. "So also if you give them to offices, honours, country, friends, children, in short to anything that lies outside the domain of moral purpose" (*Discourses* 2.17.25).

It is in relation to the death of others—to grief and loss—that the harsher side of Epictetus's Stoicism is most apparent and hardest to accept. The cultivation of serenity in the face of our own mortality is one thing; the unrelenting ideal of self-protective detachment with regard to the death of those we love is quite another. "What did you see? A man in grief over the death of his child? Apply your rule. Death lies outside the province of the moral purpose. Out of the way with it" (*Discourses* 3.3.15). Epictetus always perceives a perverse irrationality at the core of grief. Our loves are mortal, given to us "for the present, not inseparably nor for ever, but like a fig, or a cluster of grapes, at a fixed season of the year." If we hanker for such things in winter, we are fools. "If in this way you long for your son, or your friend, at a time when he is not given to you, rest assured that you are hankering for a fig in winter-time. For as winter-time is to a fig, so is every state of affairs, which arises out of the universe, in relation to the things which are destroyed in accordance with that same state of affairs" (*Discourses* 3.24.86–87). In a startling generalization in the *En-*

cheiridion, Epictetus urges his students to keep always in mind the transitory nature of the things of which they are fond. "If you are fond of a jug, say, 'I am fond of a jug'; for when it is broken you will not be disturbed. If you kiss your own child or wife, say to yourself that you are kissing a human being; for when it dies you will not be disturbed" (*Encheiridion,* sec. 3).

The ideal of detachment in the midst of even our dearest loves finds eloquent but disturbing expression again in an extended metaphor: "Just as on a voyage, when your ship has anchored, if you should go on shore to get fresh water, you may pick up a small shell-fish or little bulb on the way, but you have to keep your attention fixed on the ship, and turn about frequently for fear lest the captain should call; and if he calls, you must give up all these things, if you would escape being thrown on board all tied up like the sheep. So it is also in life; if there be given you, instead of a little bulb and a small shell-fish, a little wife and child, there will be no objection to that; only, if the Captain calls, give up all these things and run to the ship, without even turning around to look back. And if you are an old man, never even get very far away from the ship, for fear that when He calls you may be missing" (*Encheiridion,* sec. 7).

There is some good sense in these reflections on grief and loss. "If you wish to make it your will that your children and your wife and your friends should live for ever, you are silly; for you are making it your will that things not under your control should be under your control, and that what is not your own should be your own" (*Encheiridion,* sec. 14). However, the calm acceptance of loss seems, in Epictetus's Stoicism, to pass into something much harsher—a refusal of the vulnerability that comes with deep attachment. The idea that an "external" condition such as poverty is not an evil— that true evil lies in the judgment about it rather than in poverty itself—may well be a basis for serenity amid changing fortunes. To treat our love of friends, spouses, and even children in the same spirit—as a perilous concern with indifferents—seems to threaten the core of attachment to the world that makes our lives worth living.

By contrast with that apparent impoverishment of feeling, Epictetus's thought is at its richest in his treatment of the way we face our own mortality. When it is time to leave the festival, he insists, the wise man leaves willingly. How are we supposed to know the right time to die? At some points, he seems, unhelpfully, to resort to the will of God. "And now it is Thy will that I leave this festival; I go, I am full of gratitude to Thee that Thou hast deemed me worthy to take part in this festival with Thee, and to see Thy works, and to understand Thy governance" (*Discourses* 3.5.10–11). Underlying that pious acceptance of externally imposed divine will, however, is the acceptance of necessity; and that acceptance is bound up with the exercise of our own judgment. It is ours to judge—informed by reflection on the shape of a well-lived life—what is the right time to die.

Here again the acknowledgment of necessity and the exercise of freedom come together. Epictetus's constant reminders that the option of suicide is open to us may seem at odds with the resolute endurance of misfortune that we commonly associate with Stoicism. In fact, it is in his treatment of suicide that we find the fullest expression of the connections he has drawn between freedom and the appropriation of necessity. The wise mind loves the world of which it is part; but it also knows when the time has come to leave it to others. When there is too much smoke in the kitchen, Epictetus repeatedly insists, the door stands open. "If Thou sendest me to a place where men have no means of living in accordance with nature, I shall depart from this life, not in disobedience to Thee, but as though Thou wert sounding for me the recall" (*Discourses* 3.24.101). Zeus has made us high-minded and capable of patient endurance, for he has permitted us to suffer many things and still be happy, but he also opens for us the door whenever things are really not for our good. "Man, go out, and do not complain" (*Discourses* 3.8.7).

The Emperor Reflects

The thoughts of the former slave Epictetus about what constitutes a good life would come to guide the reflections of an emperor. This development is in keeping with the spirit of that egalitarian Stoicism. Marcus Aurelius, who was born in 121 CE, reigned from the death of his adoptive father, Antoninus, in 161 to his own death in a military campaign on the northern frontiers in 180 CE. Before his accession, Marcus had studied law and philosophy; he was drawn especially to the Stoics, whom he studied with his teacher Apollonius. It was at the age of twelve, we learn in Gibbon's *Decline and Fall of the Roman Empire,* that he embraced the rigid system of the Stoics, which taught him "to submit his body to his mind, his passions to his reason; to consider virtue as the only good, vice as the only evil, all things external as things indifferent." Gibbon observes that the emperor's virtue was "the well earned harvest of many a learned conference, of many a patient lecture, and many a midnight lucubration."[20]

What is most striking about Marcus Aurelius in the history of Stoicism is, however, not his scholarly achievement, but his capacity to put Stoicism to the test as a "practical philosophy" in the midst of the most arduous of demands. His life, in Gibbon's estimation, was indeed "the noblest commentary on the precepts of Zeno." Although the emperor detested war as, in Gibbon's words, "the disgrace and calamity of human nature," he nonetheless, when necessity demanded that he take up arms, "readily exposed his person to eight winter campaigns on the frozen banks of the Danube, the severity of which was at last fatal to the weakness of his constitution."[21]

The life of an emperor does seem an unlikely setting for the philosophical life; and the tumult of military headquarters in the midst of winter campaigns is an unlikely place for philosophical reflection. Marcus saw it differently; as he comments in his *Meditations,* "How ridiculous and like a stranger to the world is he who is surprised at any one of the events of his life."[22] Far from finding his life uncongenial to the pursuit of philosophy, he remarks on how vividly it strikes him that no other calling in life is so suited to the practice of philosophy as that in which he now finds himself.

Chapter headings in Marcus's *Meditations* confirm that much of the work was written in the very thick of the emperor's military campaigns—he made these jottings during pauses for reflection, and while surrounded by the horrors of war. Familiar Stoic themes—mortality, the smallness of human life within the vast cosmos; the folly of desiring what lies beyond our powers to control—take on an added immediacy and poignancy in these extraordinary reflections made in the face of disaster. Marcus's observations on the good life have an urgency and an authority that comes from living in the constant presence of death; and that presence finds its way into the text with an intensity of sensation and emotion unusual in a philosophical text. The "paltry body" of which Epictetus so frequently speaks here becomes a more graphic mixture of "clay and gore," evoking the battlefield—"the smell of corruption and blood, and dust in a winding sheet" (*Meditations* 8.37). Marcus offers a familiar Stoic reflection on pain: What we cannot bear removes us from life, whereas what lasts can be borne. Here, though, the insight is intensified by the threat of imminent death or injury. Unlike other Stoics, Marcus is not struggling to retain an awareness of mortality in the midst of normal life. His remarks on death have the air, rather, of a struggle for calm and reassurance in the constant confrontation with the reality of death.

At times the tone of Marcus's remarks on mortality suggests a numbness rather than a serene detachment: "Nature has designed

the ending of each thing, no less than its beginning and its con-
tinuance, like one who throws a ball up. What good is it to the ball
to go up or harm to come down and even fall to the ground? What
good to the bubble to be blown or harm to it to burst? The same is
true of a candle" (*Meditations* 8.20). The mood of Marcus's metaphors is darker than Epictetus's playful imagery of ball games. It is
as if human beings themselves have become like inanimate objects in the hands of Nature. The imagery with which he expresses
the ideal of selflessness, too, conveys a different mood. The disdain of praise as an "external" is familiar from earlier Stoic texts.
But Marcus links it with the delight in beauty—which is in turn
associated with a sense of transitoriness and fragility. "Everything
in any way lovely is lovely of itself and terminates in itself, holding
praise to be no part of itself. . . . Does an emerald become worse
than it was, if it be not praised? And what of gold, ivory, purple,
a lute, a sword-blade, a flower-bud, a little plant?" (*Meditations*
4.20).

This emphasis on the theme of transience—of the brevity of
all things, but especially of life, of consciousness, and of memory—
is indeed what is most distinctive in Marcus's Stoicism. "All is
ephemeral, both what remembers and what is remembered" (*Meditations* 4.35). The prospect of death gives a poignancy to transitory
beauty; but it also helps make evanescence bearable. Our own departure may be near; but so too, in the bigger picture, is that of
all who will come after us. "Brief life is the common portion of
all, yet you avoid and pursue each thing as though it will be for
everlasting. A little while and you will close your eyes, and now
another will be lamenting him who carried you out" (*Meditations*
10.34). "How swiftly eternity will cover all things, and how many
it has covered already!" (*Meditations* 6.59). "Near at hand is your
forgetting all; near too all forgetting you" (*Meditations* 7.21). "Continually run over in your mind men who were highly indignant at
some event; men who attained the greatest heights of fame or di-

saster or enmity or of any kind of fortune whatever. Then pause and think: 'Where is it all now? Smoke and ashes and a tale that is told, or not so much as a tale'" (*Meditations* 12.27).

For Marcus the closeness of death becomes bearable in the broader perspective of universal transience but also lends an urgency to the claim of virtue. Take your prescriptions for good living as "a gift from the muses," he urges himself, "and begin at last to be a human being, while life remains" (*Meditations* 11.18). What is to be dreaded is not that we will someday cease to live, but rather that we might "never at all begin to live with Nature" (*Meditations* 12.1).

Death also colors Marcus's perspective on the old Stoic theme of our place in the whole of Nature. Epictetus had already drawn connections between temporality and the structure of the universe: we should acquiesce in being replaced by others at the festival of life, make way for them with dignity. For Marcus, though, life's fleetingness intensifies the beauty of the passing spectacle. It is change that allows the world to continue "ever young and in her prime" (*Meditations* 12.23); and it is our own pending departure from it all that allows us to see that youthful beauty, and to make a virtuous response. "What a fraction of infinite and gaping time has been assigned to every man; for very swiftly it vanishes in the eternal; and what a fraction of the whole of matter, and what a fraction of the whole of the life Spirit. On what a small clod too of the whole earth you creep. Pondering all these things, imagine nothing to be great but this: to act as your own nature guides, to suffer what Universal Nature brings" (*Meditations* 12.32).

The fugitive quality of the passing show gives it a poignant beauty for the contemplating mind; but we find joy in what is fleeting precisely *because* it is: our pleasure derives from contemplating something in flux, rather than grasping it, in the way we might something permanent. "In this river, therefore, on which he cannot stand, which of these things that race past him should a man greatly prize? As though he should begin to set his heart on one of the little sparrows that fly past, when already it has gone away out of his sight" (*Meditations* 6.15).

Marcus acknowledges the gods, but his Stoicism transcends his piety. He talks of an afterlife: "Nothing is void of gods, not even in that other world." Yet he can envisage with equanimity the prospect that if he "steps ashore" to unconsciousness, rather than to a second life, he will cease to suffer pain no less than pleasure, and to be tied to the "clay and gore" that is his vulnerable body (*Meditations* 3.3). Either way, death is not to be feared; it is rather something to look forward to. It should be thought of not as a sad departure from the stage before the play is over, but rather as the goal at which he must arrive in readiness for an effortless departure. "'But I have not spoken my five acts, only three.' 'What you say is true, but in life three acts are the whole play'" (*Meditations* 12.36). What is more, for Marcus (as for Epictetus) if we are not able to continue living in accordance with Nature, it remains open to us to choose the time of our going. We should then depart as if we had met no evil fate: "The chimney smokes and I leave the room. Why do you think it a great matter?" (*Meditations* 5.29).

Stoic ethics provides the background for the important contest between two approaches to freedom and responsibility that we shall see open up later—the Cartesian emphasis on free will and the Spinozist ideal of shaping a life in accordance with necessity. To understand the contours of that opposition, however, we must first examine the emerging tensions between will and necessity in the context of Augustine's version of providence.

4 Augustine

Divine Justice and the "Ordering" of Evil

Although the Stoics idealized detachment, there was a worldliness about their ideas of nature and providence. The Stoic philosophers wanted to live at ease in a world shared with the gods. That ideal could be combined with piety; but the piety was not essential. Even when the Stoics speak in pious tones, the focus is not on the will of deities but rather on the necessary structure of the world. A Stoic may talk of acceptance of what the gods want for men; but divine providence is not perceived as an intrusion—however benign—from another world. The essence of Stoic ethical ideals was the shaping of human life in accordance with necessities that govern the world into which we are all born, and within which we must shape our lives. With the next major shift in the understanding of providence, the idea takes on distinctly otherworldly connotations. In the powerful imagination of Saint Augustine, the cosmic city of gods and men became the Christian City of God. It was a city whose existence was not exclusively either spiritual or temporal. Its dynamism—no less than its ultimate instability—derived from shifts between the two aspects of its being. Those shifts were intrinsic to Augustine's remarkable exercise of imagination in laying the foundations of the city.

Augustine was not at ease in his world. His longings for another world found expression especially in his conversion to Christianity, which is presented in his autobiographical *Confessions* as the central event of his life. Yet although his deepest desires may have been focused on a transcendent God, his experience of those desires, and his attempts to realize them, remained inextricably bound up with the necessities, and the delights, of "the flesh." Nor did Augustine deny the unresolvable tensions—the ongoing balancing act—involved in living this ideal imagined life.

Both Augustine's narrative of conversion in the *Confessions* and the later development of Christian ideals in the *City of God* are full of eloquent descriptions of the beauties of the natural world. Light, especially, was a constant source of pleasure to Augustine. In the *City of God* he talks of "the plenteousness of light and its wondrous quality," of its effects in the bright colors of birds, and of "the grand spectacle of the sea, robing herself in different colors, like garments; sometimes green, and that in so many different shades; sometimes purple; sometimes blue." Indeed Augustine seems in his reflections on beauty in the *City of God* to envisage a continuity between the temporal and the spiritual worlds. All these visual delights, he reflects, are "the mere solace of the wretched and condemned, not the rewards of the blessed! What, then, will those rewards be, if the consolations are so many and so great?"[1] Although Augustine's religious piety found expression through the otherworldliness of Neoplatonism, his desire to inhabit another world is a longing for transformation, rather than for escape from the body. "Take away death, the last enemy," he says in one of his later sermons, "and my own flesh shall be my dear friend throughout eternity."[2]

Human imperfection is a constant theme in Augustine's moral reflections, but even in its imperfections, bodily existence has for him a vivacity, a fullness, that allows him to present the longed-for perfection as a continuation rather than a replacement. His works describe human imperfection as a dynamic experience—as a constantly lived tension. His biographer Peter Brown has observed that Augustine sensed the nature of that imperfection as "a profound and permanent dislocation: as a *discordia,* a 'tension,' that strove, however perversely, to seek resolution in some balanced whole, in some *concordia.*"³ In his distinctive idea of "balance" as a lived tension, rather than an abstract proportion, Augustine made a lasting contribution to the shaping of modern ideas on both perfection and evil.

The nature of evil, and the nature of providence as divine response to evil, are recurring themes throughout Augustine's writings; but it is in one of his early works, *De Ordine,* that we can see most clearly the interconnections between his concepts of providence and of divine justice. This early work is revealing also for the light it throws on the continuities between Augustine's evolving thought and the intellectual passions of his youth. When he tells the story of his conversion in the *Confessions,* he crafts an intellectual persona that breaks radically with his past—with the unorthodox doctrines of the Manichees and with the Neoplatonic texts that had provided a content for his otherworldly yearnings. Despite the vehemence of those rejections, however, Manicheism and Neoplatonism continue to resonate in his reflections on evil and providence.

There are no simple fusions here; the appropriation of Platonism brings with it tensions that will remain unresolved. Plotinus's *Enneads,* which were a strong influence on Augustine, speak of a spark of universal Mind in human nature—a remnant that craves a unity lost when Mind unfolded into the material world. That idea resonates in Augustine's thought—along with other, darker echoes of Manichean doctrine. The Manichees saw the world's evils as the product of a malign force at odds with benign providence. Augustine would distance himself increasingly from the Manichees in his mature thought: he came to lay the responsibility for evildoing squarely on the misuse of the human capacity for free will, which is the gift of a God concerned with our wellbeing. Yet for Augustine evil seems to remain in some ways beyond human control. Divine providence is not, as the Manichees thought, engaged in conflict with a rival demiurge that has created evil; nor has God himself made evil. Still, evil remains a hostile reality that divine providence must confront and bring into order. Being all-powerful, God will succeed in this ordering; but his success will not come without a cost in human casualties.

Augustine took up with enthusiasm the call to reconcile the existence of evil with divine providence—the task of theodicy. The broad parameters of the challenge had already been set in the third century CE by the Neoplatonic philosopher Plotinus, in his third *Ennead.* Plotinus's discussion of providence had in turn been framed by Plato, who treated the theme in book 10 of *The Laws.* It cannot be assumed that Augustine, who had only a limited knowledge of Greek, was directly influenced by either of these texts. It is known, though, that he had read much of Plotinus in translation; and his own reflections on divine providence resonate with Plotinus's eloquent evocations of the encompassing unity—the "melody"—that incorporates human suffering into a beautiful whole. What made Augustine's treatment of evil distinctive was his powerful expression of the role of divine justice in responding to evil. To understand this crucial shift in the idea of providence, it is helpful to look first briefly at the treatment of providence that Plotinus offers in the third *Ennead.*

Plotinus, like many after him, is eager to reconcile the conviction that we are responsible for our own actions with the equally strong conviction that we live in an ordered and predictable world. Our free actions, he argues in a discussion of the concept of destiny in the opening sections of the third *Ennead,* are not, as the Epicureans thought, to be understood as proceeding from the unpredictable swervings of atoms. Nor are they the result of mindless universal necessity. He thinks that the world-soul of Plato's *Timaeus,* properly understood, does not absorb individual human souls into one soul with a single "destiny." Such an "excess of necessity and of destiny" would in fact do away with destiny and the "chain of causes and their interweaving," which true Platonism must preserve.[4] Each separate thing must be indeed separate: "there must be actions and thoughts that are our own; each of one's good and bad actions must come from himself" (*Ennead* 3.1.4.25). For Plotinus the resolution of the apparent tension between freedom and universal necessity lies in the distinction between thinking and unthinking action. If we think of destiny as an external cause of human action, then we can say that "the soul acts unthinkingly according to destiny"; but the best actions—the thinking actions—nonetheless "come from ourselves" (*Ennead* 3.1.10.10–12).

What then is this unthinking state that allows us to engage in acts that do not "come from ourselves"? For Plotinus it has the same general explanation as the existence of evils in the world: it is the inevitable consequence of the "unfolding" of Mind—"the All"—into the existence of a world that has the limitations of matter. What is striking about this theodicy is that it draws a conceptual link between the existence of evil and the very idea of providence. Providence is Mind providing for—looking after— the material world, including the bodily existence of human beings. It provides for us in all our inevitably conflict-ridden existence—as unthinking as well as thinking beings. No room remains for conflict in what Plotinus calls the All. Internal division within this "true and first" intellectual being is ruled out by its wholeness, which is a "kind of archetype and model" of the world we inhabit. "The whole intellect lives and thinks all together in one, and makes the part the whole and all bound in friendship with itself, since one part is not separated from another and has not become merely other, estranged from the rest, and therefore, one does not wrong another, even if they are opposites" (*Ennead* 3.2.1.30).

In Plotinus's view, evil arises from the division that is an inevitable consequence when this unified intellect unfolds into matter:

once that happens, unquiet is only to be expected. As for Plotinus's recurring metaphors of song—which resemble those we have already seen in the Stoics and will see again in Augustine—when the single melody of the unified intellectual whole separates into parts, "it is necessary that some become friendly, and others hostile." Plotinus's "All" does not contain providence within itself independently of the material world into which it unfolds; nor does that All produce evil for some purpose of its own. This is not a divine will that could be held responsible for the existence of evil; its unfolding is not to be construed as a voluntary act. Yet providence and evil require each other. Without the existence of the divided world, there would be no providence. "If everything was providence and nothing but providence, then providence would not exist; for what would it have to provide for?" (*Ennead* 3.2.9.2). Those who demand a world that contains no evil, Plotinus argues, are seeking to abolish providence itself. "For what would it be providence of? Certainly not of itself or of the better" (*Ennead* 3.3.7.7).

The very concept of providence, as Plotinus sees it, thus requires the existence of evil. Providence "ought to reach everything, and its task ought to be just this, to leave nothing neglected" (*Ennead* 3.2.6.20). It may all seem a cheap play on the semantic content of providence as needing something to "provide for." A deeper strategy is at work, however: to articulate the nature of evil in such a way that its very existence can be seen as integral to the nature of a world governed by providence. "This belongs to the greatest power, to be able to use even the evil nobly and to be strong enough to use things which have become shapeless for making other shapes. In general, we must define evil as a falling short of good; and there must be a falling short of good here below, because the good is in something else" (*Ennead* 3.2.5.26).

Plotinus's version of providence bypasses the issue of responsibility for evil. The presence of providence in the world in all its parts is a reconciling, healing force that ensures the ultimate dominance of good. Things that have happened, "if anything which follows from them is good," are "taken up again by providence, so that virtue has everywhere the mastery" (*Ennead* 3.3.5.29–30). All things have their part to play in this healing of division; and they perform their part simply by being active in their own distinctive ways. There are strong echoes here of Stoic ideas about the impulse toward self-preservation. The activity of the parts—required by life itself—"closes the wound" of division, thus gathering all things back into one (*Ennead* 3.3.5.34). Yet the structure of the whole itself depends on the opposition between and among its parts. The very existence of "rational pattern" requires internal division between opposites—and the intensification of those oppositions, "so that if in general it makes one thing different from another, it will also make them different in the extreme, and not different in a lesser degree; so by making one thing different from another in the highest degree it will necessarily make the opposites, and will be complete if it makes itself not only into different things but into opposite things" (*Ennead* 3.2.16.55–59).

Opposition thus becomes intensified. Rather than resting with a static coexistence, the antagonism of opposites means that each individual "has a greater urge to live, and there is a greater passion for unification" (*Ennead* 3.2.17.5–6). Plotinus's eloquent descriptions of the oppositions between parts of the whole evoke an internal dynamic of struggle for self-preservation that resonates with themes and imagery from early Stoicism. The "urgent straining" of the part toward the whole "draws to itself what it can" (*Ennead* 3.2.17.9). Hence the destructive power of passionate love for perishable things—lovers often destroy the objects of their passion in the pursuit of their own good (*Ennead* 3.2.17.5).

In his mature thought Augustine rejected the Neoplatonism that had so impressed him in his early intellectual development. Yet those Platonic and Stoic themes and images—especially the idea of friendship, love, and yearning as integral to the very structure of the material world—persist in his later expressions of the soul's yearning for the Christian God. The dynamism of opposition and reconciliation—the idea of a balance between opposites as an antagonistic struggle for self-preservation, rather than a pre-existing, static "harmony"—colors his version of the theme of divine justice.

Augustine's fullest development of the relations between providence and evil appears in *De Ordine*.[5] It is one of a set of early "dialogues" that emerge from a period of creative idleness after the deliberate withdrawal of a group of Christian friends into a life of communal inquiry at Cassiciacum, near Milan. The group included Augustine's mother, Monica, his eldest brother, Navigius, and his son, Adeodatus. But the key participant in the debate memorialized in *De Ordine* is Licentius, the son of Augustine's friend Romanius. These dialogues celebrate philosophical discussion—not as a rarefied scholarly activity, but as the core of a well-lived life. Augustine was here adapting older models of philosophical conversation to the inculcation of Christian doctrines and ideals. The literary form of *De Ordine* is reminiscent of Cicero's enactment of a philosophical discussion among friends in his *De Natura Deorum*. The inclusion in the debate of a couple of young students also evokes Epictetus's concern with teaching philosophy as a strategy for ethical formation.

The literary form of *De Ordine,* no less than its content, reflects the influence of earlier dialogical and pedagogical works. Augustine conjures up for his readers a communal life centered on philosophical inquiry. He and his two pupils, Licentius and Trygetius, are presented as conversing in the dark about order as they lie awake, puzzling about the intermittent noise of water in a leaf-filled drain nearby. Their interest in the idea of order—its connections with beauty and harmony, and its significance for understanding the relations between reason and the senses—frames

Augustine's treatment of the nature of evil and of divine providence.

Not surprisingly, Augustine's treatment of Platonic themes of order and beauty resonates strongly with Plotinus's treatment of similar themes in the *Enneads*. The attempts in *De Ordine* to accommodate the apparent disorder of human life into an ordered world echo themes—and also metaphors—from Plotinus and from the Stoics. But Augustine makes some significant changes to those old refrains. He places a strong emphasis, for example, on part-whole relations, but also a new emphasis on the limitations of the human perspective within the greater whole. Not only do we have distorted judgments about what matters in human life; our very perceptions of order and disorder are distorted. For the narrator of *De Ordine,* it is as if we were to say that there is no order in an inlaid pavement that is only partially perceived, and to criticize the maker for lacking skill, rather than acknowledge our own limited perception. "On this account we might think the uniformity of the little stones disarranged, just because the drawn lines, harmonizing into one integral form of beauty, could not be seen and examined all at once. Something very similar to this is found in the case of uninstructed men, who on account of their feeble mentality, are unable to grasp and to study the integral fittingness of things. They think that the whole universe is disarranged if something is displeasing to them, just because that thing is magnified in their perception" (*De Ordine* I.I.2, pp. 240–241).

As limited parts within the whole, our perspective on that whole is distorted. But what exactly do the limitations of human perception have to do with evil? Augustine's position is not that evil is an illusion, produced by distorted perception. For him, as for Plotinus, evil is a reality to which providence responds, although providence is not responsible for its existence. Augustine will be more directly concerned with the nature of evil in later works. Here in *De Ordine* his focus is on explaining the proper place of evil in an ordered world—a world ordered by providence. The idea Augustine's narrator and his pupils have reached of order—as the "integral fittingness of things"—immediately confronts the interlocutors with the challenge of evil. Is it part of the order of things? Can bad things, as well as good, be said to be "in order"? God loves order. So if evil is encompassed within order, must we then say that he loves evil? The bright young Licentius offers the answer: "This itself is the order of evils; that they be not loved by God." The narrator presents the answer as clumsy; yet it anticipates much in Augustine's own later accounts of evil, as having been brought into order by divine justice.

In the dramatic structure of *De Ordine,* Licentius's "clumsy" formulation provides a moment of insight that will shape their future discussion. With the enthusiasm of sudden realization, he shouts: "This very thing [God] loves: to love good things, and not to love evil things—and this itself is a thing of magnificent order and of divine arrangement. And because this orderly arrangement maintains the harmony of the universe by this very contrast [between good and evil] it comes about that evil things [lesser goods] must need be." Licentius goes on to suggest that this principle is borne out in the beautiful antitheses in the very discussion they are at present having in the dark. Electrified by his insight, he leaps out of bed, startling his fellow pupil by appearing beside his bed, as he demands: "I am asking you now: Is God just?" The narrator urges him to set aside this "unexpected streak of conscientiousness" until they can discuss it properly during the newly dawning day (*De Ordine* 1.7.18–20, pp. 256–257).

The old idea of cosmic justice has here entered into a new association with the idea of providence. Providence now manifests itself, not only in God's love of the good, but also and equally in his aversion to evil. This is the key to Augustine's theodicy. Divine providence is expressed, not only in his loving care for his creatures, but also in his harshness toward the evil they do. Justice is a

matter of discriminating between good and evil and giving each
its due—bringing both evil and good into order. We can now understand the point of Augustine's analogy about our perception of
the mosaic floor pattern. It is not that we discover the appearance
of evil to be an illusion; the point is rather that the proper place of
evil in the wider whole can now be discerned. That is, evil can
now be seen in its proper place, thanks to the exercise of divine
justice in punishment. The rightful order is produced by the divine response to evil. This too is providence: nothing is permitted
to be where it ought not to be. "Thus it happens that whoever
narrow-mindedly considers this life by itself alone is repelled by
its enormous foulness, and turns away in sheer disgust. But, if
he raises the eyes of his mind and broadens his field of vision and
surveys all things as a whole, then he will find nothing unarranged,
unclassed, or unassigned to its own place" (De Ordine 2.4.11, p. 287).

Assigning good and evil to their rightful place is in Augustine's
eyes the very nature of justice; but it is also the nature of providence. Good and evil are brought into order by being brought to
judgment—to reward and punishment. The theme of the right
placing of things in an ordered whole had already been discussed
by Plotinus. The evil-sounding singing of panpipes, he says in his
discussion of providence in the third Ennead, can be "beautifully
disposed" as part of a whole, even though on their own they sound
worse than other instruments. Likewise, the public executioner,
though a scoundrel, does not make the well-governed city worse.
The executioner is "well-placed" in relation to the whole city (Ennead 3.2.17.85). What was for Plotinus an observation on the way
in which things disagreeable in themselves are accommodated
into a more encompassing, harmonious whole becomes for Augustine a principle of their active ordering. "What more hideous
than a hangman?" he has his narrator ask. "What more cruel and
ferocious than his character? Yet he holds a necessary post in the
very midst of laws, and he is incorporated into the order of a well-

regulated state; himself criminal in character, he is nevertheless, by others' arrangement, the penalty of evildoers." In another example—which has become better known through being taken up by Aquinas in the *Summa Theologica*—Augustine comments on the role and rightful place of prostitutes in a well-ordered society: "Remove prostitutes from human affairs, and you will unsettle everything because of lusts; place them in the position of matrons, and you will dishonor these latter by disgrace and ignominy" (*De Ordine* 2.4.12, pp. 287–288). Everything in its place!

We see just how far Augustine is prepared to go in developing this theme of the right ordering of evil in a fuller discussion in a later dialogue from the same early period—*De Libero Arbitrio Voluntatis,* which he worked on in the period from 388 to 391, although it was not completed until 395.[6] Augustine strongly echoes Plotinus in this work. Evil, Augustine again argues, is not created by God; it results from human imperfection. Nor can God be blamed for the existence of imperfect human beings, for the world would be less perfect did it not contain such beings—capable both of sinning and of acting rightly. The interconnections between the nature of evil and the nature of providence in Augustine's analysis are here evident. God is not the author of evil; and his response to it is one of active management rather than passive acceptance.

Augustine has taken from Plotinus the idea of imperfection as a consequence of the existence of a material world. For Augustine it is of course a Christian God who plays the part of providence in relation to that world; but he articulates the Christian God's loving care of the world by means of the Platonic concept of Form. Everything that exists is governed by providence—that is, all things are given form by God, who is immutable and eternal Form. If that Form did not exist, they would not either. All existing things would cease to exist if their form were taken away; and as mutable things, they owe their continued possession of form to divine providence, construed as unchanging Form.

This appropriation of Neoplatonism to provide an explanation of Christian providence allows Augustine to present in a new way the old Stoic idea of the "debt" owed by things to Nature. The Stoics regarded it as consolation for the transience of life: individuals must die in order that others may replace them. In Augustine's version, our debt to nature becomes our obligation to live rightly. It is the failure to pay this "debt" for existence—the debt owed to the "eternal Form"—that makes possible the crucial connection between order and punishment in Augustine's treatment of evil. Another crucial appropriation, from Neoplatonism, helps to balance the apparent harshness of the allusion to our debt. Augustine adapts Platonic love of the eternal forms to a Christian narrative of the soul's journey toward its God, and central to the journey is the idea of providence, construed as the Form through which all changing things subsist. "As he gazes attentively at the whole of creation, he who travels the road to wisdom perceives how delightfully wisdom reveals itself to him on the way, and meets him in all providence. The more beautiful is the road to the wisdom toward which he hastens, the more ardently he burns to complete the journey" (De Libero Arbitrio Voluntatis 2.17.173–174).

Augustine's world pulsates with an energy, and a yearning, that derive from his Neoplatonist sources and less directly from older Stoic adaptations of the Timaeus story. From Plotinus he has taken the theme of material bodies as longing for a lost unity that can never be fully realized in the unfolding of Mind into divisible matter. At the same time, his narrative of the soul's journey resonates with ancient Stoic ideas of necessity as eliciting the soul's love. Even in the midst of misfortunes and suffering, the human soul—for Augustine as for the Stoics—is drawn by love to embrace the necessity of what it undergoes. Many of his descriptions of the yearnings of the soul echo Chrysippus's talk of its intense longings for what is necessary to it. In Augustine's version of the human soul's embrace of necessity, though, the emphasis is on the love of justice. Each human soul is part not just of a whole in which "cosmic justice" prevails as the necessary order among opposites, but of a divine ordering of evil through the exacting of punishment for the misuse of the human will. The erring soul's love of its fate is now its love of the just punishment that puts it in its rightful place. The soul—now, as a Christian soul, immortal—is supposed to love its place in the just ordering of things, even if that acceptance involves its own eternal suffering. In *De Libero Arbitrio,* Augustine offers to the erring soul a sobering reassurance: "If it is unjust for you to be more unhappy after death, you will not be more unhappy. If, however, it is just, let us praise God by whose laws you will be unhappy" (*De Libero Arbitrio Voluntatis* 3.6.65).

Augustine's emphasis on divine justice, as the active ordering principle that gives beauty to punishment, is a turning point in the history of the idea of providence. It puts an entirely new light on the accommodation of human suffering in the general goodness of the ordered whole: the enlightened soul will rejoice in justice—even in the justice of its own unhappiness. Cosmic order is for Augustine not just a rationally disposed whole but an arrangement of "just degree"—that is, one achieved through the operation of divine justice. How individual human beings fare in the universe is for him never a matter of chance or luck; it is ensured by the operation of divine justice—by punishment. Wrongdoers may appear to thrive, but they have nonetheless been assigned in some more fundamental way to their proper unhappy place in the order of things.

Punishment plays a metaphysical role in relation to order. Divine retribution is not just a means of frightening the erring into doing what they should; it is a means to equilibrium that in itself ensures the preservation of a necessary order. "Punishment is used in such a way that it places natures in their right order (that is, where it is not a disgrace for them to be), and forces them to comply with the beauty of the universe, so that the punishment of sin corrects the disgrace of sin" (*De Libero Arbitrio Voluntatis* 3.9.95). Hence the centrality of the idea of the soul as paying its debt: "If the soul does not pay its debt by doing justice, it will pay its debt by enduring unhappiness—the word 'debt' is applicable in either case. . . . If a man does not pay his debt by doing what he ought, he pays it by suffering what he ought" (*De Libero Arbitrio Voluntatis* 3.15.151–152). No one escapes from justice except into unhappiness: "The ugliness of sin is never without the beauty of punishment." The balance of sin and punishment—ugliness and beauty—may not be immediately apparent to human observers. Nevertheless, although evildoers may appear to flourish, in the judgment to come the deeds now being "secretly punished" will be disclosed, with the attendant unhappiness (*De Libero Arbitrio Voluntatis* 3.15.153).

Augustine's version of providence is in many ways a stark transformation of the ancient idea of cosmic order. It seems to require acceptance not only of Christian theology but also of the apparent ruthlessness providence exercises in bringing evil into order. The apparent harshness of the providential calculus comes out in Augustine's chilling discussion of the suffering of children in *De Libero Arbitrio Voluntatis* 3.23.229–231. Here he argues that it is right that this suffering should occur, for God works some good by correcting the sinful adults who are tortured by the sickness and death of children dear to them.

Augustine seems ready to treat the suffering of children as what we might nowadays call collateral damage from the punishment of the parents' wrongdoing. There are, however, some mitigating factors. His remarks on the suffering of children occur in the course of a discussion of original sin and the vexed issue of the need for infant baptism—a source of bitter controversy among Augustine's Christian contemporaries. Because we have all been born after the sin of Adam, Augustine thought, even newborn babies cannot be presumed to be innocent of guilt: all human beings are in need of divine grace if they are to receive the eternal rewards of heaven.

The issue of divine grace came to preoccupy Augustine in his later works, in which he refines his treatment of free will in response to the controversies surrounding the "heretical" doctrines of one of his rivals, the British monk Pelagius. According to the Pelagians, we achieve salvation or damnation through our own merits alone, rather than through any unwarranted gift of divine grace. Notwithstanding the awesome responsibilities Augustine assigns to the human will, he preached that human beings are in the end saved not through their own merits but through the unearned gift of divine grace. In his final work, the voluminous set of *Retractions,* in which he reviews all his earlier writings, Augustine insists that even in *De Libero Arbitrio Voluntatis* his version of free will is very different from that advocated by the Pelagians. Even in his treatment of the suffering of children he leaves room for the exercise of divine grace, but the argumentation seems to depend too much on accepting the inscrutability of divine judgment. Divine justice may be the arbiter of punishment, in the cause of reintegrating evil into the ordered whole; but this is not to be construed as a transparent code of punishment. We know that God is just, but we cannot expect to understand the weighing of good and evil involved in his meting out of punishment to humankind.

Evildoers may appear to escape justice, while "innocent" children suffer. But the full truth, Augustine insists, is otherwise. In response to the challenge, What evil have they done that they should suffer so? he responds: But what reason is there to believe that anyone should be rewarded for innocence when that person died before having a chance to do harm? We cannot know exactly how the suffering of children "tests the piety," or breaks down the "hardness," of their parents. Nor can we know what reward God may have reserved "in the secret place of his judgment" for the suffering children. The church after all, Augustine reminds his

readers, "commends as martyrs" the infants who were slaughtered
when Herod sought to slay the infant Christ (*De Libero Arbitrio
Voluntatis* 3.23.229–231). This is a God who bestows undeserved
grace, as well as the God of just punishment. Although such a God
allows children to suffer, we cannot presume to know exactly how
their suffering balances out in the great ordering of good and evil.

The argument cannot be expected to appeal to any but the
most pious of Christian parents; yet it is important to keep in
mind, in reading these disturbing passages, that Augustine is
speaking from within the context of a community of judgment
shared with his fellow Christians. He is not trying to offer—as the
Stoics may have—an argument to appeal to all rational minds.
Rather, he is addressing himself to a group that supposedly shares
his religious beliefs and hopes; within that framework he offers
a set of considerations that might persuade bereaved parents to
think of their suffering children as participating in the higher
ends of providence, rather than being exploited by them. Augustine is dismissive of the philosophical challenge the suffering of
children might pose to divine goodness. It arises, he complains,
from "superficial questions" posed by "careless students of such
issues" and "loquacious sophists" who "harass the faith of the less
learned." Doubters "think wickedly" about such problems and, in
failing to grasp that the "highest good" lies beyond the corporeal
world, cannot comprehend that good (*De Libero Arbitrio Voluntatis*
3.23.232–233).

Augustine is not saying that the suffering of innocent children
is of no importance; he wants to regard them as fully included in
the operations of providence. Little in his argument, however,
could persuade a nonbeliever; in the end it depends on the appeal
to a shared faith in God, as a being already assumed to care about
human well-being. The capacity to shift with such confidence between an appeal to faith and an appeal to reason is a mark of Augustine's "situated" intellectual life. He thinks not as a disembod-

ied intellect, but as a man of his place and time. He writes out of the full depths of his experience as part of a community that gives form to this thought, while at the same time he contributes to the formation of that community. The shifts between the language of faith and that of reason, which can be so disconcerting for modern readers, are not indicative of lapses in his skills of argument, but reflective of other dynamic shifts expressed in his writing—between intellect and love, between mind and "flesh," between sensuous delight in the beauty of this world and a longing for the next.

Augustine's capacity for situated thinking—imaginatively powerful and emotionally resonant—comes out also in another theme that runs through his works: that of time and the transitory nature of things. His reflections on this subject also bear on the suffering of children. In book 12 of his *Confessions* Augustine offers one of philosophy's most famous articulations of the experience of the passage of time—of the mind's poignant attempts to hold fast to a present that is always coming from a nonexistent but unavoidable future and vanishing into a nonexistent past. Echoing Stoic reflections on transience, Augustine observes in his discussion of evil in *De Libero Arbitrio Voluntatis* that it is foolish to think that temporal objects should not pass away. Those who grieve about things' passing away ought, he says, to listen to their own speech; each word of their complaint must yield its place so that the whole complaint can be made. To complain about transience can thus "be judged quite mad."

Augustine sees the remembered past as thin and insubstantial by comparison with the overwhelming reality of the present and the intense anticipation of the future. In his discussion of evil in *De Libero Arbitrio,* that temporal theme finds expression in his reluctance to allow past suffering to carry much weight when balanced against the expectation of future good. "When the sufferings of children are over, it will be as if they had never occurred for those who suffered. Either the adults on whose account the sufferings occurred will become better, if they are reformed by temporal troubles and choose to live rightly, or else, if because of the hardships of this life they are unwilling to turn their desire toward eternal life they will have no excuse when they are punished in the judgment to come" (*De Libero Arbitrio Voluntatis* 3.23.147). The metaphysical beauty of just punishment leaps over time to the consummated good end—the grand balance achieved wherein all things will be in their rightful place. The past suffering of the innocent counts, it seems, for little in that great accommodation.

It is inevitable that we now read these disturbing passages in Augustine's analysis of providence and evil through the prism of the Kantian principle that has become so crucial to modern ethics—that individual human beings must always be treated as ends in themselves, rather than as means toward the achievement of some supposedly higher end. From a post-Kantian perspective, Augustine's readiness to factor the suffering of children into the "beauty" of divine justice is unavoidably disturbing. Fyodor Dostoyevsky, in his famous reflection on the ideal of cosmic harmony in *The Brothers Karamazov,* has Ivan, in the lead-up to his conversation with the Grand Inquisitor, comment that the suffering of children is too high a price to place on harmony. Faced with that price for admission to a balanced world that demands the inclusion of such suffering, Ivan wants simply to "return the ticket." It would make little sense to offer such a response to the necessary unfolding of Platonic Mind, or to the Stoic vision of necessity; however, Augustine's providence is after all supposed to reflect a purposeful divine will, responsible for the creation of a balanced whole. To such providence, Ivan's response may well seem appropriate.

We must nonetheless be careful not to read back into Augustine's description of divine free will too much of the unconstrained autonomy that we now take for granted as pertaining to the will. Although Augustine affirms the freedom of what he calls *voluntas,* he does not think of it—whether in the case of divine or human will—as free from the constraints of necessity. Like the Stoics before him, he sees divine will and necessity as belonging together. The operations of human will are for him also framed—no less than the rest of the ordered world—by universal necessity. Indeed in a later and fuller treatment of the relations between divine will and necessity in the *City of God,* he argues that the Stoics do not insist strongly enough on universal necessity. The main source for Augustine's understanding of Stoicism, and his main target in his treatment of freedom in the *City of God,* is Cicero. The Stoics, in Augustine's view, feared necessity—feared it so much that they tried to exempt a class of voluntary causes from its sway. A Christian, Augustine argues, has no grounds for such fear of the all-encompassing necessity of providence. Providence is divine will, the divine provider; and providence encompasses human affairs no less than the order of all else.

The idea of a divine will operating beyond all necessity would for Augustine have introduced an unsettling arbitrariness into the ordering force of providence. The idea of a radically free human will—exerting its capacity for choice without any constraint from the understanding of necessity, would have been equally unsettling to his yearning for providential order. He says in *De Libero Arbitrio Voluntatis* that to reject providence is to abandon ourselves to the terrors and horrors of chance. "For some gladly believe that there is no divine providence in charge of human affairs; abandoning themselves, their spirits, and their bodies to the accidents of chance, they give themselves over to be battered and torn by lusts; they defy divine justice and evade the justice of men" (*De Libero Arbitrio Voluntatis* 3.2.16–17). Although Augustine presents providence as the domain of a benign divine will, he does not see it any less as the domain of necessity. However, that shift of emphasis, as we have seen, does leave him open to a challenge that had not risen for his Stoic predecessors: the difficulty of reconciling the existence of evil with the existence of a loving providence.

The tensions between freedom and necessity in Augustine's discussion of these concepts in the *City of God* center—as they continued to do throughout much of medieval philosophy—on the implications of God's foreknowledge of human action. Cicero, Augustine says, thought we had to make a choice between human freedom and God's knowledge of what we will do. Augustine insists, however, that because our free will is a gift of divine providence, God's knowledge of how we will exercise that freedom poses no threat to our freedom. Augustine acknowledges, in book 5, chapter 1, of the *City of God,* that his disagreement with the Stoics is partly just a matter of terminology. If anyone believes that fate was responsible for the greatness of the Roman Empire, and that person uses the word "fate" to allude to the will of God, "let him keep to this judgment but correct his language."[7]

It is striking that in quoting Seneca's version of Cleanthes in that context, Augustine presents the Stoic idea of fate as another way of talking about what he himself calls divine will. From the perspective of the Stoics, it was of course the other way round: invoking God's will was for them just a way of talking about the necessary chain of causes. Augustine's argument relies on exploiting the shifting emotional resonances of "universal necessity"; those changes in resonance serve to mark the distance between Christian providence and Stoic fate.

The Christianizing of providence came at a cost; its reconciling power would henceforth carry the moral ambiguities of an omnipotent divine will answerable for its purposes. Human freedom, too, would now assume an awesome responsibility and would increasingly break away from Augustine's framing context of universal necessity. The break will become more evident in Descartes's theory of freedom and its relation with providence, to which Spinoza will respond with a new radical rapprochement of freedom and necessity. Although Augustine's *voluntas* is an important part of the history of the emerging modern concept of the will, however, it is also in some ways very different from the will we know so well. Not least, it is still imbued with older Neoplatonic connotations of love.

Augustine shares with Plotinus, and with the Stoics, the idea of love as expressed in a striving toward the good—toward continued existence and well-being. In his *City of God,* love is the driving force governing all things—a magnetism drawing all living things, and even inanimate things, toward their rightful place. Augustine gives it eloquent expression in a passage in the *City of God:* "For if we were cattle, we should love the carnal and sensuous life, and this would be our sufficient good; and when it was well with us in respect of it, we should seek nothing else. Again, if we were trees we could not, of course, be moved by the senses to love anything; but we should seem to desire, as it were, that·by which we might become more abundantly and beautifully fruitful. If we were stones or waves or wind or flames or anything of that kind, we should, indeed, be without both sensation and life, but we should still not lack a kind of desire for our own proper place and order. For the weight of bodies is, as it were, their love, whether they are carried downwards by gravity or upwards by their lightness. For the body is carried by its weight wherever it is carried, just as the soul is carried by its love."[8]

Human beings are "drawn by their loves." And the goodness of the good man is to be understood, not in terms of the repression of desire, but rather in terms of its intensification. John Rist has argued in an excellent discussion in *Augustine: Ancient Thought Baptised,* that Augustine's notion of the will is best understood in terms of love. Human beings are driven by the "compelling pressure of what they delight in"; and the good man is driven by "blazing love." The will here is something very different from later versions of it. Rist sees Augustine's *voluntas* as the accepted set of loves that are characteristic of each human being. The freedom of *voluntas* is a matter of the "set" of the will; and that is "nothing more than the congealed sum of our loves and hates."[9] It is a concept more akin to the idea of stabilized moral character than to later ideas of an episodic mental act. Our accepted, endorsed sets of loves and desires—the habits to which we have "assented"—become what we truly are.

True freedom, for Augustine as for the Stoics, is bound up with the recognition of necessity and hence with the mind's delight in truth. Our freedom, he insists in *De Libero Arbitrio Voluntatis,* consists in submission to the truth. "What is more fragrant or more pleasant than the breath of truth? . . . Do we ask for any other happy life, when, so to speak, the silent eloquence of truth glides noiselessly into our minds?" (*De Libero Arbitrio Voluntatis* 2.13.39). Will is here closely connected with necessity. Against that background, the fact that modern free will has come to conjure up absolute autonomy—an exemption or escape from the necessities of mere nature—may indeed seem a strange transformation: a strange fate for the idea of the will. The seeds of this concept of will, although it is so far from Augustine's vision of a freedom grounded in the love of an ordered necessity, are present in his shift of emphasis away from the identification of providence with necessary order to its identification with divine will.

James O'Donnell, in an important reassessment of the legacy of Augustine, has argued that his treatment of the tensions between church and world, flesh and spirit, enact the unresolved tensions in his own life. Augustine, he says, has turned the "frictions and rivalries of the human condition" into a "cosmic conflict between armies of dubious loyalties, with angels and demons fighting alongside humankind." In the real world, O'Donnell suggests, we live with the results of those unresolved tensions. The cosmic conflict, in which angels and demons fight alongside human participants "indistinctly swarming together in a confusing world" is a powerful image to contrast with the Stoic vision of the harmonious city of gods and men. But Augustine's version of the cosmic struggle speaks to the reality of conflicted human experience, in all its unresolved loves and yearnings.[10] Whether we can accept the divine "ordering" that holds it all together—or whether the cost of the ticket is in the end too high—is of course another matter.

Providence and Fortune

What Augustine calls *liberum arbitrium voluntatis* is rightly construed as freedom. It is connected with choice and with decision. Even so, although he is concerned to affirm human freedom against the universal fatalism he associated with the Stoics, his version of freedom is, as I have just said, a long way from what we now call free will. Nowhere in his works can we really locate our idea of free will as an inner causal force, separable from "intellect" and able to counter, or compete with, external causal forces.

Concern with the nature and scope of human freedom continues over a wide range of medieval and Renaissance debates that highlight emerging tensions within ongoing attempts to synthesize Christian doctrine with classical philosophy. Many of the problems concern the antagonism of fate and providence, where providence is construed as divine will. There can be conflict between human freedom and the very idea of a providence that is responsible for the ordering of all events toward its own ends. Yet it would be misleading to cast the history of post-Augustinian treatments of freedom as a gradual but steady progress away from providence toward our modern understanding of free will. Providence remains part of the configuration of concepts out of which will emerge the modern will. Tensions within the configuration center especially on the coexistence of freedom and necessity; but it is never a simple matter of providence being rejected or surpassed.

Throughout the long history of medieval and Renaissance debates on freedom, ideas about divine will and knowledge tussle with ideas of human freedom. Many of those debates are caught up with theological disputes about divine foreknowledge and predestination and are often cast in terms drawn from ancient Greek debates about the truth of "future contingents"—about the indeterminacy of events while they are still future. Medieval writers on the issues often invoked Aristotle's famous discussion, in chapter 9 of his work *On Interpretation*, of the relations between time, truth, and necessity. If statements about a future event—such as a sea battle—are already true, Aristotle asked, does it follow that whatever happens does so of necessity? To avoid fatalism must we say that statements about the future are neither true nor false?

Such puzzles went back further into antiquity—to the famous "master argument" offered by Diodorus Cronus in the third century BCE, as a challenge to the very possibility of contingency. The exact form of the argument has been lost; but its general structure was reported by Epictetus, who commented in his Second Discourse (2.19.1–10) that if he wanted to show off, he could astonish the company at a banquet by enumerating the many thinkers who had written about the argument.

Many later commentaries, including one by Boethius, dealt with Aristotle's treatment of the logical issues. The main lines of medieval and Renaissance syntheses, bringing those old debates together with current theological disputes about freedom and predestination, were set by Boethius's famous dramatization of ethical aspects of fate, providence, and freedom in his later and more influential work *The Consolation of Philosophy*.[11] Boethius lived from about 480 to 524 CE. He was charged with treason, and composed *The Consolation* while he was confined in a kind of house arrest before his execution. Like Augustine, Boethius draws on classical sources, especially Neoplatonism, to articulate Christian ideals; and like Seneca and Cicero, he looks to philosophy as a source of solace in times of affliction. *The Consolation* combines prose and poetry, casting philosophy as a female figure, counterpoised to the deceptive ministrations of the "monstrous" and "fickle" lady Fortune.

Philosophy visits the narrator in his confinement to converse with him about the themes of fortune and providence. Boethius has Philosophy speak reassuringly of divine reason as guiding the course of the world—of God as superintending his creation, rather than leaving it to the vagaries of chance. In language that echoes that of Stoicism, she reminds the prisoner that there is final purpose in the world, toward which the whole order of Nature proceeds. It is because he has forgotten this, she suggests, that he sees the changes of fortune that have befallen him as random and unguided. Philosophy tries to coax him away from his attachment to Fortune. First, she persuades him that adverse fortune is more trustworthy than the enticements of good fortune; for adversity often drags men back to the path of the true good. Then she claims her own superiority to Fortune in any of that lady's forms. The idea of providence plays a central role in Philosophy's argument. The stability of the laws of nature—in contrast to the changeability of human power, riches, or reputation—is indicative, she says, of where man's true good and happiness are to be found.

In a lyrical hymn that echoes old Stoic celebrations of Zeus, Philosophy praises the father of all things, who steers the world by everlasting reason. Here, however, it is the Christian God who is identified with the guiding force of reason, and this God is presented as one with and the same as the highest happiness. That identification is the heart of Boethius's "consolation"; and he allows it to be challenged by his version of the problem of evil: How can providence be distinguished from the powers of blind chance if it brings suffering to the good and rewards to the wicked? Philosophy's solution rests on a distinction between providence and Fate. Providence is the divine plan for the course of events in their totality; hence it is identified with divine reason itself. Fate is subordinated to providence; it is the order imposed by providence on things that change. Providence embraces all things; but it is Fate that organizes the separate movements of individual things. When the arrangement of the temporal order is construed as a unity within the foresight of the divine mind, it is providence. When that unity is separated out and "unfolded" at various times, it is called Fate.

Echoes of Plotinus can be heard in Philosophy's talk about the order of Fate as emerging out of the indivisibility of providence; and when she talks of the "divine craftsman" as producing, stage by stage, what he originally conceives as a unity, we hear echoes also of the *Timaeus*. Providence is the unmoving, indivisible pattern of events, whereas Fate is the ordering of that pattern in time. Fate is subject to providence; but there are some things that fall—as all things must—under providence, while nonetheless transcending Fate.

That distinction is the key to Boethius's way of resolving the apparent contradiction between the purposes of providence and human freedom. Providence can accommodate free human actions into the unity of events, grasped in their entirety as part of an ordered, purpose-filled whole. Boethius's discussion involves a different—and philosophically less sophisticated—approach to evil from Augustine's resort to the ordering, restorative power of divine justice. Boethius resolves the problem of evil by denying its ultimate reality: the appearance of evil in human suffering is due to our inability to perceive, as God does, the whole order of which that suffering is part.

This resolution rests on an appeal to the power of divine intellect to comprehend hidden order, rather than on the transformative power Augustine gave to the divine will. What made *The Consolation of Philosophy* so significant in later medieval thought about freedom was the account Boethius offered in its final two books of the divine intellect's knowledge of events that, for human beings, lie in an unknowable future. He has Philosophy argue that human reason cannot attain to the simplicity of divine foreknowledge; for a divine understanding stands in a relation to human reason comparable to that in which human reason stands to sense and imagination. The divine mind, the narrator observes, is able to contemplate all things as if they are present. In an interesting twist on the range of meanings we have already seen associated with providence, the narrator suggests that God's foresight might be better construed in spatial rather than temporal terms: "It is better to term it *providentia* [looking forward spatially] rather than *praevidentia* [looking forward in time], for it is not set apart from the lowliest things, and it gazes out on everything as from one of the world's lofty peaks."[12] Philosophy concludes that God's knowledge, construed in this way, leaves intact the freedom of human acts. God, after all, is not interfering; he is simply observing us, as if from a distance. Nor is it true that his omniscience requires that "future contingents" be already true; for to him they are not—as they are to us—"future."

The nature of divine intellect and will, and of the relations between them, were to prove central to later medieval debates on the tensions between providence and freedom. Against the background of Boethius's treatment of divine foreknowledge, Anselm of Canterbury (1033–1109 CE), Saint Thomas Aquinas (1225–1274 CE), Duns Scotus (1266–1308 CE), and William of Ockham (c. 1285–1347 CE) offered widely diverging views of the implications of divine will and knowledge for freedom and necessity. The discussions continued among humanist writers on fate, fortune, and chance. Among them was Lorenzo Valla, whose work *De Libero Arbitrio,* composed in 1439, was invoked by both Erasmus and Luther. Those debates passed over into rival theological approaches within Christianity to the nature of sin, of grace and salvation, and of predestination. The debates also involved disagreements about the right relations between philosophy and theology; and they had, in their own right, a far-reaching significance for the development of philosophical concepts associated with freedom.

Aspects of those debates that connected medieval and Renaissance thinkers with ancient philosophy were reenacted in seventeenth- and eighteenth-century philosophy—in the differences between Descartes and Spinoza on the nature of freedom, and in Leibniz's attempts to reconcile concepts of design and necessity. We will see the antagonism between ideas of fortune and providence again in Descartes's use of providence as a source of strength in the struggle with the destructive force of the passions; and we will see Spinoza in turn present the idea of providence as itself subject to the superstitions and false hopes previously associated with fickle, monstrous Fortune.

Certainly, tensions exist in the syntheses of classical philosophical and literary sources with Christian theology in medieval and Renaissance thought. Many of those tensions are played out across the intersecting fault lines of distinctions between divine intellect and will, on the one hand, and between human freedom and the necessities of Nature, on the other. The Christian God's transcendence of the world he creates is mirrored in the belief in human capacity to overcome whatever natural forces cannot be accommodated into the purposes of benign providence. Christian theology is here reinforced by Renaissance humanism's celebration of human capacities to transcend passivity and take control of our own destinies. We find nonetheless an uneasy relation between Christian versions of providence and classical celebrations of human powers.

The changing understanding of human freedom is reflected in the contrasts between Boethius's figure of the lady Fortune and her reappearance in Machiavelli's famous discussion of freedom in chapter 25 of *The Prince,* composed in 1513. Machiavelli says there that the wise ruler must adapt his methods and policies to the changing times. More disturbingly, it seems that he must also be prepared to adapt his character. Machiavelli has already said in chapter 18 that those who are utterly dependent on fortune come to grief when their fortune changes. The prince should have a "flexible disposition," changing as fortune and circumstances dictate. He must learn from both the fox and the lion—from the fox to recognize tricks; from the lion to frighten off wolves. Only stupid rulers, he says, simply act at all times like either the one or the other. In chapter 25 he extends that thought into the reflection that the wise prince must be able to act contrary to his expected character when the times demand it. "Thus a man who is circumspect, when circumstances demand impetuous behaviour, is unequal to the task, and so he comes to grief. If he changed his character according to the time and circumstances, then his fortune would not change."[13]

Machiavelli's observations on the need for adapting one's character to the times rest on reflections on the nature and scope of fortune. "It is probably true," he boldly asserts, "that fortune is the arbiter of half the things we do, leaving the other half or so to be controlled by ourselves." It is not a simple division of the territory. Machiavelli's point is not that we must passively endure the things for which we are not in control. Resorting to metaphors of hydraulics, he observes that fortune, like a river, allows no possibility of resistance when in full flood; but when the river is flowing quietly, defenses can be constructed. "So it is with fortune. She shows her potency where there is no well-regulated power to resist her, and her impetus is felt where she knows there are no embankments and dykes built to restrain her."[14] The metaphors of construction and resistance serve to clarify Machiavelli's other metaphor, of the territory divided between fortune and human control. Active management can avert disaster, although the unprepared— the inflexible—will perish. When the changeability of fortune is

met by the wisely flexible character of the prince, the prospects
of prospering are better than fifty-fifty; for the balance changes
when we accept that we must shape our fortunes, rather than passively endure them.

We will see the struggles between fortune and human control
reenacted—in very different ways—in the seventeenth-century
"remedies" Descartes and Spinoza offered for the destructive effects of passion. For Descartes, fortune will be displaced by providence. Spinoza in turn will replace Descartes's version of providence with his own version of the ethical force of necessity.
Meanwhile, at the end of his discussion of freedom in chapter 25
of *The Prince,* Machiavelli gives his own distinctive twist to the fig-
uring of fortune as a woman:

> I conclude, therefore, that as fortune is changeable whereas
> men are obstinate in their ways, men prosper so long as for-
> tune and policy are in accord, and when there is a clash they
> fail. I hold strongly to this: that it is better to be impetuous
> than circumspect; because fortune is a woman and if she is
> to be submissive it is necessary to beat and coerce her. Ex-
> perience shows that she is more often subdued by men who
> do this than by those who act coldly. Always, being a wo-
> man, she favours young men, because they are less circum-
> spect and more ardent, and because they command her with
> greater audacity.[15]

Machiavelli has here abandoned his metaphors drawn from hydraulics, in order to embrace—like many Western thinkers before and since—the imagery of male sexual dominance to articulate the relations between human beings and the forces of nature.
Rather than being cast as a fickle goddess to be placated, Fortune
is now to be courted; and the model for the courtship is not the
pining of unrequited love, but the taming of the shrew.

5 The Philosopher and the Princess

Descartes and the Philosophical Life

Over the final six years of his life, the philosopher René Descartes exchanged letters with a young princess-in-exile at The Hague. Elisabeth was one of the thirteen children of the more famous Elizabeth of Bohemia—the "Winter Queen," so called for the shortness of her reign—whose picturesque but disaster-ridden life was caught up in the tragic events of both the Thirty Years' War and the English Civil War.[1] That older Elizabeth was the daughter of James I of England; her brother Charles would become Charles I. The troubled trajectory of her life was set by her dazzling marriage in 1613 to Frederick, the elector palatine. Elizabeth and Frederick were both sixteen at the time of their marriage. Fortune—in the guise of ceremonial extravaganza—shone on their extended and elaborate nuptials. John Donne was the author of one among several epithalamia written in their honor. Legend has it that Shakespeare's *Tempest* was refurbished for the occasion; and other theatrical events were not lacking. James I is reported to have complained that if a planned performance of yet another masque—called "The Marriage of Thames and Rhine"— went ahead, they would have to bury him quickly, for he could last no longer. The young couple made a triumphal journey to take up residence at Heidelberg Castle, in a Paris-built coach—a wedding gift from James. But within five years the fairy tale was to end.[2]

In 1618, in the aftermath of the famous defenestration of the Hapsburg emperor's advisers from the parliament buildings in

Prague, Frederick accepted from the Protestant insurgents the crown of the deposed king of Bohemia. It was an ill-fated decision, which bound his family's fortunes thereafter to the power struggles and religious discord of the Thirty Years' War. By late 1620, Elizabeth had been forced to flee Prague after the defeat of Frederick's armies in the Battle of White Mountain. Her husband had lost both Bohemia and the Palatinate. It was the beginning of a lifelong struggle on Elizabeth's part to maintain the fortunes of her ever-growing family. After a succession of futile campaigns, the debilitated Frederick died of fever in Germany in 1632. Elizabeth's brother Charles invited her to return to England, but Elizabeth declined—determined to continue the struggle to restore her children's lost palatine heritage.

The story of Frederick and Elizabeth that frames the philosophical correspondence of Descartes and the younger Elisabeth is no ordinary story of ups and downs in family fortunes. In its own time it took on an emblematic character—became a contemporary fable of fate and fortune. Carola Oman, in her excellent biography of the older Elizabeth, gives a fascinating summary of the flood of caricatures on the subject of the young couple's impoverishment and exile, published in pamphlets in the winter of 1620–21. Frederick is represented as riding on top of the famous Heidelberg barrel, for economy's sake. He might, the onlookers suggest, be made king of Lapland: "Winter is long there." He is also shown climbing up a wheel of Fate, from the top of which he falls into an ocean of troubles, only to be hauled ashore by a Dutch fisherman, who will display him as a new monster. The fertility of the queen is also caricatured; she is depicted as a lioness with her many cubs, for whom Frederick is unable to provide.[3] Some of the lampoons present them as victims of a fate beyond human control; other examples present them as having brought their misfortunes on themselves through their follies: Elizabeth is ridiculed as having pressured Frederick into accepting the Bohemian crown.

Either way, the extreme reversal of their fortunes is highlighted—the plunge from the heights to the depths.

Elisabeth, the third of Frederick and Elizabeth's children, was born in 1618. Throughout much of the drama of the gain and loss of the Bohemian crown, she was left in the care of her paternal grandmother, to rejoin her parents only when they had found secure but disconsolate refuge after accepting the hospitality of the Prince of Orange at The Hague. From an early age the princess was burdened by her awareness of the family's troubles. Carola Oman reports that before her arrival in The Hague the little girl had been solemnly warned that her parents had suffered many sorrows and trials, and that it would be her duty to annoy them as little as possible. Her solemn demeanor when she was presented to her relatives was so similar to that of her widowed grandmother that it occasioned laughter among the assembled courtiers. She looks very serious indeed in a portrait with a few of her siblings in which she is depicted as Diana, receiving the gift of a dead hare from her brother Charles Louis. Their family's exile loomed large in the children's consciousness. They were said to have enjoyed dressing up in their mother's past finery and playing a favorite game in which they pretended to be staying at an inn on their longed-for journey back to Heidelberg.[4]

Thanks to monthly grants both from England and from the Dutch, the family was by no means poor. The struggles of the impoverished Winter Queen on behalf of her children throughout the Thirty Years' War do not bear comparison with the hardships of Brecht's Mother Courage. Yet the natural generosity of the Queen of Hearts—as she also came to be known—combined with a lack of practical wisdom in household management to produce an atmosphere of constant crisis. According to the testimony of the British ambassador, the couple's entourage numbered two thousand persons, of whom many were old men, women, and children. It also included large numbers of pet dogs and monkeys, to which the queen was strongly attached.[5] The older Elizabeth was intent on keeping up appearances; but it was also true that she struggled to maintain some of the structures of cultured conviviality that were for her among the essentials of life. "Though I have cause enough to be sad," she is quoted as saying, "yet I am still of my wylde humour to be as merrie as I can in spite of fortune."[6] Frederick was largely absent, and despondent when present. The queen's reputation for cheerful hospitality continued, despite the lack of adequate funds to sustain the gaiety of ongoing feasts and masques. For the intellectually gifted young Elisabeth it must have been a confusing and unhappy milieu, but one that also gave her access to cultured conversation—to association with the learned; and it brought her eventually into contact with Descartes.

It was in the winter of 1643, when he was forty-seven and the princess twenty-three, that Descartes first visited the court of the queen of Bohemia at The Hague. There has been speculation that the princess may, like some other young women of her circle, also have visited Descartes in his by no means solitary philosophical seclusion at a nearby château. She was at any rate already well acquainted with his works when Descartes's friend the French soldier and courtier Alphonse Pollot mediated their first exchange of letters. Pollot, who had himself corresponded with Descartes about some of his earlier writings, was at this stage gentleman-in-waiting to the Prince of Orange, the family's host at The Hague.

Pollot's philosophical thoughts are not relevant to the correspondence that ensued between the philosopher and the princess—of whose "outstanding intelligence," Descartes has already, he tells his friend in a letter of 6 October 1642, had "remarkable reports."[7] One striking aspect of the relations between Descartes and Pollot, however, anticipates what will become the central theme of the philosopher's correspondence with Elisabeth—how human beings can combat the oppression of the passions. The remedy that Descartes sketches throughout his letters to Elisabeth—and later refines in his final work, *The Passions of the Soul*—has been framed in an earlier letter to Pollot, of mid-January 1641, on the occasion of the death of Pollot's brother. In it Descartes offers his friend a remedy for grief that has, he claims, served him well in his own recent loss of two people very close to him. As sympathy letters go, this one is memorable for its apparent mix of genuine fellow feeling and crass insensitivity—of common sense and an almost grotesque inappropriateness. The informal treatment of the passions that Descartes offers here allows us to follow more readily the elements of the more complex and subtle version of the "remedy" that he goes on to develop in his correspondence with Elisabeth.

Descartes is not, he tells Pollot, among those who think tears and sorrow are appropriate only for women; Pollot's grief is justified—it would be barbaric not to be distressed when we have due cause. Yet it is wrong, Descartes goes on, to abandon ourselves to grief; we should rather strive to free ourselves from such a troublesome passion. To try, through an effort of will, to suppress the internal agitation immediately might only make things worse. Yet it would also be a mistake to leave all to the supposedly healing effects of time. Rather, we should try to alleviate the pain, little by little, by looking at what has happened from whatever perspective can make it appear more bearable. At the same time, we should take our minds off it, as much as we can, through other activities.

So far, the advice may sound sensible enough; but the example Descartes provides for attaining the required positive perspective is disconcerting. He tells his soldier-friend, "There is, it seems to me, a very great similarity between losing one's hand and losing one's brother; you have previously suffered the former without my ever noticing you were afflicted by it; why should you be more so as regards the latter? For, if it is for your own interest, it is certain you can better repair this latter situation, inasmuch as acquiring a faithful friend can be as valuable as the affection of a good brother. And if it is for the interest of him whom you are lamenting—as your generosity undoubtedly does not allow you to be touched by anything else—you know that neither reason nor religion gives cause for fearing evil after this life to those who have lived as people of honour, but that, on the contrary, both promise joys and rewards" (104).

Descartes's advice to Pollot reads like a mix of good sense, conventional piety, and sheer insensitivity. The elements of his later, subtler versions of the remedy for the passions are, however, already there. In his advice to his bereaved friend the separation of roles between will and understanding is implicit: we cannot subdue the passions through an impromptu act of will; a crucial role is played by thought—by the shift to a more positive perspective. This involves in turn a belief in a providential God and in immortality. Although it breaks up into disparate elements, a unifying strategy is already at work here: a tactical separation is required within the self. All our afflictions, Descartes tells Pollot, depend only very slightly on the reasons we give for them. They depend rather on "the emotion and internal disturbance which nature arouses within us." Once that emotion has subsided, although all the "reasons" for our distress may remain the same, we no longer feel ourselves afflicted. We have little immediate power to check our internal agitations. By understanding what is going on, however, and looking at things from whatever perspective makes them appear more bearable, we can alleviate the pain little by little.

Under the pressure of Elisabeth's thoughtful objections—and at times barely disguised incredulity and frustration—Descartes goes on to refine the crude advice he first gave to Pollot; and in the final work of Descartes, *The Passions of the Soul,* his treatment of the power of reason over the passions will become yet more subtle. In the intervening correspondence with Elisabeth the strategic separation within the self, which he recommended to Pollot, becomes much more clearly articulated. That articulation is in some ways at odds with the now received understanding of Descartes, for the remedy that Descartes eventually proposes in response to Elisabeth's challenges to his philosophy rests not on a radical separation of mind from body, but rather on a complex balancing of the mind's belief in its future immortality with an equally strong insistence on understanding of its present embodiment. As with Augustine's treatment of providence, we encounter a juxtaposition here of what we now see more readily as distinct approaches—reason and religion. But in the end it is not the reassuring Christian belief in immortality that bears the weight in Descartes's remedy. It is rather an understanding of the idea of providence—centered on the relations between parts and whole—that links the remedy with ideas drawn from ancient Stoicism.

The theme of embodiment runs right through Descartes's and Elisabeth's letters. Descartes gives it charming expression in his gallant tributes to the princess in his opening letter of 21 May 1643. Her embodiment of strength of intellect in conjunction with remarkable physical beauty, he tells her, evokes wonder in him. Later, in *The Passions of the Soul,* he will describe wonder as "a sudden surprise of the soul," leading it to "consider with attention the objects that seem to it unusual and extraordinary."[8] The princess, if we are to believe him, has such an effect on the movement of Descartes's animal spirits. Had he been able to see her in person at that point, he says in that first letter, he would have had too many wonders to admire at the same time: "Seeing a discourse more than human flow from a frame so similar to those painters bestow upon angels, I would have been ravished, just as, it seems to me, are bound to be they who, in coming from earth, enter for the first time upon heaven" (107). Descartes pays similar tribute to the princess later, in his dedication to her of his *Principles of Philosophy.* Her intellect, he says there, is unique in finding everything equally clear. "And when I consider that such a varied and complete knowledge of all things is to be found not in some aged pedant who has spent many years in contemplation but in a young princess whose beauty and youth call to mind one of the Graces rather than gray-eyed Minerva or any of the Muses, then I cannot but be lost in admiration."[9]

From the evidence of family letters and comments of visitors to the court of the Palatines in exile, Descartes's respect for Elisabeth's intellectual powers may have more basis than his extravagant praise of her physical beauty. "La Grecque," as her mocking siblings nicknamed their scholarly sister, was not renowned for her beauty. She did indeed, however, have a capacity to see to the heart of philosophical issues. She shrewdly observes in her first letter that things radically different, as Descartes supposes minds and bodies to be, could not also causally interact with one another, as he claims they must. She challenges Descartes to explain how the soul—if it is, as he says, only a "thinking substance"—can causally interact with material particles. In this objection she anticipates the key issue that will later prompt Spinoza to a less polite expression of skepticism in the *Ethics,* where he remarks that he cannot wonder enough that a philosopher of Descartes's caliber should have produced such a nonsensical doctrine.

In response to Elisabeth's objection, Descartes, rather than defend his metaphysics of mind and body, quickly moves to an elaboration of the deeper truth, in his view, of his often misunderstood distinction. The human mind, he believes, is separable from the body and will indeed exist separately after death. During life, however, the mind is embodied; and it is in understanding ourselves as embodied beings that we will find the remedy for our passions. For Descartes the apparent contradiction between two distinct truths—the separateness of mind and body and their embodiment—is to be resolved not through contorted abstractions, but rather through the realization that the two truths must be grasped by different kinds of thought. The pursuit of a more concrete form of thinking to grasp the truth of embodiment also figures in his remedy for the passions. Descartes and Elisabeth embark together not on the task of tidying up his metaphysics of mind-body relations, but rather on a shared exploration of how they can put philosophy to work in their lives.

Descartes and Elisabeth are in search of a philosophy that is practical, in the sense that is applicable to the deliberations of the ancient Greek philosophers: What is the good life for human beings, and how is it to be attained in the midst of the affliction caused by human passions and the vicissitudes of fortune? The philosopher and the princess are trying to understand mind-body union in order to understand better how they, and human beings in general, can deal with the turmoil of their passions. Both are happy to think of this practical philosophy as a form of "medicine." Descartes had already spoken, in part 6 of his *Discourse on Method*, of his philosophy as connected with medicine, construed as a way of living well and prolonging life. Elisabeth in her first letter charmingly refers to Descartes as her doctor. This way of thinking of philosophy goes back to the Stoics. It is appropriate, then, that "doctor" and patient should agree to ground their reflections in the shared reading of a text from Roman Stoicism—*De Vita Beata,* by Seneca. Although they soon abandon this exercise in textual commentary, their appeal to it highlights a thread in Descartes's philosophy that is often overlooked. It is often regarded as a completely fresh start—as the beginning of a distinctively modern approach to philosophy, centered on criteria for certainty. Yet it is no less true that Descartes's philosophy is a reworking of the ancient concern with describing the good life—a concern that has largely receded from modern philosophy.

Descartes's practical philosophy starts from a model of Stoic detachment familiar from the neo-Stoics of his own times—an exercise in training the will to exert control over the passions. From his correspondence with Elisabeth, however, something different emerges. His version of practical philosophy (as I call it here) is distinctive in the emphasis he gives to human embodiment. In his early letters to Elisabeth, Descartes attempts to initiate a style of thinking. This is the rationale for passages—often quoted but rarely given close consideration—where Descartes advises Elisabeth, in a letter of 28 June 1643, that if she really wants to understand the union of mind and body, as opposed to merely comprehending their separate natures, she must turn away from abstract intellectual thought and turn instead to the kinds of thought that depend on bodily awareness. "The metaphysical thoughts that exercise the pure understanding serve to render the notion of the soul more familiar to us; and the study of mathematics, which principally exercises the imagination in considering figures and movements, accustoms us to form very distinct notions of body; and finally, it is by availing oneself only of life and ordinary conversations, and by abstaining from meditating and studying things that exercise the imagination, that one learns to conceive the union of the soul and the body" (113–114).

Descartes was undoubtedly aware of the apparent affront in this response; Elisabeth may well have been taken aback. Having struggled to keep her mind engaged in the midst of the tiresome prattle of court life and the overwhelming sadness and anxiety attending her domestic responsibilities and tragedies, she has now, to all intents and purposes, been told not to bother. "I almost fear," he continues, "that your Highness may think that I am not speaking seriously here; but that would be contrary to the respect I owe her and shall never fail to render her. And I can truly say that the principal rule I have always observed in my studies, and of which I believe I have made very good use in acquiring some knowledge, has been that I have never employed save very few hours each day at thoughts that occupy the imagination, and very few hours per year at those that occupy the understanding alone, and that I have devoted all the rest of my time to the respite of my senses and the repose of my mind; I even reckon among the exercises of the imagination all serious conversations, and everything that requires attention" (114).

How seriously should we take Descartes's advice on time management for the aspiring philosopher? Some playfulness is of course evident in his proffered regime for the well-spent life: it cannot be literally true that this is how the prolific philosopher has passed his time. But Descartes is also making a point. Something of more significance is happening here than the stuff of biographical anecdote. Far from making fun of Elisabeth's intellectual pretensions, Descartes is attempting to shift their discussion onto a plane more appropriate for the consideration of the good life. If they are to understand the predicaments of passion, they must consciously reflect as the embodied minds they indeed are. Elisabeth has been construing the philosophical life as a life of abstract thought. Descartes is trying to offer a different way of conceiving of it. In drawing an analogy that initially puzzles the princess—between understanding mind-body union and understanding the weight of bodies—his point is not, as she initially thinks, that something in the theoretical understanding of the nature of bodily weight and movement can cast light on the theoretical understanding of the nature of mind-body union. The point is rather that we understand bodily weight and movement quite well when we are not engaged in theoretical thinking—when we are simply aware of ourselves as embodied beings subject, as other bodies are, to physical forces.

With this shift of emphasis, Descartes is also trying to reassure Elisabeth that the undoubted distractions of her life should not prevent her from engaging in the kind of philosophical thinking requisite for attaining his version of the good life. On the contrary, he insists, her situation leaves her well placed to engage in the kind of thinking needed for dealing with the passions.

Descartes does not foresee, however, that Elisabeth, in putting his recommendations to the test, will force him to recognize some serious asymmetries in his supposed universally accessible remedy for the passions. Elisabeth struggles to articulate just how much they are divided by bodily awareness. As differently sexed bodies, they have different self-knowledge—even in the shared social space in which their lives have converged. Thought grounded in bodily awareness is one thing for a male philosopher, leading the life male philosophers typically do; it is quite another for a princess encumbered as she is by the restraints and demands of a bizarre court life. Idle, yet constantly busy, Elisabeth is struggling to make sense of a life that, through no fault of her own, consumes her time, while keeping her ever more out of touch with both the fully human solitude and the meaningful social interaction that she craves.

Descartes and Elisabeth both experience their frustrations in their efforts to find release through philosophy from the burden of the passions. References to illness and family misfortunes run through her letters; references to the "chicaneries" of his philosophical enemies run through his. She is wearied by the many distractions of her anomalous court life; he is distracted by the misunderstandings and machinations of "messieurs les docteurs," as he calls them—the caviling pedants and scheming theologians with whom he must constantly deal. Their frustrations are asymmetrical. The princess regrets being endlessly distracted from the kind of thought she views as the key to freedom from oppressive passion; the philosopher is tired of the pettiness and silliness that seem inevitably to accompany that concentrated theoretical thought to which she aspires.

In this context of shared but asymmetrical frustration Descartes tries to articulate the kind of thought in which he sees the path to freedom. Yet every attempt meets with a new stubborn resistance, as Elisabeth reports back on her efforts to apply the "doctor"'s remedy. She has been unable, she tells him, to banish the confusions of mind and body that she believes his philosophy

requires her to treat as the source of error. In her letter of 10 or
20 June 1643, she says: "The life I am constrained to lead does not
allow me enough free time to acquire a habit of meditation in accordance with your rules. Sometimes the interests of my household, which I must not neglect, sometimes conversations and ci-
vilities I cannot eschew, so thoroughly deject this weak mind with
annoyances or boredom that it remains, for a long time afterward,
useless for anything else" (111).

At one level, Elisabeth's plaintive response is directed at her
own apparent inability to apply Descartes's remedy. As the pattern of restatement from Descartes and resistance from Elisabeth
unfolds, though, another level of difference appears: the embodied thinking that is the key to the remedy yields different results
for each of them. Embodied thought brings out crucial contrasts
between the lived experience of male and female embodiment.
Descartes's and Elisabeth's multilayered interaction divides along
lines of culturally embodied sexual difference, played out in different temperaments; and also along lines of religious differences
amid shared habitual pieties. It is, after all, an exchange about the
passions, enacted between Catholic and Protestant in the midst
of the religious hatreds of the Thirty Years' War.

Descartes is perplexed by the stubborn resistance to his remedy
that Elisabeth reports as arising from her debilitating passions.
Such a wonder-inspiring example of embodied intellect should,
after all, be the happiest of souls. Elisabeth's resistance comes
from her taking more seriously than Descartes has yet done the
theme of embodiment on which he has insisted. The more Descartes attempts to focus her attention on embodiment, the more
they are driven apart. The remedy, Descartes advises in a letter of
18 May 1645, requires of her only that she reflect on the positive
aspects of her situation—comparing the value of the goods she
possesses and that can never be taken from her with those "fortune has stripped from her." She will then find contentment in

"the goods in her very own person" (120). But that self-satisfaction, Elisabeth insists, in one of her most poignant and startling observations, is not available to her.

Descartes has granted the complexities of bodily resistance to the efforts of the autonomous, rational will. Elisabeth goes further, however, in recognizing the implications of embodiment. If bodily awareness is the key to the remedy, then the differences between male and female bodies become crucial to its prospects: "Know then," she says in a letter of 24 May 1645, "that I have a body filled with a great many of the weaknesses of my sex; it very easily feels the afflictions of the soul and does not have the force to bring itself into harmony with the soul, since it is of such a temperament as to be subject to obstructions and remains in a condition that very much contributes to them" (121).

Elizabeth attributes her problems to female bodily weakness, but the predicament she goes on to describe is as much mental as physical. For her, harsh limits exist to the power of positive thinking Descartes recommends. Although she has accepted that her family's misfortunes will be permanent, she says, she finds herself unable to consider them as anything but evil. She cannot countenance the redescription of undoubted evils as good. As for finding satisfaction, as Descartes has urged her to do, in her efforts to help her distressed family, their misfortunes seem to follow so quickly on one another that she finds little time between her "useless efforts," in which to attain the desired state of self-contentment. The countervailing healing satisfaction of the altruistic is not for the likes of her. Not for her the triumphal narrative of self-confident reason turning adversity into self-satisfied virtue. "I think that if my life were entirely known to you, you would find more strange than the causes of this present malady, that a sensitive mind such as mine, when so thwarted, remains conserved for so long a time in so frail a body" (122).

Elizabeth does not elaborate on this more personal "thwarting" which has cast her life into such lonely depths. She is sufficiently concerned about keeping it private that she warns Descartes in a postscript that she trusts his discretion to commit the letter to the fire should it risk falling into "bad hands" (123). The bleak self-portrait she paints is that of a woman with a permanently "thwarted" mind trapped in a frail body, subject to all the "weaknesses of her sex." In her sad words it is possible to hear something of the sexually differentiated ambiguity evident in Samuel Johnson's famous comparison, in the next century, between hearing a female preacher and seeing a dog walk on its hind legs. The amazement that it is done at all—which, coming from a man, can be heard as a sexist putdown of female capability—can also sound, when uttered by a woman, like a cry from the heart. It can be heard as an expression of rueful self-reflection, as if to say: "The wonder is not that I did not do it better, but that I did it at all."

Elisabeth repeatedly insists that the remedy Descartes proposes is for her unworkable; and he is dismayed—as he indicates in a letter of May or June 1645—that "a virtue so rare and accomplished" as hers should be so sadly unaccompanied by health or happiness. Under those pressures, Descartes increasingly distances himself from the neo-Stoic belief that detachment is attainable through the efforts of rational will. Such a "multitude of displeasures" as she speaks of, he says, can often not be dispelled by directly opposing them. They must be thought of as "domestic enemies": since one is compelled to converse with them, one must constantly maintain one's guard in their presence, to avoid being harmed. It is a fitting metaphor. The princess, after all, sees herself as "thwarted" in that nonmetaphorically "domestic" sphere which is the only one she can in fact inhabit. She has just been talking of the tiresomeness of domestic civility—of an enforced sociability that gets in the way of the philosophical life she longs to pursue. To motivate his patient to adopt his remedy, Descartes must re-state the ideal of detachment in such a way that he shifts the emphasis away from a simple assertion of will. A subtler management of different elements in a complex structure of thought is called for, grounded in the realities of bodily awareness: we must learn to deploy the resources of sense and imagination, rather than driving them away.

To clarify this complex balancing act, Descartes has recourse to the experience of the theater. Watching the lugubrious events of theatrical tragedies, we can induce in ourselves the physical effects that accompany real disasters. This ability gives us a clue, he suggests, to how we might engage in a comparable dislocation in response to genuine misfortune. The emotion we call up in ourselves in the theater arises from the engagement of our senses and imagination in the spectacle. Conversely, in response to actual misfortune, we can pull back our senses and imagination, by postponing their consideration until a time when our numbed understanding can better deal with them. From the experience of engagement with unreal misfortune, we can learn how to disengage from what is actually happening. While going through an infinity of genuine subjects for displeasure, we can turn our imagination from them, thinking of them only when we must, and employing our remaining time considering objects that bring us contentment and joy. In this way we can, Descartes insists, not only judge more sanely the things that are important to us by regarding them without passion; we can also restore ourselves to physical health. In another striking metaphor drawn from the experience of the theater, in a letter of 18 May 1645, Descartes tells Elisabeth that the "greatest souls" can detach themselves from their misfortunes in a way similar to that in which we can all regard the events of the theater as occurring in a subsidiary narrative, esteeming this life "so little in relation to eternity that they consider its eventualities only as we consider the things that come to pass in comedies" (119).

The crucial skill is to divert our imagination and senses from the "domestic enemies," meanwhile employing only the under-standing to consider them, and only at a time when it is prudent to do so. But to do this we need to apply our senses and imagina-tion to other pursuits. Descartes recommends that Elisabeth should, while taking the spa waters, occupy herself with such ef-forts to deliver herself from sad thoughts; he also advises, endors-ing her real doctors' advice, that she should at that time abstain "even from all serious meditations regarding the sciences" and ap-ply herself to imitating those who in looking at the greenness of a wood, the colors of a flower, the flight of a bird, convince them-selves that they are not thinking of anything. To do so is not to waste time, he insists, but to employ it well. For in the process she can satisfy herself with the hope that by this means she will re-cover perfect health, which is the foundation for every other good one can have in this life.

The asymmetry that has divided them previously, however, now manifests itself at another level. It is all very well for the male phi-losopher, with an apparent abundance of time for intellectual pursuits, to claim that this is the method he has employed to ward off early death. Elisabeth's attempts to follow it in response to her own "domestic enemies" have a more forlorn outcome. "I con-fess," she says with gentle irony, in her reply of 22 June 1645, "I find difficulty in separating from my senses and imagination the topics continually represented there by the conversation and the letters I could not avoid without sinning against my obligations" (127). The occupations that for Descartes can offer a healthy di-version from abstract thinking represent for her the loss of a pre-cious respite from the throngs of real and metaphorical domestic enemies. The problem is that she seems to have both too much and too little sense of reason for her own good. "Were I able to profit, as you do," she says, "from everything that presents itself to the senses, I would divert myself without thinking of it. But it is at that very time that I feel the inconvenience of being a little reasonable. For were I not at all reasonable, I would find pleasures in common with those among whom it is necessary for me to live, and thus take this medicine [of diversion from reason] with profit. And were I as reasonable as you, I would cure myself as you have done" (127).

The activities Descartes regards as a diversion are for Elisabeth the inescapable stuff of life. For her the "diversion" is her all-too-rare escape into undistracted pure thought. Descartes seems genuinely to try to treat Elisabeth as his equal in the pursuit of his remedy, but the inequities and asymmetries in their situations keep breaking through. Would a man, living in that anomalous court, have comparable difficulties? Would one of the princess's brothers, given a similar philosophical bent, find his life equally intolerable? The source of Elisabeth's despair is not something that can be removed by her trying harder. Between the lines we can see insight on her part into the ways in which, in her context, domestic enemies have more power to thwart women than men of access to philosophy. The repeated insistence that someone with such a fine mind and body is deserving of happiness and must therefore be able to attain it sounds hollow—no matter how often Descartes refines it—when confronted with realities of female life he can only dimly comprehend.

Elisabeth has great difficulty also in applying another crucial aspect of Descartes's remedy, which, as we shall see later, relates more directly to our theme of providence: for her it seems an impossible task to disentangle which things depend on herself alone and which misfortunes come from outside. The pain that twists back into one's being, rather than coming straightforwardly from outside, can often be the hardest to bear with equanimity; and for her the inward and the external are often intertwined in painfully convoluted ways. In a letter of 30 November 1645, Elisabeth is particularly distressed by a family calamity that, she touchingly says, she can discuss at all with Descartes only because she knows he has "more charity than bigotry." This latest misfortune, which causes her such apparently disproportionate pain, is the conversion of one of her younger brothers to Catholicism. The event, as she sees it, is a complex mix of folly and misfortune, of the weak credulity of her brother and the devious machinations of their family's enemies. Her brother's foolishness in being caught in their enemies' traps, she writes, has more disturbed the health of her body and the tranquillity of her soul than all the unfortunate things that have previously happened to her. "It is necessary that I see a person, whom I loved with the greatest tenderness possible, subjected to the contempt of the world and (according to my belief) to the loss of his soul" (171).

Descartes's response, in January 1646, echoes the apparent insensitivity he showed toward the loss felt by his bereaved amputee friend. The philosopher expresses surprise at the extent of her distress over a matter that those in most of Europe, which shares his own religion, would regard as a good rather than as an evil. Even those who are not Catholic can hardly complain, he goes on, for they would not be Protestants had not they or their fathers or grandfathers formerly belonged to the Roman religion. Descartes crashes on—with a blunt pragmatism, concerning issues of religious conviction, that the devout and principled Elisabeth must have found even more inappropriate in the circumstances. He suggests that perhaps the people who persuaded her brother to convert may really have had his best interests at heart. Those who already have fortune on their side, he says, may do best to "stay with her and press to join their forces together to prevent her from escaping them" (174). By contrast, members of an unfortunate household such as Elisabeth's may do best to go in different directions, in the hope that at least one of them might find good fortune. With belated tact, Descartes decides to leave it at that, lest he arouse Elisabeth's resentment. Even so, the exchange may well have confirmed the princess's general skepticism about Descartes's version of the power of positive thinking.

Under the pressure of Elisabeth's misgivings, Descartes is forced to clarify the structure of his remedy. Central to it are the interconnected strategies of detachment and engagement: sense and imagination are to be withdrawn and redeployed; understanding is to be held in abeyance and brought to bear only at the appropriate time. In the midst of tumultuous passion, frequently the only resort is sleep, Descartes cautions, with refreshing realism, in June 1645. Only when the movement of the blood has subsided can we begin to restore our minds and render them tranquil through the exercise of thought (128). Of course, he must give to his version of detachment some fuller content than the resort to oblivion. Here we come to the role of the idea of providence in Descartes's remedy.

In some ways the views Descartes expresses on detachment strongly echo ancient doctrines of necessity. We must, he says in a letter of 4 August 1645, accept that "maladies and misfortune" are no less natural to humankind than are prosperity and health. Why, he asks, should we desire to be free of them any more than we desire "to have more arms or tongues than we have?" (133–134). Our mistake is to think either that we have control over things that in fact we cannot control, or to think that our health and fortune are somehow owing to our nature. Descartes has greater difficulties than the ancient Stoics had, however, in combining this route to acquiescence with the recognition of human freedom. For his philosophy is influenced not only by the Stoics but by Augustine. He must leave room for the responsibility of the human will. His solution is to make room for the will by carving up the territory of affliction. Some misfortunes—and even some recurring maladies—are within our power to control; but others are not. It now becomes crucial, in Descartes's reworking of Stoic detachment, to learn to distinguish what lies within our power from what does not. We have already seen one source of Elisabeth's difficulty with this exercise: the bonds of sympathy that unite her to others make it difficult to discern the sources of her own pain. Another great divide separates the temperaments of the relatively self-assured philosopher and the self-questioning princess, and it is also related to gender: How, Elisabeth asks, can we possibly determine that we have indeed done all that lies within our power?

Elisabeth sees herself as constantly thwarted by failed efforts, by unexpected outcomes. The crucial decision about what does and what does not lie within her power is as elusive as the tranquillity it is supposed to bring. For Descartes, the solution seems simple: we must simply do our best and, having done it, refrain from useless regrets. He insists in a letter of 6 October 1645, "One has no subject for repentance when one has done what one judged best at the time one had to make a decision to act, even though in rethinking the matter afterward, when one has more leisure, one judges oneself to have failed" (158). The very process of deliberation, culminating in the recognition that one has "done one's best" depends on a self-possession that is not accessible to one for whom being "thwarted" has become almost a defining trait. Elisabeth cannot recognize herself in Descartes's picture of resolute persistence combined with a judicious letting-go when the time for decision has come. For someone whose life consists in a struggle to address constant demands that can never be satisfactorily met, the good sense that allows the mind to let go of things is not attainable. Never does her conscience testify that she has "taken all possible precautions," she writes in a letter of 13 September 1645. "For always one plagues one's mind with the things that remained to consider." Elisabeth can never be confident that her best is good enough. Nor can she see why having tried to do her best should be a source of tranquillity: "I have always been in a condition that rendered my life very useless to persons I love," she sadly reflects in a letter of 28 October 1645 (167).

Descartes's remedy seems by this point to have come a long way from Stoic acceptance of necessity. The maladies and misfortunes he urges us to accept are not unavoidable necessities within the nature of things. They are the misfortunes that remain when we have done our best to avoid trouble. After all our efforts, are we back in the hands of a malign fate or fickle fortune? It is difficult to read these passages now without being struck by what seems a succession of commonplaces in Descartes's advice to Elisabeth. From her exasperated tones we may suspect that even at the time she may have seen the philosopher's recommendations as empty clichés—as the complacent optimism of the self-assured. It is not just Descartes's greater self-assurance that emerges here, but also the crucial role that his version of providence plays in the remedy. Under further challenge from Elisabeth, this element in the remedy develops into something more than a pious platitude. The appeal to providence will allow Descartes to insist that free will can coexist with the acceptance of necessity.

Let us now look more closely at Descartes's version of providence and the role it is supposed to play in controlling the passions. Elisabeth's resistance to the role of providence is one of the things that makes her objections more than just a succession of self-deprecating reports of failure—laced at times with a certain ironic skepticism. She offers also a more targeted challenge. It comes out especially in her comments about the self and others, about the contrasts between those who seek the good life in pursuing their own interests and those who seek it in pursuing the good of others. Faced with that choice, she asks, in her letter of 13 September 1645, how can the "good sense" or "right reason" on which Descartes depends be trusted to deliver a true verdict? Elisabeth, as we have already seen, regards herself as forever caught in the morass of trying to meet the needs of others. She lacks the self-possession that might set limits to her "doing her best." Now, though, it is evident that she has taken the division between the self-seeking and the altruistic yet further: Do we, she ponders, perhaps confront equal and irreconcilable convictions about the direction in which "right reason" points? What if neither of them can prevail sufficiently to assure us that we have truly "done our best"?

An issue emerges here that transcends the expression of different temperaments. Elisabeth has seen with a more discerning eye than Descartes at this stage the logical gap in his proposal. A person must rely on true reason or good judgment at the point of determining whether she has done her best, yet reason and judgment seem unable to adjudicate the differences between self-fulfillment and altruism as a means to the good. Both people who favor other-directed action and those who principally pursue their own needs, both apparently following "right reason," will have equal confidence in the value of the good they pursue. So the question about which is the better life will remain unresolved; and the conviction of having "done one's best," which is crucial to the proposed remedy—will remain unfounded.

What is this "right reason" on which it all depends, and how can we rely on it? Elisabeth demands to know what its status is. It seems to be a "sentiment," but not a "passion," for we are born with it. It is not something we are subjected to by causes outside ourselves. "Tell me, . . . if you please," she asks, "how far it is necessary to follow this sentiment (since it is a gift of nature) and how does one correct it?" (149). With prescient insight, she refers to it as a "quiet sentiment." Its status will later become a crucial issue between Spinoza and the Cartesians in their differences over the relations between reason and the passions; and Spinoza's idea of a kind of reason that is itself an emotion will be developed further in the next century in Hume's talk of the love of truth as a "calm passion."

More important for us here, however, is that Elisabeth's probing on the issue of what "right reason" is and how we know that we can rely on it brings to the surface the role of providence. "Right reason" is for Descartes a gift of God. It is the belief in providence that allows him to rest assured that he need not worry about outcomes—provided he feels sure that he has done his best. Echoing his pious remarks about the sustaining role of the belief in immortality, with which he tried to comfort the grieving amputee, he writes to Elisabeth on 15 September 1645 that in looking forward to life beyond death, we are able to so detach our affections from things of the world that "we regard only with disdain everything in fortune's power" (151). Reliance on a providential God helps give Descartes confidence about having reached his own limits. Near enough is good enough—for the man of basic goodwill, living in a world he sees as structured in accordance with the purposes of a wise and loving providence. Where does this leave the remedy as a whole? By detaching ourselves from all that depends on fortune, we were supposed to focus better on what depends on us alone. Now, however, Christian trust in the will of a loving God seems essential to the remedy. Rather than trusting to "fortune," we are to trust in the Christian God. Knowing that there is a good God on whom all things depend—a God whose "perfections are infinite, power immense, decrees infallible"— teaches us, Descartes says, to "accept in good spirit everything that comes to us as being expressly sent from God." We are then able to "extract joy even from our afflictions by thinking it his will that they have come to us" (150–151).

Descartes's continuation of the project of the ancient philosophers—finding the good through the exercise of reason—seems to have led us into the shallows of conventional piety. What is more, with the shift to anticipation of an afterlife, the emphasis on embodiment—which has been so important an element in the remedy—now seems to recede. Elisabeth, notwithstanding her own piety, is clearly unimpressed by this apparent outcome of their intellectual journey. She continues the challenge to Descartes; and what emerges is something more interesting—and of greater consequence for later intellectual history—than Descartes's initial pious platitudes. Passion and providence enter into a new relationship that will set the scene for Spinoza's treatment of the transformative power of the love of necessity in freeing us from the turmoil of the passions.

Elisabeth resists Descartes's lunge toward the afterlife—not because she does not believe in providence and immortality, but because she wants to hold out for a viable version of the gift promised by the ancient philosophers—access to the greatest human good through the pursuit of reason in this life. If the ideal of detachment involves nothing more than a focus on immortality, she reflects, why bother with the present life at all? Why, she asks, in a letter of 30 September 1645, would we prefer a troublesome life to an advantageous death? Knowledge of our immortality, she observes, might make us just as readily seek death as loathe it. This response highlights the need for Descartes to emphasize the other strand in the idea of God—the role of providence in this life. Rather than preoccupy himself with individual immortality, the philosopher must stress the consideration of our selves as part of an ordered whole—as small parts within the vast expanse of the universe.

In his reflections in his letter of 15 September 1645 about parts and whole, Descartes continues his earlier discussion with Elisabeth about the two competing concerns, self-interest and the interests of others; but he also gives a new twist to the role of providence in his remedy. We should, he says, be less concerned with that little bit of the universe that satisfies our own needs. If we turn our attention to the whole of which we are but part, we will be less likely to be devastated by misfortune, for we will no longer expect that events should respond to our needs or desires. We should consider "that one could not subsist alone and is, in effect, one of the parts of the earth, and more particularly, of this state, of this society, of this family, to which one is joined by one's residence, by one's oath, and by one's birth. And it is necessary to prefer always the interests of the whole, of which one is a part, to the interests of one's own person in particular" (151–152).

This aspect of providence brings us back from the supernatural to the natural world, from faith to reason, and from future immortality to present embodiment. The idea of providence is here linked with the mind's efforts to understand its relations with the body through which it is connected to the rest of the world. The Stoic echoes are strong here. The theme of the self as part of a whole introduces an idea that Descartes will develop more fully in *The Passions of the Soul*: it allows him to draw a close connection between the idea of providence and the very nature of love. For Descartes defines love as the forming of a whole, comprising oneself together with the loved object. The power that reason holds over the passions becomes linked in a new way with the affectivity of reason: thought, in the form in which it can engage with the passions, is itself a kind of love.

This shift in Descartes's formulation of his remedy is sketched in the closing letters of his correspondence with Elisabeth. It is more fully explored in another letter—the remarkable letter on love he wrote on 1 February 1647 to his friend Chanut—which marks a poignant and fateful change, both in his relationship with Elisabeth and in the trajectory of his remaining life. Chanut is the go-between for a new relationship between Descartes and female nobility; this time it is with a woman possessing more direct relations with power—Christina, the queen of Sweden. Christina, by Chanut's testimony, is also a female marvel with astonishing force of mind.

Descartes seems to have been no less wonderstruck with Christina than he had shown himself to be in his first letters to Elisabeth. He writes to Christina on 26 February 1649: "If a letter was sent to me from heaven and I saw it descending from the clouds, I would not be more surprised than I was to receive the letter which your highness so graciously wrote me; and I could not receive such a letter with more respect and veneration than I feel on receiving your letter."[10] Descartes did not see himself as having rejected or replaced Elisabeth, who was again very ill; he was confident that no jealousy would arise between his two female wonders. Writing enthusiastically to Elisabeth, on 6 June 1647, he suggests that the two women should become friends. Being both of noble birth and both endowed with intellect, they should be worthy of each other's conversation.

In his letter to Chanut on 1 February 1647, which frames his correspondence with Christina, Descartes gives eloquent expression to his account of love as a relationship of the part to the whole. The version of reason implicit in Descartes's practical philosophy is evolving in the direction of emotion. Love, he says, comes in two forms: "love that is purely intellectual or reasonable" and "love that is a passion." In intellectual love the soul willingly joins itself to something perceived as good; the soul considers itself, together with this good, as a whole. The movement of will involved in forming this part-whole relation is the soul's joy. It is not itself a passion; it is rational thought, which could exist even if the soul were not embodied. Where, however, the soul is embodied, in our day-to-day human lives, this rational love is usually accompanied by sensual or at any rate sensuous love—by love as passion.

The two kinds of love—intellectual, or reasonable, love and

love as passion—come together in an intriguing and moving passage, where Descartes talks of the joy the soul must have felt before birth, in its first union with body. Probably, he speculates, the
soul feels at that moment first joy and then love (204). Human
love is thus closely connected with a basic bodily joy—a sensuous
delight in embodied being, in being embodied. Intellectual love,
although it can occur without passion—as it will, presumably, for
Descartes in an afterlife—is in human life closely accompanied by
the basic joy of embodied being. The whole package centers on an
understanding of the nature of embodied human love. This understanding of love is in turn closely connected with the interrelation of parts and whole, and hence with the ancient idea of providence as an ordered whole.

In response to a question on the issue from Christina, Descartes assures her that we can love God out of reason alone, without recourse to faith. We can attain to this love merely by reflecting on the nature of God, on the infinity of his power, "through
which he has created so many things, of which we are the least
part; the extension of his providence, that makes him see in one
thought alone everything that has been, shall be, and could be."
An important strand in this conception of the love of God is that
we heed both our insignificance and the "grandeur of all created
things," by noting the manner in which they depend on him. Understanding these things, says Descartes, fills us with "extreme
joy" (206–207). The recognition of our status as parts of an ordered whole, which Descartes has adapted from the ancient Stoics, is here integrated—through the emphasis on embodiment—
with the consideration of human passion. Our passions, rather
than being just the problem to be overcome, now become part of
the remedy.

In response to Elisabeth's probing, Descartes has developed a
role for providence in his practical philosophy. Rather than redi-
recting hope toward an afterlife, his "remedy" now reflects the

transforming power of love—construed as the joyful forming of part-whole relations in the here and now. Yet his remarks on the remedy still echo conventional piety. He tells Christina through Chanut that if the wise man "does not refuse evils or afflictions, because they come to him from divine providence, he refuses still less all the goods or licit pleasures one can enjoy in this life, because they too issue from that providence; and accepting them with joy, without having any fear of evils, his love renders him perfectly happy" (207).

The verbose pieties that had already irritated Elisabeth would later be scorned by Spinoza—and would prompt his radical reworking of the idea of love of God and of its role in the remedy of the passions. Spinoza went on to offer a powerful portrayal of reason itself as emotion, and of the intellectual love of God as the mind's understanding of itself as a mode of God as substance—part of an infinite, ordered whole. Already present in Descartes's treatment of the interconnection of love and providence, however, are the seeds of that transformation of Stoic ideas of necessity.

Descartes has in effect, by his own admission, made the Christian God an object of the human passion of love. If that seems strange, he remarks to Chanut, it is just because we are not accustomed to talking in this way of a love for something superior to ourselves—speaking rather of respect, honor, or esteem. As philosophers, he insists, we should nevertheless resist giving different names to things that share the same definition. In an amusing passage—which may bear on his own attachment to intellectually gifted noblewomen—Descartes teasingly suggests that Chanut's own feelings toward the wondrous Christina might perhaps be more truly called love than respect or esteem: "And if I asked you, candidly, do you love this great Queen upon whom you now wait, it would be idle for you to protest you have for her only respect, veneration, and astonishment—for I should not hesitate to judge you have a very ardent affection as well. For the style which flows so felicitously when you speak of her, that although I believe everything you say about her, because I know you are truthful and I have also heard others speak of her, nevertheless I do not believe you could have described her as you have unless you feel a very great devotion, nor that you could have attended so great a light without receiving of its warmth" (209).

In one of his last letters to Elisabeth, on 22 February 1649, Descartes expresses excitement about his new life in Sweden, as well as attempting to say something helpful about her latest family misfortune—the execution of her uncle, Charles I of England. Putting this violent death "in its best light," as is his wont, he suggests that Charles's mode of death is "more glorious, more happy, and more calm" than dying in one's bed. Without this final ordeal, the king's virtues might never have been so noticed or esteemed. Moreover the pain of a blow from a hatchet would have been short-lived in comparison with what his dying might have been had his murderers been able to afflict him with a fever, or "whatever other maladies nature is wont to use to put men out of this world."

We do not know what Elisabeth, with her habitual forbearance, may have made of this latest attempt at positive thinking. Their correspondence soon came to an end, and Descartes's own death was not far off. Fortune did not treat him well in Sweden, with regard to either body or soul. His final letters to other friends express a sadness and loneliness in that place where, as he puts it, people's thoughts, "like the water," are frozen in winter and his desire to return to his solitude "grows stronger with each passing day."[11] Thoughts of mortality, and of his own dealings with fortune, occupy him in his final letters. "I have never wished to expect anything of Fortune," he tells Chanut, "and I have tried to conduct my life in such a way that she has never had any power over me." That was after all, the core of his remedy for the passions. He adds a rueful reflection, though: "This has, it seems, made Fortune jealous of me, for she never fails to disappoint me whenever she has any chance to do so."[12]

In his final letter to Elisabeth, on 9 October 1649, he writes that although he has "a great veneration" for Queen Christina, he does not think that anything is capable of keeping him in Sweden longer than the next summer. Descartes died at Stockholm on 11 February 1650. At the time of his death, Elisabeth was in the midst of a particularly distracting set of family responsibilities, trying to arrange the betrothal of one of her younger sisters, Henrietta, to a Transylvanian prince. The reinstatement of their brother Charles Louis to the title of elector palatine, with the end of the Thirty Years' War and the Peace of Westphalia, had come too late for there to be much hope of marriage for the older sisters. It fell to Elisabeth to handle the frustrating diplomatic maneuvers to persuade Charles Louis of the suitability of this match, as well as to overcome the doubts of the nervous Henrietta and assemble a meager trousseau. It seems Elisabeth was greatly affected by Descartes's death. When she joined her siblings on a visit to Charles Louis, after accompanying Henrietta to her betrothal, her brother Edward is reported as asking their younger sister Sophia, "What has become of her spirits?" and "Whither has her entertaining conversation vanished?" Sadly, even the satisfaction of getting her sister's life organized was to prove short-lived. Henrietta, who had, after overcoming her initial reluctance, become an enthusiastic bride, died of a fever only five months later.[13]

At the age of forty-two, Elisabeth became a canoness at Hertford, an ancient Westphalian convent, and at the age of forty-nine its abbess. She died in her sixty-second year, after a long illness. It would be good to be able to believe that she found at last a calm life of satisfying scholarship, contemplation, and companionship. From Carola Oman's account, however, it seems to have been in fact a rather dreary community—as distant from her mother's lively court as it was from the serene philosophical life for which the princess had longed.[14]

Although Charles Louis eventually regained the palatine title, the long desired restoration of the family fortunes did not occur in the lifetime of the Winter Queen. Through the marriage of her youngest daughter, Sophia, and through Charles Louis's descendants, the older Elizabeth nonetheless became the ancestor to descendants of most of the royal houses of England and of Europe. Perhaps Fortune shone posthumously also on the frustrated intellectual hopes of the young Elisabeth. She was rightly skeptical about Descartes's conviction that she too could have access to the good life through philosophy; yet the influence she exerted on Descartes's thinking about the passions through her sharp critical comments and her relentless testing of his theories against concrete lived experience significantly shaped *The Passions of the Soul*. Transformed by Spinoza, and articulated afresh by Hume, the ideal of affective reason—of a form of thinking that participates in the dynamics of emotion—became a rich strand in intellectual history and a resource for our own attempts to understand and deal with contemporary forms of fate and fortune.

The "friend and correspondent of Descartes"—as she is now identified in the British National Portrait Gallery—merits more than an incidental footnote in the history of abstract philosophical theories of mind-body relations. Her search for a version of the philosophical life that might accommodate and sustain her in her daily struggles has helped open up a way back into those rich ancient sources of practical philosophy—a path that the more conventional caviling critics about whom Descartes complained might otherwise have denied us forever.

6   Living with Necessity

Spinoza and the Philosophical Life

On 27 July 1656, a Jewish edict of separation—a *cherem*—was read in Hebrew in the synagogue of Amsterdam. The authorities, it said, having failed to get Baruch de Spinoza to "mend his wicked ways," and receiving more information daily about his "abominable heresies" and "monstrous deeds," had decided to resort to more drastic action, by expelling him "from the people of Israel." Spinoza, "with the consent of God," was accordingly cursed and damned. "Cursed be he by day and cursed be he by night, cursed be he when he lies down and cursed be he when he rises up. Cursed be he when he goes out and cursed be he when he comes in."[1]

The *Cherem* and Its Aftermath

The exclusion was to be absolute. The congregation was warned not to communicate with him, stay with him under the same roof, or come "within four cubits in his vicinity." Nor were they to read any treatise written by him. The language of the condemnation evoked the separation of death: the Lord would "blot out his name from under heaven" and "separate him unto evil out of all the tribes of Israel." Removed from all that sustained the cultural life of the community, the cursed Spinoza—then twenty-three years old—was as if expelled from the ranks of the living. In stark contrast with those to whom the edict was read, whose life would continue as before, Spinoza was talked of as if he were already dead. "But you that cleave unto the Lord your God are alive every one of you this day."[2]

The stark words of separation came as the definitive end to an already troubled relationship between Spinoza and the community whose life centered on the synagogue. Lucas, the author of what has come to be known as the "oldest biography" of Spinoza, reported that one night when the philosopher was leaving the synagogue, he had been attacked by a man brandishing a knife. Spinoza's unorthodox beliefs had already caused controversy in the community. The authorities' treatment of other men who had expressed unpopular views must have alerted the young man to the dangers of open communication. The *cherem* would not have come as a surprise. Nevertheless, Spinoza probably did not attend the synagogue to hear it delivered. Although he would have been permitted to do so, he did not reply in his own defense; he asked for no intercession, no reconsideration. Lucas attributes to him the following words on hearing of the condemnation: "All the better; they do not force me to do anything that I would not have done of my own accord if I did not dread scandal. But, since they want it that way, I enter gladly on the path that is opened to me, with the consolation that my departure will be more innocent than was the exodus of the early Hebrews from Egypt."[3]

The response attributed to Spinoza is as multilayered as the man himself. It resonates with youthful bravado; yet we can also discern in the response the wily anticipation of trouble—the watchfulness—that would be a lifelong trait of the philosopher. *Caute* was the motto that would later be inscribed on his signet ring. In one of the most commonly reproduced portraits of the philosopher, his long, narrow, finely sculpted features loom out of the surrounding darkness with luminous intensity over a white starched collar. "Caute!" he might well be saying. Yet the look is anything but timid; and the curl of the lip conveys a touch of amused irony that offsets a sadness lurking in the eyes. It is doubt-

ful that the painting was from life, but it may well be an indication
of how his character was perceived.

His philosophy was audacious—often outrageous; Spinoza ventured into territory it had previously been unthinkable to explore.
That intellectual courage, however, coexisted with a capacity to
lie low. Spinoza's caution is not timidity but rather a form of
steadfastness in the pursuit of truth. Later, in *The Ethics,* he will
claim that courage can manifest itself in recognizing the wisdom
of timely retreat no less than in giving battle. The conjunction of
apparently limitless intellectual courage with shrewdness in nego-
tiating the politics of truth would be a persistent thread in his
intellectual character. Fiercely independent and audaciously original though he was in his thinking, he was nonetheless profoundly
cautious about its public expression.

Other tendencies come through in the response Spinoza made
to the *cherem.* We recognize the same intellectual agility he was
to display throughout his writings—his skill in shifting positions,
in ironically appropriating stances that were not really his own.
He was—in ways that are often ignored by his commentators—
a master, not just of philosophical thinking, but of the art of philosophical writing. Spinoza often turned the tables on his opponents, undermining them by apparently embracing their views,
while transforming these into doctrines his critics would have
found outrageous. He could also at other times draw out the unexpected depth and beauty of doctrines that were commonly
loathed. He is the master of the unexpected outcome. Here, in
comparing his departure from the synagogue to the exodus of the
ancient Hebrews from Egypt, he positioned himself as belonging
to the Jewish tradition at a level too deep to be threatened by the
machinations of the local Jewish authorities. Exclude him as they
would, they could not separate him from the deep Jewish resonances that enrich his philosophy.

Something else, too, can be glimpsed through the bravado, the watchfulness, and the irony of those words attributed to the accursed Spinoza. His response expresses a joy in the acceptance of how things are—an emotional identification with what must be. We can see here a conscious rapprochement between freedom and necessity that accords with a central strand in Spinoza's mature philosophy. It is one of his greatest—though also least understood—legacies to modern thought. We can already discern here the contours of his mature articulations of that theme. He responds to his exclusion by appropriating it, by accommodating his desires to his changed circumstances. He is not just making the best of a bad situation. In recasting his exclusion as necessary, he transforms it, thereby making his future continuous with what he already is.

Spinoza's accommodation of the *cherem* gives greater clarity to the direction of the life he was already implicitly leading; it serves to constitute the identity he would thenceforth live out. Spinoza becomes what he most deeply is by shaping the story of his future life around the *cherem* as a central event. Despite his bravado, there can be no denying the significance of the changes that came from embracing, rather than resisting, the *cherem*. He may, as his words suggest, have welcomed the loss of the restraints of religious orthodoxy; even so, the *cherem* threatened not only his freedom of thought but also the external forms that had provided his life with structure and meaning. From having been a busy merchant, Spinoza went on to become a secluded, though by no means solitary, scholar. In the immediate aftermath of the *cherem,* his brother Gabriel took over the family business, while Spinoza continued his studies. Yet he reshaped his life in a direction that was by no means alien to him: Baruch the merchant became Benedictus the philosopher. In adapting his mode of living he was not passively accepting events outside his control; he was rendering explicit underlying tendencies that were already present. What I want to stress here is that in bringing the deeper currents of his life into

closer conformity with its external forms Spinoza was—in terms
of his own mature philosophy—acting out of both freedom and
necessity. He appropriates to himself this formative event, whose
necessity is as much something of his own making as it was an im-
position of external authority.

The convergence of freedom and necessity would become a
central concern in Spinoza's philosophy. It was one of his principal departures from the Cartesian philosophy that was in many
ways his starting point. But before considering what is distinctive
about Spinoza's approach to freedom and the good life, it is helpful first to examine a little more of the shape Spinoza's life took
on in the aftermath of the *cherem*.[4] Like Descartes, Spinoza highly
valued his intellectual friendships, but Spinoza was much more
explicit than Descartes in drawing connections between the virtuous life and the cultivation of such friendship. The framework
for this view of the good life was set by the transition from the
community life centered on the synagogue to the cultivation of
his own intellectual circle.

In 1661 Spinoza took up residence in Rijnsberg, a small village
near Leiden. According to Lucas, the move was motivated by a
love of solitude—by the hope of disengaging from the madness
of a large city, when people started bothering the philosopher.
The life Spinoza led in Rijnsberg, however, was in fact far from
reclusive. He had frequent visitors, some of whom traveled to the
Netherlands to discuss scientific matters with him. He kept up
close contact with a group of disciples who read his work together—first his commentary on Descartes, then his own developing
philosophy. At least one student, Casearius, also lived in his house
while Spinoza instructed him in Cartesian philosophy. Spinoza's
problems with Casearius display a pattern that would recur
throughout his life—the tension between response to the demands of intellectual generosity, on the one hand, and vulnerability to the hazards of sociability on the other. Writing about Case-

arius to his friend Simon de Vries in March 1663, Spinoza remarked: "There is no need for you to envy Casearius. No one is more troublesome to me, and there is no one with whom I have to be more on my guard. So I should like to warn you and all our friends not to communicate my views to him until he has reached greater maturity. He is still too childish and unstable, more anxious for novelty than for truth. But I hope that in a few years he will correct these youthful faults. Indeed, as far as I can judge from his native ability, I am almost certain that he will. So his talent induces me to like him."[5]

Openness to a shared pursuit of truth—in a context where tolerance of unorthodox views cannot be taken for granted—requires caution about premature communication. Another source of anxiety for Spinoza, however, was the encroachments would-be friends made on the time and energies he required for his own scholarly pursuits. During this period, Spinoza—whether out of scientific curiosity or financial necessity—was developing his expertise at grinding lenses and making microscopes and telescopes, occupations that would provide his livelihood for the rest of his life. He was anxious about time taken away from his studies by the collegial demands of other truth seekers. More is at stake here than the common challenge of dealing with enervating distractions while trying to write. The pursuit of truth represented for Spinoza not just the time-consuming accumulation of a body of work but a whole way of life. The "true method," he says in a letter to his friend Johannes Bouwmeester on 10 June 1666, requires "incessant thought and a most constant mind and purpose. To gain these, it is first of all necessary to adopt a definite mode and plan of life, and to set before one a definite end" (*The Correspondence of Spinoza*, 228). Fine words—that goal itself, as Descartes and Elisabeth well knew, though, is constantly liable to be thwarted by practical distractions and by the attention of fools; and Spinoza's life was subject to similar frustrations.

The competing demands of solitude and friendship in the life of the mind became a recurring motif in Spinoza's letters. It is an old theme, which would have been familiar to him from ancient Greek thought. We have seen that Epictetus used it in illustration of the Stoic ideal of appropriating necessity, finding contentment in whatever life presents: "You ought, when staying alone, to call that peace and freedom, and to look upon yourself as like the gods; and when you are in the company of many, you ought not call that a mob, nor a tumult, nor a disgusting thing, but a feast and a festival, and so accept all things contentedly."[6] In the vision Spinoza develops of the life of the mind, solitude and friendship jostle as equal but competing preconditions. As he sees it, in a shared pursuit of truth the communication of thought does not merely accelerate the accumulation of knowledge through a division of labor; such communication is essential to the good life. In his mature philosophy the shared love of truth will be presented as crucial to the strengthening of intellect, which passes over into the mind's resistance to the rival force of destructive passions. Yet securing the right conditions for that shared love of truth is an ongoing source of frustration.

For the young Spinoza, sustaining the solitude necessary for scholarly studies was a constant challenge, but he had also been alerted to the dangers of careless communication by his early experience of the wrath of religious orthodoxy. His generosity with ideas with friends had to be balanced with caution toward those who had not earned his confidence. Friendship was already central to his vision of the life of the mind as the fully virtuous life; but finding the right friends could be a matter of time-consuming trial and error. Spinoza's exchanges with the obtuse grain broker William van Blijenberg provide an amusing illustration of the difficulty of finding the right kind of intellectual friend. Van Blijenberg had contacted Spinoza after reading his commentary on Descartes, the publication of which had been organized by Spi-

noza's trusted friend Lodewijk Meyer. In his reply to Van Blijenberg of 5 January 1665 Spinoza agreed, on the basis of what he
perceived as Van Blijenberg's "great love of truth," to do all he
could to develop with him "a closer acquaintance and genuine
friendship" (Collected Works, 357–358).

Spinoza enters on the correspondence with enthusiasm: "To
me, of the things outside my power, I esteem none more than
being allowed the honour of entering into a pact of friendship
with people who sincerely love the truth; for I believe that of
things outside our power we can love none tranquilly, except such
people. Because the love they bear to one another is based on the
love each has for knowledge of the truth, it is as impossible to destroy it as not to embrace the truth once it has been perceived.
Moreover, it is the greatest and most pleasant that can be given to
things outside our power, since nothing but truth can completely
unite different opinions and minds" (Collected Works, 357–358).

The mind may be unable to refrain from embracing the truth it
perceives. But finding the right minds with which to share the
pursuit of truth is another matter. After responding patiently to a
long series of defenses of the Christian religion, Spinoza eventually retreats. When Van Blijenberg complains, in a letter of 19
February 1665, of his "touchy reproofs" that seem at odds with his
initial pledge of friendship, Spinoza, on 13 March 1665, conveys
his decision that he would be "ill advised" to neglect his own studies for the sake of "things that can be of no use." He adds, "This
does not contradict my first letter, . . . because there I considered
you as a pure philosopher who (as many who consider themselves
Christians grant) has no other touchstone of truth than the natural intellect and not theology. But you have taught me otherwise
and shown me that the foundation on which I intended to build
our friendship was not laid as I thought" (Collected Works, 387).
The obtuse Van Blijenberg had proved incapable of grasping the
central guiding principle of Spinoza's thinking—that "pure phi-

losophy," with its appeal to "the natural intellect," can and must be kept separate from theology. The depth of Spinoza's commitment to this principle would in the end, as we will see, prove difficult even for more powerful minds than Van Blijenberg's to accommodate.

Good intellectual friendships, according to Spinoza, strengthen the life of the mind and hence the life of virtue. The interconnections between freedom and necessity are crucial to his version of the good life; and the idea of providence is in turn crucial to Spinoza's alignment of freedom and necessity. Let us now see how his philosophy articulates the convergence of freedom and necessity that was already being enacted in his own life.

Freedom, Necessity, and Providence

In Descartes's treatment of freedom, an inherently free will forces back ever further the limits of what must be accepted as beyond human control. The prevailing imagery is of border skirmishes. The will conducts forays out from the inner space of mind into the less secure territory beyond, where minds and bodies intermingle; the territory of what lies within human power is thus constantly expanded. Spinoza offers instead a vision of freedom as the joyful acceptance and appropriation of what must be. Such acceptance was to be as central to Spinoza's idea of the good life as the doctrine of free will was to Descartes's.

The closeness of freedom and necessity was, as we have seen, a favorite theme in ancient Stoic thought. Spinoza himself repudiated neo-Stoic ideas circulating in his own time that asserted the human will's absolute power over the passions—a view he attributed also to the Cartesians. But his own treatment of freedom and necessity—however far it may have been from contemporary neo-Stoic doctrines—resonates with ancient Stoic thought. For him freedom does not reside in a limited domain where the will escapes the encroachments of necessity; freedom derives rather from the active engagement of the mind with necessity, an engagement that flows from understanding of the truth. For Descartes, freedom pertains to the will, though attaining freedom requires that the will maintain an appropriate relationship with the understanding; for Spinoza the gaining of freedom is the work of the understanding alone.

Princess Elisabeth might well have found Spinoza's approach to the philosophical life more congenial than the one Descartes offered her. She herself had, after all, anticipated the core objection that Spinoza would later make to Descartes's version of mind-body relations; and under the force of her questioning Descartes had already, in his last work, *The Passions of the Soul,* moved a considerable distance toward the kind of knowledge-centered version of freedom that Spinoza would develop. Elisabeth longed for a "remedy" for the passions that would rely on the cultivation of her understanding rather than on the limited power she found in her will. Spinoza offers such a remedy, grounded in the convergence of freedom and necessity.

Necessity, for Spinoza as for the Stoics, held a powerful attraction for the mind, of a kind that can be difficult for us to comprehend. It may well strike us now as strange to talk of the mind as finding its freedom in acceptance of the unavoidable. In this respect we are Cartesians. Stoic talk of an "impulse" toward necessity can seem startlingly at odds with modern ideas of autonomy. The idea of shaping our lives around the necessities we cannot avoid—of learning to live with what we cannot change—may still resonate with us. We may think of it as a commendable form of endurance, patience, or resignation—even of what we now call Stoicism. We do not readily, though, think of it as the content of freedom.

The tensions between freedom and necessity were already familiar to the ancient Stoics. Cicero in his work *On Fate* describes

Chrysippus as trying to reconcile the apparent contradictions through appeal to the analogies of a spinning top and of a cylinder rolling down hill. "These cannot begin to move without a push, but once that has happened, he holds that it is thereafter through their own nature that the cylinder rolls and the top spins." Another source, Gellius, gives a fuller account of the analogy. "Just as [Chrysippus] says, 'if you push a stone cylinder on steeply sloping ground, you have produced the cause and beginning of its forward motion, but soon it rolls forward not because you are still making it do so, but because such are its form and smooth-rolling shape—so too, the order, rationale and necessity of fate sets in motion the actual types of causes and their beginnings, but the deliberative impulses of our minds and our actual actions are controlled by our own individual will and intellect.'"[7]

Although Descartes saw freedom and necessity as being reconciled in his account of the interrelations of will and understanding, his account of freedom does give scope to the will as a free-ranging causal force. The conceptual preconditions are present for the separation of freedom and necessity. By the time Spinoza formulated his own account of human freedom in *The Ethics,* his arguments for the interdependence of freedom and necessity would be subtle and ingenious. His views on this issue, however, were to remain throughout his life a source of consternation to his friends, no less than to his strident critics. His treatment of human freedom is grounded in the "free necessity" he ascribes to his version of God; and the key to this rapprochement of the free and the necessary in God is Spinoza's rejection of conventional ideas of providence.

Spinoza scathingly rejects the idea of providence in the appendix to part 1 of *The Ethics.*[8] What he rejects there, however, is a version of providence—which he attributes to both Descartes and the Stoics—associated with the belief in free will. For Descartes, ideas of providence, divine will, and purpose are closely connected; and Spinoza rejects the whole package—along with the belief in the absolute power of the human will, which he sees as grounded in the idea of divine will.

In his early *Commentary on Descartes's Principles,* we already find signs of a radical departure from traditional ways of thinking about providence, and more generally about divine will. In the appendix to that work, Spinoza says that it is ridiculous for "the Philosophers" to "take refuge in the will of God whenever they are ignorant of the causes of things." Turning his attention to ordinary people, he says (in the appendix, part 2, chap. 7) that they too "have found no stronger proof of God's providence and rule than that based on the ignorance of causes. This shows clearly that they have no knowledge at all of the nature of God's will, and that they have attributed a human will to him, i.e., a will really distinct from the intellect." He concludes darkly, "I think this misconception has been the sole cause of superstition, and perhaps of much knavery" (*Collected Works,* 326).

A form of divine will that is not separated from intellect is something quite different, for Spinoza, from one that is; and the providence that accompanies it is also transformed. Earlier, in the *Short Treatise on God, Man and His Well-Being,* Spinoza had presented providence as an "attribute" of God. It is, he says there, "nothing but that striving we find both in the whole of Nature and in particular things, tending to maintain and preserve their being." In that remark we see him already drawing a very close connection between the idea of providence and a concept that will become one of the most important in his mature philosophy—that of *conatus,* or striving. The *Short Treatise* definition of providence allows him to put his own mark on the old distinction between universal and "special," or "particular," providence; and the relations between parts and whole is also already central to this shift. Universal providence, Spinoza says, is that through which each thing is produced and maintained, insofar as it is part of the whole of Na-

ture. Particular providence, by contrast, is that striving which pertains to each particular thing for the preservation of its being,
insofar as it is considered not as part of Nature but as a whole.
"Thus," he says in illustration, all man's limbs are "provided and
cared for, insofar as they are parts of man. That is universal providence." By contrast (part I, chap. 5), particular providence is "that
striving that each particular limb (as a whole, not as a part of
man) has to preserve and maintain its own well-being" (*Collected
Works*, 84).

With those definitions and distinctions in place, Spinoza can
go on to present the belief in "particular providence"—which had
in earlier theological thinking become associated with God's special interventions in the world on behalf of human beings—as
amounting merely to ignorance of the whole of which each thing
is in fact part. Belief in a particular providence becomes the deluded thought of individual things as self-contained wholes. Spinoza more fully explores the ramifications of that delusion implicit in the conventional idea of providence, and delivers a
trenchant dismissal of the idea, in his mature work. In the appendix to part I of *The Ethics* he ridicules the "prejudices" that
make human beings think of "natural things" as depending on the
will of a purposeful God. Having found many things helpful in
seeking their own advantage—"eyes for seeing, teeth for chewing,
plants and animals for food, the sun for light, the sea for support-
ing fish"—people conclude foolishly that the whole of nature is
directed by a purposeful God in accordance with the needs, the
"blind desires," and the "insatiable greed" of human beings. Seeking to show that "nature does nothing in vain," they "seem to have
shown only that nature and the Gods are as mad as men" (*Collected
Works*, 440–441).

The supposed "will of God" turns out to be nothing but a refuge, a sanctuary for human ignorance. The truth is that all things
happen of necessity. We need not, then, ponder why "evil" things

exist, Spinoza continues. For the perfection of things is to be judged not according to whether they please or are of use to us, but "solely from their nature and power" (*Collected Works,* 446). As he mischievously goes on, the only adequate answer to the question why God allows the existence of things we find evil is that "'he did not lack material to create all things from the highest degree of perfection to the lowest'; or, to speak more properly, 'because the laws of his nature have been so ample that they sufficed for producing all things which can be conceived by an infinite intellect.'" Not only does this God not act out of concern for human well-being; this is a God who does not act for "ends" at all—a God with no will, either benign or malign.

Spinoza's caustic remarks here may offer a fair commentary on some aspects of prevalent versions of providence, articulated in terms of the idea of divine will; but his own idea of human beings as necessarily interconnected parts of the whole of Nature strongly echoes older Stoic ideas about providence as the ordered unity of the cosmos. It is striking that those ancient Stoic ideas about a necessarily unified cosmic order resurface in Spinoza's thought, despite his vehement rejection of what he calls providence. The Stoics, as we have seen, liked to talk about the world of gods and men as the "cosmic city"—and of divine and human alike as subject to the rational necessities that govern the whole of nature. There was providence in that Stoic world, but it resided not in the presence of a divine will not governed by necessity, but precisely in a necessity that pervaded everything. The assurance that arose from trust in providence came from the sense of being part of that necessary whole.

The history of Stoic providence has here followed what is in some ways a surprising path—having been absorbed into later theological ideas of a benign divine will, only to resurface in the necessarily unified whole about which Spinoza talks in rejecting the divine will. Spinoza regards the idea of providence that prevails in his own times as the mark of irrationality or superstitious ignorance. Rather than being the frame of the cosmic city of rational necessities, the conventional idea of providence as benign divine will has yielded, as he sees it, a world in which gods and men are all mad together. Hence the "knavery" that he thinks arises from belief in divine will, for in conditions of ignorance the voices of authority are all too willing to offer specious and oppressive interpretations of divine purpose.

In *The Ethics,* then, we see Spinoza vehemently reject prevailing ideas of providence, along with the supposed free will of gods and of men. Throughout the work we nonetheless find intimations of that older Stoic concept of providence, though Spinoza does not call it by that name. We can hear reverberations from Stoicism in his claim that the wise knowingly participate in the necessity of the whole of nature, and—paradoxical though it may initially sound now—that they find their true freedom in understanding themselves as part of that necessary whole. Spinoza's treatment of human freedom expresses a perspective that has its origin in those ancient Stoic sources, although he has set his own distinctive mark on it. Despite his rejection of providence as it was conceived in his own time, he had his own version of providence—a providence without the will.

More is at stake, however, than a simple reenactment of Stoic themes. Epicurean echoes are present also in Spinoza's rejection of superstitious belief in a world conformable to human needs. Moreover, another way of thinking about providence surfaces here, which has different origins. For Spinoza's ethic of freedom shows continuities also with ideas of providence from the Jewish tradition. Steven Nadler has argued convincingly that terminological differences notwithstanding, Spinoza drew on Jewish sources—especially Maimonides and Gesonides—to develop a nonteleological version of divine providence. The view of providence that emerges is grounded in necessity and expressed in terms of the ethical consequences of a rational understanding of Nature. As Nadler sums it up, this version of providence amounts to "the natural benefits of intellectual knowledge as this is achieved by particular human beings." According to this reading, Spinoza has retained from the Jewish rationalist tradition the crucial idea that "universal epistemic arrangements" are in place that will benefit those virtuous individuals who take advantage of them.[9]

Not surprisingly, the common construction of Spinoza by his contemporary critics and enemies did not rest on any clear understanding of—or sensitivity to—the relations between his philosophy and earlier Jewish thought. Providence in the thought of Maimonides and Gesonides differed in crucial ways from Christian preoccupations with a benign divine will answering to human needs and purposes. Nor would Spinoza's contemporaries have been particularly attuned to the ancient Stoic background of his version of providence. It is not surprising, then, that even before the posthumous publication of *The Ethics* the name Spinoza had come to be associated, as we shall see in more detail later, with a godless rejection of the very idea of providence.

In place of the conventional conception of providence as the inscrutable purpose of a benign divine will, Spinoza proposes a different way of thinking of the divine nature and its relations with the world. In place of trust in the will of a transcendent creator, he offers the challenge of coming to an ever greater understanding of ourselves as part of the whole of nature. What are the implications for freedom of this way of thinking about God and Nature? In a letter of 1674 to Hugo Boxel, Spinoza observes that the terms "fortuitous" and "necessary" are contraries, but that "necessary" and "free" are not. In defense of this alignment of the free and the necessary, he appeals to familiar ideas (in his intellectual context) about the necessary existence of God. To say that the world is the necessary effect of the divine nature is, he observes, to deny that the world was made by chance, for it is to deny that the world resulted from a contingent act of divine will.

This is one of those moments in Spinoza's philosophy when apparently orthodox religious positions are turned upside down. Unless God acts of necessity, he claims, the world exists by chance. To avoid that unthinkable conclusion, it must be admitted that the world is the necessary effect of the divine nature—that no room exists for divine will as distinct from divine intellect. In other words, whatever God conceives as possible must come to be. Nevertheless, Spinoza continues, to insist that what God does, he does of necessity, is in no way to detract from God's freedom. Both terms—"necessary" and "free"—are appropriately applied to God. To think otherwise, Spinoza says, would be to confuse God's freedom with "a freedom of indifference"—a false freedom, a wavering that arises from ignorance or doubt.

That model of God's freedom as coexisting with necessity sets the scene for Spinoza's treatment of human freedom. Human beings, because they lack necessary existence in their own right, lack the freedom that God has necessarily. They are necessarily "determined by an external cause to exist and to act in a definite and determinate manner." Lacking necessary existence, human beings lack also the kind of freedom that comes with it. The lack does not mean that they are not free; it means, rather, that their freedom must be rethought.

To illustrate the point, Spinoza asks his correspondent to engage in a thought experiment. Imagine, he says, a stone that is conscious of its own movement but ignorant of the external causes of that motion. The stone will believe, falsely, that its movement is not imposed by necessity—that it continues its motion for no other reason than that it wants to. For Spinoza the "free will of which men boast" is like the illusory freedom of the moving stone. Men, he says, are conscious of their desires and ignorant of the causes by which those are determined. "So the infant believes that it freely wants milk; the boy when he is angry that he freely wants revenge; the timid man that he wants to escape. Then too the drunkard believes that, by the free decision of his mind, he says those things which afterwards when sober he would prefer to have left unsaid. So the delirious, the garrulous, and many others of the same sort, believe that they are acting in accordance with the free decision of their mind, and not that they are carried away by impulse" (*The Correspondence of Spinoza,* 295). Wittgenstein once offered a similar illustration of the illusion of supposedly inner states of volition in an analogy of leaves blowing in the wind, saying to themselves, "Now I'll go this way, now I'll go that way."[10]

The approach to freedom Spinoza develops more fully in *The Ethics* has—at any rate initially—a certain starkness to it. Our belief that we do things of our own free will, he argues, is foolish—no less foolish than the familiar follies in which, we think, we engage of our own free will. Are our supposed virtues then no less determined than our follies? They are indeed determined, he says. But just as freedom and necessity are not, for Spinoza, at odds within the divine nature, so true human freedom—as distinct from the illusory freedom of the will—coexists with necessity. We gain true freedom by coming to understand our own natures as parts of the whole of nature, which is in turn the complete, free, and necessary expression of the divine nature. It is another of those cunning reversals of orthodox theology that Spinoza relishes. The coexistence of freedom and necessity in the divine nature becomes the key to understanding our own lack of free will. God is our model, not—as Descartes would have said—in his all-powerful free will, but precisely in his not having a will at all. For freedom and necessity come together in the understanding of our own status as parts of the whole of nature—that is, in Spinoza's terminology, as "modes" of God or Substance.

Spinoza has here completely reversed the Cartesian character ideal, centered on free will, which is now so familiar to us—regardless of whether we have actually read Descartes. Descartes bequeathed to us the familiar figure of post-Enlightenment man, and even (with some maneuvering) woman: an individual thinking thing, a self-contained center of consciousness and autonomous will, able to exert control, at least over its immediate environment, without constraint from the necessities that govern the rest of nature. Spinoza, cunningly but also profoundly, undercuts that Cartesian ideal, and offers in its place the alternate ideal of a free life shaped around the recognition of necessity.

The development of this ideal of a freedom that accommodates and finds joy in necessity is the climax of Spinoza's *Ethics*. Like Descartes's account of freedom as residing in the will, Spinoza's is integrated with an account of the nature of human passions and the search for a way of avoiding their destructive force. We have here, then, two rival practical philosophies—two alternate approaches to the challenges of living well under the onslaught of the passions.

Spinoza's Remedy

Descartes's method for dealing with the passions, as Spinoza saw it, relied on an outrageous claim—one Descartes made along with the Stoics—that the will had absolute power to control the passions. According to that approach, simply by strengthening our wills we can bring our passions under our command. Spinoza's interpretation may not have done full justice to the subtle rapprochement between will and understanding that characterizes Descartes's treatment of the passions in *The Passions of the Soul*. Spinoza was nonetheless correct in identifying the power of the will as central to the Cartesian remedy.

As Spinoza saw it, Descartes had placed at the center of his radical philosophy the doctrine of free will. To accommodate the many points of inconsistency between it and common experience, Descartes had then to surround an incoherent theory with excessively complex qualifications: the human will had absolute power but was nonetheless subject to severe limitations in its exercise because of the mind's limited knowledge. Moreover, as Spinoza saw it, the whole approach rested on a still more problematic incoherence in Descartes's treatment of the relations between minds and bodies. In *The Ethics* Spinoza expresses, though with less politeness, essentially the same objection Elisabeth raised to Descartes: How could there be causal relations between things as utterly distinct in kind as Descartes claimed minds and bodies were? How could an act of the will have causal efficacy on the passions, which Descartes regards as involving bodily changes?

According to Spinoza, Descartes's very definition of a passion— as a movement of the bodily spirits caused by something happening in the soul—was incoherent. Spinoza delivers a scathing attack on this aspect of Descartes's philosophy in the preface to part 5 of *The Ethics*. The claim that the will has the power to exert a causal effect on part of the brain, he suggests, is a grotesque doctrine. "I would hardly have believed it had been propounded by so great a Man, had it not been so subtle. Indeed, I cannot wonder enough that a Philosopher of his calibre—one who had firmly decided to deduce nothing except from principles known through themselves, and to affirm nothing which he did not perceive clearly and distinctly, one who had so often censured the Scholastics for wishing to explain obscure things by occult qualities—that such a Philosopher should assume a hypothesis more occult than any occult quality" (*Collected Works,* 596).

Spinoza regarded Descartes's misguided belief in the "absolute" power of the will as a Stoic doctrine. Although his ridicule may have been an appropriate response to some neo-Stoic views on the passions circulating at the time, his own treatment of freedom and necessity, as we have seen, has much in common with the thought of the ancient Stoics; and his own remedy for the passions is in some ways a new version of the ancient Stoic ideal of appropriating necessity. We have seen in earlier chapters that the ancient Stoics found in the acceptance of necessity not bleak endurance but intense joy. In this respect, Spinoza was their heir. He argues in *The Ethics* that from the mind's understanding of necessity arises a powerful affirmation that is, by definition, joy: the mind's transition to greater activity. This affective intensity is the key to Spinoza's version of the struggle between reason and the passions: reason can prevail only because it can come to have a greater emotional power than the passions with which it contends, transforming them into a version of active joy, rather than passive despondency. "No affect," he says, in part 4, proposition 14, "can be restrained by the true knowledge of good and evil insofar as it is true, but only insofar as it is considered as an affect" (*Collected Works,* 553). The passions are to be overcome not through the power of will, but through confrontation with a more powerful intellectual joy.

In practice, the alternative remedies for the passions offered by Descartes and Spinoza may often converge. Like Descartes, Spinoza stresses the importance of knowing that we have "done our duty." But the context in which Spinoza talks in those terms makes his recommended path to acquiescence very different from that of Descartes. "We do not have an absolute power to adapt things outside us to our use," he says at the end of the appendix to part 4 of *The Ethics.* "Nevertheless, we shall bear calmly those things which happen to us contrary to what the principle of our advantage demands, if we are conscious that we have done our duty, that the power we have could not have extended itself to the point where we could have avoided those things, and that we are a part of the whole of nature, whose order we follow. If we understand this clearly and distinctly, that part of us which is defined by understanding, i.e., the better part of us, will be entirely satisfied with this, and will strive to persevere in that satisfaction" (*Collected Works*, 593–594).

For Descartes the assurance that we have "done our duty" allows us to surrender all that lies outside our control to the benign divine will that holds our well-being in its providential care. Acquiescence and tranquillity come from realizing our limitations in relation to the all-powerful will of God. For Spinoza, by contrast (*Ethics*, part 4, app., sec. 32), acquiescence is grounded in the understanding of universal necessity. "For insofar as we understand, we can want nothing except what is necessary, nor absolutely be satisfied with anything except what is true" (*Collected Works*, 594).

The contrast between the two approaches is in fact even more marked; for according to Descartes, our limited power is not a matter of some lack in the power of the human will. The power of the Cartesian will is no less absolute in its human version than in the divine. The undeniable constraints on human power derive not from the relative weakness of our wills, but from the deficiencies of the understanding in conjunction with which the human will must operate. For Spinoza the difference between human and divine power resides solely in the fact that we are part of nature, limited by the causal determination exerted on us by the rest of the whole. Whereas Descartes emphasizes the absolute power of the human will, which sets us apart from the rest of nature, Spinoza emphasizes our lack of insulation from that totality.

To find positive emotional resonances in the understanding of necessity may well now strike us as strange. Part of the residue of Stoicism in our own thought is the idea that it is futile to waste emotion on what cannot be avoided or changed. That commonsense response is reflected in Spinoza's observation that we can often lessen the power of passion by recognizing our circumstances as necessary. To the extent that (as Spinoza's philosophy demands) we come to accept that all things are necessary, we become less subject to futile dissatisfaction. Spinoza confirms this in

part 5, proposition 6, of *The Ethics:* "Insofar as the mind understands all things as necessary, it has a greater power over the affects or is less acted on by them." In the accompanying Scholium
he elaborates on the point: our sadness over some good that has
perished lessens as soon as we realize that "this good could not in
any way have been kept." In one of his more fanciful examples, he
goes on to suggest that "we see that no-one pities infants, because
of their inability to speak, to walk, or to reason, or because they
live so many years, as it were, unconscious of themselves. But if
most people were born grown up, and only one or two were born
infants, then everyone would pity the infants, because they would
regard infancy itself, not as a natural and necessary thing, but as a
vice of nature, or a sin" (*Collected Works,* 599–600). Understanding that infancy is not a rare affliction but a necessary stage of a
human life, we accept its limitations with equanimity, rather than
seeing it as something to be pitied or deplored. Thus, we should
not rail at things we know to be unavoidable, but rather endure
them—as we might now say—stoically. In recognizing necessity,
we are able to defuse pointless passion.

Yet this is not all there is to it—either for Spinoza or for the
ancient Stoics. Directly from an understanding of necessity also
comes a positive intensification of emotion; and this, rather than
lack of emotion, is the key to Spinoza's remedy for the passions.
When the mind comes to fully understand things as necessary,
far from disengaging from the world, it engages more intensely
with it. Again, despite his hostility to what he thinks of as Stoicism, Spinoza's description of the intense intellectual joy associated with the recognition of necessity connects him with those
ancient sources.

Spinoza's Critique of Religion

Spinoza's rethinking of providence, and more generally of the relations between the human and the divine, in addition to being

the basis for his account of the good life, had ramifications in his responses to the political events of his time. The political implications are illuminated by letters written throughout his long intellectual friendship with the scientist Henry Oldenburg. Spinoza's dissatisfactions with conventional religious beliefs and his antagonism toward the theologians are a recurring theme in their letters. Here too, the difficult balance between caution and confidence frames the exchange.

Oldenburg repeatedly urges Spinoza to publish his philosophical views. In April 1662 Spinoza wrote to Oldenburg, then resident in England, of putting aside a short work he was engaged in writing (probably the *Short Treatise*) because he did not yet have any definite plan for its publication. "I fear, of course," he says, "that the theologians of our time may be offended and with their usual hatred attack me, who absolutely dread quarrels." Oldenburg, inspired by enthusiasm for the developing community of learning—the Republic of Philosophers—in which he saw Spinoza as having a major part to play, was frustrated by Spinoza's caution. Why, he asks the following July, should Spinoza begrudge other scholars the knowledge he has arrived at through the acuteness of his understanding? "Let it be published," he says, "whatever rumblings there may be among the foolish Theologians. Your Republic is very free, and gives great freedom for philosophising. And your own prudence will suggest to you that you express your concepts and your opinions as moderately as possible. For the rest, leave the outcome to Fate" (*Collected Works*, 189).

Oldenburg's confidence in the future of the Republic of Philosophers was initially well founded. His own efforts to disseminate scientific knowledge in England were sustained by what he describes as a "Philosophical Group." The informal gatherings of scientists to which he alludes could provide not only intellectual friendship but also legitimation in the form of public acceptance. Meetings had been held in London and Oxford since about 1645, and the groups were about to be incorporated as the prestigious

Royal Society. The exuberance with which Oldenburg urged publication on Spinoza reflects that success: "Come, then, excellent
Sir, banish all fear of arousing the pygmies of our time. Long
enough have we appeased ignorant triflers. Let us set full sail for
true knowledge, and penetrate more deeply into nature's myster-
ies than anyone yet has. Among your people, I think, your meditations can be published with impunity, nor should you fear that
they will give any offense to the Wise. . . . I will not leave you
in peace, honoured Friend, until I prevail on you, nor will I ever,
so far as it depends on me, allow your Thoughts, which are of
such great weight, to be concealed in eternal silence" (*Collected
Works,* 189–190). The importunate Oldenburg would be true to
his word, continuing to entreat Spinoza to throw aside his misguided caution. But Spinoza's judgment—both regarding the limitations on freedom in the Dutch Republic and about the likely
reception of his developing philosophy—was to prove better than
Oldenburg's.

The tussle with Oldenburg about publication goes on for years.
Clearly, Oldenburg sees his Republic of Philosophers as transcending both geographical boundaries and the restraints of orthodoxy. A man of Spinoza's talent and understanding, he insists
in a letter of 3 April 1663, must look to the reception of his work
by "Men who are really learned and wise," rather than being concerned with "the things that please the Theologians of our age
and fashion," who "have an eye more to their own interest than
to truth" (*Collected Works,* 200). His appeal is always to "the com-
pact of friendship" between himself and Spinoza, which he sees as
grounding a duty to increase and spread knowledge. He talks of
his desire to see Spinoza's efforts to establish the principles of
things through the acuteness of his mathematical understanding
complement the painstaking experiments and observations of
others, especially Oldenburg's friend Boyle. "You see, Dearest
Friend," he says in a letter of 4 August 1663, "what I am striving

for. I know that in this Kingdom our native Philosophers will not shirk their experimental duty. I am no less convinced that you in your Country will zealously do your part, however much the mob of Philosophers or Theologians may growl, whatever accusations they may make" (*Collected Works,* 218).

The wily Spinoza may well have been skeptical about Oldenburg's confidence in the freedoms of the Dutch Republic. Spinoza may well also have had some well-founded misgivings about the extent of Oldenburg's understanding of the direction in which his philosophy was moving. Oldenburg, focused as he was on his admiring vision of Spinoza as theorist of the emerging new science, failed at first to grasp the radical nature of Spinoza's way of thinking of the nature of God and his relations to the world. Indeed by 1665 Oldenburg was perplexed by Spinoza's apparent preoccupation with issues of religion. "I see," he says, in a letter of September or October of that year, "that you are not so much philosophizing as, if I may say so, theologizing; for you are writing down your thoughts about Angels, prophecy and miracles." He adds hopefully, "But perhaps you are doing this in a philosophical manner" (*The Correspondence of Spinoza,* 204). As Oldenburg sees it, Spinoza, in turning his thoughts to religion, seems to be abandoning his honorable place in their Republic of Philosophers.

To Oldenburg's disappointment, Spinoza had set aside the work that would eventually be published posthumously as *The Ethics* in favor of the controversial book whose publication would make him notorious in his lifetime—*A Theologico-Political Treatise.* The interrelation of the two works is, however, much more complex than the simple separation between the philosophical and the theological that Oldenburg invokes. Together the two works would bring about a new integration of the two activities. It is an integration that requires more than sorting out their conceptual differences and relations. It also involves a political intervention on Spinoza's part, and one on which, as he sees it, depends the future—perhaps

the very existence—of the Republic of Philosophers to which
Oldenburg is attempting to recall him.

At this stage in their long correspondence, Oldenburg and Spinoza are exchanging letters in difficult circumstances—both for
the Dutch Republic and for Oldenburg's treasured dream of the
Republic of Philosophers. The ravages of the plague of 1664–65,
and of the Dutch-English War of 1665–1667, form the backdrop
to their exchanges. Some letters open with an expression of relief
and pleasure that each of them is still alive, and that other learned
friends have also survived. The plague still hinders nearly all traf-
fic, Oldenburg reports in September 1665. "In addition there is
this most dreadful war, which brings in its train a very Iliad of
evils, and all but wipes out all human kindness from the world"
(*The Correspondence of Spinoza,* 203). Both Spinoza and Oldenburg
deplored the irrationalities of the war, though not surprisingly
they sometimes differed in their evaluations of how it was unfolding. "Here we are daily expecting news of a second naval battle,"
Oldenburg continues, "unless perhaps your Fleet has again retired
into port. The courage with which you hint that your men fight is
brutish not human. For if men acted under the guidance of reason, they would not rend one another in pieces, as is obvious to
everybody. But why do I complain? There will be wickedness as
long as there are men; but that is not unrelieved, and is counterbalanced by the intervention of better things" (*The Correspondence
of Spinoza,* 204).

Oldenburg's reflections on war express a fairly conventional
conviction about the balance of good and evil. The comforting
presence of benign providence is not far below the surface of his
sad remarks on the times. Spinoza's response is equally revealing
about the direction in which his own, less conventional, thoughts
are moving. A chasm is opening between the two men about the
nature of good and evil, and about the relations between the divine and the human—a chasm about which Spinoza was already

clearer than Oldenburg. Oldenburg was more sanguine than Spinoza could be, both about the role of God in the chaotic affairs of men and about the likely reception of Spinoza's philosophy in a social and intellectual context where providence, construed as benign divine will, was generally accepted.

Spinoza's reactions to the war are revelatory of the role that his thoughts on religion played in the way he was coming to see his practice of philosophy. He responds to Oldenburg's dismay at the savagery of their times—probably referring to Democritus: "If that famous scoffer were alive today, he would surely die of laughter." As for himself, he insists, the current disorders of their world move him neither to laughter nor to tears, "but rather to philosophising, and to the better observation of human nature" (*The Correspondence of Spinoza*, 205). Oldenburg is frustrated by Spinoza's apparent abandonment of philosophy. For Spinoza the shift toward what his friend calls theologizing is, however, the essence of the philosophizing that allows him to contemplate the madness of their times with detachment, while recognizing that both tears and laughter are inappropriate.

Anger and irony are barely concealed in Spinoza's show of tolerance for the grotesque follies of war. Philosophizing will, as he says, serve as his alternative to futile laughter or tears at human folly. As is often the case throughout his work, we can nonetheless hear a dark laughter in the philosophizing of the voice of reason. Yet dark though the mood is, it is also clear that Spinoza is already finding, in his emphasis on the theme of human beings as part of a necessarily unified whole, his own alternative to the conventional view of the relations between the divine and the human.

Spinoza's transformation of the idea of providence is the key to his rethinking of the relations between philosophy and theology. In presenting philosophizing as a constructive alternative to both laughter and tears, he makes no explicit mention of providence. We might well have been surprised if he had, since as we have already seen, it is not an idea that receives sympathetic treatment in his works. The idea of providence can nonetheless illuminate the apparent shift from philosophy to theology that perplexed Oldenburg. This is a philosophizing that has reabsorbed some of the traditional theological concerns that Oldenburg wanted to keep separate from the agenda of the Republic of Philosophers. The divine to which Spinoza had apparently turned, however, was not that of the orthodox preachers. At the heart of his concerns is the preoccupation that will drive his philosophy—the theme of human beings as part of the whole of nature.

Spinoza's apparent shift to theologizing and his new stance regarding the follies of the times both rest on his reconnection with the old Stoic idea of the unified whole of nature. Spinoza identifies as the foundation of his refusal to laugh or weep at human folly the insight that "men, like the rest, are only a part of nature, and that I do not know how each part is connected with the whole of it, and how with the other parts. And I find that it is from the mere want of this kind of knowledge that certain things in Nature were formerly wont to appear to me vain, disorderly and absurd, because I perceive them only in part and mutilated, and they do not agree with our philosophic mind. But now I let every man live according to his own ideas. Let those who will, by all means die for their good, so long as I am allowed to live for the truth" (*The Correspondence of Spinoza,* 205–206).

It is a remark that is often quoted but little understood. The content of Spinoza's ideal of "living for the truth" is not transparent. Spinoza here connects it directly with his recognition of himself as part of a whole and hence as liable to partial and "mutilated" perception. The full articulation of the ideal of "living for the truth" will come only with the completion of *The Ethics.* The immediate effect of Spinoza's new insight, however, is to motivate him to engage more closely with the politics of truth in the Dutch Republic. To Oldenburg's bewilderment, Spinoza sees such en-

gagement as requiring that he turn his attention to what Oldenburg dismissively refers to as theological matters.

Spinoza's "living for the truth" demands both caution and courage—caution, to avoid what can disrupt the mind's free activity;
courage, to trust to that free intellectual activity as the sole arbiter
of truth. Spinoza saw the free activity of the mind as essential to
its access to truth and hence to its freedom; and he saw that freedom as at stake in the political exigencies of his time and place.
The well-lived life—construed as the life lived "for the truth"—
thus called first of all for understanding of the political preconditions of the life of the mind. Only when philosophizing could be
extricated from theologizing would the mind be enabled to give
the necessary assent to truth wherein its true freedom would be
attained.

The Politics of Truth

Spinoza is driven to write a treatise about the interpretation of
Scripture for three reasons, he tells the disgruntled Oldenburg in
a letter of September or October 1665: "1. The prejudices of the
Theologians; for I know that these are among the chief obstacles
which prevent men from directing their mind to philosophy; and
therefore I do all I can to expose them, and to remove them from
the minds of the more prudent. 2. The opinion which the common people have of me, who do not cease to accuse me falsely of
atheism; I am also obliged to avert this accusation as far as it is
possible to do so. 3. The freedom of philosophising, and of saying
what we think; this I desire to vindicate in every way, for here it is
always suppressed through the excessive authority and impudence
of the preachers" (*The Correspondence of Spinoza*, 206).

Spinoza has at this time shifted his attention away from the
work that will eventually become *The Ethics*; he is now occupied
with what will become *A Theologico-Political Treatise*.[11] The treatise

is a work about politics, no less than it is about the theologizing
that perplexed Oldenburg. On one level, Spinoza's interruption
of the *Ethics* was, as he said, an attempt to ensure that his own
philosophical views, when he eventually published them, might be
received with greater understanding. But he was also driven by a
broader political concern. He wanted to address what he saw as
the growing intolerance of free speech in the Dutch Republic—
the growing influence of the prejudiced preachers and the damag-
ing effects of their superstitions on the common people. A *Theologico-Political Treatise* was as much a political intervention as it was a
strategic move in Spinoza's own scholarly agenda. The politics
surrounding the threatened Dutch Republic provided a powerful
incentive for this shift in Spinoza's concerns. His writings would
increasingly reflect the vulnerability of the republic, and with it
the tradition of tolerance and freedom that—whatever its limitations—had indeed provided relative security for scholarly pursuits.

The mix of topics addressed in A *Theologico-Political Treatise* can
seem no less strange to political theorists of our own times than
it did to Oldenburg. He was bewildered by Spinoza's apparent
abandonment of serious concern with the metaphysical foundations of science to address "theological" issues. Modern readers
of the treatise are also often perplexed at finding political theory
together with issues of textual interpretation, prophecy, and miracles. The nature of the work makes more sense, however, in its
own political context.

The apparent tolerant attitudes of the Dutch Republic masked
complexities of which Oldenburg had no inkling; and the vexed
question of the relation between philosophy and theology lay at
their core. Spinoza would have been well aware that the politics of
debate on this issue were caught up with the future of intellectual
freedom in the republic—indeed with the future of the republic
itself. His shift of focus reflected concern with a changing political

situation that threatened the very possibility of the kind of intellectual life that he later presents in *The Ethics* as the life of virtue
and freedom.

The Cartesians had taken a skeptical attitude toward scriptural
accounts of miracles and, more generally, toward literal interpretations of biblical texts. Jonathan Israel, in his study of the Dutch
Republic, shows how the authority of Scripture had become not
just a scholarly issue but a political one. The Grand Pensionary,
Johan de Witt—well informed on Cartesian mathematics and attuned to the broader ramifications of Descartes's philosophy—
had strong political reasons to defuse the tensions surrounding
religious authority. He had sufficient insight into the philosophical issues to be able to mediate in overheated debates at the uni-
versities between the new philosophy and the powerful forces of
religious orthodoxy. By Israel's account, "De Witt wished to preserve freedom to philosophize, and philosophers, from the censorship of preachers and synods; but took the view that to achieve
this the States needed to enforce the separation of philosophy and
theology implied in Cartesian teaching."[12] Under De Witt's influence, compromises were reached that allowed agreement on an
edict that in effect gave political force to the separation of philosophy and theology, thus defeating attempts to restrict philosophical freedom. It was, however, a tenuous standoff.

This was the political context for Spinoza's apparent shift of
focus toward what Oldenburg saw as theologizing. In arguing in
A Theologico-Political Treatise for an approach to Scripture that separated the role of imagination in biblical narrative from the role
of intellect in philosophical understanding, Spinoza was acting in
the spirit of the earlier political endeavors of De Witt, while also
pursuing strategies for the reception of his own future publica-
tions. The future of the Dutch Republic had been increasingly
bound up with the personal fate of its Grand Pensionary, who had
been responsible for that edict enforcing the separation of phi-

losophy and theology; and both Spinoza's personal future and the
fate of his works were in turn tied to the fate of De Witt. Distrusted by the Dutch public, De Witt was attacked in anonymous
pamphlets blaming him for the humiliating capture of Utrecht by
the French. His brother Cornelis was arrested for allegedly plot-
ting against William of Orange, who had been elected Stadtholder
for Holland and Zeeland. Although Cornelis was acquitted, an
angry crowd gathered on 20 August 1672 outside the prison at
The Hague. Johan was led to believe that his brother had asked
him to come and escort him from the prison. While the brothers
were together in the prison the angry mob broke in to drag them
away to be hanged. In the violence that followed the brothers died
before reaching the scaffold; their bodies were then strung up and
torn to pieces by the crowd.

The massacre of the De Witts had a powerful impact on contemporary supporters of the republic; it was also to become an
image that epitomized for the European imagination the horrors
of mob violence. Alexandre Dumas fictionalized the incident in
his novel *The Black Tulip.* Spinoza's own shocked reaction was recorded by Leibniz, who visited him in 1676: "I have spent several
hours with Spinoza, after dinner. He said to me that, on the day of
the massacre of the De Witts, he wanted to go out at night and
post a placard near the site of the massacre, reading *ultimi barbaro-
rum.* But his host locked the doors to keep him from going out, for
he would be exposed to being torn to pieces."[13]

In *Spinoza: A Life* Steven Nadler has documented ways in which
Spinoza's name was already associated with the De Witts by Johan's Orangist opponents. It is doubtful that he actually had any
close connections with the Grand Pensionary, but an anonymous
pamphlet circulated in 1672 alleged that De Witt had offered him
the protection that made possible the publication of *A Theologico-
Political Treatise,* and that De Witt had in his possession a copy of
that book "brought forth from hell by the fallen Jew Spinoza, in

which it is proven, in an unprecedented, atheistic fashion, that the word of God must be explained and understood through Philosophy, and which was published with the knowledge of Mr Jan."[14]

In the immediate aftermath of the massacre the town councils were purged, and De Witt sympathizers replaced with Orangists, who supported Calvinist orthodoxies. Spinoza had now to deal with condemnation by the political as well as the religious authorities. In this poisonous context the hostile attacks that came from the Cartesians were not just differences of opinion about scholarly minutiae. They were caught up in broader political conflicts that threatened the very way of living that Spinoza was defending in his philosophical writings and trying to enact in his life. The Cartesians meanwhile were differentiating their views from his, not only in response to the inexorable demands of the truth as they perceived it, but also in response to political exigencies. The Republic of Philosophers was unraveling, no less than the political republic that had enabled it to flourish locally.

The initial reception of A Theologico-Political Treatise outside the Netherlands must have been for Spinoza no less disappointing than the hostility he encountered at home. He thought of himself as showing the way to true religious belief and to the true freedom of virtue. Even his loyal friend Oldenburg, however, was eventually disconcerted by the revelation of Spinoza's views on the divine nature. On 8 June 1675 Oldenburg wrote to Spinoza that certain things in the treatise seemed to him to "tend to harm religion." Oldenburg was clearly shocked by his initial reading of the work; but he came to revise his interpretation of it after discussions with their mutual acquaintance Tschirnhaus, who had also corresponded with Spinoza, especially about issues of freedom and necessity. Oldenburg's initial dismay gave way to a conviction that Spinoza was engaged in an extraordinarily important rethinking of the existence and nature of God. Oldenburg urged Spinoza to explain his views more fully to him—his "old and sincere friend, who whole-heartedly wishes the happiest issue of so divine an enterprise" (*The Correspondence of Spinoza*, 302–303).

Despite his renewed loyalty, it is now Oldenburg who expresses anxiety about the likely reception of Spinoza's new work, *The Ethics*. He urges caution in a letter of 22 July 1675. "Since I understand from your answer to me . . . that you intend to publish your Five-Part Treatise, allow me, I pray, to advise you out of your sincere affection for me not to include anything which may appear to undermine the practice of Religious virtue. Especially so since there is nothing for which this degenerate and wicked age seeks more eagerly than the kind of doctrines whose conclusions seem to give the encouragement to flagrant vices" (*The Correspondence of Spinoza*, 303). In an ironic reversal of his previous exasperation at Spinoza's apparent timidity, Oldenburg offers to distribute some copies of the book only on condition that Spinoza take the precaution of sending them covertly to "a certain Dutch merchant, settled in London" (*The Correspondence of Spinoza*, 304).

Oldenburg's newfound caution was understandable. He had been imprisoned in the Tower of London in 1667 on charges of espionage, arising from his correspondence with a French scientist. Clearly Spinoza had nonetheless been irritated by Oldenburg's reactions to *A Theologico-Political Treatise*. Asked to identify the sections of the work likely to give offense, Oldenburg mentions in a letter of 15 November 1675 Spinoza's allegedly ambiguous references to "god and nature," his apparent denial of the authority of miracles, and his having "concealed" his opinion about the status of Christ, his incarnation, and his atonement. Spinoza complains in a letter of November or December 1675 that Oldenburg has identified only the sections of the work that have in fact "tormented" the select group of readers who are his special concern. He has not made good his claim that the work is likely to undermine the practice of religious virtue. Spinoza's efforts to extricate the wisdom of true religion from doctrinal intolerance have clearly not been successful in Oldenburg's case. Whether his explanations of the work will please the Christians whom Oldenburg knows, Spinoza says curtly in conclusion, Oldenburg will be better able to judge than he (*The Correspondence of Spinoza*, 342–344).

Events closer to home after the circulation of *A Theologico-Political Treatise* had in any case already made Spinoza rethink his plans to publish *The Ethics*. In his letter of September 1675 to Oldenburg he had told him that while Spinoza was trying to get the work printed, a rumor circulated that he was about to publish a book in which he tried to show that there is no God. Certain theologians—perhaps those who had spread the rumor—had seized the opportunity to bring complaints against him before the Prince of Orange and the magistrates. Moreover, the "dull-witted Cartesians," in order to free themselves of suspicion, were continuing to denounce the opinions of Spinoza. He had therefore decided to postpone publication (*The Correspondence of Spinoza*, 334). The work would be published only after Spinoza's death, which was now not far off.

"True Religion" and "Free Necessity"

We saw earlier that the nature of God, his role in human life, and the nature and scope of human freedom are interconnected themes in Spinoza's philosophy and that they converge in his treatment of necessity. Oldenburg's alarm about Spinoza's emerging views on religion centered on the understanding of divine freedom and necessity. In maintaining that all things happen of necessity, Spinoza seemed, Oldenburg thought, to make God subject to fate. Spinoza responds in December 1675 that, on the contrary, to say that everything follows with inevitable necessity from the nature of God is to utter nothing more threatening to religious belief than a familiar and accepted doctrine: that it follows necessarily from the divine nature that God understands himself. No one,

Spinoza says, thinks that the necessity of such divine self-under-standing is a restriction on God's freedom; God understands him-self "absolutely freely, although necessarily." Nor, Spinoza insists, do his doctrines imply that we can shift the blame for human con-duct to God. Elaborating the point in a later letter, of 7 February 1676, Spinoza says that none of us, after all, can blame God for having given us "an infirm nature or an impotent mind." That would be no less absurd than for a circle to complain that God has not given it the properties of a sphere.

Spinoza extends this analysis to more plausible—though to his mind, no less absurd—complaints involving responsibility for human frailty. A child tormented by a kidney stone cannot com-plain that God has not given him a healthy body. Nor can a weak-minded man complain that God has denied him strength or the true knowledge and love of God, or that he has given him a na-ture so weak that he cannot restrain or moderate his desires. The central point here is that neither necessity nor excusability is at odds with responsibility. Spinoza criticizes Oldenburg for imply-ing that "if men sin from the necessity of their nature, they are excusable." Just as a horse is "excusable" for being a horse and not a man, Spinoza says, men can be "excusable" and nevertheless lack blessedness and be tormented in many ways. "He who goes mad from the bite of a dog is, indeed, to be excused, and yet is rightly suffocated." And he who is unable to control his desires and re-strain them through fear of the laws, "although he must be ex-cused for his weakness, is nevertheless unable to enjoy peace of mind, and the knowledge and love of God, but necessarily per-ishes" (*The Correspondence of Spinoza,* 357–359). It is hardly surpris-ing that Oldenburg was shocked by Spinoza's having broken the connection between responsibility and the will. Although Olden-burg was impressed by the awesome possibilities opened up by Spinoza's rethinking of the divine nature, he found the immedi-

ate conflicts with prevailing views of religion and morality disturbing.

Despite the hostile reception of the ideas expressed in *A Theologico-Political Treatise,* Spinoza seems to have been firmly convinced
that his philosophy was indeed the foundation of "true religion"
and virtue. Responding in February 1671 to one particularly vitri-
olic attack, Spinoza counterattacked with a scathing description
of the "bog" in which his critic was mired. "Namely, he finds nothing to please him in virtue itself and in understanding, but would
rather live under the impulse of his feelings, if it were not for this
single obstacle, that he fears punishment. Thus he abstains from
evil deeds, and follows the divine commands as a slave, unwillingly, and with a vacillating mind, and for this servitude he expects
to be honoured by God with gifts, far pleasanter to him than the
divine love itself, and the more so in proportion as the good which
he does is so repugnant to him, and he does it unwillingly. Hence
it comes that he believes that all those who are not restrained by
this fear, lead unbridled lives, and cast aside all religion" (letter to
Jacob Ostens, February 1671, *The Correspondence of Spinoza,* 256).

It is a shrewd diagnosis of the emotions motivating his more
vehement critics; and there is no doubting the strength of Spinoza's own emotions in response. His vision of true religion as resting on the necessity of philosophical thought—on the ideal of
"living for the truth," rather than on superstition—was intense.
"Does that man, I pray," he asks indignantly in his own defense,
"cast aside all religion who declares that God must be recognised
as the Highest Good, and that He must be loved as such with a
free spirit? And that in this alone does our highest felicity and supreme liberty consist? That, furthermore, the reward of virtue is
virtue itself? And the punishment of folly and weakness is the
folly itself?" (*The Correspondence of Spinoza,* 255). It was not, however,
only the self-serving preachers and superstitious zealots who were

disturbed by Spinoza's doctrines. They were also disconcerting to
some of his sympathetic fellow scholars who had not been able to
follow as far as he tried to lead them, even if they admired his
forthrightness. John Aubrey, in his essay on Hobbes in his *Brief
Lives,* quotes him as saying that A *Theologico-Political Treatise* "cut
through him a bar's length, for he durst not write so boldly."[15] Only
in the next century would the obvious next step be taken, most
boldly by David Hume—toward the idea that an atheist might be
no less capable than a religious believer of leading a virtuous life.

From the perspective of our own times, it may seem that Spinoza was undoubtedly an atheist. We have no reason, though, to
think that his rejection of the charge of atheism was not genuine.
He frequently insisted that rather than rejecting belief in God, he
was freeing that belief from the accretions of superstition; and it
is the treatment of theological matters in A *Theologico-Political Treatise* that allowed him to drive that wedge. He could be scathing in
his attack on superstition, and sarcastic at the expense of the religious zealots; but as he saw it, his criticisms were directed not at
religious belief as such, but at the distorted forms it takes on in
the popular imagination. His criticism of superstition could be
playfully skeptical as well as savagely sardonic. In a letter to Hugo
Boxel of September 1674 Spinoza adopts a teasing tone about his
friend's belief in ghosts. "On the one hand, you do not doubt the
existence of spirits of the male sex, but, on the other hand, you
doubt whether there are any of the female sex. This seems to me
more like fancy than a doubt. For if this really were your opinion
it would resemble rather the popular imagination which makes
God masculine and not feminine. I am surprised that those who
have seen naked spirits did not turn their eyes to the genital parts,
perhaps from fear or from ignorance of this difference" (*The Correspondence of Spinoza,* 277).

In A *Theologico-Political Treatise* Spinoza tried to offer a rationale
for separating the theological out from the philosophical, and with

it a strategy for removing superstitious accretions from the essence of religious belief; however, if his aims in publishing the work were to lessen hostility toward his metaphysical views and to strengthen the cause of free speech and thought in the ailing Dutch Republic, he must have been disappointed on both counts. His critique of superstition and the accompanying defense of freedom of thought and speech became themselves the target of savage attacks.

We have seen that Spinoza's rejection of more conventional ideas of providence in favor of divine "free necessity" was both a philosophical riposte to the Cartesians and a political intervention. It was a savage denunciation of the "impudent" religious zealots and an attempt to reclaim the freedoms of the Dutch Republic as the territory of what Spinoza saw as "true" religion—freed from superstition and resting on the clear grasp of necessary truth by means of the resources of the mind itself, rather than subject to external authority. It was an attempt to defend the two republics by bringing them both under the banner of true religion; and he is at the same time trying to defend himself against the zealots by nailing his colors to the mast as the defender of that true religion. Rather than being Spinoza the pernicious atheist, he would be Spinoza the true man of God. It was not to be. Spinoza the unbeliever he would remain—both in his contemporary context and in the subsequent history of Enlightenment thought.

I have argued that it was his version of providence as "free necessity" that allowed Spinoza to envision the writing of *A Theologico-Political Treatise* as a political intervention. This was crucial to his reshaping of the relations between philosophy and theology. De Witt had kept the anti-Cartesian zealots at bay, providing a space for the Republic of Philosophers by keeping apart the realms of the theological and the philosophical. That conceptual distinction was clearly visible to Oldenburg, as is evident in his consternation at Spinoza's apparently having forsaken philosophy for theology.

De Witt had given institutional force to their uncoupling, thus making room for the Republic of Philosophers within the Dutch Republic. Spinoza, apprehending with dread the destruction of both republics, set himself a daunting task. Rather than simply accepting the separation of theology and philosophy, as two warring armies—the two-worlds approach of De Witt—he would bring them together again; but the fusion would proceed in the opposite direction from the one that had been familiar before the intellectual and political challenges from the new philosophy.

The authority theology had once claimed over philosophy would now shift to philosophy—but only with respect to philosophy's proper concerns: access to truth and wisdom. Theology would now be aligned with the constructions of imagination. In the view of Spinoza such realignment was not dismissive of the proper claims of theology, for the imagination—as he would go on to demonstrate more fully in *The Ethics*—was not to be treated as a source of error. The individual mind does not err merely because it imagines; and as he insists in *A Theologico-Political Treatise,* theology is not to be regarded as erring because it presents the collective imaginings of a community. Imagination does not have the direct access to truth that Spinoza attributes to higher forms of knowledge; but its products are not to be treated lightly.

This was no simple reversal, then, of the relation of dominance between philosophy and theology. It had all the marks of a radical deconstruction of the old hierarchy of dominance. For Spinoza it was no insult to theology to associate it with the imagination, in contrast to philosophy's association with reason. True religion does not spurn imagination in favor of reason. But it is philosophy that now claims the authority to determine how our imaginings are to be understood. The authority of the theologians must give way to the philosophical ideal of living for the truth. The full content of that ideal will be given in *The Ethics* taken as a whole. In the *Treatise* Spinoza has already made it clear that he thinks that neither theology nor philosophy is subservient to the other. Wherever either one tries to dominate the other, he says in chapter 15, "one party will run wild with the aid of reason, and the other will run wild without the aid of reason" (A Theologico-Political Treatise, 190).

Theology is not bound to serve reason, nor reason theology; each has its own domain: the sphere of reason is "truth and wisdom"; the sphere of theology is "piety and obedience." They are not competing sources of access to truth. Theology, he insists, neither aims nor has the power to oppose reason. "She defines the dogmas of faith . . . only in so far as they may be necessary for obedience, and leaves reason to determine their precise truth: for reason is the light of the mind, and without her all things are dreams or phantoms" (A Theologico-Political Treatise, 195).

The theological zealots, as Spinoza thought of them, did act as if theology had the power to oppose philosophy, but in doing so the zealots failed to distinguish between the disciplines properly, and "absurdities, inconveniences and evils" were the result. For Spinoza, such dogmatists were among those he describes in chapter 20 as exhibiting "an inordinate desire for supremacy," rather than "the love of truth." They are among "the real disturbers of the peace," who "in a free state, seek to curtain the liberty of judgement which they are unable to tyrannize over" (A Theologico-Political Treatise, 264).

De Witt's attempted separation of theology and philosophy was a significant moment in the history of Enlightenment attempts to contain but also accommodate religion. It was a milestone in the emergence of the secular as an Enlightenment ideal. Spinoza's attempt to bring conceptual clarity to that distinction, and to bring the two realms of thought into new harmony, is another turning point in that history. Disconcerting though Spinoza's version of "true religion" was in the eyes of Oldenburg, it was not, as Spinoza himself saw it, irreligious. Just as Spinoza was to retain the repu-

tation of a notorious atheist rather than a true man of God, the
Enlightenment persona of the philosopher in general would never
be equated with that of the true man of God. Perhaps in the long
run it was just as well for both philosophy and religion. Spinoza's
account of their relation nonetheless forms an important thread
in our own heritage from Enlightenment thought on the idea of
the secular.

Spinoza rejected the view of providence as divine free will; he
thought it amounted to seeing the whole world as irrational—to
seeing gods and men as all mad together. His own idea of God's
"free necessity" offered a vision of a world in which natural and
man-made disasters—the miseries of plague and the madness of
war alike—called forth neither despairing tears nor scoffing laughter. A world freed from the supposed attentions of a transcendent,
purposeful God was for Spinoza also a world liberated from superstition and from the "excessive authority and impudence of
the preachers." To minds that could "live for the truth" it offered
an ideal that had some affinities with ancient ideas of gods and
men living in a shared "free necessity." It was no longer the gods
that mattered, but the truth. Spinoza offered a way for the Republic of Philosophers to reconnect with the Stoic cosmic city: it
is no longer the benign or malevolent divine will that matters, but
the truth, which governs the minds of men and gods alike.

7   Designer Worlds

In early Enlightenment thought, ideas of providence stood at the center of controversies about a range of issues that on the surface had little to do with what we now recognize as philosophy—issues of governance, of the authority of the state, of free speech and censorship, and of the nature and scope of science. As long as philosophy—not seen at this stage as sharply differentiated from science—had been subservient to theology, it had been possible for philosophical controversy to remain, for the most part, just that—disputes that divided the learned. Not that those discussions were by any means dispassionate. Rival theologies, and the rival philosophies attendant on them, could be hotly debated. With the shift in philosophy's traditional inclusion within theology, disputes about divine providence and about the nature of human and divine will became more frequently tied in with intense political power struggles.

Leibniz's *Theodicy*

The crossover between philosophical, theological, and political disputes was not in itself new. The Roman Stoics were often embroiled in political intrigues; and the theological disputes that framed Augustine's views on providence were part of a broader context in which the politics of church and state were entangled. There was something different, however, about the learned dis-

putes over divine providence in the hundred or so years starting
in the midseventeenth century. Philosophy and science had gained
a new intellectual autonomy, which could no longer be readily
controlled by the religious authority vested in theology. Freed
from those constraints, the "New Philosophy" could be a source
of radical challenge—not only to church authority but, in unpredictable and volatile ways, to the power of civil authorities.

Amid this ferment, the name Descartes was to become the symbol of an ominous break with tradition. It was also to become the
signifier of an even more threatening shift. Descartes would make
possible Spinoza—the symbol of disorderly atheism, of the repudiation of God, with all the chaos that such a rejection presaged;
and the two could not be easily distinguished. Whatever the real
differences between the two philosophies might be, Descartes
would come to represent the disturbing "New Philosophy" which
made possible the terrible disorder represented by Spinoza—the
rejection of the prevailing, ordered structure of the intellectual
and political worlds.

The idea of providence would be at the center of the intellectual upheaval that ensued; and in relation especially to this concept, Leibniz would come to be seen as the great synthesizer and
reconciler. Leibniz would come to represent the more moderate
forces of the Enlightenment—the reconciliation between religion
and philosophy. The contested concept of providence would mark
out the terrain on which the intellectually and politically tumultuous conflict between "radical" and "moderate" forces of Enlightenment would be fought out.

In some respects, the centrality of the idea of providence has
a clear rationale. Providence—at least in the sense of "special"
providence—was readily associated with the idea of miracles, and
hence with the eruption of the supernatural into the natural world.
The "new Science" seemed at least implicitly to deny the possibility of miracles and hence to threaten religious beliefs that drew

support from them. Of course special providence, with its connotations of divine intervention in the natural processes of the world, could be rejected without rejection of broader ideas of providence as immanent in the natural order of the world itself. Such ideas of an immanent providence—providence without divine intervention—seemed to hark back to non-Christian ideas of a godless providence. Although Spinoza himself saw his philosophy as a rejection of Stoic, no less than Cartesian, ideas of providence, some of his critics—not without reason—saw "Spinozism" as a reversion to an older pagan philosophy.

Inadequate though much of the contemporary interpretation of Spinoza's philosophy undoubtedly was, the symbolic force of the name Spinoza took on a life of its own as a perceived threat to the established order of religion and civil authority. Even thinkers who were broadly sympathetic to the break with the past that the "new Science" represented took "Spinoza" as a symbol of the more extreme, more radical wing of Enlightenment thought. Jonathan Israel, in his study *Radical Enlightenment: Philosophy and the Making of Modernity, 1650–1750,* has traced the fascinating dynamics of the triangulation process through which thinkers would use Spinoza as the foil against which they could identify themselves, by opposition, with the more moderate versions of Enlightenment aspirations. Europe's war of philosophies during the early Enlightenment, he observes, was not confined to the intellectual sphere; nor was it a straightforward two-way contest between new enlightened thinking and older tradition. "Rather, the rivalry between moderate mainstream and radical fringe was always as much an integral part of the drama as that between moderate enlightenment and conservative opposition. In this triangular battle of ideas what was ultimately at stake was what kind of belief-system should prevail in Europe's politics, social order and institutions, as well as in high culture and, no less, in popular attitudes."[1]

As is often the case in the history of philosophy, the symbolic force of Spinoza's philosophy came to diverge considerably from its actual content. It is true, as we have seen, that the *Ethics* contains a scathing attack on the idea of providence. But we have also seen that Spinoza was able nonetheless to develop an ethic of freedom and virtue based on the acceptance of necessity—an ethic that was continuous in important ways with ancient versions of providence. In the immediate reception of his thought, however, the nuances of his critique of prevailing ideas of providence, and more generally of religion, were largely lost.

Leibniz, unlike many of Spinoza's contemporary critics, had read and given serious attention to the actual content of Spinoza's philosophy; and he was in a better position than most to grasp its connections with earlier traditions. In responding to Spinoza's rejection of providence, however, he was responding to the symbolism of Spinozism and to the political significance of that potent construct, no less than to the philosophy itself. It is ironic that, for all his attention to detail, Leibniz's own philosophy was later to be simplified and satirized by Voltaire as the ridiculed doctrine that we are living in "the best of all possible worlds." Spinoza had come to symbolize atheistic rejection of God's concern for the world. Leibniz would come to epitomize facile optimism about the world and the place of human beings within it.

Out of the Labyrinth: "Christian Fate" in Leibniz's Theodicy

Leibniz's *Theodicy* (1710) was the only work by this extraordinarily productive mathematician, philosopher, and diplomat published during his lifetime. It was largely a polemical work, directed against the critique of divine providence offered by Pierre Bayle, the French author of the famous *Critical and Historical Dictionary*, published in 1697. As its name suggests, Leibniz's set of essays attempts to reconcile divine providence with the existence of evil; but Leibniz also sets himself the broader task of reconciling freedom with necessity. In the preface to the work he declares his intention to examine one of the two "famous labyrinths" where human reason often goes astray. This first labyrinth is the "great question of the Free and the Necessary, above all in the production and the origin of Evil." Leibniz addressed the other "labyrinth" in his famous discussion of mathematical and metaphysical aspects of continuity and of "the indivisibles which appear to be the elements thereof." That labyrinth, he remarks in the preface to *Theodicy*, exercises only philosophers. The labyrinth of freedom, necessity, and evil, by contrast, "perplexes almost all the human race."[2]

The ambitious project of reconciliation that Leibniz sets himself in *Theodicy* is nothing less than to articulate a Christian version of the ancient concept of fate that had always seemed so opposed to Christian doctrine. He approaches the task with verve, presenting it facetiously in his preface as if it is itself a contribution to the wars against the enemies of Christianity. There is, he says, a false conception of necessity which, applied in practice, yields the "lazy reason" associated with *Fatum Mahometanum*—"fate after the Turkish fashion," so called because it is said of Turkish soldiers that they do not shun danger or even abandon places infected with the plague. In a later section, Leibniz mischievously observes that although the supposed fearlessness of the Turks may rest partly on the sophism of "lazy reason," hashish may well be a more important factor—and that in any case their "resolute spirit" seems to have greatly diminished in his own times (*Theodicy*, sec. 55, p. 153).

The version of fate that Leibniz, by way of contrast, calls *Fatum Stoicum* was less bleak than Stoicism was often painted in his times. Stoicism, he says in the preface, "did not divert men from the care of their affairs," but it did tend to bring them tranquillity with regard to what happened in their lives—through the consideration of necessity, which "renders our anxieties and our vexations needless." In that respect, Leibniz suggests—with generosity toward the ancient pagans—the Stoics were not far removed from the teachings of Christ, who compares anxieties regarding the morrow with the needless troubles a man would incur in laboring to increase his stature. The Stoics, he continues, lacked the Christian conviction that God, "being altogether good and wise, has care for everything." Lacking the sources of entire confidence that are available to the Christian, they could therefore impart only a "forced patience," rather than true contentment. The Christian not merely endures necessity; he knows that it is not even possible for him to wish for anything better than what his God has provided for him. "It is as if one said to men: Do your duty and be content with that which shall come of it, not only because you cannot resist divine providence, or the nature of things (which may suffice for tranquillity, but not for contentment), but also because you have to do with a good master. And this is what may be called *Fatum Christianum*" (preface, *Theodicy,* 54, 55).

At the core of Leibniz's "Christian Fate" is the sense of fittingness—the sense of things being as they are because they are the best possible, the best even thinkable as able to exist. To give content to this version of providence, Leibniz must be able to attribute to his God a kind of freedom that is not subject to the absolute necessity that governed both Stoic providence and Spinoza's God as substance. Free action, Leibniz insists, must be exempt not only from constraint but also from real necessity. "God himself, although he always chooses the best, does not act by an absolute necessity" (preface, *Theodicy,* 61). Leibniz also insists that this freedom from "absolute necessity" is not a freedom of "equipoise" between competing options. What God does he does freely but not from indifference.

This is Leibniz's way out of the labyrinth of freedom, necessity, and evil. Evil has a source other than the will of God; he does not choose it, but he does in his infinite wisdom permit it. The old dilemma that Augustine faced—of reconciling faith and reason, grace and free will—finds its resolution for Leibniz in the intricate interplay of divine will and infinite knowledge. "Faith . . . is a gift of God, who has predestined the faith of the elect, for reasons lying in a superior decree, which dispenses grace and circumstance in accordance with God's supreme wisdom" (preface, *Theodicy,* 62). God's knowledge of the infinite possibilities for the worlds he might make incorporates not only what human beings will freely do, but also all the operations of his healing grace in response to the evil they do.

From Leibniz's perspective, the scourge of Spinozism resides in its denial of true freedom to God. Spinoza, he says, insists more or less that "all has come from the first cause or from primitive Nature by a blind and geometrical necessity, with complete absence of capacity for choice, for goodness and for understanding in this first source of things." For Leibniz, by contrast, the nature of "active force and the laws of motion" is such that they have no "geometrical necessity"; they are dependent, rather, on "the fittingness of things," on God's choice in accordance with "the principle of the best" (preface, *Theodicy,* 67, 68).

Having ridiculed Spinoza's treatment of necessity as allegedly extending to everything the absolute necessity of mathematical truths, Leibniz now offers his own version of universal mathematical order. Just as there are appearances of irregularity in mathematics, which nonetheless issue finally in "a great order" when one has finally reached full understanding of them, so too apparent disorder in the world would, if we only knew enough, be seen as part of the great encompassing order in accordance with which God has chosen what will be. Whereas Spinoza, in Leibniz's view, would see no difference between the necessity of mathematics and the necessity of individual events, Leibniz sees individual events as resulting from the exercise of the divine will, choosing the best possible order. "According to my principles all individual events, without exception, are consequences of general acts of will" (*Theodicy,* sec. 241, p. 277).

In elaborating his version of the ordered world, Leibniz takes up and extends the old Stoic idea of the interconnections of all things within an ordered whole. His world is the whole collection of contingent things, all so interconnected that the lack of any one of them would involve the existence instead of a different possible world. There is an infinity of other such possible worlds—all equally possible, each holding equal claim to existence with the one we have. The existence of the actual world, Leibniz reasons, presupposes that an intelligent being has fixed upon one of them—a god who must have both *understanding* to consider the alternatives and *will* to choose among them. Leibniz cleverly grafts his adaptation of Stoic ideas about interconnection onto traditional Christian ideas of the divine attributes. "Power relates to *being,* wisdom or understanding to *truth,* and will to *good*" (*Theodicy,* sec. 7, p. 127). God as intelligent cause is infinite and perfect in power, wisdom, and goodness. His divine understanding is the source of *essences;* and his will is the source of *existences.* Divine providence here becomes the exercise of a loving, all-powerful will, guided by infinite wisdom.

Leibniz's reasoning is a powerful synthesis of Christian doctrine with philosophical principles. Its roots go back to pre-Christian sources. Plato, he reminds his readers in section 20 of *Theodicy,* said in the *Timaeus* that the world originated in Understanding united to Necessity; and other ancient thinkers united God and Nature (135). He gives those ancient ideas "a reasonable meaning": God will be the Understanding; Necessity will be the essential nature of things—the "eternal verities" that are the objects of the divine understanding. In this inward and abiding object of the divine understanding are to be found both the primitive form of good and the origin of evil.

Whereas the Neoplatonists located evil in the unfolding of the eternal ideas into matter, Leibniz allows it to inhabit the "Region of the Eternal Verities." These eternal verities will contain the "ideal" cause of evil as well as good, although, properly speaking, evil consists in privation rather than in anything positive. Thus God, for Leibniz as for Augustine, is not responsible for the existence of evil. But for Leibniz the "eternal verities" that are the object of God's understanding contain the possibility of evil. "As this vast Region of Verities contains all possibilities it is necessary that there be an infinitude of possible worlds, that evil enter into divers of them, and that even the best of all contain a measure thereof. Thus has God been induced to permit evil" (*Theodicy*, sec. 21, p. 136).

Not all evils pose the same degree of difficulty in the challenge of reconciling God's goodness with what he is prepared to "permit." Leibniz distinguishes three forms of "evil." The term may be taken metaphysically, physically, and morally. *Metaphysical evil* consists in mere imperfection, *physical evil* in suffering, and *moral evil* in sin. It is the categories of *physical* and *moral* evil that pose the real challenge of reconciliation with God's goodness. God does not directly create them; but he does "permit" them. Moral evil is the price of the great good of human freedom. As for *physical* evil, it can be said that God wills it, though not "absolutely." He does not will it for itself, but as part of something else that he does directly will, often as a penalty owing to guilt, and often also as a means to an end—that is, to prevent greater evils or to obtain greater good. In choosing physical evil as a penalty, God might also want it to serve as "amendment and example." For "evil often serves to make us savour good the more; sometimes too it contributes to a greater perfection in him who suffers it, as the seed that one sows is subject to a kind of corruption before it can germinate: this is a beautiful similitude, which Jesus Christ himself used" (*Theodicy*, sec. 23, p. 137).

In Leibniz's view of human suffering serving a "higher end" are echoes of Augustine, but Leibniz has pushed much further than either the Stoics or Augustine the idea of the interconnection of things as an active ordering on the part of providence. Whereas divine justice was for Augustine the attribute under which God was concerned with the ordering of things, Leibniz's God seems driven by a desire more akin to the challenge of solving a mathematical challenge. Augustine saw divine justice as putting things in their rightful place by aligning punishment with guilt. Leibniz's God, by contrast, acts out of a desire to achieve the greatest possible good. Achieving that good, however, involves solving a challenge of infinite complexity: he must bring together compossible things in such a way that the greatest possible reality is achieved with the greatest possible harmony among the component parts. Leibniz's God strives to create as much reality as possible, without falling into the contradictions which would demand that some realities prevent others from existing.

The creation of the best possible world requires the exercise of divine judgment, and that includes provision for the inevitable consequences of the existence of imperfection. For Leibniz divine judgment—to the extent that it is comprehensible to us—is more akin to the choices of a wise provider, reconciling competing needs for continued existence, rather than the decisions of an Augustinian almighty judge, tasked with balancing evil with the compensatory good of punishment. "God being inclined to produce as much good as possible, and having all the knowledge and all the power necessary for that, it is impossible that in him there be fault, or guilt, or sin; and when he permits sin, it is wisdom, it is virtue" (*Theodicy*, sec. 26, p. 138).

Leibniz insists that God is no more the cause of sin than, as he puts it, the current in a river is the cause of the drag on a heavily loaded boat; the cause of what is defective in human action is not God but the limitations in our receptivity to his causal force (*Theodicy*, sec. 30, p. 140). In part 2 of *Theodicy*, Leibniz responds to Bay-

le's ridicule of the supposedly all-good God who nonetheless allows evil in the world for whose existence he is responsible. God,
Leibniz says there, permits evil "justly" and directs it willingly toward the good. In contrast to the ancient gods, Leibniz's God cannot be compelled by any higher necessity to comply with evil. He
is not like Jupiter, who fears the Styx when he swears by it. His
own wisdom is "the greatest judge he can find, there is no appeal
from its judgements: they are the decrees of destiny." Moreover,
"the eternal verities, objects of his wisdom," Leibniz continues,
"are more inviolable than the Styx. These laws and this judge do
not constrain: they are stronger, for they persuade. Wisdom only
shows God the best possible exercise of his goodness: after that,
the evil that occurs is an inevitable result of the best. I will add
something stronger: to permit the evil, as God permits it, is the
greatest goodness" (*Theodicy,* sec. 121, pp. 194–195).

Leibniz's system thus aims to preserve human freedom despite
the ordering of the entire universe by divine providence, and to
preserve divine providence despite the manifest reality of the evil
of human sin and suffering. Nothing necessitates one course of
action over another for either God or human beings. True, God
has chosen to make real the possible world in which we would do
whatever we do; but our choice is not canceled by God's; rather, it
is taken into account in God's choice. Whatever we do is included
in the complete integration of events into the Leibnizian world,
which God, knowing what would happen freely, chose to make
real. "Thus, if the smallest evil that comes to pass in the world
were missing in it, it would no longer be this world; which, with
nothing omitted and all allowance made, was found the best by
the Creator who chose it" (*Theodicy,* sec. 9, pp. 128–129).

The only necessity to which we are subject here, Leibniz repeatedly insists, is of the kind he calls hypothetical necessity. In
fuller discussion of this point in chapter 13 of his *Discourse on Metaphysics,* and in his extensive correspondence on that work with

the French philosopher Antoine Arnauld, he illustrates his view of human freedom with reference to Caesar's momentous act of freely crossing the Rubicon. Nothing is in itself impossible about Caesar's not crossing; but he does so in conformity with divine anticipation of his doing so. It is therefore impossible ex hypothesi for it not to happen. Yet this is no restriction on human free will. To accord with God's choice of the best of all possible worlds, all we have to do is to do what we want. The connection between causes and effects, in accordance with which God has made this actual world, finds reflection in the conscious choices made by human beings. Still, Leibniz insists again in *Theodicy,* this preordained interconnection of all things only inclines us to act, without necessitating our actions. The events remain in themselves contingent. The maxim that "the prevailing inclination always triumphs" remains intact (*Theodicy,* sec. 53, p. 152).

The appeal to providence is thus central to Leibniz's *Fatum Christianum.* The kind of tranquillity it represents is supposed to be found in the recognition of the order of the universe. Every detail of the future is determined, but because our limited understanding cannot grasp it, we must fall back on doing our duty "according to the reason that God has given us; and according to the rules that he has prescribed for us; and thereafter we must have a quiet mind, and leave to God himself the care for the outcome" (*Theodicy,* sec. 58, p. 154). In contrast to what Leibniz dismisses as *Fatum Mahometanum,* his version of acquiescence is experienced not as passivity, but as a "wonderful *spontaneity.*" The "lazy reason" associated with fatalism "overthrows forethought and good counsel" in its assertion of a "preposterous and unendurable fatality" (*Theodicy,* sec. 59, p. 155). That fatality is thrust on us from outside. His own version of the tranquillity that resides in the acceptance of necessity, by contrast, involves a "spontaneity" that comes from recognizing our own place in the system of preestablished harmony.

The Stoics, in Leibniz's interpretation, drew a blasphemous conclusion from the principle that the evil that exists in the world serves to augment the good. For them, evils must be endured with patience because they are necessary—not only to the well-being and completeness of the universe, but also to the felicity, perfection, and conservation of God himself. Marcus Aurelius, he observes, was not at his most reasonable when he endorsed this view in his *Meditations*. For it was foolish to think that a thing somehow becomes pleasing just because it is necessary (*Theodicy,* sec. 217, p. 203). Furthermore, something that is evil for me will not cease to be so just because it is for my master's good, unless this good somehow reflects back to me. The Stoics' error, in Leibniz's diagnosis, resides in their assumption that the good of the universe must please God himself, because they imagined God as the soul of the world. His own God, by contrast, is *intelligentia extramundana,* or rather *supramundana* (*Theodicy,* sec. 217, p. 264). He is not identified with the world. Moreover, he acts to do good and not to receive it. His bliss is perfect and can receive no increase, either from within or from without.

Although the God of Leibniz transcends the world, his accentuation of the Stoics' doctrine of interconnection means that human choices become part of God's choice of the particular world he will create. *Fatum* now takes on for Leibniz a new quality—a "good" sense, which is not contrary to freedom. Providing his own perhaps eccentric etymology, he suggests the word derives from *fari:* to speak or "pronounce." For Leibniz *fatum* signifies "a judgement, a decree of God, the award of his wisdom" (*Theodicy,* sec. 228, p. 269). This modification to the idea of fate reinforces Leibniz's conviction of the ethical superiority of his version of the acceptance of necessity over that offered by the Stoics: "It is no small thing to be content with God and with the universe, not to fear what destiny has in store for us, nor to complain of what befalls us. Acquaintance with true principles gives us this advantage, quite other than the Stoics and the Epicureans derived from their philosophy. There is as much difference between true morality and theirs as there is between joy and patience: for their tranquillity was founded only on necessity, while ours must rest upon the perfections and beauty of things, upon our own happiness" (*Theodicy*, sec. 254, pp. 282–283).

The Leibnizian Synthesis

The Spinoza attacked in *Theodicy* is a more subtle construct than the versions of *Fatum Mahometanum* and *Fatum Stoicum* that Leibniz ridicules. He does nonetheless present Spinoza's version of necessity as a grotesque doctrine—as an "opinion so bad, and indeed so inexplicable" that it is barely worth wasting time refuting it. Spinoza, according to Leibniz, "appears to have explicitly taught a blind necessity, having denied to the Author of Things understanding and will, and assuming that good and perfection relate to us only, and not to him" (*Theodicy*, sec. 173, p. 234). In claiming that all things exist of necessity, Spinoza has denied any act of choice to God (*Theodicy*, sec. 372, p. 349).

Leibniz enlists Bayle as an ally in his attack on Spinoza, quoting his ridicule of the Spinozists for their alleged embarrassment at having to say that it was as impossible from all eternity that Spinoza should not die at The Hague as it is impossible for two and two to make six. It is a conclusion, Leibniz sneers, that "disheartens, affrights and stirs the mind to revolt, because of the absurdity it involves, diametrically opposed to common sense" (*Theodicy*, sec. 173, p. 235). Leibniz wants his God to be neither caught in the stasis of indifference nor compelled, as he thinks Spinoza's God is, to compulsively produce all that is possible. Leibniz's God is "inclined" rather than "compelled" to act; drawn toward what is clearly the best, rather than fixed in indifferent equipoise.

Unlike Spinoza, Leibniz insists on a distinction between will and understanding; and in contrast to Descartes he insists that the divine will is restrained by the necessities of the laws of reason. The freedom of his God is grounded in necessity; and human freedom is modeled on that convergence of freedom and necessity. The will's freedom is exercised in the effort to act in accordance with judgment. Understanding and will may fail to coincide. There can be a long passage "from mind to heart," but there is no "freedom of indifference." A soul that perversely acted against what it perceived as its own good would have to be seen as more imperfect and less free than a soul that lacked such freedom.

It is all an ingenious synthesis of elements from Cartesianism and Spinozism—of will and understanding, freedom and necessity. An all-powerful will, acting in accordance with infinite wisdom, has chosen this world from an infinity of possibilities; and—on the hypothesis of that free choice—every detail of the world necessarily follows. In the end, though, it all seems to rest on another synthesis—of reason and faith: of rational argument and trust in a divine providence that lies outside and beyond what we can ever fully comprehend. "I have proved," Leibniz insists, "that God cannot fail to produce the best; and from that assumption it follows that the evils we experience could not have been reasonably excluded from the universe, since they are there" (*Theodicy,* sec. 218, p. 264). Given that things are this way, it must be the case that all is for the best.

Powerful though this all-inclusive system may be—once the starting point is granted—it also seems undeniably circular. Supreme wisdom, "united to a goodness that is no less infinite" can only have "chosen the best." Once we grant the infinity of possible worlds confronting such a divine understanding, it is no surprise that God must needs have chosen the best, since all he does is in accordance with supreme reason. With all that conceptual machinery in place, the resolution of the apparent inconsistency be-

tween divine goodness and human misery is straightforward: a
world without sin and suffering would not be a "better" world, for
the existence of evil is connected with the existence of all else in
this world that an all-powerful, infinitely loving and knowing God
has chosen as the best possible.

Leibniz's appeal to the conformity between faith and reason
seems to bolster the circularity in the reasoning about good and
evil. The city of God must be, he says, "the most perfect of all possible states," for it was formed and is perpetually governed by "the
greatest and best of all Monarchs." According to this reasoning, it
can only be through misperception, through an appeal to imperfect "appearances," that anything can seem to be at odds with the
belief that we live in the best possible world. Rejection of Leibnizian optimism must involve opposition to "the proofs of reason
and the revelations of faith" (*Theodicy*, sec. 221, pp. 265–266). It
is all a remarkable intellectual construct. A committed Spinozist
might well find in the audacious blend of faith and reason that
characterizes Leibniz's version of providence yet another illustration of the ways in which gods and men can be all mad together.

In contrast with Spinoza's rejection of the supernatural, Leibniz's idea of God retains something impenetrable. Leibniz rejects
the Cartesian idea that the will of God is the source of the eternal
truths. That would suggest, he thinks, that they are valid only so
long as God so wills. "The Will of God," he insists, "is not independent of the rules of Wisdom" (*Theodicy*, sec. 193, p. 247). Unlike Spinoza's God, however, Leibniz's version of the deity acts for
a reason; and his purposes are not accessible to us. Bayle had caus-
tically noted that the glory derived from the unhappiness of others by someone who is their master is a false glory. Leibniz's response was, "If we knew the city of God just as it is, we should see
that it is the most perfect state which can be devised"; but of
course we do not know that city in its entirety and cannot grasp
the "supreme order" governing the reasons that have determined
its existence (*Theodicy*, sec. 124, p. 198).

Throughout much of *Theodicy* runs a tone of pious trust that echoes some of the quainter convictions of all-pervasive purpose that Cicero has his Epicurean persona ridicule in his *On the Nature of the Gods*. According to Leibniz, Nature needs animals and plants in order to provide marvels for intelligent creatures to wonder at, so that they can exercise their capacity for reason.

Intellectually ingenious though the Leibnizian synthesis is, its persuasiveness ultimately rests on emotional resonances—on the appeal of an emotional, even an aesthetic, stance toward human suffering, without which the intellectual structure would remain an empty shell. Leibniz himself comes close to acknowledging this in a passage in *Theodicy* where he describes the "intellectual plea-sure" human beings can take in the contemplation of the unpleas-ant—and in the zest that the disagreeable can add to what might otherwise be bland experience. "A little acid, sharpness or bitter-ness is often more pleasing than sugar; shadows enhance colours; and even a dissonance in the right place gives relief to harmony. We wish to be terrified by rope dancers on the point of falling and we wish that tragedies shall well-nigh cause us to weep. Do men relish health enough, or thank God enough for it, without having ever been sick? And is it not most often necessary that a little evil render the good more discernible, that is to say, greater?" (sec. 12, p. 130).

It all rests on our readiness to be reconciled, for the sake of God's higher purposes, to the existence of the shadows in the beautiful picture—to find a "fittingness" in even the most nega-tive aspects of our lives. The sense of fittingness that Leibniz as-cribes to the creator's choices has its human emotional analogue. Leibnizian optimism seems in the end as much a precondition for our being persuaded by his reasoning as it is a rational conse-quence of it. It was for this determination to look on the bright side that the figure of Leibniz would later be pilloried. The intri-cate intellectual synthesis in which Leibniz brings together ele-ments taken from the Stoics, from Descartes, and from Spinoza

would be generally ignored in favor of Voltaire's caricature of him
as the intellectual hero Pangloss—the inane tutor and mentor of
the hapless Candide.

Voltaire on the "Wretched Gamble" of Life

Unfair though Voltaire's caricature may be to the subtlety of Leibniz's metaphysics, *Candide* does offer a powerful challenge to the
emotional upshot of Leibnizian optimism. Written at white heat,
this short satire, in which the young, eternally trusting Candide
wanders through the horrors of the "best of all possible worlds,"
offers a devastating critique of the accommodation of human
misery in a world supposedly chosen by an all-good and all-powerful God.

It was the Lisbon earthquake of 1 November 1755 that focused
Voltaire's anger on the grotesqueness of attempting to justify human suffering through an appeal to its place in an all-encompassing providential order. The earthquake was what we would now
call a natural disaster—in the category Leibniz would have called
physical rather than moral evil. As the story of Candide unfolds,
that distinction is deliberately blurred. Physical evils are compounded by the inadequate responses of human beings, by their
failure to do what lies within their control to alleviate human misery; and that failure is fed by the folly of philosophical interpretations of evil. The anger of the satire is directed at those who offer
as a response to human suffering the idea that evils are permitted
by divine providence because they somehow contribute to a better world overall. *Candide* is a savage critique of the idea that human misery serves the purposes of divine justice—or indeed any
divine purpose.

The Lisbon earthquake had at the time a profound impact on
the collective imagination. Clerics fulminated about its significa-
tion as the manifestation of divine wrath. For them, Lisbon repre-

sented divine justice wreaked on a wicked cosmopolitanism—on a society suffering from the erosion of traditional morals and religion. The philosophical responses were more complex. Some saw in the event itself a challenge to the ideas of contemporary Deists—to belief in a "natural" religion answering to the empirical experience of an ordered world, rather than sustained by revelation. For the critics of the Deists Lisbon posed a challenge to the idea of a providential order inherent in the world itself—as distinct from a transcendent, purposeful creator. How, they asked, could there be such misery in the world if benign purpose is immanent in it? But not all the philosophers who grappled with the significance of the earthquake saw it as a refutation of the idea of divine order. Rousseau argued only that it showed the folly of human beings, responsible for their own misfortune because they had gathered together in such a big city.[3]

Voltaire's analysis of the event was different both from Rousseau's and from that of critics of the Deists. He was no Deist, though he did give limited support to some of their views. In a letter to d'Alembert, he defined Deism as "the pure adoration of a supreme being, freed from all superstition."[4] He resisted in Deism its tendency to go beyond that, in the attempt to read the natural world as somehow expressing a divinely endowed moral law. Voltaire's critique of responses to the earthquake was in any case directed not at the idea of divine providence but rather at the moral deficiency in responding to such a catastrophe with philosophical justifications for human misery. His main target was not the belief in God as such, but the superstitious belief in a moral law based on the recognition of purposeful design.

Voltaire wrote his *Poem on the Disaster of Lisbon* within a month of the earthquake. His immediate response to the catastrophe provided the catalyst for the philosophical debate that ensued. The terms of his response were clear from the start: our gaze should be focused on human folly, for which we can own responsibility; the issue of divine justice has no place in the consideration of human misery.

Whereas Rousseau bemoans the error of life in the city, Voltaire's wrath is directed at those who avoid taking responsibility for what we ourselves can control, in directing the blame toward natural disasters. In a letter written soon after the earthquake, he wrote that men "do themselves more harm on their little mole-hill than does nature." "More men are slaughtered in our wars," he says there, "than are swallowed up by earthquakes."[5] The enormity of the earthquake, Voltaire thought, should direct our attention to the madness of the avoidable misery we inflict on one another. "What a wretched gamble is the game of human life," he comments in another letter about the earthquake. "That ought to teach men not to persecute each other, for while a few holy scoundrels burn a few fanatics, the earth swallows up one and all."[6] It is a perspective he will later exploit in *Candide,* in presenting horrific instances of inhumanity against the backdrop of the dramatic disappearances and reappearances of his characters—swallowed up as the earth swallows its prey, and just as randomly resurrected.

Misguided philosophers, Voltaire complained in his poem on Lisbon, tranquilly seek the causes of the event; they would do better to weep. He already had Leibnizian optimism in his sights:

> One day all will be good, that is our hope;
> All is good today, that is the illusion.[7]

In place of philosophical speculation, Voltaire urged a response of simple pity. That did not stem the tide of philosophizing—and his poem itself, of course, went beyond the recommended response of weeping—but it set the scene for his more sustained and virulent attack on philosophies of optimism in *Candide,* published in 1759. In the story of the wanderings of the naive Candide, Voltaire weaves the Lisbon earthquake into a narrative of disasters—both "natural" and man-made—which afflict his characters with endless miseries. The suffering caused directly by storms and shipwrecks, earthquakes and plagues, may be classifiable as what Leibniz would call physical rather than moral evils; however, the human responses of Voltaire's characters to the succession of tragedies render the philosophical distinction meaningless.

Candide's friend James, the lovable Anabaptist, goes to the rescue of a frenzied sailor who has been thrown into the sea in a storm as their boat approaches Lisbon. Human responsibility and accident are interconnected in this catastrophe: the sailor has lost his balance after assaulting James, who was trying to help prevent the ship from sinking. The rescued sailor allows the good James to perish without even deigning to look at him. Candide sees his friend reappear for a moment before sinking, but is stopped by Pangloss from leaping into the sea after him. The Lisbon harbor, Pangloss reasons, was "formed expressly for the Anabaptist to drown in."[8] As he is offering his a priori proof of this view, the ship splits open and everyone perishes except Pangloss, Candide, and the brutal sailor. And so it all goes on.

Pangloss's idiocies reflect the Leibnizian accommodation of evil into the best of all possible worlds. Voltaire takes aim here not only at the insensitivity of that response to human suffering, but also at ready rationalization of inaction. Pangloss engages in pompous philosophizing when he might instead take appropriate action. "All is for the best," he assures the wounded and distressed Candide. "For if there's a volcano at Lisbon, it couldn't be anywhere else. For it's impossible for things not to be where they are. For all is well" (Candide, 30).

Each character in the tale has his or her own recitation of horrors. The old woman who recites to Candide her tale of appalling atrocities predicts, rightly, that he will hear similar tales from all the passengers on the ship that is taking them to Cádiz—that all will claim to be the most miserable of human beings. In response to their narrated horrors, Candide regrets the loss of Pangloss, who has—temporarily, it seems—suffered death by hanging in an auto-da-fé: "He would have told us admirable things about the physical and moral evils that cover the earth and the sea" (*Candide,* 50). Pangloss himself, once he reappears in the final stages of the story, admits that he has always suffered horribly, but "having once maintained that all was for the best, he still maintained it, without believing it" (*Candide,* 117).

Throughout, Voltaire's focus remains not on the issue of whether good in fact outweighs evil but on the grotesqueness of presenting such debates as a response to human suffering. "I don't know what scales your Pangloss would use to weigh the misfortunes of men and judge their sorrows," says Candide's friend the Manichean Martin, who is skeptical about all possibility of human happiness. "'You're a bitter man,' said Candide. 'That's because I've lived,' said Martin" (*Candide,* 98).

Political and religious events, as well as "natural" disasters, form the backdrop to Voltaire's parade of misery. In letters commenting on, among other things, the execution of the British admiral Byng—for allegedly having made insufficient effort to kill the enemy during the Seven Years' War with the French—Voltaire declared that the world was "completely mad."[9] He revisits that specific form of madness with particularly black irony in *Candide.* "He fought a battle with a French admiral," Martin tells the perplexed Candide, as they watch the execution from their boat off the coast of England, "and it was decided that he wasn't close enough to him." "'But,'" said Candide, "'the French admiral was just as far away from the English admiral.' 'That's undeniable' was the answer. 'But in this country it's good to kill an admiral now and then, to encourage the others'" (*Candide,* 92–93).

Through all the horrors of their lives Voltaire's characters maintain an unquenchable enthusiasm for life. "I've wanted to kill myself a hundred times," the old woman tells Candide, "but I still love life. That ridiculous weakness is perhaps one of our most pernicious inclinations. What could be more stupid than to persist in carrying a burden that we constantly want to cast off?"

(*Candide,* 49). Such pessimism is not, however, in the end the message of the story, and her stance is belied by the old woman's zest for living. *Candide* is a condemnation of facile optimism—the "mania for insisting everything is all right when everything is going wrong"—but it is not a defense of pessimism (*Candide,* 73). Voltaire's characters are carried along in the flow of life—joyous, even against their will; always ready for a celebratory feast, for a lively conversation. And they do, in the end, reach some measure of self-reflective contentment in taking responsibility for what they can control: they agree to cultivate their garden.

For Voltaire's characters, their exuberantly shared humanity is the final defense against the "madness" of those who would try to accommodate their suffering to a higher good. Voltaire, like Hume, repudiates the folly of holding beliefs in such a way that they interfere with our human nature. Bertrand Russell, in his short essay "Voltaire's Influence on Me," says that Voltaire influenced not so much his opinions, as the way in which he held them and the tone of voice in which he advocated them. "I cannot find words," he says, "in which to express my delight in his sharp, swift wit which penetrates in a moment to the inner core of humbug beneath pretentious trappings. I wish the world contained more of his deft light-heartedness. But we have all grown serious and forgotten how to laugh."[10] In *Candide,* Voltaire's target is the obstinate resort to supposed certainties that have become a substitute for—or a rationale for overriding—a more direct human response of compassion or pity. In sharing his outraged, incredulous laughter, we recover our own capacity for empathetic weeping.

Hume on the Distance between the Human and the Divine: Reworking Old Themes

David Hume's final work—the wonderful *Dialogues concerning Natural Religion*—was modeled on Cicero's dialogue *On the Nature of the Gods;* and the choice of models was not incidental. The dialogues can be read as a tribute to the spirit of "academic"—nondogmat-ic—skepticism that was Cicero's favored approach to philosophy. It is Hume's final expression of the skeptical spirit he had made his own, refining ancient philosophical ideals into a modern style of thinking and of living. This is Hume's version of the Enlight-enment ideal of intellectual character, which—misunderstood though it was in his own times—would become his lasting legacy.

The dialogues were composed and revised over an extended period, but published only posthumously.[11] They originated in the period from 1751 to 1755. Hume revised them in 1761 and re-turned to them, with passion, in 1776 in the final months of his life. He hoped, for a time, that he would be able to publish them himself. When it became clear that illness would make this proj-ect impossible, he took considerable pains to ensure that they would be published after his death—with as little discomfort to others as possible, given that they were likely to cause offense to his contemporary critics.

The dialogue form—in conjunction with his masterful use of irony—made it possible for Hume to distance himself shrewdly from the views articulated in the work. Even so, there can be no mistaking the intended assault on the superstitious character of contemporary religious belief, as he saw it. No less important, however, is that the dialogues represent an equally resolute attack on dogmatic atheism. It is the uncritical spirit of both assured re-ligious belief and unshakable atheism—the shared assumption that certainty is possible about the ultimate nature and origins of the world—that comes under challenge. Hume's objective is not to demolish the possibility that God exists; it is to deny the possi-bility of certainty about such matters. He also aims to show that it is possible to live—with decency and with pleasure—in the lack of such certainties.

The theme of providence plays a crucial part in Hume's project, both in the content of the dialogues and—in more subtle, and in some respects surprising, ways—in the literary enactment of his ideals of intellectual character. Like Cicero, Hume combines his endorsement of skepticism with a generous infusion of Stoicism. There are striking continuities between ancient Stoic views of providence and Hume's treatment of human nature in his first and still most famous work, *A Treatise of Human Nature;* and those continuities persist into *Dialogues concerning Natural Religion.*

In the short autobiographical work *My Own Life*—also written as he approached death—Hume reports that neglecting his studies in law for the pursuits of philosophy and general learning, he read the ancient classics with enthusiasm in his youth. While his family fancied he was "poring upon Voet and Vinnius," in fact Cicero and Virgil were the authors he was "secretly devouring."[12] More was at stake for the young Hume, however, than acquiring "general learning." The works of the ancient philosophers became for him a guide to strenuous efforts for his own moral improvement. In his childhood, religious devotion had motivated him to test his character by reference to the catalogue of vices enumerated in the Calvinist text *The Whole Duty of Man.* As a young man, by his own account, he subjected himself to a similar exercise in trying himself against the moral recommendations of the pagan philosophers. In an early letter to Francis Hutcheson, Hume wrote, "Upon the whole, I desire to take my Catalogue of Virtues from *Cicero's Offices,* not from the *Whole Duty of Man.* I had, indeed, the former Book in my Eye in all my Reasonings."[13]

The ancient philosophers' recommendations for the good life would remain a strong influence on Hume's developing philosophy and on his intellectual character. His mature version of the "philosophical life" would be a less harsh, more genial ideal than his early attempts to combine pietist fervor with the resources of ancient wisdom. Hume would articulate in his philosophy, and enact in his way of life, an Enlightenment version of the old ideal of the "smooth flow of life." He insists in the concluding sections of Book One of *A Treatise*, "I may, nay I must, yield to the current of nature, in submitting to my senses and understanding, and in this blind submission I shew most perfectly my sceptical disposition and principles."[14] Yet submission to the current of nature—an attitude he saw as compatible with, and indeed required by, his skepticism—is also inimical to dogmatic certainty. In an ironic exercise in self-criticism, Hume goes on to chide himself for lapses in which he forgets his skepticism—for his indulgence in such terms as "'tis evident," "'tis certain," "'tis undeniable." His use of such expressions, he reassures his readers, implies "no dogmatical spirit, nor conceited idea of my own judgement, which are sentiments that I am sensible can become no body, and a sceptic still less than any other."[15]

In the *Dialogues concerning Natural Religion*, as he faces his own death, Hume returns to his preoccupation with finding the right style and character for intellectual pursuits—the right way of holding beliefs. This issue of the modality of belief that runs through the dialogues is no less important to understanding the work than is its direct content: the philosophical consideration of issues of divine providence and design.

Hume's philosophical engagement with questions about divine design and providence originated in conversations he had as a young man with a group of French Jesuits at the college of La Flèche in Anjou. He had withdrawn to France, he says in *My Own Life*, with a view of pursuing his studies in a country retreat. It was during this period that he wrote *A Treatise of Human Nature;* and his conversations with the Jesuits formed the basis for his famous critique of the belief in miracles, which he originally intended to include in that work. Hume, to his later chagrin, let himself be persuaded to omit it, for fear that his reflections would "give too much offence, even as the world is disposed at present." In a letter to Henry Home of 1737, when he was arranging the publication of *A Treatise*, Hume described this act of omission as "castrating" his

work—"cutting off its nobler parts," so that it should give as little
offense as possible. "This is a piece of cowardice," he says, "for
which I blame myself, though I believe none of my friends will
blame me."[16]

Hume later incorporated those "nobler parts" of *A Treatise* as
chapters—"On Miracles" and "On a Special Providence and a Future State"—in *An Inquiry concerning Human Understanding,* published
in 1748. He hoped that by giving greater attention to literary style
in this new work he might secure a better reception for his philosophical ideas. *A Treatise,* in Hume's estimation in *My Own Life,* had
fallen "*dead-born from the press* without reaching such distinction, as
even to excite a murmur among the zealots."[17] Sadly, he reports,
the reception of *An Inquiry* was little better. Disappointing though
their scholarly reception was, Hume's early reflections on religion did, however, serve to reinforce his reputation as a scurrilous
atheist.

The "Miracle" of Religious Belief

There can be little doubt that Hume's treatment of miracles and
of providence was intended to undermine prevailing forms of religious belief. His apparently gentle irony at the expense of religious believers packs a punch. Yet his purpose here goes beyond
the exposure of the epistemological foolishness involved in attempting to base religious belief on unreasonable acceptance of
the miraculous. In arguing against taking the belief in miracles as
a justification for religion, Hume intends to lay bare the nature of
belief itself, and to articulate the conditions in which a belief can
be regarded as reasonable.

Hume's fundamental principle in the evaluation of beliefs is
that a belief should be proportionate to the available evidence.
Applying that principle, he says in the opening sections of part 1
of his chapter on miracles in *An Inquiry,* he has found with respect

to miracles, he thinks, an argument that will serve with the wise and learned as "an everlasting check to all kinds of superstitious delusion," and will consequently be "useful as long as the world endures." Accounts of miracles and prodigies will, he presumes, be found that long in all history, sacred and profane. A wise man "proportions his belief to the evidence." Echoing the ancient Stoics, Hume urges his readers to withhold judgment where the evidence is not clear. That ancient ideal, which was for the Stoics bound up with the attainment of tranquillity, with the goal of resting content with "appearances," now takes on a new dimension. When his wise man at last "fixes his judgement," the evidence "exceeds not what we properly call probability."[18] He neither stops at "appearances"—refraining from judgment—nor holds out for certainty. The wise man, knowing that certainty is not attainable, founds his judgments on probability and adapts them reasonably to the strength of the evidence available.

Although Hume's approach to belief is different from the Stoics' recommendation of a sustained suspension of judgment, Hume has taken over much of their language. This borrowing is particularly apparent in his argument about the belief in miracles. The evidence for the occurrence of a miracle, he points out, depends on testimony. An inevitable "counterpoise," he says in part 1, exists between the probability of the miracle's having occurred as claimed and the probability that the testimony about its occurrence is false. "The very same principle of experience which gives us a certain degree of assurance in the testimony of witnesses gives us also, in this case, another degree of assurance against the fact which they endeavour to establish; from which contradiction there necessarily arises a counterpoise and mutual destruction of belief and authority" (*An Inquiry*, 121).

The argument is ingenious. It echoes ancient themes of suspension of judgment—of the attaining of "equipoise" as a basis for an idealized state of "detachment." Hume is replaying those

themes, however, with an eye to modern concern with probabilities. The balance of probabilities, he argues, is such that the reli-
ability of the testimony is inevitably outweighed by the unlikeli-
hood of the miracle's having occurred. "A miracle is a violation of
the laws of nature; and as a firm and unalterable experience has
established these laws, the proof against a miracle, from the very
nature of the fact, is as entire as any argument from experience
can possibly be imagined." Hume concludes that no testimony is
sufficient to establish a miracle unless "the testimony be of such a
kind that its falsehood would be more miraculous than the fact
which it endeavours to establish" (*An Inquiry,* 122, 123).

Hume's final words on the matter, at the end of part 2 of the
chapter, are carefully crafted; they can be read either as ironic
comment, at the expense of religious believers, or as a pious insistence that religion must be grounded not in experience but only
in faith: "So that, upon the whole, we may conclude that the
Christian religion not only was at first attended with miracles, but
even at this day cannot be believed by any reasonable person without one. Mere reason is insufficient to convince us of its veracity.
And whoever is moved by *faith* to assent to it is conscious of a continued miracle in his own person which subverts all the principles
of his understanding and gives him a determination to believe
what is contrary to custom and experience" (*An Inquiry,* 141).

It is a theme that Hume will develop in greater detail—and
with no less elegance and irony—in his *Dialogues concerning Natural
Religion,* along with related issues of providence, which he has discussed in chapter 11 of *An Inquiry.* In the treatment of providence
in *An Inquiry,* Hume's focus is on a principle of "proportion" that
parallels the one to which he appeals in his discussion of miracles.
When we infer causes from effects we must again be careful to
adapt our beliefs in relation to the available evidence. "We must
proportion the one to the other and can never be allowed to as-
cribe to the cause any qualities but what are exactly sufficient to

produce the effect." Moreover, "the knowledge of the cause being derived solely from the effect, they must be exactly adjusted to each other, and the one can never refer to anything further or be the foundation of any new inference and conclusion" (*An Inquiry,* 145–147).

In keeping with his general emphasis in *An Inquiry* on literary strategies, Hume resorts, in his discussion of providence in section 11, to the distancing effects of reported conversation to allow a robust engagement with sensitive issues of religion. His critique of providence is presented in the words of "a friend who loves sceptical paradoxes," who will argue in the persona of Epicurus— that ancient critic of ideas of providence—while the narrator takes on the role of the Athenian people, who will judge whether "Epicurus"'s denial of providence and a future state should be regarded as undermining the foundations of society. Philosophers who talk of divine purpose, says Hume's Epicurus, have "aided the ascent of reason by the wings of imagination." Otherwise, they could not have changed their usual manner of inference. Rather than arguing from causes to effects, they here draw fallacious conclusions about the nature of the gods from observation of the world (*An Inquiry,* 147–148).

Not just a fallacious mode of reasoning is under attack here, but a whole mentality. For Hume's Epicurus, those who argue in favor of providential design—instead of regarding the present scene of things as the sole object of contemplation—willfully turn our attention elsewhere. They interpret this life as "merely a passage to something further—a porch which leads to a greater and vastly different building, a prologue which serves only to introduce the piece and give it more grace and propriety" (*An Inquiry,* 150).

Arguments for providential design, Epicurus concludes, are useless. They do not provide any warranted additions to the "common and experienced course of nature" that could allow us to establish any principles for conduct and behavior (*An Inquiry,* 151). It is not those who deny providence and a future state who undermine the foundations of society, but rather those who try to turn our attention away from the effort to ground our conduct in experience.

Design and Providence

When Hume returns to themes of design and providence in his *Dialogues concerning Natural Religion,* it is with a more fully developed sense of the possibilities of the dialogue form as a vehicle for expressing his form of skepticism in the sensitive and hotly contested area of religious belief. The issues unfold through the interactions of Philo, the skeptic; Cleanthes, the exponent of religious belief based on experience; and Demea, the more orthodox believer, who backs religion with the deductive certainties of argumentative reason. The dialogue form allows Hume to construct a model of reasonable debate that serves, taken as a whole, as his answer to the religious zealots whose prejudices and superstitions had plagued his public intellectual life. Hume saw them not only as his own adversaries but as enemies of the free spirit of intellectual inquiry, which was his answer to the ancient question: What is the good life for a human being?

Much, then, was at stake for Hume in this last attempt to express the real nature of his much-misunderstood and maligned skepticism. The persona of Philo, as Hume himself acknowledged in correspondence, comes closest to his own stance on the issues. But it is the conversation as a whole—with its shifting emphases and alliances and its surprising reversals in argument—that is the real vehicle for Hume's skepticism. It is by no means incidental to Hume's purposes that he chooses to have the work resonate with ancient arguments and rhetorical maneuvers, in appropriating the form of Cicero's dialogue *On the Nature of the Gods.* The interactions of the three protagonists are framed by the observations of the

youthful and all too easily impressed Pamphilus, whose edification provides the rationale for the learned discussion. The skeptic
Philo is given the mediating role, cleverly shifting between apparent support for the experience-based approach to religion advocated by Cleanthes and the more traditional a priori approach of
Demea, while seeing that the terms of this modern debate are en-
riched by resonances from their ancient analogues.

Hume had already addressed the relations among ancient versions of the good life in a remarkable set of essays—"The Epicurean," "The Stoic," "The Platonist," and "The Sceptic"—published
in his *Political Discourses* in 1752.[19] There, he reworked those old ideals into modern versions appropriate to his own times. Each of
these intellectual personas reflects the dynamic shifts of their interaction in Hume's reconstruction. We find, in particular, strong
elements of Stoicism in Hume's figure of the modern Skeptic.
Those elements are carried over into Hume's creation of the persona of Philo in the dialogues. For all of Philo's skepticism, the
Stoic's embrace of necessity is recognizable in his intellectual
style and character. As Philo himself acknowledges in part 1, "To
whatever length any one may push his speculative principles of
scepticism, he must act, I own, and live, and converse like other
men; and for this conduct he is not obliged to give any other reason than the absolute necessity he lies under of so doing" (*Dialogues*, 134).

Siding initially with Cleanthes, Philo argues against Demea that
it is only through experience that we can reason from facts about
the world to conclusions about a designing mind behind it all.
From a priori reasoning alone, we have no more reason to think
that the world is a product of mind than that its exquisite arrangement springs from some unknown cause internal to matter. As
Cleanthes' arguments from experience to the existence of a divine
designer unfold, however, they are quickly shown to be in breach
of the fundamental principle of the proportioning of belief to evi-

dence, on which his whole approach is supposed to rest. Since we have no experience of other worlds, we cannot draw from our observations of this world any inferences about how it came to be. As the arguments unfold, Hume's seditious intent against the prevailing forms of religious belief becomes clearer. Again, Hume's discussion has a parallel in his ancient sources. In *On the Nature of the Gods,* Cicero has the Stoic Cotta rebuke the Epicurean Velleius for placing the gods at too great a distance from human beings. Cotta alleges that the Epicurean, in his eagerness to undermine the anthropomorphism of Stoic ideas of providence, has removed the gods so far from concern with human beings that he has actually abolished them.

In the early sections of the dialogues, Hume shrewdly avoids controversy by highlighting the distinction between consideration of the existence of God and consideration of his nature. The issue of God's existence is deftly put out of consideration—as if it is assumed by all the protagonists. "Surely," says Philo, in part 2, "where reasonable men treat these subjects, the question can never be concerning the *being* but only the *nature* of the Deity. The former truth, as you [Demea] well observe, is unquestionable and self-evident" (*Dialogues,* 142). For Hume, however—as for Cicero's Cotta—the two issues cannot really be separated; and Hume has Philo exploit the false security created by their apparent separation.

Finding the right distance between the divine and the human is a constant theme in the dialogues; and Hume explores it in evaluating prevailing tendencies in "natural religion" that anthropomorphize the supernatural. The strategy yields an initially surprising alliance between Philo and Demea against Cleanthes' readiness to assimilate the divine into familiar concepts of human agency and design. Where Cleanthes desires knowability, Philo sides with Demea on "the adorable mysteriousness of the divine nature." Cleanthes sees Demea's insistence on God's unknowability as "mystical"; Demea sees Cleanthes' craving for knowability as "anthropomorphism." Philo cunningly shifts his allegiance between the two. He argues in part 2 against Cleanthes that anthropomorphism taints the very idea of arguing from experience to the claim that the world exists by design: "What peculiar privilege has this little agitation of the rain which we call thought, that we must thus make it the model of the whole universe? Our partiality in our own favor does indeed present it on all occasions: But sound philosophy ought carefully to guard against so natural an illusion. . . . And if thought, as we may well suppose, be confined merely to this narrow corner, and has even there so limited a sphere of action, with what propriety can we assign it for the original cause of all things? The narrow views of a peasant, who makes his domestic oeconomy the rule for the government of kingdoms, is in comparison a pardonable sophism." For Hume's Philo, as for Spinoza in the *Theologico-Political Treatise,* it is folly to think of human reason as if it were somehow the principle of the whole world (*Dialogues,* 148).

The ready alliance between Philo and Demea on the "adorable mysteriousness" of the divine nature may well seem at first sight a strange accommodation for Philo to make. It is, however, an important thread in Hume's own version of skepticism. It accords with his emphasis on resisting all claims to certainty. With regard to religious belief, the skeptical spirit demands that possibilities remain open—that we give space to the free play of intellect and imagination, while denying that they yield any certain knowledge. The realm of "adorable mysteriousness" is not alien to Hume the skeptic. He has Philo insist, though, that we must recognize this as the domain of the imagination, not of religious certainty. It is a space of fanciful hypotheses about the divine nature that are no less plausible—no less a product of our limited experience of worlds—than Cleanthes' hypothesis of a divine artificer.

The truth, Philo argues, is that we have no adequate experiential data to establish any system of cosmogony. If we are going to engage in such exercises, he asks in part 7, why give preference to the model of the world as a cleverly constructed machine? "Does not a plant or an animal, which springs from vegetation or generation, bear a stronger resemblance to the world, than does any artificial machine, which arises from reason and design?" (*Dialogues*, 177). Why, Philo demands, should we privilege reason rather than generation as a standard for the whole of nature? "Reason, in its internal fabric and structure, is really as little known to us as instinct or vegetation; and perhaps even that vague, undeterminate word, nature, to which the vulgar refer everything, is not at the bottom more inexplicable. The effects of these principles are all known to us from experience. But the principles themselves, and their manner of operation, are totally unknown. Nor is it less intelligible, or less conformable to experience to say, that the world arose by vegetation from a seed shed by another world, than to say that it arose from a divine reason or contrivance" (*Dialogues*, 178).

Demea is clearly delighted by the rout of Cleanthes, but the dynamic of the argument now turns against Demea. Cleanthes rehearses the familiar arguments against the significance of a priori arguments in matters of religion: we cannot move by reason alone from concept to existence; everything we can conceive of as existing can just as readily be conceived as not existing. In part 9 Philo, joining forces with Cleanthes, points out that the necessity that characterizes a priori reasoning is a dangerous idea to introduce into the consideration of religious belief, for that kind of reasoning readily affords "an inference directly opposite to the religious hypothesis." Perhaps the whole economy of the universe could be conducted by a like necessity to which human algebra cannot yet furnish the key. In a world governed by the necessity to which lovers of abstract reasoning are accustomed, might not a deity become superfluous?

Hume's own commitment, of course, is to the reasonableness

of reasoning from probability: much though those who engage in mathematical reasoning may delight in a priori abstractions, these have no place in the consideration of religion. Of far greater importance for Hume, however, is a more concrete theme that is much less comfortable for Demea: the bearing divine providence has on human misery. It is to this issue that Philo now cunningly directs the conversation. Philo's maneuvers at this point echo the caustic remark that Cicero put in Cotta's mouth—that the Epicureans remove the gods so far from human beings that the gods have nothing to do with our well-being or suffering. Hume has Philo also indulge in a scathing aside on Leibniz's theodicy. In part 10 Philo reminds his friends that it was Leibniz who first ventured on the "bold and paradoxical" denial of "the sense of human misery"—or at least who first made it essential to a philosophical system. In the spirit of Leibniz's theodicy Demea attempts to grapple with the apparent tensions between divine providence and human suffering. Philo and Demea, in their rejection of Cleanthes' resort to anthropomorphism—their shared insistence that we must see ourselves as but part of a whole—were previously united, but that very view now divides them. Demea says in part 10: "This world is but a point in comparison of the universe: This life but a moment in comparison of eternity. The present evil phenomena, therefore, are rectified in other regions, and in some future period of existence. And the eyes of men, being then opened to larger views of things, see the whole connection of general laws, and trace, with adoration, the benevolence and rectitude of the Deity, through all the mazes and intricacies of his providence" (*Dialogues,* 199). Philo's earlier appeal to the perception of ourselves as but part of a whole was, by contrast, an attack—in the spirit of Spinoza—on the anthropomorphic delusion that human reason, a mere "ripple of rain," can be the basis for understanding the nature and origins of the universe as a whole.

The scene is now set for Philo's separation from Demea, dramatized in Demea's own quiet physical withdrawal.

Hume is again careful not to let Philo overstate the skeptic's case: If we are already committed to a belief in divine providence, he has Philo say, we may on that basis be able to explain away the sense of evil; but we cannot find in the sense of evil any good reason for religious belief. Demea and Cleanthes can now be seen as standing at opposite ends of an unsustainable shared method of argument. To prove a consistency with God's existence is in no way to provide a reason for belief in his existence. Demea has allowed himself to be drawn into the trap, in that he emphasizes the miseries of experience in order the better to appeal to God's providence as the resolution. "The whole earth, believe me, Philo," he rants in part 10, "is cursed and polluted. A perpetual war is kindled amongst all living creatures. Necessity, hunger, want, stimulate the strong and courageous: Fear, anxiety, terror, agitate the weak and infirm. The first entrance into life gives anguish to the new-born infant and to its wretched parent: Weakness, impotence, distress, attend each stage of that life: And it is at last finished in agony and horror" (*Dialogues,* 194).

Philo is only too willing to join in the rant, with ever-direr depictions of the human condition, setting Demea against Cleanthes, who now struggles to deny the miseries of the world that fuel Demea's doomed appeal to providence. Philo's victory is now assured. In part 11 he concludes: "All that belongs to human understanding, in this deep ignorance and obscurity, is to be skeptical, or at least cautious, and not to admit of any hypothesis whatever; much less, of any which is supported by no appearance of probability" (*Dialogues,* 205). The triumph, Philo has claimed throughout the dialogues, lies with the skeptic. At the end of part 8, he insisted that total suspension of judgment is on these issues our only reasonable resource. "And if every attack, as is commonly observed, and no defence, among theologians, is successful; how complete must be *his* victory, who remains always, with all mankind, on the offensive; and has himself no fixed station or abiding city, which he is ever, on any occasion, obliged to defend?" (*Dialogues,* 187).

Neither Cleanthes nor Demea is allowed to prevail. It is the humane spirit of inquiry that Hume celebrates in the final sections of the work—not the defense of an alternative position, but the enactment of a new version of the critical spirit of skepticism. In part 12 Philo observes that the dispute concerning theism is left irremediably in ambiguity. "The theist allows, that the original intelligence is very different from human reason: The atheist allows, that the original principle of order bears some remote analogy to it. Will you quarrel, Gentlemen, about the degrees and enter into a controversy, which admits not of any precise meaning, nor consequently of any determination?" He pleads with them: "Consider then, where the real point of controversy lies, and if you cannot lay aside your disputes, endeavour, at least, to cure yourselves of your animosity" (*Dialogues,* 218–219). The true antagonists in the dialogue finally emerge as two mentalities—those of the skeptic and of the dogmatist. Philo acknowledges a "peculiar pleasure" in pushing superstition to the point sometimes of absurdity, sometimes of impiety. "And you are sensible, that all bigots, notwithstanding their great aversion to the latter above the former, are commonly equally guilty of both" (*Dialogues,* 219).

The dialogues engage with intricate arguments about design and providence—about what can be known of the existence and nature of God. They also engage, at a deeper level, in an evaluation of different kinds of mentality—of the varying structures of thought, imagination, and emotion that can either sustain religious belief or confirm the resistance to it. Underlying the argumentation are structures of emotions, needs, and desires. The emotional undercurrents are not inconsistent with the content of religious belief; nor, however, can they provide a rational basis for becoming a believer.

The highest zeal and the deepest hypocrisy, Philo comments, are far from being inconsistent; they are often united in the same individual character, and darker emotions are also involved. Both fear and hope enter into religion, but terror, he says toward the end of part 12, the passion that predominates in it, "admits but of short intervals of pleasure." Even the joy in religion comes at a cost, for its excess tends to exhaust the spirits and yields inevitably to fits of "superstitious terror and dejection." The mentality susceptible to religion, as Philo sees it, is far from the happiness that characterizes the "calm and equable." It is hardly surprising that devout people are generally so gloomy and melancholy, for it is impossible to be tranquil when we believe ourselves to be precariously poised between an eternity of happiness and an eternity of misery. To believe in religion, Philo concludes, is to live in profound darkness and uncertainty. "For as death lies between the eye and the prospect of futurity, that event is so shocking to nature, that it must throw a gloom on all the regions which lie beyond it; and suggest to the generality of mankind the idea of Cerberus and Furies; devils and torrents of fire and brimstone" (*Dialogues*, 225).

These are words we will see Hume echo, wittily, in writing of his own impending death. When he speaks in his own voice, Hume is willing to make explicit his own lack of belief in the Christian afterlife. In the final sections of the dialogues, he is more circumspect, though the irony of Philo's last piece of advice to Pamphilus is scarcely in doubt: "To be a philosophical sceptic is, in a man of letters, the first and most essential step towards being a sound, believing Christian" (*Dialogues*, 228). The dialogues leave open the possibility of a religious belief that rests on faith rather than either a priori reason or the appeal to experience. The celebration of skepticism in the concluding sections of his final work, however, echo the masterly irony of Hume's earlier evaluation of miracles in his *Inquiry.* Religious belief, he said in that earlier work, requires a continuing miracle in the mind of the believer. It is an observation that will be greeted with amused agreement by the skeptics among Hume's readers. Yet the religious believers could hardly disagree with the description of their faith as involving a continuing unfolding of the supernatural into the realm of nature. We can make of the continuing miracle either a cause for rejoicing or a cautionary reminder of human foolishness.

Hume remains careful to hide his own voice, in the concluding lines of his *Dialogues,* in a clever reflection of Cicero's judicious masking of his allegiances at the end of *On the Nature of the Gods.* "Here the conversation ended, and we parted," explains Cicero's narrating voice, "Velleius thinking Cotta's discourse to be the truer, while I felt that of Balbus approximated more nearly to a semblance of the truth." Hume's voice is even more concealed in the conversation. The argument is left to reverberate in the developing consciousness of the young Pamphilus, for whose benefit it has been conducted; and it is clear that what he has really learned is not so much the truth of any position but the importance of continually weighing the arguments and suspending premature belief: "Cleanthes and Philo pursued not this conversation much farther; and as nothing ever made greater impression on me, than all the reasonings of that day; so I confess, that, upon a serious review of the whole, I cannot but think, that Philo's principles are more probable than Demea's; but that those of Cleanthes approach still nearer to the truth" (*Dialogues,* 228).

Death of a Philosopher

In the voice of the young Pamphilus we can hear Hume's hope for the youthful spirit of the Enlightenment. His desire to nurture this spirit spurred him on as he labored in his last weeks to put his

Dialogues into its final form, and to negotiate carefully the arrangements needed to ensure the posthumous publication of the work. This was Hume's final engagement with what he regarded as the prevailing superstition of his times—not religious belief as such, but an unenlightened mode of believing. The dialogues were to be his final articulation of the ideal of the "calm and equable" against the darker spirit of the "zealots" and hypocrites.

Hume himself, from the reports of his friends, was able to remain calm and equable to the end. Adam Smith reported: "Poor David Hume is dying very fast, but with great cheerfulness and good humour and with more real resignation to the necessary course of things, than any shining Christian ever dyed with pretended resignation to the will of God." Writing more fully of Hume's death after the event, Smith reported to friends a conversation that makes poignant reference to Hume's self-deprecating wish to nourish the Enlightenment spirit. Hume had been reading Lucian's *Dialogues of the Dead* and pondered with amusement on the excuses he might make to Charon for not readily entering his boat to make the trip to the underworld. He had no house to finish, no daughter to provide for, no enemies on whom to take revenge. He had done everything of consequence that he ever meant to do. "He then diverted himself with inventing several jocular excuses, which he supposed he might make to Charon, and with imagining the very surly answers which it might suit the character of Charon to return to them. 'Upon further consideration,' said he, 'I thought I might say to him, "Good Charon, I have been correcting my works for a new edition. Allow me a little time, that I may see how the Public receives the alterations." But Charon would answer, "When you have seen the effects of these, you will be for making other alterations. There will be no end of such excuses; so, honest friend, please step into the boat." But I might still urge, "Have a little patience, good Charon, I have been endeavouring to open the eyes of the Public. If I live a few years longer, I may have the satisfaction of seeing the downfall of some of the prevailing systems of superstition." But Charon would then lose all temper and decency. "You loitering rogue, that will not happen these many hundred years. Do you fancy I will grant you a lease for so long a term? Get into the boat this instant, you lazy loitering rogue.""""[20]

One person who was particularly interested in and perplexed by the demeanor of the dying Hume was James Boswell. Having talked his way in for a deathbed chat, Boswell interrogated Hume on whether he still maintained his disbelief in an afterlife. Incredulous at Hume's cheerfully persisting in his disbelief, Boswell, by his own account in his journal, asked Hume if it was not after all possible that there might be a future state. True to his principles on probability and evidence, Hume conceded that a piece of coal put upon a fire might not burn, and added that "it was a most unreasonable fancy that he should exist for ever." Pressed by Boswell as to whether the thought of annihilation never gave him any unhappiness, Hume responded: "Not the least; no more than the thought that he had not been, as Lucretius observes." Boswell left him, he says, "with impressions which disturbed me for some time."[21] Boswell records in his *Life of Johnson* that he mentioned to Johnson his shock at Hume's persisting in his attitude of infidelity when he was dying. In an interesting play on Hume's own emphasis on probability and testimony, Johnson insisted that it was more probable that Hume was only assuming "an appearance of ease" and added—with an apparently perverse streak of logic—that according to Hume's own "principle of annihilation," the philosopher had no motive to speak the truth.[22]

Without disregarding the principles Hume enunciated on probability and testimony, we cannot confidently reject Johnson's claim that Hume's cheerfulness in the face of death was a show of vanity or bravado. The desire for a cheerful acceptance of the necessity of death was in keeping, however, with the ideals of the ancient philosophers that he had always tried to incorporate into his own style of skepticism. What are we to make of the anxious incredulity of his critics? There are precedents in the earlier history of the Enlightenment for their preoccupation with Hume's composure in the face of death. The death of Spinoza—no less notorious an alleged atheist than Hume—had also given rise to a clamor of conflicting testimony and speculation among religious believers. The infamous Pierre Bayle, whose *Dictionary* had been the main source for the dissemination of Spinoza's ideas throughout Europe, claimed in his earlier work, the *Pensées diverses sur la comète,* that Spinoza had lived virtuously and died showing great fortitude, while cheerfully maintaining his disbelief in providence. Spinoza, according to Bayle's report, gave instructions as he was dying that no clergyman should be admitted, lest he, Spinoza, lapse into a delirium and say something that could subsequently be used to damage his philosophical reputation.

The issue whether Spinoza had indeed been "a true Spinozist"— and whether he could have maintained such a stance in the face of death—was hotly disputed. Some claimed that he became a Christian on his deathbed, in acknowledging at the last his belief in divine providence. His biographer Colerus, however, keen though he was to reclaim Spinoza as a believer, concluded that the evidence was in favor of Spinoza's having died serenely with no change of heart.[23]

Both philosophers had to negotiate the obstacles put in their way by religious intolerance. Both had strongly rejected conventional ideas of providence associated with religious belief. Yet for each of them a deeper sense of providence connected his thought to that of the ancient philosophers. "One considerable advantage that arises from philosophy," Hume said at the beginning of his essay "On Suicide," "consists in the sovereign antidote which it affords to superstition and false religion." In his philosophy, however, runs an acceptance of providence deeper than that defended in the "superstition and false religion" he struggled to expose. The life of a man, he says in that essay, is "of no greater importance to the universe than that of an oyster." Yet for all that, a providential necessity encompasses human life and death. "When I shall be dead, the principles of which I am composed will still perform their part in the universe, and will be equally useful in the grand fabric, as when they composed this individual creature. The difference to the whole will be no greater than betwixt my being in a chamber and in the open air. The one change is of more importance to me than the other, but not more so to the universe. It is a kind of blasphemy to imagine that any created being can disturb the order of the world, or invade the business of providence."[24]

For Hume, as for the Stoics, the goodness of a life can find expression in knowing when it is good to die.

8   Providence as Progress

"Something thus it must have been!" Plotinus, inspired by the te-
merity of Plato's *Timaeus,* was confident that he too could tell a
convincing story of cosmic origins. As we have seen, later philosophers have not held back either from offering ingeniously constructed fictions through which their readers might glimpse truths
about the origins and nature of the world. It was Jean-Jacques
Rousseau who was in the eighteenth century to offer perhaps the
boldest of crossovers between philosophical argument and imaginative storytelling.

Rousseau: Providence and Paranoia

In the preface to his *Discourse on the Origins of Inequality,* published
in 1755, Rousseau argued that to answer the question of what is
natural to human beings demands that we "form a true idea of a
state which no longer exists, perhaps never did exist, and probably
never will exist; and of which it is, nevertheless, necessary to have
true ideas, in order to form a proper judgement of our present
state."[1] The state of nature was for Rousseau a philosophical fiction; so too was its companion concept—the social contract,
through which human beings emerged from the state of nature
into the state of society. A deeper and more influential intellectual
construct, however, was to prove such a lasting legacy of Rousseau's thought that we now barely notice that it is a fiction: the

mapping of the history of the human species onto the model of
the growth of a human individual.

In *Emile*—published in the same year as the *Discourse on the Origins of Inequality*—Rousseau sketches the ideal development of an
imaginary young man, educated in accordance with a method intended to draw out what lies dormant within his own nature. In
the *Discourse on the Origins of Inequality* Rousseau traces the development of capacities latent in the human species. Human potential-
ities unfold into a golden age of innocently self-reflective achievement, which is meant to contrast with the more individualistic
forms of self-love that have become familiar in the conditions of
modern life.

The *Discourse* has had a far greater impact on the history of
political and social philosophy than *Emile* has had on the philosophy of education, but the two works mirror one another; and it is
their interconnection that is significant for understanding distinctive eighteenth-century developments in the idea of providence. Once Rousseau grafted the history of the species onto the
imagined history of an individual human being, the conceptual
framework was in place for temporalization of the idea of providence: it could be embedded in human history, to yield the modern idea of progress.

The ancient ideal of a cosmic polis—one comprising citizens of
the world, rather than just of a particular place—underlies Rousseau's version of "nature." It echoes in his ringing call toward the
end of the opening section of the *Discourse on the Origins of Inequality*:
"O man, of whatever country you are, and whatever your opinions
may be, behold your history, such as I have thought to read it, not
in books written by your fellow-creatures, who are liars, but in nature, which never lies." It is the life of the human species that
Rousseau promises to narrate. Yet the narrative centers on an exercise in moral imagination based on the familiar experience of
reflection on the stages of individual life: "There is, I feel, an age

at which the individual man would wish to stop: you are about to inquire about the age at which you would have liked your whole species to stand still" (*Discourse,* 46). That imagined temporal stage will then be expanded to become the apogee of the development of the species. What saves Rousseau's story from being a nostalgic tale of the decline of the species is that his vision of that golden age becomes a model for the transformation of contemporary society. The future lies in a new "natural" sociability—grounded in reflective reason, guided by the ideal of remaining close to nature.

Rousseau complains in the opening sections of the *Discourse on the Origins of Inequality* that although the philosophers who have inquired into the foundations of society have all felt the necessity of going back to a state of nature, not one of them has gotten there. Dwelling on the flaws that have characterized human beings in corrupt societies, philosophers have transferred to the state of nature traits that were in fact acquired in society. "In speaking of the savage, they described the social man." The account Rousseau gave of the development of the species was, by contrast, supposed to reveal true, uncorrupted human nature. His disaffection with the corruption inherent in contemporary society he expressed by the positioning of his own present—and of the terrible future that can be expected to follow it—in relation to the whole story of humanity. At the end of the introductory section he says: "Discontented with your present state, for reasons which threaten your unfortunate descendants with still greater discontent, you will perhaps wish it were in your power to go back; and this feeling should be a panegyric on your first ancestors, a criticism of your contemporaries, and a terror to the unfortunates who will come after you" (*Discourse,* 45–46).

Rousseau derived some cause for optimism from his belief in providence; his story reveals glimpses of positive transformations in corrupted social institutions to yield a new closeness to nature.

He elaborated that positive vision of the future of the species in *The Social Contract*; his overall treatment of the future prospects of the human species is not pessimistic, but his version of human "progress" in the *Discourse on the Origins of Inequality* emphasizes the relative bleakness of the condition of humanity in his own time.

Rousseau's vision of the future allows for an enlightened cultivation of the human garden. His novel *Julie, or the New Heloise* includes a description of actual cultivation of a "natural" garden that is clearly intended as a model for the metaphorical development of individual lives and social institutions in accordance with the ideal of closeness to Nature. Rousseau, unlike Voltaire and Hume, envisaged that desired social transformation as taking place under the firm guidance of a purposeful providence, overseeing human history. The *Discourse on the Origins of Inequality* also resonates with the old debates Leibniz tried to resolve, on the balance of good and evil in human life. In the state of nature, Rousseau claims in the appendix to the work, "man would have been seen to be subject to very few evils not of his own creation." It is the state of society that has multiplied human evils: "It has indeed cost us not a little trouble to make ourselves as wretched as we are" (*Discourse*, 106).

Rather than seeing the unfolding of human history as essentially a steady, benign advance, Rousseau considered any "progress" as negative: we are traveling a downward path. Yet in the conclusion to the appendix of the *Discourse*, he makes it clear that a countervailing optimism is possible, reflecting belief in a divine being who has "called all mankind to be partakers in the happiness and perfection of celestial intelligences." That religious vision informs the morality of Rousseau's ideal society. Guided by it, virtuous human beings will "respect the sacred bonds of their respective communities," love and serve their fellow citizens, scrupulously obey the laws, and honor particularly those "wise and good princes, who find means of preventing, curing, or even palliating" all the evils and abuses that constantly threaten human beings (*Discourse,* 113).

In the *Discourse on the Origins of Inequality* Rousseau offers his most sustained construction of the philosophical fiction of human history as guided by providence; but it is in book 4 of *Emile* that he gives his most fully developed account of the providence that underpins that fiction. There he presents a natural religion permeated with reflection on the operations of providential purpose in the world, rather than with the authority of the organized churches. In a long section relating the religious beliefs of a supposed priest of Savoy, the tutor of the young Emile is introduced to this religion. Rousseau resorts to narrative devices to conceal his own voice. The principles of natural religion are embedded in a fictional conversation within the story of the development of a young man educated in accordance with nature. At the time of its publication, the "Creed of a Savoyard Priest" nonetheless occasioned much controversy among the religiously orthodox.

"In my exposition," Rousseau has his imaginary priest say, "you find nothing but natural religion; strange that we should need more!"[2] Nor does the tutor make any attempt to conceal his own interpretation of the creed he has heard expounded. It seems, he says in response, very like "that theism or natural religion, which Christians profess to compound with atheism or irreligion which is their exact opposite." The tutor, who throughout the work acts as the spokesman for Rousseau's preferred approach to education, makes his own allegiances clear: "So long as we yield nothing to human authority, nor to the prejudices of our native land, the light of reason alone, in a state of nature, can lead us no further than to natural religion; and this is as far as I should go with Emile" (*Emile,* 278). Emile's religious education—if it is to conform with the general principle of taking nature, rather than authority, as a guide—must follow the lines suggested in the priest's creed.

This is a religion based on "natural" sentiments—on feeling and on reasoning that confines itself to reflection on feeling. What applies to religious education applies also to moral education in *Emile*: conscience itself belongs in the realm of feeling. "The decrees of conscience are not judgements but feelings." Taking the point even further, Rousseau claims: "To exist is to feel, our feeling is undoubtedly earlier than our intelligence and we had feelings before we had ideas." Accordingly, the vicar tells the tutor, "I do not wish to philosophise with you, but to help you to consult your own heart. If all the philosophies in the world should prove that I am wrong, and you feel that I am right, that is all I ask." For the vicar, morality is well rid of philosophy: "Thank heaven we have now got rid of all that alarming show of philosophy; we may be men without being scholars" (*Emile*, 253–254). The tutor will follow the same principles when he comes to instruct Emile in religion.

The version of argument from design that grounds the belief in providence in *Emile* would have carried little weight against the critique of natural religion that Hume would later offer. The consideration of matter in motion, the vicar says, points him to a will; and his reflection that this motion accords with fixed laws points him to an intelligence. "To act, to compare, to choose, are the operations of an active, thinking being; so this being exists. Where do you find him existing, you will say? Not merely in the revolving heavens, nor in the sun which gives us light, not in myself alone, but in the sheep that grazes, the bird that flies, the stone that falls, and the leaf blown by the wind." Listening to the "inner voice of feeling" and looking at the world through eyes not blinded by prejudice will suffice, he thinks, to allow us to see that "the visible order of the universe proclaims a supreme intelligence" (*Emile*, 237).

The vicar has no hesitation judging that all things are made for human beings. That conclusion follows, he argues, from the obvious fact that human beings alone have the intellectual capacity to

relate all things to themselves. The vicar has no difficulty reconciling providence with the existence of evil: "Providence does not
will the evil that man does when he misuses the freedom given to
him; neither does Providence prevent him doing it, either because
the wrong done by so feeble a creature is as nothing in its eyes, or
because it could not prevent it without doing a greater wrong and
degrading his nature." Providence has made human beings free so
that they can choose good and refuse evil. The thought is by no
means new. Rousseau has the vicar add a corollary, which is elaborated in the *Discourse on the Origins of Inequality*—the connection between evil and progress. "O Man!" cries the vicar, "seek no further
for the author of evil; thou art he. There is no evil but the evil you
do or the evil you suffer, and both come from yourself. . . . Take
away our fatal progress, take away our faults and our vices, take
away man's handiwork, and all is well" (*Emile*, 243–245).

Despite Rousseau's distrust of progress, however, the optimistic, forward-looking strand in his understanding of the development of the species persists. The vicar's attitude toward providence seems to bring together an Augustinian trust in divine
justice with the optimism of a Pangloss. "O God, merciful and
good, whatever thy decrees may be I adore them; if thou shouldst
commit the wicked to everlasting punishment, I abandon my feeble reason to thy justice; but if the remorse of these wretched beings should in the course of time be extinguished, if their sufferings should come to an end, and if the same peace shall one day be
the lot of all mankind, I give thanks to thee for this" (*Emile*, 247).
Whatever betides, all shall be well.

By putting the natural religion of the vicar of Savoy together
with the tale of loss and renewal in the *Discourse on the Origins of
Inequality*, we can glimpse in Rousseau's philosophy a convergence
of the idea of providence with the idea of progress; but the full
articulation of that convergence was not to be realized by Rousseau. Although in the *Discourse on the Origins of Inequality* the belief in

providence was supposed to offer hope for future happiness, the fulfillment of that hope rested on its projection beyond human history into a Christian afterlife. Although he offers a more optimistic view of the present state of humanity in *The Social Contract,* it is never really integrated with his appeal to providence. In his last work, the *Reveries of a Solitary Walker,* we find instead a more disconcerting convergence—of providence with paranoia.

The account of natural religion in *Emile* brought upon Rousseau a tide of condemnation and persecution—real and imagined. The condemnation was real, though the persecution was largely in Rousseau's imagination; he became increasingly incapable of telling the difference. His ongoing torments and panic-stricken flights from anticipated reprisals drew sympathy and support from many of his literary admirers, including David Hume, who provided Rousseau with hospitality, only to find himself cast as one of the alleged persecutors.

In the twisted logic of the final ruminations Rousseau records on his life, his conviction that there was a conspiracy against him joins forces with an intense faith in providence to yield a bizarre variety of tranquillity. The accumulation of so many misfortunes, he reasons at the end of the second "Walk," is too extraordinary to be mere coincidence: it must represent the outcome of a universal conspiracy. The conspiracy involves such a "striking and incredible combination of circumstances" that it must, moreover, be "heaven's eternal decree" that his enemies' designs should be crowned with success. He must then regard as "a divine secret beyond the reach of human reason" the plot that he had previously seen as nothing but the fruit of human malevolence.[3]

In the eighth "Walk" Rousseau presents himself as having escaped his anguish and despair to recover his "serenity, tranquillity, peace and even happiness" by learning to "bear the yoke of necessity without complaining." His trust in providence, however, has itself undergone a transformation into a poignantly twisted form of self-reliance. "Where previously I strove to cling on to a host of things, now, when I have lost hold of them all one after another and have nothing left but myself, I have at last regained a firm footing. Under pressure from all sides, I remain upright because I cling to nothing and lean only on myself" (*Reveries,* 126).

It is one of the strangest turns in the history of providence; the tranquillity that derives from understanding oneself as part of a purposeful whole becomes, through a relentless but perverse logic, the supposed serenity of trusting no one but oneself. The divine purpose seems inscrutable indeed in this lonely cul-de-sac of the cosmic city. It was left to Immanuel Kant to retell the Rousseauian story of human history as a positive Enlightenment version of the old cosmopolitan ideal.

Kant's *Idea for a Universal History with a Cosmopolitan Purpose*

Tales once told can be retold with variations; and philosophical tales can be adapted to express very different philosophical insights. Kant's essay *Idea for a Universal History with a Cosmopolitan Purpose,* published in 1784, adapts Rousseau's story of progress to offer both a more positive view of Kant's own present and a celebration of the future.[4] Within the shared framing device of a story of development, Kant tells a very different story from Rousseau's. Kant's version of social hope looks forward to an intensely imagined future "cosmopolitan" stage of human history. This era of cosmopolitanism is a construct of the imagination, imagined not as a utopia but as an achievable—and indeed inevitable—future. Rousseau had taken the social antagonism of his times to indicate the corruption of the species under conditions of supposed social progress. Kant, by contrast, treats it as a necessary stimulus that will bring out the nascent, distinctively human capacity for reason. Without the "asocial qualities," which cause resistance among self-seeking individuals, "man would live an Arcadian, pastoral existence of perfect concord, self-sufficiency and mutual love." All human talents, however, would then lie dormant. Human beings, "as good-natured as the sheep they tended, would scarcely render their existence more valuable than that of their animals. . . . Man wishes concord, but nature, knowing better what is good for his species, wishes discord" (*Political Writings,* 45).

Kant's description of the limitations of a conflict-free mode of life displays a gentle irony. In its wistful allusion to the idyllic period of bucolic simplicity that Rousseau depicts in the second part of the *Discourse on the Origins of Inequality,* the Kantian account evokes the golden age of human development—the era when men and women, frolicking around the oak trees, enjoyed the pleasures of sociability without the conflict-ridden competitiveness that emerges in more fully developed society.

Kant makes the Rousseauian overtones even more explicit in a later passage, where he directly challenges Rousseau's descriptions of social corruption. The differences between the two writers lie in the way each positions his present in relation to the narrative of progress. In Kant's version of the story, a "little beyond the halfway mark in its development" human nature has to endure the "hardest of evils under the guise of outward prosperity" (*Political Writings,* 49). Rousseau's preference for "the state of savagery," Kant says, does not appear so very mistaken—if we leave out of consideration that human beings, in the condition he finds so deplorable, are as yet in an immature stage of development. The modern human beings whom Rousseau regards as miserable have not yet reached the "moral maturity" that Nature has in store for them. Cultivated though they may be in the arts and sciences, and civilized in "social courtesies and proprieties," their present is still a long way from the fullness of development that Nature intends for them.

Discussion of the "purposes" of Nature runs through Kant's essay; he writes in the language of providence, and the text resonates with the history of providence. This is a providence cleverly adapted to a rich sense of history, which was not present in earlier versions of the concept. We hear echoes of Leibniz in Kant's remarkable opening passages on the hidden order of our apparently chaotic human world. The "order" Leibniz presents, however, was static by comparison—even atemporal. His focus was on the beautiful mathematical structure that the informed eye can discern in an apparently random distribution of numbers. Kant's emphasis right from the start, by contrast, is on the temporal unfolding of human lives in all their messy unpredictability. The qualities in the actions of individuals that strike us as "confused and fortuitous" can be recognized in the history of the entire species, Kant says, as "a steadily advancing but slow development of man's original capacities." Elaborating the vision, he goes on, "Individual men and even entire nations little imagine that, while they are pursuing their own ends, each in his own way and often in opposition to others, they are unwittingly guided in their advance along a course intended by nature. They are unconsciously promoting an end which, even if they knew what it was, would scarcely arouse their interest" (*Political Writings,* 41).

We can hear in those remarks echoes not only of Leibniz's fascination with the hidden order of the apparently random, but also of his desire to reconcile the freedom of the individual human will with the divine choice of the best, which benignly encompasses our decisions. Leibniz, like the Stoics, saw the free acts of human individuals against the background of the totality of interconnected events; however, Kant's way of reconciling freedom and necessity engages more deeply with the temporal aspects of human existence: each act occurs against the background of the whole of history. Kant considers his present as bearing within it the past of the entire human species, and as reaching out into the distant future of that species. It is a dizzying perspective from which to contemplate human action; and Kant acknowledges that it is in some ways a bleak one. Human activities, he says, may display an occasional apparent wisdom; but, taken as a whole, they are "made up of folly and childish vanity, and often of childish malice and destructiveness." The good news is that the worse things are, the better they are becoming. Human destructiveness has its part to play in the emergence of moral maturity. It serves a higher purpose, which goes beyond any individual or collective human decision making. Behind the apparently "senseless course of human events" lies a profound "purpose in nature" (*Political Writings*, 42).

The ancient dispute between Epicurean and Stoic cosmologies—between chance and all-pervasive purpose—is here recast as a contrast between rival modern hypotheses about history and politics. On the one hand, there is what Kant considers the "implausible" hypothesis that cosmopolitan order could emerge through "random collisions" of states. On the other, there is Kant's own preferred hypothesis—that Nature develops the capacities of the human race by a regular process within apparent disorder. A third hypothesis—that it could be that nothing rational will emerge from the actions and counteractions among men as a whole—is dismissed as unthinkable. Within Kant's preferred framework of purpose in nature, the old controversies about the place of the human capacity for evil within providential harmony now find a new resolution. Kant offers a positive view of the evils that arise within human societies. Unlike many earlier resolutions of the "problem" of evil through appeal to the idea of providence, his approach does not attempt to redescribe human suffering so that it is subsumed under the higher agenda of some agent other than ourselves.

As became clear in Chapter 7, although Leibniz strongly affirmed the freedom of the human will, his reconciliation of human evil with cosmic harmony involves a trust in purposes other than our own—the purposes of divine goodness and justice. For Kant, by contrast, although Nature is purposive, the only "end" it has for human beings is the self-realization that is implicit in their own nature. Through crises of "unsocial sociability," the human species is led gradually upward to attain its own highest level; man is forced to "employ an art which is nonetheless his own" (*Political Writings*, 48). Leibniz sought to reconcile human freedom with divine purpose by incorporating human inclinations and desires into the best of all possible worlds—already understood and chosen by God. Our cooperation in the divine plan involves trustingly accepting our place in a bigger picture, which we can only dimly understand. Kant's reconciliation strategy is different: our antagonisms and the suffering they produce are the necessary catalyst for the emergence of dormant rational capacities that distinguish us from the rest of the universe. Human suffering is no longer collateral damage in the achievement of the agenda of a higher agent. The higher ends of Nature now coincide with our realization of our own natures as human beings. If we are to cooperate with "the wisdom of nature" it is above all expected that we exercise our minds—that we use our reason. In the slogan about enlightenment that Kant made famous in his companion essay to *Idea for a Universal History*—"*What Is Enlightenment?*" published in the same year—we must dare to know: "Have courage to use your *own* understanding" (*Political Writings*, 54). By exercising our minds, we realize our humanity in participating in the public realm of emerging reason—a participation that marks our progress toward full achievement of our humanity.

Something new has here entered the history of ideas of providence. Rather than trusting mindlessly, like Pangloss in Voltaire's
Candide, in the unfathomable aims of a higher being, we fulfill the
ends of Nature by learning to think for ourselves. It can all be read
as an adaptation of old Stoic ideas about cosmic purpose to the
understanding of human history; yet this philosophy rests on a
distinctly modern preoccupation with what separates human nature from the rest of creation.

Kant, emphasizing the temporal dimensions of providence, presents it as unfolding in human history. Keeping in mind this crucial shift in thinking about providence can help us more clearly
discern the role his tale of origins will play in the overall line of
argument of the *Idea for a Universal History.* Of course, more is going
on here than the retelling of a philosophical tale. The essay audaciously mixes genres. It brings together a literary device—the construction of a fiction—with an apparent testing of hypotheses
in the manner of science, although it is a highly a priori kind of
scientific reason. The essay is structured as a set of foundational
"propositions" and methodically arranged elaborations on these,
which together present different aspects of the relations between
the human individual and the human species. Despite the deliberate evocation of scientific method, however, the essay as a whole
reads like a sustained work of imaginative fiction, which takes into
account considerations of emotional plausibility. Although Kant
makes few explicit references to Rousseau's tale of origins, the
whole essay is permeated with its influence. The background philosophical story provides an imaginative frame against which the
series of "propositions" is to be assessed.

Kant's tale of origins demands that we evaluate its fittingness—
makes an appeal, in other words, to an integrated response from
reason, emotion, and imagination. This does not mean that Kant's
arguments are merely subjective or emotional. Affect and imagination are brought into interaction with the procedures of ratio-

nal argument; but Kant by no means abandons the appeal to reason. The tale of development, which engages our imagination and
emotions, is incorporated into Kant's argumentation and cannot
readily be separated from it. Thus, Kant insists, in accepting that
human beings do not act from instinct, we grant that human reason can develop its potential only within the species, not in the
individual. Having accepted that premise, we are supposed to acknowledge also that afflictions befalling the human race are intelligible in relation to the story as a whole. That human beings depend on the labors and sufferings of their forebears appears as
necessary as it is puzzling, once we "simply assume that one animal species was intended to have reason, and that, as a class of rational beings who are mortal as individuals but immortal as a species, it was still meant to develop its capacities completely" (*Political
Writings*, 44).

In *Idea for a Universal History* the demands of logic and the persuasive force of the tale of origins come together. Kant, like many
philosophers before him, makes use of literary strategies for philosophical ends; but in bringing philosophical fictions together so
directly with the logical structuring of his "propositions," he is
also doing something that is distinctively his own. Philosophers in
the past had used tales of origin to elicit a sense of necessity—not
just to offer a pleasing story but to instill a sense of fittingness, a
sense of the way things *must* be. Plato in the *Timaeus* used a tale of
origins to give persuasive expression to his convictions about how
human society should be organized. He tried to show how things
should be in the present, on the basis of how they must have been
at their beginning. We have already seen how that "must" itself
expresses a sense of fittingness rather than an absolute demand of
reason. The fiction is enhanced by its orientation toward the
past—at least an imagined past. Kant's tale, in contrast, presents
itself as reaching into the future. The genre of the philosophical
tale of origins has here taken a bold leap—into the idea of a "phil-

osophical history" that is concerned as much with the future as with the past or the present. This is a "history" in which the issue of truth will be assessed according to "how world events must develop if they are to conform to certain rational ends" (*Political Writings*, 51).

"Dare to know," indeed! Kant in effect calls on his readers to dare to know how things *must* be in the future. He repeatedly insists that some conclusions about the future of humanity are simply inconceivable. It is unthinkable, he says in the eighth proposition, that out of contemporary disorder nothing rational will emerge—unthinkable that things might simply remain as they have been. It is also unthinkable that after the current discord humanity—no matter what its cultural progress to date—should be overtaken by "a hell of evils." Emotion and imagination here come into close engagement with rational argument—not in order to subdue it, but to produce an integrated, fully human style of reasoning. For Kant, the ultimate barbaric devastation of all civilization and cultural progress achieved up to that point was simply inconceivable. It is, he says, "a fate against which it would be impossible to guard under a rule of blind chance, with which the state of lawless freedom is in fact identical, unless we assume that the latter is secretly guided by the wisdom of nature" (*Political Writings*, 48).

The philosophical tale becomes in itself an exercise in the creative conjoining of freedom and necessity. The sense of fittingness evoked by philosophical stories has entered new territory. The philosopher shows how the development of human history—at least in its broad outlines—must unfold. In the defense of his final proposition, Kant acknowledges that it may seem absurd to suggest that such an exercise should yield anything more than "a novel." He nonetheless insists that the ultimate aim of the exercise is truth: this is how things must be if we are ever to uncover a rational aim behind the spectacle of the world. This is how things must be if human destiny is to be "fulfilled here on earth," rather than "only in some other world" (*Political Writings*, 52–53).

The sense of necessity that emanates from Kant's telling of the tale of origins is accompanied by a self-fulfilling optimism, which expresses itself in a resolve to shape the future, rather than passively waiting for it to unfold. That optimism is grounded in a conviction that providential purpose is at work in the world. This purpose, however, is not understood as divine intervention; it is immanent in the efforts of human beings to fulfill their natures. Kant does not merely offer a description of this unfolding of human nature. His strategic use of the tale of origins demands of his readers that they position themselves with him as participants in the ongoing narrative of enlightenment.

An essential part of the story is that in any period of history the stirrings of the cosmopolitan future can be temporarily thwarted by human folly. In daring to engage in the process of enlightenment, however, Kant's readers are given the opportunity to cooperate with the wisdom of nature. In the final sections of the essay, Kant issues a rhetorical challenge, calling on readers to seize their historical moment and position themselves in their present as contributors to the cosmopolitan future, rather than place obstacles in the way of its onward flow. But Kant's transformation of the tale of origins into a tale of the future goes even further: the call to enlightenment is addressed not only to his present readers but also to future generations—the remote descendants of his contemporaries, who will in turn have to take up "the burden of history" (*Political Writings*, 53).

Whereas Rousseau in his tale speaks in pitying terms of the "unfortunates" who will come later, Kant embraces future generations as fellow participants in the achievement of the cosmopolitan goal. Their own future conflicts will elicit in turn an accompanying process of enlightenment—a process that they too will be able either to thwart or to facilitate. "No doubt they will value the history of the oldest times, of which the original documents would long since have vanished, only from the point of view of what interests *them,* i.e. the positive and negative achievements of nations and governments in relation to the cosmopolitan goal" (*Political Writings,* 53). His contemporaries, he insists, owe it to their descendants—to us—not to stand in the way of the maturing of human reason, as we will in turn owe it to our descendants.

In *Idea for a Universal History* the interplay of content and genre is an exercise of imagination in which Kant invites his readers to participate. His essay embraces both the ancient past and the distant future. In his temporalized version, he transforms the old Stoic idea of the cosmic city into the ideal of a universal cosmopolitan existence, to be realized as "the matrix within which all the original capacities of the human race may develop" (*Political Writings,* 51). Full human moral maturity will be achieved within the framework of an international cosmopolitan order, which will stand in a relation to states similar to that in which civil society stands to individuals.

In making these proposals, Kant follows a guiding assumption (which he shared with many of his predecessors in the history of the idea of providence)—that the "spectacle of the world is properly understood only in terms of imminent, rational purpose." Like many of them too, he is concerned to offer a justification of providence. At the end of the essay, he declares: "Such a *justification* of nature—or rather perhaps of providence—is no mean motive for adopting a particular point of view in considering the world" (*Political Writings,* 53). The justification of providence, rather than working against the forward-looking hopes and dreams of Enlightenment reason, has joined forces with them. Kantian optimism is founded on the hope that human beings can improve their world. Kant's optimism, tested against Voltaire's dictum, is not the irrational conviction that all is well; it is rather the rational hope that all may yet be well. The optimism resides in the conviction that "although folly and caprice creep in at times, *enlightenment* gradually arises" (*Political Writings*, 51).

Later, in the introductory sections of *The Contest of Faculties*—his work on the organization of the branches of learning published in 1788—Kant, returning to the issue of progress, asks whether the human race is continually improving. The French Revolution he takes as a sign of the emerging moral maturity of the human species as sketched in the *Idea for a Universal History.* The stirring of the cosmopolitan future can already be discerned, he claims, in the enthusiastic response he has witnessed among his contemporaries to the Revolution, which, he reflects, has no guarantee of success. "It may be so filled with misery and atrocities that no right-thinking man could ever decide to make the same experiment again at such a price, even if he could hope to carry it out successfully at the second attempt." Yet the Revolution has nonetheless aroused in "the hearts and desires" of its spectators a sympathy that could have been caused by nothing other than "a moral disposition within the human race" (*Political Writings*, 182).

Kant insists that it is not the event itself that matters here, but rather "the attitude of the onlookers." Grasping this special, future-imbued significance of the event as "spectacle," however, demands a rather special set of observers—able to read events as pointing to things not yet realized. In responding to events in that way, the spectators are already positioning themselves as sharing in the unfolding of Enlightenment reason, which he celebrated in the *Idea for a Universal History.* Kant's optimism is directed not to the actual future outcomes of events, but to the emerging "moral maturity" that can be discerned in those who contemplate those events in their own present. It was this perception that allowed Kant to sustain the conviction that his bold history of the future was something more than "a novel." The realization of the "cosmopolitan goal" may not have been imminent, but it was, he thought, at any rate within his contemporaries' imaginative reach.

He was no Pangloss. Considering our own "burden of history," we may nonetheless wonder at the exultant optimism expressed in his daring tale of human progress.

Hegel: From Providence to "Absolute Spirit"

Kant's bold leap of imagination into a grand future of cosmopolitan moral maturity is a fitting point at which to end the trajectory I have traced of the idea of providence. It would be an exaggeration to say that the idea of providence disappears from philosophical thought after Kant, but something does end there. After Kant, it is no longer possible to discern a continuing succession of philosophical adaptations of the idea of providence to articulate a sense of being at ease in the world.

The philosophy of late modernity and the idea of providence do not readily coexist. The dominant themes of post-Kantian philosophy will not deal with the accommodation of human life to universal necessities; they will concern rather the human attempt to modify those necessities—to extend their limits ever further, and to challenge the very necessity of limits. Hegel's philosophy has been central to that restructuring of the challenge of being human. The history of providence is by no means irrelevant to understanding the Hegelian project. But in that project the idea of providence was to be absorbed into the grand and relentless unfolding of Nature into Absolute Spirit.

Strong echoes of Stoic philosophy can be heard in much of Hegel's work—in the convergence of necessity and contingency; in reason's recognition of itself in the world; in the pervasive presence of purpose that drives the natural world no less than the drama of consciousness. Hegel's "Spirit" owes much to earlier ideas of providence—not least to Kant's temporalized version of providence as progress, but the Hegelian transformation of the idea of providence is so complete that it has no room to operate independently. Hegel himself gives it little explicit attention; however, in the sections on logic in his *Encyclopaedia of the Philosophical Sciences,* he does offer some succinct and illuminating reflections on the contrasts between ancient and modern attitudes to necessity in relation to the idea of providence.

The perception of the world as ruled by necessity, Hegel says there, by no means excludes the belief in a divine providence. It is true that a contrast exists between the apparent "blindness" of necessity—the apparent randomness of scattered circumstances—and the foreknowing and forewilling of teleological design. Even so, providence or design—here identified by Hegel with his concept of "the notion"—is in fact "the truth of necessity," and "necessity is blind only so long as it is not understood." In attempting to understand the necessity of every event, the philosophy of history, rightly understood, takes on for Hegel the status of a Theodicy. On the other hand, those who think they honor divine providence by excluding necessity from it are really reducing it to "a blind and irrational caprice."[5]

There are echoes here of Leibniz's rejection of the "freedom of indifference" as a model of the divine will. Hegel's interest in the relations between providence and necessity, however, focuses more on the contrasts between the emotional structures that distinguish modern consciousness from ancient attitudes toward necessity. His concern is with the contrasts between the "sentiments and behaviour" that divide the human beings of modernity from the ancients. Whereas in the "creed of the ancients" necessity "figured as Destiny," its place in the modern point of view is that of "Consolation."[6]

For Hegel, consolation is the prospect of receiving compensation for our having given up our aims and interests. Destiny, by contrast, leaves no room for consolation. Yet the ancient feeling about destiny, he observes, far from carrying any sense of "bondage," is the reverse; it imparts a sense of freedom, for the ancients experienced no contradiction between what happened and what *ought* to be or happen. The sense of bondage springs from an inability to surmount a perceived antithesis between the two. In the ancient conception, by contrast, "because such a thing is, it is, and as it is, so ought it to be." Hegel remarks, "Here there is no contrast to be seen, and therefore no sense of bondage, no pain, and no sorrow."[7] It is an attitude void of consolation, but at the same time a frame of mind that does not call for consolation.

From Hegel's perspective, this contrast marks the crucial stress on "personal subjectivity" that divides the "ancient sentiment" from that of the modern and Christian world. He acknowledges the appeal of the ancients' "tranquil resignation" before destiny as a "much higher and worthier mood" than that of the moderns, who "obstinately pursue their subjective aims," while consoling themselves with the prospect of a reward in some other shape when they have to resign those aims. True to his confidence in the onward march of the transformation of nature into spirit, though, Hegel sees this as a lesser form of the subjectivity of modernity. A higher consolation, Hegel insists, is to be achieved in Christianity—in the recognition of the "absolute subjectivity" of God's self-knowledge.[8]

God's self-knowledge represents for Hegel a higher form of personality than that figured in the personifications of the ancient gods, who were themselves subject to destiny. Knowledge that this higher personality exists holds out for Christian consciousness a form of "absolute" consolation that bears comparison with the tranquillity of the ancients. In this higher state of consolation, human consciousness realizes itself in the true freedom that transcends the sense of chance we experience in the disagreeable things that befall us. In this higher consciousness, whatever happens to us ultimately derives from ourselves alone.

The confidence Hegel brings to his exalted sense of the future—his conviction of its eventual attainment in the inexorable unfolding of Absolute Spirit—goes well beyond the shy hope expressed in Kant's vision of a gradual emergence of moral maturity achieved through struggle with the setbacks of history. The Hegelian convergence of freedom and necessity may well lie beyond our imaginative reach; and it may be alien to our emotional sensibilities. Yet we do not have to follow him into that vision of the human future to appreciate his insight that "it is their view of necessity . . . which is at the root of the content and discontent of men, and which in that way determines their destiny itself."[9]

We have now tracked a succession of ideas of providence structuring that sense of necessity which governs human content and discontent. Providence has played a central role in the conceptual formations that sustain and shape our emotional lives. The idea of providence has for us largely retreated from philosophical and political thought into the realm of theology and religious belief. It now remains to explore how its departure from the public space of Enlightenment reason, as Kant would say, affects our contemporary ways of thinking of our contents and discontents.

9   Providence Lost

We have seen the concept of providence, in a succession of forms, in the crossovers between religion and philosophy throughout the history of Western thought. The presence of providence in philosophy was in the past not regarded as an alien incursion. Yet if we look for it now as a living concept—one that might give rise to lively disputation or to rival accounts or approaches—we turn not to the works of contemporary philosophers but to religious discussion. Providence is now the stuff not of philosophical seminars but of sermons. Despite its departure from "secular" public discourse, however, the idea of providence exerts an influence on our thought and our lives. Through its very absence from the configurations it once formed with other concepts, the idea of providence continues to affect our lives, structuring our attitudes toward our contents and discontents, and thus, as Hegel suggested, shaping our destiny. Nowhere is this influence more evident than in the effects of the disappearance of providence from our legacy from Descartes's treatment of the freedom of the human will. To bring out the effects of this absence, I want now to return briefly for a closer look at Descartes's final words on the importance of the idea of providence.

Descartes's Legacy: The Fate of the Will

In his final work, *The Passions of the Soul*, Descartes returned to the challenge he had first taken up in his correspondence with Elisabeth—to find a practical philosophy that might provide a remedy for the turmoil caused by human passion. The idea of providence plays a central role in his final version of the remedy and allows him to put forward a subtler version of the advice that frustrated Elisabeth: Know when to cease your efforts; remain confident in the judgment that you have done your best. In the version of the strategy for finding contentment that he proposes in *The Passions of the Soul*, the ideas of providence and necessity draw closer together. Reflection on providence is the key to freedom from the tyranny of the passions; and to reflect on providence is to reflect that "nothing can possibly happen other than as Providence has determined from all eternity."[1]

Providence, Descartes says in *The Passions of the Soul*, is "so to speak, a fate or immutable necessity." We must set this idea over against that of fortune, which is a "chimera" arising solely from error: when we do not know the causes of things, we think of them as dependent on fortune. If we did know the causes completely, we would recognize that the things we wrongly think of as depending on fortune are in fact absolutely impossible. We would then never wish for them. In place of the misguided idea of fortune—which lures us into the folly of vain desires—we must, he insists, install the idea of providence. We will then consider everything that happens to us as occurring "of necessity and as it were by fate," so that it would be wrong to want things to happen in any other way (*Passions of the Soul*, part 2, sec. 146, p. 380).

All this, however, as Descartes acknowledges, leaves us with a difficulty. Amid the uncertainties of life—and lacking, as we do, complete knowledge of causes—we must first form a clear judgment about which of our longings we should consign to fate. We avoid the folly of vain desire by learning to distinguish what depends wholly on ourselves, so that we can limit our yearnings to that alone. Descartes's suggestions on how to do so are a more refined version of the advice that had already failed to satisfy Elisabeth: in the lack of complete knowledge, we are to trust to our

reason and simply do our best; but it is through reflection on the
idea of providence that we learn to surrender inappropriate efforts of will.

In an interesting but by no means transparent example, Descartes considers the quandary of a traveler who has to choose between two different routes, one usually much safer than the other.
Providence may, on a particular occasion, decree that the apparently safer route will lead us into danger, while the one that is
more likely to be dangerous would bring us safely to our destina-
tion. Yet this is no excuse for indifference or passive fatalism.
"Reason insists that we should choose the route which is usually
the safer, and our desire in this case must be fulfilled when we
have followed this route, whatever evil may befall us." All that was
required of us is "to do the best that our intellect was able to rec-
ognise." It is certain, Descartes concludes, that "when we apply
ourselves to distinguish Fatality from Fortune in this way, we easily acquire the habit of governing our desires so that their fulfillment depends only on us, making it possible for them always to
give us complete satisfaction" (*Passions of the Soul,* part 2, sec. 146,
p. 381).

The skeptical Elisabeth might well have still been dissatisfied
with this strategy for avoiding the dissatisfaction attendant on
futile desires. Self-doubt may still plague those conscientiously
struggling to do their best. Perhaps with Elisabeth's debilitating
self-doubt in mind, Descartes recommends complementing the
tactic of frequent reflection on providence by cultivating an appropriate self-esteem—a trait he calls, strangely to our ear, "generosity." This is a noncompetitive form of self-regard, which can
celebrate—rather than envy—the development of virtue in others
as well as in ourselves. His discussion of this characteristic brings
out clearly the interrelation of Descartes's treatment of divine will
and his account of human free will (*Passions of the Soul,* part 3, secs.
152–155, pp. 384–385). The proper use of our free will, he insists,

is the only thing for which we can rightly esteem ourselves, for it is the only thing for which we can be reasonably praised or blamed. The virtuous respect themselves only for the good exercise of their free will.

For the whole Cartesian strategy to work, it must be possible at least in principle to draw a clear distinction between the things that depend on divine will and those which depend on human will; between what we must deal with ourselves and what can be left to providence. Princess Elisabeth, as we know, had her difficulties with Descartes's strategy; it was all too easy for her to doubt that she had ever done "all that lay within her power." Her difficulties might have been regarded as reflecting a temperamental tendency toward self-doubt, or even—as she herself was inclined to think—more general weaknesses of her sex. As a committed Cartesian and a committed Christian, though, she may well have benefited from access to the more elaborate strategic appeal to providence that Descartes later offered in *The Passions of the Soul.*

Descartes's contemporaries—whatever difficulties they may have had with his method—could at least grasp the role he assigned to providence. The appeal to providence was available to them not just as an expression of piety, but as a viable philosophical concept—able to bear the strategic weight he accorded it. For us, in contrast, providence is akin to those evocative but ghostly ideas Wittgenstein describes as wheels that turn without moving any part of the conceptual mechanism.

For Descartes and his contemporaries, a viable—even if contestable—distinction could be drawn between the things that depend on the human will and the things that do not. It was possible to dispute exactly where the border lay, but the distinction itself was meaningful. In that early modern conceptual frame, with a clear sense of which matters could be regarded as lying within human power, it made sense to talk of leaving the rest to providence. In the lack of a complete knowledge of causes, providence ensured that the best efforts of the human will would not lead human beings completely astray. Human reason, sensibly applied, could assume that it would not be unreasonably held responsible—not at any rate in the court of appeal that really mattered: the ultimate court of divine justice, to which fallible human courts would eventually answer. Divine and human will existed in an accepted balance that guaranteed all was well. The sad fate of the human will under conditions of late modernity was to be left with a legacy of unlimited responsibility. It is as if the self-doubt of the fragile Elisabeth, plagued by the thought of all that always remained undone, had been let loose to haunt an entire culture.

Spinoza offered a drastic simplification of the unwieldy structure of the Cartesian remedy for destructive passion, as he saw it. Descartes located virtue in the proper exercise of human free will; Spinoza located it in the active exercise of intellect. Descartes emphasized justifiable self-esteem, arising from the proper exercise of the will in accordance with right judgment about its limits; Spinoza shifted the emphasis to the free appropriation of necessity. He vehemently rejected Descartes's distinction between knowledge and will; he saw that as a cumbersome distinction, operating across an equally awkward divide between divine and human, supernatural and natural. The scorn Descartes had directed at the ill-conceived notion of fortune, constructed out of human ignorance, Spinoza redirected at the Cartesian concept of providence. Providence, construed as divine will, is for Spinoza, as he says in the appendix to part 1 of the *Ethics,* the "sanctuary of ignorance"—an illusory haven to which we retreat when we do not know the causes of things.

Might it now be possible to think back through Spinoza to reconnect with ancient Greek approaches to necessity? Or would that require a greater sense of inexorable necessity than is available to "us now"? Are we now on the other side of a great divide— the belief in human power to control nature—that separates us from our own intellectual past, thus making it impossible to think

our way into the acceptance of necessity that Spinoza shared with
the Stoics?

The term "us now" is of course itself multiply ambiguous. At
the level of individual existence, wherever and whenever we are,
the basic necessities that structure a human life remain to some
degree as unavoidable as they have always been. We are born, do
what is needed to stay alive, fall ill, live—as we must—lives vulnerable to chance, and we die. In reading ancient Greek tragedies we
recognize the contours of necessity that lie not far beneath the
surface of any human life. It is the capacities and prospects of human collectivities that have changed enormously—at any rate for
those privileged to enjoy the advances and advantages of the modern West. Yet it is not our "progress" that most clearly divides us
from the ancient Greeks; it is rather the misfit between the individual and collective possibilities of life under conditions of modernity. The interplay between contingency and necessity in individual lives is no longer readily mapped onto their interplay at the
collective level. In that dislocation we can recognize what is most
distinctive in our modern mentality about attitudes toward necessity.

We now live out our individual lives against the background of
an implicit collective belief—however irrational it may be—that
the borders between the controllable and the necessary are indefi-
nitely shiftable. Our lives are subject to different anxieties and
frustrations from those presented in Greek tragedy. Given the assumption that death is always in principle avoidable, it becomes
easy to think that, when it comes, someone or something can always be held responsible. Often it is in states of dislocated consciousness—in the shock of grief—that the deeper disjunction
between individual realities and collective assumptions becomes
noticeable. Joan Didion, in her remarkable memoir on grief, *The
Year of Magical Thinking*, comments on the jarring insight into collective irrationality in the aftermath of sudden bereavement—the
shock of recognition of the falseness of the general assumption

that death can always in principle be averted. Recalling her obsession with retrospective strategies by which her husband's heart attack might have been avoided, she comments: "As I recall this I realize how open we are to the persistent message that we can avert death. And to its punitive correlate, the message that if death catches us we have only ourselves to blame."[2]

The withdrawal of providence deprives a Cartesian will of its framing sense of necessity—of the sense of a definite limit to its responsibilities. In the absence of providence, moreover, we have no assurance that what does lie beyond our control is nonetheless accommodated to human needs and well-being. It becomes possible to believe in limits to human mastery without believing that a benign divine will attends on our behalf to all that lies beyond those limits. Without benign providence, the uncontrollable can become metaphysically threatening. Indeed, when human self-esteem rests on its capacity for control, anxiety arises at having to admit the very existence of the uncontrollable. In the lack of any firm boundary, the uncontrollable can always break into our lives. Borders in themselves fuel the fear of trespass—of the eruption of the unknown into the familiar.

The philosophy of Spinoza was of course not opposed to the extension of human powers; it was notoriously congenial to "the new science." His affirmation of universal necessity does not exclude human agency or ethics, any more than ancient Stoic doctrines of necessity did. To reject the Cartesian concept of will is not thereby to embrace passivity or fatalism. But the two philosophies do represent different ways of joining ideals of freedom with the recognition of necessity. Cartesianism and Spinozism offer different models for the place of human beings in the world, and different ways of remedying the passions—all linked with different attitudes toward necessity. Descartes's approach prevailed; and the fate of the Cartesian will has been to outlive the model of providence that once made it emotionally viable.

A common form of the narrative of necessity and progress goes as follows: history traces the gradual emergence of human beings from the passive acceptance of necessity into active control over their destiny. The dream of modernity, in this narrative, depends on human ability to push back ever further the limits of what human ingenuity and strength of will can achieve. The story is one of advancing dominion—of ongoing conquest of what has hitherto been the realm of necessity. We have here a way of thinking that fits neatly Descartes's model of virtue as extending the reach of the will, through a foray out into the world. The image is a reflection of his recommended strategy for individual happiness, writ large on the screen of human collectivities. Once again, models of individual and collective progress have converged.

Spinoza offered an alternate approach—another route, which was not taken, into the mentality of modernity. There can be no real going back. Too much makes Spinoza's ideal of living with necessity alien to our way of thinking. His vision of human minds as parts of "the mind of God," corresponding to the unified whole of Nature, requires a totalizing sense of interconnection that goes well beyond our contemporary understanding of ourselves as "part of nature." We need not accept all of Spinoza's worldview, however, to learn from it. The ideal of shaping a life in accordance with necessity is intelligible even if we don't believe every detail of our lives to be integrated into a relentlessly ordered whole. In trying to make such reconnections now through Spinoza to ancient ideals of necessity—of freedom without free will, acceptance without passivity—we might rediscover the capacity to be reassured rather than terrified by necessity. We might again find delight in the mind's recognition of its own movement in perceiving how things must be. Perhaps that might serve us better, individually and collectively, than the increasingly fearful—endless because illusory—pursuit of human mastery over necessity.

If we do try to reconnect through Spinoza with the ancient

Stoic ideal of living with necessity, we will no doubt face some of the same ambiguities I talked about in Chapter 6 with regard to Spinoza's stance on providence. Did he reject the concept of providence, or did he reconstruct it in ways that connect his thinking with that of the Stoics? In trying to restate now an ideal of living in accordance with necessity, would we be learning how to live without providence? Or would we be, rather, reconnecting with ancient versions of providence—providence-without-the will? If we have no religious commitments, we might be reluctant to use the language of providence; however we describe it, though, it would clearly represent a radical departure from the Cartesian legacy concerning the will in both its divine and its human forms.

Descartes himself—despite his aspirations to a form of practical philosophy that might increasingly resist the encroachments of nature—did have a healthy sense both of the general limits of human power and of his own mortality. In a letter to his friend Chanut on 16 June 1645 he reports that whereas he once devoted himself to finding ways to preserve life, he has now found another much easier and surer method of disarming death, which is not to fear it. He knew there was a time to die, just as there was always a time to acknowledge that we have done all we can and leave the rest to providence. But Descartes could still map the limits of an individual life onto the limits of collective human power over nature. Sadly, his legacy to "us now" has been the pervasive illusion of unlimited human control. Perhaps, by imaginatively reaching back through Spinoza to the ancients, we can recover something of the acceptance of necessity, the forgotten strand in the conceptual history of the will.

From "The Best of All Possible" to "Collateral Damage"

What is Leibniz's legacy in modern attitudes toward necessity? By the time the eighteenth century was little more than half over,

Voltaire had already pilloried the optimistic belief that we were living in the "best of all possible worlds." Candide's weary insistence that we must instead "cultivate our garden" has itself, however, often been taken up as an Enlightenment slogan—as an expression of hope that a harsh world can be transformed by good sense and diligence; that reason, if only we can avoid its foolish excesses, will ultimately prevail, to the good of suffering humanity. Candide's comment is a commonsense reaction—a mantra for small-scale achievement, rather than an alternative grandiose project of reason. Yet in some ways Leibnizian grandeur lingers disconcertingly in the modern conviction that good outweighs evil in the cultivated garden—and in the assumption that it is always possible in principle to find the right balance between competing versions of the good. Here again, as with the legacy of Descartes, we have inherited the optimistic vision, without the accompanying restraints that held it in check in its original version.

Leibniz's world is imbued with providence; it is maintained and sustained by the presence of a unified center of omnipotent will and omniscient knowledge. What happens when that site is no longer occupied by such a perfect convergence of power and knowledge? The balanced interrelation of knowledge and will that is crucial to the Leibnizian synthesis depends on the idea of divine perfection. Take away the unifying force of perfection, and there is nothing left that can determine the right balance between will and intellect, power and knowledge. Without the perfection of the divine creator, no balancing of competing elements is feasible that could otherwise unite them in the best possible whole. Without the perfection of divine will, we are left not simply with an inferior version of the Leibnizian interconnected totality: without the infallible maker, we have no interconnected whole at all, but merely a jumble of disparate fragments.

The balance of intellect and will, of power and knowledge, depends on the idea of unified perfection; with its departure from the scene we also lose the delicate balancing act that kept the best of all possible worlds coherent. Without perfection, there is no "best of all possible"—only the best that we can manage on any occasion with our limited resources of intellect and will. The patient voice of Candide reminds us that we may not really be worse off because we have lost the conviction that our world is the best one possible. We may be better without the illusion of perfection. Still, the remnants of the Leibnizian vision—the disconnected elements of the grand synthesis—haunt our understanding of human agency and its effects in the world. The idea of achieving a balance among competing ends, interests, or "values" is one such locus of confused collective memory; the idea of "higher ends" that can justify the damage wrought by our imperfect actions is another.

In the absence of a perfect being, all agency is fallible. Leibniz of course allowed for the existence of fallible agents in his best of all possible worlds: whatever they chose to do, providence had it covered—accommodated within a world that in its totality was the best of all possible wholes. But what happens to that conceptual scheme when fallible human agency is all there is? The predicament that the loss of providence throws up for a Leibnizian worldview is that there is no longer a systematically interlocking whole into which inadequate and malevolent actions can be accommodated. All agency, whether individual or collective, is now all too fallible. The best of all possible worlds has become the best we can manage in a world of our own making. Yet the framing idea of an infallible choice of higher ends persists in our illusion that the morally good intention somehow cancels out harm done.

As with the Cartesian legacy, we seem to have inherited bits of the Leibnizian worldview without the accompanying concept of providence that made it work. From the celebration of the best of all possible worlds, we have moved to the celebration of the best action possible. A human will, being human, must inevitably act without full knowledge of past events, present conditions, and future consequences. It is not wise for such a will to model itself on the infallible choices of a perfect will—unless the human will can incorporate that accompanying divine will effectively into a coherent ethic. Human fallibility, rather than being the imperfect antithesis of the divine omniscience and omnipotence that framed it for Leibniz, now occupies the place of all-knowing, all-providing divine agency. Lack of knowledge—no longer a limitation on prudent action that must be taken into account—has become a mitigating excuse for harm done. Recognition of vulnerability to fallible decision making is swallowed up in a sense of moral rectitude, resting on good intentions. The "shadows in the beautiful picture" now become the "necessary evils" that accompany the execution of our higher ends. The suffering of the innocent, which was for Augustine and for Leibniz the terrible but beautiful cost of divine justice, lives on in confused contemporary ideas of "collateral damage." Anything not encompassed by a pure intention is allowed to pass as not really having been "done," even when the unintended consequences—as in the case of civilian casualties of military air strikes—occur too commonly to be considered unforeseeable.

Leibniz, echoing Augustine, resolved the "problem" of evil by appealing to the wise decisions of a benign divine will intent on providing for human needs and interests. Spinoza contemptuously dismissed the supposed problem, in the appendix to part 1 of the *Ethics*. To the questions "Why are things corrupt to the point where they stink? so ugly that they produce nausea? why is there confusion, evil and sin?" his caustic response is that matter was not lacking for everything conceivable to an infinite mind to come into being. "Things are not more or less perfect because they please or offend men's senses, or because they are of use to, or are incompatible with, human nature." On the issue of the free human choice of evil, Spinoza is equally dismissive. "To those who ask 'why God did not create all men so that they would be governed by the command of reason?'" he will answer, he says, only: "'Because he did not lack material to create all things, from the highest degree of perfection to the lowest' or, to speak more properly, 'because the laws of his nature have been so ample that they sufficed for producing all things which can be conceived by an infinite intellect.'"[3]

Leibniz saw Spinoza's treatment of the supposed problem of evil as an insult to providence, which reduced divine will to the compulsion of fate. "We now" may well have more patience with Spinoza's sardonic dismissal of the problem than with his contemporaries' attempts to "justify the ways of God to man," in Pope's phrase. We might also look to Spinoza for an alternative way of thinking of the conjunction of good intention and fallible knowledge to the one that lingers in contemporary ideas of "collateral damage." The suggestion that wars happen because "matter was not lacking" may better capture contemporary realities of power and knowledge than appeals to supposedly higher ends. Spinoza's philosophy opens up a different approach to responsibility, in allowing us to consider lack of relevant knowledge as itself a locus of responsibility—as something we may need to answer for, rather than as an excuse for harm we have occasioned. More generally, it focuses attention on the suffering we cause, rather than on the alleged higher good to which our intentions are directed.

Public discourse is, for the most part, little concerned these days with seeking to reconcile divine providence with the presence of evil in the world. But the tones of Leibnizian optimism can still be heard in justifications of public policy on war or torture, and in the prevailing rhetoric about finding a balance among different "values." When we are told that we must surrender basic freedoms in the name of "finding the right balance" between such values as liberty and security, we should be wary. Talk of the right balance makes sense in a case where competing demands can be encompassed within a meaningful totality. Such rhetoric makes little sense in a situation where the rival forms of the "good" are incommensurable, and it can readily mask a specious alignment of frames for judging an action or policy that are in fact incompatible. One shrewd commentator on recent Australian government policy on the treatment of refugees and asylum seekers observed wryly that the authorities seem to think they have found the right balance between cruelty and compassion. It is an observation in the spirit of Voltaire responding to the moral optimism of Leibniz.

Moral Luck

Some of the philosophical tensions in our contemporary ways of thinking of intention and morality have been fruitfully addressed through the concept of moral luck—as explored especially by Bernard Williams and Thomas Nagel.[4] As Nagel sums up the concept, moral luck is appropriately invoked when a significant aspect of what someone does depends on factors beyond his or her control, yet we continue to subject that person's action to moral judgment. Acknowledging that certain situations call for such a concept appears, on the face of it, at odds with the common assumption—which has strong connections with our heritage from Kantian ethics—that good or bad luck is irrelevant to our moral judgments of people and actions.

Much of the debate around moral luck focuses on predicaments similar to those which arise in Euripides' dramas—situations where decisions must be made under conditions of uncertainty, or where the full nature of what is done becomes clear only in retrospect, in the light of how things turn out. The preoccupation with the will—with purity of moral intention—that is central to modern ethical consciousness may intensify such ethical predicaments. We are tempted, in Nagel's words, "to feel that some decision must be possible in the light of what is known at the time, which will make reproach unsuitable no matter how things turn out." We are drawn toward thinking that our responsibility extends only to the limits of our control.

The idea that we might be, in Nagel's phrase, "morally at the mercy of fate" is indeed disconcerting if we think of it within a framework that emphasizes the will as the site of moral responsibility. I talked earlier of the limitless responsibility that seems to ensue once loss of providence eliminates any sense of a firm line between matters that do and those which do not lie within human control. To be given control that is in principle limitless is to be given also responsibility in principle limitless. The retreat to pure intention—to the idea of what we "really" do, as distinct from the consequences that lie beyond our intention—can be regarded as reinstating a sense of limitation on our responsibility. The limits of actions and results for which we are responsible are now relocated within the mind, rather than, as in the Cartesian model, at the mind's borders with the changing world. In the absence of providence in the role Descartes assigned to it, the entire weight of responsibility falls on the will. "Collateral damage" is then considered to be harm caused beyond the bounds of our intentions. The conceptual boundaries of intention may themselves be too imprecise to bear the weight needed here.

To some degree the modern concept of the will generates the need for a clear line between the pure intention and the compromised outcome. The challenges, and the quandaries, of the concept of moral luck arise from its uneasy situation of simultaneously inhabiting two different moral landscapes. It evokes, on the one hand, the ancient notion of human vulnerability to chance and necessity, and on the other the moral landscape of modernity, with its emphasis on will and control. It is within the arena of the will that the idea of moral luck gives rise to discomfort. Within the moral framework of the modern will, we are preoccupied with the conditions under which we can be *held* responsible—often at the expense of attention to the conditions in which it is appropriate for us to *take* responsibility. Both concerns are of course applicable within both the ancient and the modern moral perspective—and it is of course possible to be held responsible within both for not taking appropriate responsibility. Yet it is the modern emphasis on the will, with its accompanying focus on issues of praise and blame, that makes the idea of moral luck so discomforting.

The narrative of providence I have offered in this book is oriented toward acceptance rather than denial of the possibility of moral luck; but it also suggests that the discomfort induced by the idea of moral luck derives largely from the ambivalent power exerted by our Cartesian legacy of an autonomous human will. To consider moral luck a problem is already to position ourselves on "our" side of the divide that separates "us now" from the ancient conception of acceptance of necessity.

Facing the Future

Kantian optimism about the future rested on a daring adaptation of the idea of providence—its embodiment in human history. Kant's grand vision of the cosmopolitan goal was secured by a confidence in the ultimate achievement of nature's design for the realization of the fullness of human reason. It was crucial, however, to the Kantian vision of the future that the kind of reason that would represent that noble fulfillment was not primarily "theoretical" reason, but what he called practical reason: the capacity to formulate, and act in accordance with, universal moral laws. Reason, thus construed, was Kant's version of true freedom.

It was the antithesis of indecision—of the state Leibniz had called the "freedom of indifference," the passivity of a will unable to choose between equally appealing alternatives.

Kant's extraordinary account of the unfolding of providence in human history, in *The Idea for a History with a Cosmopolitan Purpose,* was based on his earlier treatment of design and purpose in the *Critique of Judgement.* There, Kant had appealed to nature's purpose, in giving an account of human reason and of its relations with the rest of the world. "Without man," he says in the *Critique of Judgement,* "the whole of creation would be a mere wilderness, a thing in vain, and have no final end." It is not, however, man's cognitive faculty, his "theoretical reason," that forms the "point of reference which alone gives its worth to the existence of all else in the world—as if the meaning of his presence in the world was that there might be some one in it that could make it an object of *contemplation.*" It is rather the presence of moral beings—autonomous agents acting on universally binding principles—that represents the fulfillment of the rest of nature.[5] The *Idea for a Universal History* completes that picture of the realization of nature's purposes: the achievement of the "cosmopolitan goal" for humanity will realize in turn nature's intentions for the world as a whole.

It is a grand vision, and one that lends to individual human struggles—to borrow George Eliot's phrase in the prelude to *Middlemarch*—"a certain spiritual grandeur." The audacity of Kant's appropriation and adaptation of Rousseau's imaginative mapping of the history of the human species onto individual human development is breathtaking. Whereas Rousseau assimilated human history to individual growth, the emotional force of Kant's assimilation goes in the other direction: the individual struggle for moral maturity is imbued with the grandeur of the unfolding of Nature's purposes for the whole species and for the world as a whole.

However, this exalting of the individual in Kant's representation of providence as progress comes at a cost. Hannah Arendt articulated the problem at the conclusion of her *Lectures on Kant's Political Philosophy.* There she calls attention to an apparent contradiction at the heart of Kant's crucial linking of the particular and the universal in his treatment of progress: "In Kant himself there is this contradiction: Infinite Progress is the law of the human species; at the same time, man's dignity demands that he be seen (every single one of us) in his particularity and, as such, be seen—but without any comparison and independent of time—as reflecting mankind in general. In other words, the very idea of progress—if it is more than a change in circumstances and an improvement of the world—contradicts Kant's notion of man's dignity. It is against human dignity to believe in progress. Progress, moreover, means that the story never has an end. The end of the story itself is in infinity. There is no point at which we might stand still and look back with the backward glance of the historian."[6]

As a moral being, each of us represents the full realization of nature's purposes; yet that achievement also depends on the unfolding of human history. Nature's ends are achieved in the fullness of history, yet each individual is, in Kant's famous slogan, to be treated as an "end in itself." Hence the paradox that Arendt perceives at the heart of the Kantian vision of progress. The end in itself is also a work in progress. It seems, moreover, that for Kant there can be no actual present in which the fruition will come to pass. The achievement of the goal is deferred to an infinite future.

Troubling though that paradox may be for the ultimate coherence of Kant's broader moral theory, it is this very tension between particular and universal, individual and species—and between present actuality and the yet-to-be-realized future—that gives Kant's version of optimism a greater resilience than the Cartesian or Leibnizian treatments of free will and necessity. The hope of achieved purpose at some indefinite point in an infinite future may—in its very distance from the present—sustain human hope more effectively than can trust in an impenetrable providence, supposedly operating in the here and now. An inherent indeterminacy characterizes the Kantian vision of the future—a built-in skepticism about when nature's goals might ever be accomplished. The elusive end of human fulfillment is always still to come. In this sense of uncircumscribed futurity "we now" can perhaps find some emotional and argumentative resonances with Kant's vision.

Jacques Derrida—so often maligned as a supposed "postmodern" enemy of Enlightenment ideals—in many of his later works explored the legacy of Kant's vision of enlightenment in contemporary paradoxes—aporias—of the indeterminate future. The concept which fascinates Derrida is that of the "perhaps," which he elaborates as a nexus of considerations of time and modality. Here the relations among past, present, and future intersect with those of actuality, possibility, and necessity. The experience of the "perhaps"—the state of eager anticipation of what may happen—brings a way of thinking of the future that cannot be reduced to the thought of a future present whose actual arrival we anticipate or expect. The futurity associated with Derrida's "perhaps"—like the future of Kant's unfolding providence—is always still to come. It contrasts with thinking about the future based on probable outcomes—a way of thinking associated with more conventional ideas of human control of contingencies.

Derrida's treatment of the future is associated with another strand in his later works—his emphasis on the singularity of "the event": the utter particularity of "that which comes to pass." The "event" comes to us always with an element of surprise—of the utterly unexpected, the unique occurrence: "Unheard of, totally new, that very experience which no metaphysician might yet have dared to think." It is an experience akin to risk—an "addressing of oneself to the possible."[7] In its uniqueness, its singularity, this experience of the "perhaps" locates us at a crossroads of chance and necessity: the thought of the one becomes the thought of the other. The utter contingency of something so singular that it cannot be repeated becomes the utter necessity of something that, being unique, cannot be different from what it is. Although chance and necessity can seem to be radically antithetical—the completely random, as opposed to the completely determined— they converge in our emotional response to facing the indeterminate future. Both chance and necessity elicit a sense of vulnerability to that which cannot be brought under human control—and with it a fear of passivity, which is the dark flip side of the prized autonomy of the modern will.

Derrida's "event" is the element of chance at the heart of all thought of the future. His articulation of the concept evokes the breathless sense of futurity in Kant's temporalized version of providence. But in the shifting emotional resonances of this paradoxical "perhaps," we can also recognize the instability of our contemporary orientation toward the future—the strange mixture of delighted anticipation of the unknown, and the accompanying sense of dread; the ambivalence in the sense of boundless possibilities. We find echoes here of the theme of openness to the unexpected that we saw, at the beginning of this book, in early Greek tragedy. That theme of openness to the unexpected reverberates also in Arendt's remarks about Kant's sense of an indefinite future that resists the backward glance of the historian. In an earlier work, her wonderful *Life of the Mind,* Arendt foreshadowed her later reflections on judgment in a celebration of "the thinking will" in its capacity for an "enlarged mentality" able to embrace— among many other things—the openness of the future. Her later thoughts on judgment bring the open-ended, nonformulaic character of Kantian judgment together with ancient Greek ideals of contemplative thought—and in particular with Epictetus's description of the spectators' perspective on "the fair of life," which I discussed earlier.

For Kant, judgment was a way of thinking that deals with particulars—with specific situations—without subjecting them to general rules that can become ossified. Arendt, too, considered that judgment is different from established knowledge. It is unprogrammed, uncircumscribed thinking—"a manifestation of the wind of thought." The metaphor, which has special resonances in relation to the mind's confrontation with the indeterminacy of the future, fits well with the metaphor Charles Taylor invokes in *A Secular Age* when he talks of the "buffered" disenchanted self and the predicaments it faces in the modern world. I have argued that the loss of providence exposes that buffered modern self to new vulnerabilities. It is no less true, however, that this loss offers new possibilities of reconnection with older ideals that preceded the philosophical construct of *the will*.

Bernard Williams, as I mentioned in the introduction, suggested in *Shame and Necessity* that now that many of the intervening assumptions of modernity are falling away, we can find some striking affinities between the mentality of the ancient Greeks and our own. Williams's point was that many of the central beliefs which have structured modern philosophical thought, and indirectly sustained modern lives, have been rejected or simply fallen away from consciousness. We no longer readily believe that the world was made for us, that our history tells a purposive story, that there is a "redemptive Hegelian history or universal Leibnizian cost-benefit analysis to show that it will all come out well enough in the end."[8] I have argued in this book that lurking beneath modernity's much celebrated mastery of Fortune is an incapacity to think coherently either about the necessities that frame human life or its uncontrollable contingencies. To see now more clearly our separation from ancient Greek attitudes to necessity—and the unprecedented affinities we nonetheless have with them—let us turn, in conclusion, to one more of the timeless dramas of Euripides.

Chosen Death: The Sacrifice of Iphigenia

Iphigenia at Aulis was Euripides' final play. It seems patchy by comparison with the *Bacchae,* a work of consummate artistry. It is even more difficult here than with his earlier plays to determine exactly which bits can be attributed to Euripides himself, and which are the work of later "revisers." Revisions were made even before the play's first performance, after Euripides' death; the process of reconstruing and culturally appropriating Iphigenia's sacrifice seems to have started before the play was even performed. Even with the parts we can be confident were written by Euripides himself, it is more difficult than usual to judge what his own stance may have been toward his characters and the action of the play. Because of the textual ambiguities of the work—its fragmentation, the uncertainty of its overall rationale—it epitomizes the challenges of interpreting ancient texts. Yet it is not difficult to regard the story of Iphigenia as in many ways a parable for our own times.

Like many other classical Greek dramas, including many of Euripides' earlier works, *Iphigenia at Aulis* retells the story of the siege of Troy. This time, the action takes place on the Greek coast, before the Greeks have set sail on their mission. The context is provided by the preconditions—of the most direct kind possible—of that momentous embarkation. Becalmed at Aulis, apparently abandoned by the gods, the Greeks, in growing unease, await a favorable wind. They have already formed the patriotic resolve to avenge the seizing of Helen. Agamemnon and his men are now poised in an unnerving hiatus between the intent and the act. They are powerless to resolve their dilemma; the movement of the winds is not theirs to control; the fate of their mission is entirely in the hands of the gods. According to the seer Calchas, the goddess Artemis is angry; and she will be placated only if Agamemnon sacrifices his daughter Iphigenia in appeasement.

How widely, if at all, the oracle of Calchas has been communicated to the troops is one of the contested issues in scholarly debate about which sections of the play can be attributed to Euripides himself. Inconsistencies in the text make it even more difficult than in the earlier plays to decide what might have been the aging Euripides' own attitude toward the demands of the gods, Agamemnon's compliance, or the patriotism implicit in the mission. At the core of the drama—vivid amid the ambiguities of the text— is Iphigenia's own transformation of her predicament into an act of chosen self-sacrifice.

Iphigenia's dying enacts the appropriation of necessity—the transformation of fate into freedom. Agamemnon has lured Iphigenia and her mother Clytemnestra to Aulis with the promise that she is to be married. Achilles, unknown to himself, has been chosen as the supposed husband-to-be. Clytemnestra's provocative overtures toward her putative future son-in-law, and Achilles' puzzled embarrassment in response, provide an interlude of comedy in a dark story. But the misunderstandings and accommodations that unfold between them have a deeper significance. Their intrigues confront us with another variation on the themes of truth, action, and necessity observed in Euripides' earlier plays. The unstable illusions of Achilles and Clytemnestra—along with Agamemnon's vacillations—throw into relief the clarity of intent in Iphigenia's self-sacrifice, her luminous acceptance of necessity.

Agamemnon's equivocations—his failure either to accept the will of the gods or to make any serious attempt to defy them— produce an atmosphere of confusion. "What a yoke of necessity have I fallen under!" he cries, as he swings irresolutely from one command to another, dispatching and recalling his message summoning Iphigenia to Aulis. "The god has attacked me stealthily and proved far craftier than my craftiness."[9] Craftiness, rather than clear action, is Agamemnon's style of response to crisis. His initial deception of his wife and daughter creates a cruel confusion; he cannot even speak clearly to his bewildered daughter about her fate. In the lack of any clear engagement with the truth, his actions are unstable. Under the withering questioning of Iphigenia and Clytemnestra, after they have discovered his real intentions, he defends himself by recourse to an acceptance of fate that could be a model for what Leibniz dismisses as *Fatum Mahometanum:* "I understand what calls for pity and what does not, and I love my children: I would be mad otherwise. It is a terrible thing to steel myself to this deed, but a terrible thing likewise not to. For my fate will be the same" (*Iphigenia at Aulis,* lines 1255–1259).

Under the pressure of his daughter's and his wife's demands for clarity, Agamemnon articulates his own kind of acceptance of necessity; it consists in recognizing the overriding demands of loyalty to the Greek state, as opposed to individual needs or desires. "See how large a seagoing army is here, how many Greeks with panoplies of bronze! They cannot go to the towers of Ilium or capture the glorious plains of Troy unless I kill you: so Calchas says. A great longing runs riot in the Greek army to sail with all speed to the land of the barbarians and stop the abduction of Greek wives. The Greeks will kill my girls in Argos and the two of you and me if I make void the goddess's oracle. It is not Menelaus who has enslaved me, nor have I gone over to his purposes: it is Hellas. To her I must sacrifice you, whether I will or no: she is my ruler" (*Iphigenia at Aulis,* lines 1259–1275).

Clytemnestra's responses, in comparison, show determination and clarity of purpose, but the foolish plot she hatches with the perplexed but compliant Achilles displays a different kind of lack of engagement with truth—one both more complex and more poignant. Achilles is already ineffectually agitated about the effects of the enforced delay on his own interests; he is trying to keep his restless Myrmidons in check as they press him: "Achilles, why are we waiting?" (*Iphigenia at Aulis,* line 814).

"Join your right hand with mine, to mark the beginning of blessed nuptials!" demands the deluded Clytemnestra. "Perhaps we are both being tripped up with words," responds Achilles. Clytemnestra is abashed at discovering that she has been "eager for a non-existent marriage." The nonexistent nuptial plans now become for her a weirdly real basis for an alliance with Achilles in the attempt to oppose the will of Agamemnon. Freed from the illusion of her daughter's impending marriage, and informed of Agamemnon's real intentions, she turns to Achilles for help. He is, after all, her daughter's nonhusband; even an illusory husband has obligations to his putative wife and mother-in-law! "Help me in my misfortune, son of the goddess," she pleads, "help her who was called, even if falsely, your wife. It was for you that I decked her out and brought her to be married, but now I'm bringing her to be slaughtered. It will be a reproach to you if you do not help her. For even if you were not married to her, you were at least called the poor maiden's beloved husband" (*Iphigenia at Aulis,* lines 903–909).

The illusory husband agrees to honor his hypothetical responsibilities. Not surprisingly, his attempts to rally support among the troops for the bizarre project to defend the honor of his non-wife find no favor with the frustrated Greeks. They threaten to stone him to death, as even his own Myrmidons turn against him. The nonexistent marriage itself is turned to ridicule.

> Achilles: They said that I was a slave of marriage.
> Clytaemnestra: And what did you reply?
> Achilles: I begged them not to kill my future wife . . .
> Clytaemnestra: As is only fair.
> Achilles: . . . whom her father promised me.
> Clytaemnestra: Yes, and summoned from Argos.
> Achilles: But I was drowned out by the shouting.
> Clytaemnestra: The multitude are a terrible bane.
>
> (*Iphigenia at Aulis,* lines 1355–1359)

The nonexistent marriage becomes a grotesque parody of the saga of love and betrayal, honor and vengeance, that is being played out in the drama of the becalmed Trojan expedition. For Agamemnon, when he is eventually forced to bring to clarity his confused intentions, it is not the goddess Artemis but Hellas that necessitates the act of sacrifice. It is Hellas also, in a more prosaic form—in the volatile frustration and impatience of the Greek soldiers, massed on the shore, awaiting the saving breeze—that determines the fate of Iphigenia.

What then of Iphigenia? A very young woman, plunged from the heights of delighted nuptial expectations to the depths of confrontation with untimely death, she has little time to form her attitude toward necessity. She pleads to Agamemnon: "Do not kill me before my time: to see the light of day is sweet. And do not compel me to look upon the Underworld" (*Iphigenia at Aulis*, lines 1215–1219). Iphigenia is soon able, though, to position her own fate in the larger context of the saga of love, grief, and revenge in which her individual life is caught up. The breath that Zeus has blown against the current is, in Iphigenia's lament, identified with the all-encompassing whirling breeze of fate—

> different for different mortals,
> a joy for the sails of some,
> for others grief, for others harsh necessity,
> for some a setting forth, for others the furling of sail, for
>   others delay.
> How vexed, how vexed, it seems, is our race,
> we who live but a day! It is fated
> that men must have trouble for their lot.
> (*Iphigenia at Aulis*, lines 1329–1332)

The hapless Achilles has urged Clytemnestra to hold her daughter fast while he, the brave warrior, will resist the force of her father

and the multitude. Iphigenia has the wisdom to recognize the futility of resistance, to realize that her mother is angry "to no purpose" (*Iphigenia at Aulis,* line 1369). Iphigenia seizes the only option
still available to her—the free choice of a noble death. "It is determined that I must die: but to do so gloriously—that is the thing I
want to do, clearing myself from all taint of baseness" (*Iphigenia at
Aulis,* lines 1375–1377).

What exactly is the content of this noble death? Iphigenia's
speech is strong in patriotic sentiment, as well as in pragmatism.
She points out to her mother that Achilles' foolhardy resistance is
unlikely to improve their lot. But might the young woman's concern be also a more self-centered one—that Achilles, in dying to
no avail, would deprive Iphigenia herself of the possibility of a
noble death? Achilles' chosen death would not be, in Iphigenia's
eyes, a noble surrender to necessity, but rather an act of silliness.
Her own self-sacrifice, by contrast, will do honor to Hellas. It will
allow the expedition to succeed; it will save other women from
Helen's fate.

Iphigenia has already lamented the fact that her own fate is
caught up in the saga of Helen's abduction. By now embracing her
fate, she can turn the pathos of her place in the story of Helen
into a position of honor in the triumphal tale of Greek revenge.
"All this rescuing is accomplished by my death, and the fame I win
for freeing Hellas will make me blessed," she tells her grieving
mother. "Truly it is not right that I should be too in love with my
life: you bore me for all the Greeks in common, not for yourself
alone. Countless hoplites and countless rowers will dare, since
their country has been wronged, to fight bravely against the enemy and die on behalf of Hellas: shall my single life stand in the
way of all this?" (*Iphigenia at Aulis,* lines 1383–1391).

From Iphigenia's perspective, the issue of gender roles also demands attention. The foolish Achilles would do battle with all the
Greeks and be killed for a woman's sake. "Better to save the life of
a single man than ten thousand women!" she cries. "If Artemis has

decided to take my body, shall I, who am mortal, oppose a god-dess? That is impossible: I shall give myself to Greece" (*Iphigenia at Aulis,* lines 1394–1397). Exactly what Euripides might himself have thought of this pious, patriotic, and perhaps misogynist fervor is obscured—by the corruptions of the text, as well as by his own masterly irony. The whole expedition, after all, is also about the destruction of many male lives for one woman. In the comment of the chorus leader we can detect a hint of Euripides' detachment from both the piety and the patriotism that Iphigenia expresses: "Your conduct, maiden, is noble. Yet ill is the fate the gods have sent you" (*Iphigenia at Aulis,* lines 1402–1403).

In a beautiful twist to the unfolding drama, Achilles, witnessing the nobility of Iphigenia, is moved to a true declaration of love and commitment: "Hellas I consider enviable because she has you, and you I consider enviable because you have her" (*Iphigenia at Au-lis,* lines 1405–1406). In promising to stay nearby to defend her, in case she changes her mind before the sacrifice, Achilles gains his own place in her noble death. He will ensure that if she dies, it will not be by her folly. He will intervene only if she herself aban-dons her project to claim a noble death. His protection will ensure that she will die either nobly or not at all. Even the weak, wavering Agamemnon is given a part in the patriotic pageant. Iphigenia, in her final interpretation of her father's "unholy act," explains: "He killed me for Hellas' sake against his will" (*Iphigenia at Aulis,* line 1456). Iphigenia dies a glorious death, declaring that she is "de-parting, to give the Greeks salvation and victory" (*Iphigenia at Aulis,* line 1476). But the revisers—apparently unwilling to miss any op-portunity to turn her into a patriotic emblem—introduced a last-minute reprieve. In the final, triumphant scene, the audience is told that a doe has miraculously been substituted as the sacrificial victim, while Iphigenia flies off to dwell among the gods.

Although the death is in the end ambiguous, we are left in no doubt about the glory. What should we now make of Iphigenia's self-sacrifice? What drove her to her resolute embrace of her fate?

To try to reconnect with the mentality that found this tale emotionally intelligible is in some ways as difficult for "us now" as it is
to comprehend the motivation of contemporary suicide bombers.
Our own distant cultural origins can seem as strange and alien as
the mystifying "values" we confront in that other readiness to embrace death.

When the actions of others are a mystery to us, it is easy to fall
back on simple models of reward and punishment. The "instant
reward" of paradise is often cited to explain suicide bombings. Although the will to martyrdom does figure in the self-descriptions
of some suicide bombers, and in the narratives of their deaths offered by those close to them, it may be in general no more adequate an explanation for the phenomenon than it would be to describe Iphigenia as being driven by a desire to live among the gods.
The closing *deus ex machina*—*ex machina ad deos*—of Iphigenia is the
most superficial of many layers of representation of her complex
choice. It is not commonly accepted as belonging to Euripides'
original text; and in any case the context makes it clear that the
desire for a life spent among the gods was not her motive. To what
extent she was genuinely driven by piety, by patriotism, or by a
combination of the two is left unresolved. Was patriotic love of
Hellas her real motivation? Or might it have been a gloss she offered to reconcile Clytemnestra—and perhaps also to impress the
illusory husband in whose eyes she regards herself as shamed?

All these questions remain unclear. It is clear, however—as well
as more important in relation to the history of ideas of providence
and necessity—that Iphigenia has come, amid the disarray and
confusion that surround her, to the sad recognition that she has
no way out. Having rejected the desperate maneuvers of her advisers, she apprehends that the only way of salvaging her hopes for
a purposeful, joyous life reside in an effort to make her own way
of dying. Whether her fate has been determined by the gods, the
winds, her father's weakness or her father's strength, or the vola-

tile emotions of "the multitude"—all that is in the end irrelevant. All that matters to her is that she freely embrace the necessity of her death. Iphigenia's death is not a suicide. But it is a death that evokes the ancient Stoic image of the door that is always open—the free acceptance of the ultimate necessity.

The transmutation of necessity into noble death is an old ideal. It remains in many ways foreign to a modern mentality. Hegel, however, transformed that ideal into the aspiration to achieve a higher selfhood through struggle to the point of death; and the concept lingers on in much contemporary patriotic rhetoric. The hope of turning meaningless death into something of grandeur is still with us; and it still makes the young vulnerable to the patriotism of the powerful.

Something else too—very different in mood—connects us with the dying thoughts of Iphigenia, as the troops gather to await the winds that will carry them on to the unpredictable triumphs and horrors of Troy. *Iphigenia at Aulis* speaks timelessly to us of our vulnerability to forces beyond human control; of human foibles and frailties; of the fickleness of the gods to whom we have given our trust. It speaks to us also in yet another way. In Iphigenia's sad tones we can hear something akin to the bleak yet strangely reassuring cadences of Samuel Beckett in *Waiting for Godot*, his evocation of endless waiting for a desired presence that will never arrive. We can detect that tone too at the end of his *Trilogy* when he narrates the struggle, in the strange realm of "the unnamable," to find meaning in continuing, when no other meaning is left. In the concluding lines of *The Unnamable*, Beckett shows us not only the tenuous struggles of an individual consciousness, but also the struggle of the contemporary collective mind, which has outlived the conceptual configurations that once gave form to its contents and discontents.[10] All that remains open to it is the inexorable sense of futurity, which is also a sense of necessity: "In the silence you don't know, you must go on, I can't go on, I'll go on."

Notes

Introduction

1. Bernard Williams, *Shame and Necessity* (Berkeley: University of California Press, 1993), 166.

2. Charles Taylor, *A Secular Age* (Cambridge, Mass.: Harvard University Press), 20.

3. Taylor discusses the concept of "social imaginaries" in relation to secularity and modernity especially in chap. 4, ibid., 159–211.

1. Euripides, Philosopher of the Stage

1. Fragment 44, Charles Kahn, *The Art and Thought of Heraclitus: An Edition of the Fragments with Translation and Commentary* (Cambridge: Cambridge University Press, 1962), 49.

2. Fragment 37, ibid., 45.

3. Fragments 125 and 94, ibid., 85 and 71.

4. The fable of Euripides giving Socrates a copy of Heraclitus is cited by Jonathan Barnes in his book *The Presocratic Philosophers* (London: Routledge & Kegan Paul, 1982), 57–58.

5. Euripides, *The Women of Troy*, in *Euripides: The Bacchae and Other Plays*, trans. Philip Vellacott (Middlesex: Penguin Books, 1954), 110.

6. The fragment is cited and discussed by Paul Décharmes in his *Euripides and the Spirit of His Dramas,* trans. J. Loeb (Port Washington, N.Y.: Kennikat Press, 1968), 21–34.

7. Euripides, *Alcestis,* ed. and trans. David Kovacs, Loeb Classical Library 12 (Cambridge, Mass.: Harvard University Press, 2001). Subsequent quota-

tions are accompanied, in parentheses, by line references in text to that edition (unless otherwise noted).

8. *Euripides in a Version by Ted Hughes: Alcestis* (London: Faber and Faber, 1999).

9. Ibid., 37.

10. Jacques Derrida, *The Politics of Friendship,* trans. George Collins (London: Verso, 1997), 67.

11. Leo Tolstoy, "The Death of Ivan Ilyich," in *The Death of Ivan Ilyich and Other Stories* (London: Penguin, 1960), 137.

12. George Eliot, *Middlemarch* (London: Oxford University Press, 1947), 455.

13. Hughes, *Alcestis,* 15.

14. Ibid., 22.

15. Ibid.

16. Ibid., 5–6.

17. Ibid.

18. Euripides, *Helen,* ed. and trans. David Kovacs, Loeb Classical Library 11 (Cambridge, Mass.: Harvard University Press, 2002), lines 309–310. Subsequent quotations are accompanied, in parentheses, by line references in text to that edition.

19. In Edmund Keeley and Philip Sherrard, trans., *Four Greek Poets: C. P. Cavafy, George Sefaris, Odysseus Elytus, Nikos Gatsos* (London: Penguin, 1966).

20. Euripides, *Orestes,* ed. and trans. David Kovacs, Loeb Classical Library 11 (Cambridge, Mass.: Harvard University Press, 2002), lines 974–980.

21. Euripides, *Bacchae,* ed. and trans. David Kovacs, Loeb Classical Library 495 (Cambridge, Mass.: Harvard University Press, 2002), lines 201–209. Subsequent quotations are accompanied, in parentheses, by line references in text to that edition.

22. Cicero's account of Epicurus on pleasure is from his work *On Ends.* The quotation is given in A. A. Long and D. N. Sedley, eds., *The Hellenistic Philosophers* (Cambridge: Cambridge University Press, 1987), 1:113.

2. The World of Men and Gods

1. Plato, *Timaeus,* ed. R. M. Hare and D. A. Russell, trans. Benjamin Jowett, in *The Dialogues of Plato,* vol. 3: *Timaeus and Other Dialogues* (London: Sphere, 1970). Subsequent quotations are accompanied, in parentheses, by references in text to that edition.

2. Roberto Calasso, *The Marriage of Cadmus and Harmony*, trans. Tim Parks (London: Vintage, 1994), 97. The Plato reference is to *Republic* 616c.

3. Plato, *Critias,* 121c, in Benjamin Jowett, trans., *The Dialogues of Plato,* 3:314.

4. Quotations are from the version of Cleanthes' hymn in A. A. Long and D. N. Sedley, eds., *The Hellenistic Philosophers,* 1 (Cambridge: Cambridge University Press, 1987), 1:326–327.

5. Ibid.

6. Ibid.

7. Ibid.

8. The quotation from Stobaeus on Zeno is cited in Kempe Algra, Jonathan Barnes, Jaap Mansfield, and Malcolm Schofield, eds., *The Cambridge History of Hellenistic Philosophy* (Cambridge: Cambridge University Press, 1999), chap. 13, p. 465.

9. Quoted in Long and Sedley, *Hellenistic Philosophers,* 336.

10. Ibid., 337.

11. Ibid., 337–338.

12. Ibid., 339.

13. Ibid., 323.

14. Cicero, *On the Nature of the Gods,* trans. H. Rackman, Loeb Classical Library 268 (Cambridge, Mass.: Harvard University Press, 1951), bk. 1, secs. 15–16, pp. 41–43. Subsequent quotations are accompanied, in parentheses, by section references in text to that edition.

15. Cited from Philodemus, *On Piety,* in Algra, Barnes, Mansfield, and Schofield, *The Cambridge History of Hellenistic Philosophy,* 461–462.

16. Lucretius, *De Rerum Natura* 2.1052–1104, 5.156–234, as given in Long and Sedley, *Hellenistic Philosophers,* 58–59.

17. Ibid.

18. Ibid.

19. Epicurus, *Letter to Menoecus* (133–134), as given in Long and Sedley, *Hellenistic Philosophers,* 102.

3. Agreeing with Nature

1. Quoted in A. A. Long and D. N. Sedley, eds., *The Hellenistic Philosophers* (Cambridge: Cambridge University Press, 1987), 1:331.

2. Ibid., 346.

3. Ibid., 347.

4. Ibid., 317.

5. Ibid., 348.

6. Ibid., 356.

7. Ibid., 386.

8. Ibid., 388.

9. Ibid., 394.

10. Ibid., 412.

11. Ibid., 395.

12. Seneca, Letter 89, ibid., 344.

13. Seneca, Letter 120, ibid., 370.

14. Seneca, *Ad Lucilium Epistulae Morales*, Letter 46, in *Epistles*, trans. Richard M. Gummere, Loeb Classical Library 75–76 (Cambridge, Mass.: Harvard University Press, 1917). Subsequent quotations from Seneca's letters are taken from this edition.

15. Plato, *Theaetetus* [144b], trans. M. J. Levett, in Myles Burnyeat, *The Theaetetus of Plato* (Indianapolis, Ind.: Hackett, 1990), 261–262.

16. Seneca, *On Providence*, in Seneca, *Moral Essays*, trans. J. W. Basore, Loeb Classical Library 310 (Cambridge, Mass.: Harvard University Press, 1958), 1:7–9, 27–29.

17. Ibid., 38–39.

18. Seneca, *Consolation to Helvia*, in C. D. N. Costa, ed. and trans., *Seneca: Dialogues and Letters* (London: Penguin, 1997), 28.

19. Epictetus, *The Discourses as Reported by Arrian, The Manual,* and *Fragments*, trans. W. A. Oldfather, 2 vols., Loeb Classical Library 131 (Cambridge, Mass.: Harvard University Press, 1925), 1.12.9. Subsequent quotations are accompanied, in parentheses, by references in text to that edition.

20. Edward Gibbon, *Decline and Fall of the Roman Empire*, abridged by D. M. Low (London: Penguin, 1960), 45.

21. Ibid.

22. Marcus Aurelius, *Meditations*, trans. A. S. Farquarson (London: Dent, 1961), bk. 12, sec. 13. Subsequent quotations are accompanied, in parentheses, by book and section references in text to that edition.

4. Augustine

1. Augustine, *Augustine: The City of God against the Pelagians,* trans. R. W. Dyson (Cambridge: Cambridge University Press, 1998), book 22 (chapter 24), 1164–1165.

2. Sermon 155 is quoted in Peter Brown, *Augustine of Hippo: A Biography* (London: Faber and Faber, 1969), 366.

3. Ibid.

4. Plotinus, *Ennead III,* trans. A. H. Armstrong, Loeb Classical Library 442 (Cambridge, Mass.: Harvard University Press, 1967), 3.1.4.9. Subsequent quotations are accompanied, in parentheses, by references in text to that edition.

5. Augustine, *De Ordine (Divine Providence and the Problem of Evil),* trans. Robert P. Russell, in vol. 5 of Ludwig Schopp, ed., *The Fathers of the Church* (New York: CIMA, 1948), 229–332. Subsequent quotations are accompanied, in parentheses, by references in text to that edition.

6. All quotations are from the Library of Liberal Arts version. Augustine, *De Libero Arbitrio Voluntatis (On the Free Choice of the Will),* trans. Anna S. Benjamin and L. H. Hackstaff (Indianapolis, Ind.: Bobbs-Merrill, 1964). Subsequent quotations are accompanied, in parentheses, by references in text to that version.

7. *City of God,* 187.

8. Ibid., 487.

9. John Rist, *Augustine: Ancient Thought Baptised* (Cambridge: Cambridge University Press, 1994), 175.

10. James O'Donnell, *Augustine Sinner and Saint: A New Biography* (London: Profile, 2005), 307.

11. Quotations are from the Oxford World's Classics Series. Boethius, *The Consolation of Philosophy,* trans. P. G. Walsh (Oxford: Oxford University Press, 1999).

12. Ibid., 112.

13. Niccolò Machiavelli, *The Prince,* trans. George Bull (London: Penguin, 2003), 79–81.

14. Ibid.

15. Ibid.

5. The Philosopher and the Princess

1. My account of biographical details of the lives of Princess Elisabeth and her mother, Elizabeth of Bohemia, draws extensively on Carola Oman's excellent biography, *Elizabeth of Bohemia* (London: Hodder and Stoughton, 1938), and also on L. M. Baker's edition of *The Letters of Elizabeth of Bohemia* (London: The Bodley Head, 1953).

2. Oman, *Elizabeth of Bohemia,* 84–117.

3. Ibid., 236–240.

4. Ibid., 319–333.

5. Ibid., 250–252.

6. Ibid., 279–280.

7. Quotations from the letters of Descartes and Elisabeth and other letters of Descartes are, unless otherwise indicated, as given in John Blom, ed., *Descartes: His Moral Philosophy and Psychology* (Hassocks, U.K.: Harvester, 1978). Page references to this collection are given in parentheses in text.

8. René Descartes, *The Passions of the Soul,* trans. John Cottingham, Robert Stoothoff, Dugald Murdoch, vol. 1 in *The Philosophical Writings of Descartes* (Cambridge: Cambridge University Press, 1985), 353.

9. Ibid., 1:192.

10. René Descartes, *The Correspondence,* trans. Cottingham, Stoothoff, Murdoch, and Kenny, vol. 3 in *The Philosophical Writings of Descartes,* 3:369.

11. Descartes to Bregy, 15 January 1650, in *The Correspondence,* trans. Cottingham, Stoothoff, Murdoch, and Kenny, ibid., 3:383–384.

12. Descartes to Chanut, 31 March, 1649, ibid., 371.

13. Oman, *Elizabeth of Bohemia,* 379–388.

14. Ibid., 382–384.

6. Living with Necessity

1. For details on the *cherem* pronounced on Spinoza, I have drawn on Asa Kasher and Shlomo Biderman, "Why Was Baruch de Spinoza Excommunicated?" in David S. Katz and Jonathan Israel, ed., *Sceptics, Millenarians and Jews* (Leiden: Brill, 1990), 98–141.

2. Ibid., 98–99.

3. Jean Maximilien Lucas, *The Oldest Biography of Spinoza,* ed. and trans. A. Wolf (London: Allen and Unwin, 1927), 51.

4. My account of biographical details of Spinoza's life at the time of the *cherem* and in its aftermath draws on the biography by Steven Nadler, *Spinoza: A Life* (Cambridge: Cambridge University Press, 1999), especially chapters 6 and 7.

5. Edwin Curley, *Collected Works of Spinoza* (Princeton, N.J.: Princeton University Press, 1985), 1:193–194. Where possible, quotations from Spinoza's correspondence are taken from this translation by Curley. For letters written after 1665, I have used the translations in A. Wolf, *The Correspondence of Spinoza* (London: Frank Cass, 1966). Subsequent quotations are accompanied, in parentheses, by page references in text to that edition.

6. Epictetus, *Discourses,* trans. W. A. Oldfather, Loeb Classical Library 131 (Cambridge, Mass.: Harvard University Press, 1925), 1.22.21.

7. Both quoted in A. A. Long and D. N. Sedley, ed., *The Hellenistic Philosophers* (Cambridge: Cambridge University Press, 1999), 1:388.

8. Quotations from Spinoza's *Ethics,* his *Commentary on Descartes's Principles,* and his *Short Treatise on God, Man and His Well-Being* are all taken from the translations in Curley, *Collected Works of Spinoza.* Again, quotations are accompanied, in parentheses, by page references in text to that edition.

9. Steven Nadler, *Spinoza's Theory of Divine Providence: Rationalist Solutions, Jewish Sources,* Medelingen Vanwege Het Spinozahuis 87 (Budel, The Netherlands: Damon, 2005), 29.

10. Attributed by Elizabeth Anscombe to notes on a lecture by Wittgenstein. The quotation is from her book *Intention* (Oxford: Blackwell, 1957), 6.

11. Also known as *Tractatus Theologico-Politicus.* Quotations, accompanied in parentheses by page references in text, are taken from Baruch Spinoza, *A Theologico-Political Treatise and A Political Treatise,* trans. R. H. M. Elwes (New York: Dover, 1951).

12. Jonathan Israel, *The Dutch Republic: Its Rise, Greatness, and Fall, 1477–1806* (Oxford: Oxford University Press, 1995), 893.

13. Quoted in Steven Nadler, *Spinoza: A Life,* 306.

14. Ibid.

15. John Aubrey, *Brief Lives,* ed. Andrew Clark (Oxford: Clarendon, 1898), 1:357.

7. Designer Worlds

1. Jonathan Israel, *Radical Enlightenment: Philosophy and the Making of Modernity, 1650–1750* (Oxford: Oxford University Press, 2001), 11.

2. Preface, Gottfried Leibniz, *Theodicy: Essays on the Goodness of God, the Freedom of Man and the Origin of Evil,* ed. Austin Farrer, trans. E. M. Huggard (London: Routledge & Kegan Paul, 1951), 53–54. Subsequent quotations are accompanied, in parentheses, by section and page references in text to that edition.

3. Rousseau's letter of 18 August 1756 to Voltaire, attacking Voltaire's poem on the Lisbon earthquake, is discussed in Theodore Besterman, *Voltaire* (Oxford: Blackwell, 1976), 210–211.

4. Letter to d'Alembert, 4 February 1757, quoted in Besterman, *Voltaire,* 225.

5. Letter of 16 December 1755, ibid., 372.

6. Letter of 24 November 1755, ibid., 366.

7. Ibid., 369.

8. Voltaire, *Candide,* trans. Lowell Blair (New York: Bantam, 1959), 28. Subsequent quotations are accompanied, in parentheses, by page references in text to that edition.

9. Letters of 1756–1758, mentioned in Besterman, *Voltaire,* 372.

10. Bertrand Russell, "Voltaire's Influence on Me," *Studies in Voltaire* 6 (1958): 157–162.

11. Quotations are from David Hume, *Dialogues concerning Natural Religion,* ed. Norman Kemp Smith (Indianapolis, Ind.: Bobbs-Merrill, 1947 [1779]). They are accompanied, in parentheses, by page references in text to that edition.

12. Hume's short autobiography *My Own Life,* originally published in 1777, is included as a supplement in the Library of Liberal Arts version of *Dialogues,* 233–240.

13. David Hume, letter to Francis Hutcheson, 17 September 1739, in J. Y. T. Grieg, ed., *The Letters of David Hume* (Oxford: Oxford University Press, 1932), 1:34.

14. David Hume, *A Treatise of Human Nature*, ed. L. A. Selby-Bigge (Oxford: Oxford University Press, n.d. [1739]), 269.

15. Ibid., 274.

16. Letter to Henry Home, 2 December 1737, in *Letters of David Hume*, 1:25.

17. Hume, *My Own Life*, 234 (emphasis in the original).

18. David Hume, *An Inquiry concerning Human Understanding*, ed. Charles W. Hendel (Indianapolis, Ind.: Bobbs-Merrill, 1955), 118. Subsequent quotations are accompanied, in parentheses, by page references in text to that edition.

19. The essays can be found in David Hume, *Selected Essays*, ed. Stephen Copley and Andrew Edgar (Oxford: Oxford University Press, 1993).

20. Letter from Adam Smith to William Strahan, 9 November 1776, in Grieg, *Letters of David Hume*, 2:450–452. The letter is also included in the Library of Liberal Arts version of the *Dialogues concerning Natural Religion*, 243–245.

21. Extract from the private papers of James Boswell, reprinted as an appendix in the Library of Liberal Arts version of the *Dialogues concerning Natural Religion*, 76–79.

22. James Boswell, entry for 16 September 1777, *Life of Johnson*, ed. R. W. Chapman (Oxford: Oxford University Press, 1970), 838–839.

23. The controversy surrounding Spinoza's death is described in Israel, *Radical Enlightenment*, 295–301.

24. "On Suicide," in Hume, *Selected Essays*, 315–323.

8. Providence as Progress

1. Jean-Jacques Rousseau, *Discourse on the Origins of Inequality*, trans. G. D. H. Cole, rev. J. H. Brumfitt and John C. Hall (London: Dent and Sons, 1973), 39. Subsequent quotations are accompanied, in parentheses, by page references in text to that edition.

2. Jean-Jacques Rousseau, *Emile*, trans. Barbara Foxley (London: Dent

and Sons, 1911), 259. Subsequent quotations are accompanied, in parentheses, by page references in text to that edition.

3. Jean-Jacques Rousseau, *Reveries of a Solitary Walker,* trans. Peter France (Middlesex: Penguin, 1979), 44–45. Subsequent quotations are accompanied, in parentheses, by page references in text to that edition.

4. Quotations from Kant's *Idea for a Universal History with a Cosmopolitan Purpose, An Answer to the Question, "What Is Enlightenment?"* and *The Contest of Faculties* are from Hans Reiss, ed., *Kant: Political Writings,* 2nd ed., trans. H. B. Nisbet (Cambridge: Cambridge University Press, 1991). Quotations are accompanied, in parentheses, by page references in text to that edition.

5. From the discussion of providence in the first part of G. W. F. Hegel, *Encyclopaedia of the Philosophical Sciences,* in *The Logic of Hegel,* 2nd ed., trans. William Wallace (Oxford: Oxford University Press, 1959), sec. 147, p. 269.

6. Ibid.

7. Ibid.

8. Ibid., pp. 269–271.

9. Ibid., p. 271.

9. Providence Lost

1. René Descartes, *The Passions of the Soul,* trans. John Cottingham, Robert Stoothoff, and Dugald Murdoch, in *The Philosophical Writings of Descartes,* vol. 1 (Cambridge: Cambridge University Press, 1985), part 2, sec. 146, p. 380. Subsequent quotations are accompanied, in parentheses, by section and page references in text to that edition.

2. Joan Didion, *The Year of Magical Thinking* (London: Harper, 2006), 206.

3. Benedict de Spinoza, *Ethics,* in Edwin Curley, ed. and trans., *Collected Works of Spinoza* (Princeton, N.J.: Princeton University Press, 1985), 1:446.

4. The papers by Bernard Williams and Thomas Nagel, both called "Moral Luck," were originally published in *Proceedings of the Aristotelian Society,* supplementary vol. 1, 1976. Nagel's paper is republished in his collection *Mortal Questions* (Cambridge: Cambridge University Press, 1979), 24–38.

5. Immanuel Kant, *Critique of Judgement,* trans. James Creed Meredith (Oxford: Clarendon, 1952), 108.

6. Hannah Arendt, *Lectures on Kant's Political Philosophy,* ed. Ronald Beiner (Chicago: University of Chicago Press, 1982), 77.

7. Jacques Derrida, *The Politics of Friendship,* trans. George Collins (London: Verso, 1997), 29 and 67.

8. Bernard Williams, *Shame and Necessity* (Berkeley: University of California Press, 1993), 166.

9. Euripides, *Iphigenia at Aulis,* ed. and trans. David Kovacs, Loeb Classical Library 10 (Cambridge, Mass.: Harvard University Press, 2002), lines 443–445. Subsequent quotations are accompanied, in parentheses, by line references in text to that edition.

10. Samuel Beckett, *The Beckett Trilogy: Molloy, Malone Dies, The Unnamable* (London: Picador, 1979), 382 (quotation).

Acknowledgments

Earlier versions of some passages in this book appear in the following essays: "Providence Lost: 'September 11' and the History of Evil," in Robert Sinnerbrink, Jean-Philippe Deranty, Nicholas H. Smith, and Peter Schmiedgen, eds., *Critical Today* (Leiden: Brill, 2006), 23–43; "Busy Lives: Descartes and Elisabeth on Time Management and the Philosophical Life," *Australian Feminist Studies* 21, no. 51 (2006): 303–313; "Shaping a Life: Narrative, Time, and Necessity," in Kim Atkins and Catriona Mackenzie, eds., *Practical Identity and Narrative Agency* (New York: Routledge, 2008), 255–268; "Providence as Progress: Variations on a Tale of Origins," in Amélie Rorty and James Schmidt, eds., *History as Philosophy: Essays on Kant's Idea for a Universal History* (New York: Cambridge University Press, forthcoming).

I am grateful to Amélie Rorty and Natalie Staples for very helpful comments on earlier drafts, and also to three anonymous reviewers.

Further Reading

Introduction

I discuss the operations of imagination and emotion in philosophical texts more fully in the introduction to the edited collection Genevieve Lloyd, ed., *Feminism and History of Philosophy* (Oxford: Oxford University Press, 2002). More generally, recognition is growing in contemporary history of ideas about the interconnections between intellect and emotion in the operation of some of the most central concepts in the Western philosophical tradition. Lynn Hunt, for example, in a fascinating study, has argued that shifts in emotion are at play in appeals to "what is self-evident," which are central to the history of the idea of "universal human rights." Human rights, she argues, are difficult to pin down because their definition, indeed their very existence, depends on emotions as much as on reason. Lynn Hunt, *Inventing Human Rights: A History* (New York: Norton, 2007), 26.

1. Euripides, Philosopher of the Stage

On the reputation of Euripides as "the philosopher of the stage," see the rich treatment of his plays in Paul Décharme, *Euripides and the Spirit of His Dramas*, trans. J. Loeb (Washington: Kennikat Press, 1968), esp. 21–34.

I am indebted to the informative discussion of the fragments of Heraclitus in Charles Kahn, *The Art and Thought of Heraclitus: An Edition of the Fragments with Translation and Commentary* (Cambridge: Cambridge University Press, 1962). See especially his illuminating juxtapositions of Heraclitus and Anaximander with respect to the idea of cosmic justice, pp. 206–210; and the introduction, p. 18, where he discusses Anaximander's reference to opposing forces "making amends." I have also found very useful the comprehensive commentary in G. S. Kirk, *Heraclitus: The Cosmic Fragments* (Cambridge: Cambridge University Press, 1962). Another useful commentary on Heraclitus—including a discussion of the relations between his concept of cosmic justice and the thought of Anaximander—is Philip Wheelright, *Heraclitus* (Princeton, N.J.: Princeton University Press, 1959). On the idea of the human mind and the cosmos as sharing a common structure, see especially Kirk, *Heraclitus, the Cosmic Fragments,* 367–368; and Kahn, *The Art and Thought of Heraclitus,* 261.

On *Alcestis,* Justina Gregory offers a very interesting analysis of Admetus's reprieve as bringing a shift toward death by "prearrangement and consent," in *Euripides and the Instruction of the Athenians* (Ann Arbor: University of Michigan Press, 1991), 19–50. For a useful discussion of modern readings and interpretations of *Alcestis,* see John R. Wilson, ed., *Twentieth Century Interpretations of Euripides'* Alcestis: *A Collection of Critical Essays* (Englewood Cliffs, N.J.: Prentice-Hall, 1968).

For Derrida's treatment of hospitality and its conceptual connections with chance, contingency, and necessity, see especially Jacques Derrida, *Politics of Friendship,* trans. George Collins (London: Verso, 1997). Derrida elaborates on the connections between the "perhaps" and the theme of hospitality in his contribution to Giovanni Borradori, *Philosophy in a Time of Terror: Dialogues with Jürgen Habermas and Jacques Derrida* (Chicago: University of Chicago Press, 2003). For a very useful discussion of Derrida's notion of the "perhaps" in relation to chance and to death, see John D. Caputo, *The Prayers and Tears of Jacques Derrida: Religion without Religion* (Bloomington: Indiana University Press, 1997), esp. 81–88. I discuss Derrida's treatment of these themes more fully in "Fate and Fortune: Derrida on Facing the Future," *Philosophy Today,* SPEP supplement 1999, 27–35, and "Providence Lost: 'September 11' and the History of Evil," *Critical Horizons* (special issue, *Critique Today*) 6, no. 1 (2005): 23–43.

For an interesting treatment of the complexities of interpreting Euripides' attitude toward the gods in the *Bacchae,* see R. P. Winnington-Ingram, *Euripides and Dionysus: An Interpretation of* The Bacchae (Amsterdam: Adolf M. Hakbent, 1969). I also found his treatment of the transformation of emotions in the passage on the fawn very useful—see pp. 106–113.

2. The World of Men and Gods

The issues surrounding the dating of the *Timaeus* and its relations to Plato's other dialogues are comprehensively discussed in G. E. L. Owen, "The Place of the *Timaeus* in Plato's Dialogues," in *Logic, Science and Dialectic: Collected Papers in Greek Philosophy,* ed. Martha Nussbaum (Ithaca, N.Y.: Cornell University Press, 1986), 65–84. There is a useful, brief discussion of the dating issue in Richard Kraut, "Introduction to the Study of Plato," in Richard Kraut, ed., *The Cambridge Companion to Plato* (Cambridge: Cambridge University Press, 1992), 1–50. For useful overviews of the *Timaeus,* see F. M. Cornford, *Plato's Cosmology: The* Timaeus *of Plato* (London: Kegan Paul, 1937); and A. E. Taylor, *A Commentary on Plato's* Timaeus (Oxford: Oxford University Press, 1928).

For useful commentary on the *Timaeus* view of the generation of the universe as a mixed result of reason and necessity, see Cornford, *Plato's Cosmology,* 162–177; and Glen R. Morrow, "Necessity and Persuasion in Plato's *Timaeus,*" *Philosophical Review* 59 (1950): 147–164, repr. in R. E. Allen, ed., *Studies in Plato's Metaphysics* (London: Routledge & Kegan Paul, 1965), 421–437.

Wittgenstein talks of the "hardness of the logical must" in Ludwig Wittgenstein, *Philosophical Investigations,* trans. Elizabeth Anscombe (Oxford: Basil Blackwell, 1958), part I, sec. 437. There are echoes of Platonic and Stoic ideas on the common order of thought and world in the following passage from the *Philosophical Investigations,* part I, sec. 97, p. 44e, where he refers to similar comments in his *Tractatus:* "Thought is surrounded by a halo—Its essence, logic, presents an order, in fact the a priori order of the world: that is, the order *of possibilities,* which must be common to both world and thought. But this order, it seems, must be *utterly simple.* It is *prior* to all experience, must run through all experience; no empirical cloudiness or uncertainty can be allowed to affect it—It must rather be of the purest crystal. But this crystal does not appear as an abstraction; but as something concrete, indeed as the most concrete, as it were the *hardest* thing there is (*Tractatus Logico-Philosophicus* No. 5.5563)."

My summaries of Greek myths, in relation to the transformations of Zeus, draw especially on Robert Graves, *The Greek Myths,* rev. ed., 2 vols. (London: Penguin, 1960), and Roberto Calasso, *The Marriage of Cadmus and Harmony,* trans. Tim Parks (London: Vintage, 1994). Robert Graves's discussion of Tyche and Nemesis appears in the section "Sky, Sea and Underworld," in Graves, *The Greek Myths*, 1:125–127. Calasso also discusses Zeus's dealings with Tyche and Nemesis in chapter 4 of *The Marriage of Cadmus and Harmony*, esp. 124–126. On the identification of Cleanthes' Zeus with other versions of the deity, see the commentary on the hymn in A. A. Long and D. N. Sedley, *Hellenistic Philosophers* (Cambridge: Cambridge University Press, 1987), 332.

My discussion of the relations between the Stoics and Heraclitus, and of the contrasts between Stoic providence and the versions of providence offered by Plato and Aristotle, owe much to David Furley's excellent discussion in his chapter "Cosmology," in Kempe Algra, Jonathan Barnes, Jaap Mansfield, and Malcolm Schofield, eds., *The Cambridge History of Hellenistic Philosophy* (Cambridge: Cambridge University Press, 1999), part 4, chap. 12, esp. 448–451.

Issues of freedom and necessity in Stoic thought are comprehensively discussed in Susanne Bobzien, *Determinism and Freedom in Stoic Philosophy* (Oxford: Clarendon, 1998). See especially the sections on the concept of fate in relation to determinism, pp. 38–58, and on Epictetus's treatment of freedom, in chap. 7, pp. 330–50. Long and Sedley offer a very useful commentary on the contrasts between Stoic doctrines and the less rigid traditional Greek picture of fate in *The Hellenistic Philosophers*, 1:342–343.

For a useful commentary on the Epicurean doctrine of "swervings" and its bearing on ideas of free will and responsibility, see Long and Sedley, *The Hellenistic Philosophers*, 1:107–112; and for a useful discussion of Stoic cosmology and its contrasts with Epicurean doctrine, see David Furley, "Cosmology," 412–451.

3. Agreeing with Nature

Helpful treatments of the broader ethical issues arising from the doctrines of the ancient Stoics include Malcolm Schofield, "Stoic Ethics," in Brad Inwood, ed., *The Cambridge Companion to the Stoics* (Cambridge: Cambridge University Press, 2003), 233–256; Gisela Striker, "Following Nature: A Study in Stoic Ethics," *Oxford Studies in Ancient Philosophy* 9 (1991): 1–73, reprinted in Striker, *Essays on Hellenistic Epistemology and Ethics* (Cambridge: Cambridge University Press, 1996), 221–280; and Brad Inwood and Pierluigi Donini, "Stoic Ethics," in Algra, Barnes, Mansfield, and Schofield, *The Cambridge History of Helle-nistic Philosophy,* 675–736. Long and Sedley provide a useful overview of the Stoic concepts of impulse and appropriation in *Hellenistic Philosophers,* 350–354, and of the Stoic treatment of "indifferents," 357–359.

On related issues of the connections between Stoic cosmology and ethics, the following are particularly useful: A. A. Long, *Stoic Studies* (Cambridge: Cambridge University Press, 1991); A. A. Long, ed., *Problems in Stoicism* (London: Athlone, 1971); J. M. Rist, *Stoic Philosophy* (Cambridge: Cambridge University Press, 1969); J. M. Rist, ed., *The Stoics* (Berkeley: University of California Press, 1969); Malcolm Schofield, *The Stoic Idea of the City* (Cambridge: Cambridge University Press, 1991). See also the comment on morality and the "cosmic plan" in Long and Sedley, *Hellenistic Philosophers,* 394.

I have focused primarily on Stoic sources for the idea of necessity as having ethical force. The Stoics were the main sources through which that idea became important in later debates about freedom and necessity in modern philosophy. A full history of the ethical connotations of providence would also address other sources in ancient Greek philosophy, including the two philosophical poems of Empedocles, *Poem on Nature* and *Purifications,* composed in the middle of the fifth century BCE. In Empedocles' version of the role of necessity in the origins of the world, the four elements—fire, earth, air, and water—are mixed together in "reciprocal replacements" under the rival powers of Love and Strife. For an overview of his thought, and an assemblage of fragments from the poems, see John Burnet, *Early Greek Philosophy,* 4th ed. (New York: Meridian, 1930), chap. 5, pp. 197–250. F. M. Cornford, *From Religion to Philosophy: A Study in the Origins of Western Speculation* (New York: Harper, 1957), also includes a commentary on relevant aspects of the two poems, in secs. 118–125, pp. 224–242.

For an excellent general commentary on Epictetus's life and thought, see A. A. Long, *Epictetus: A Stoic and Socratic Guide to Life* (Oxford: Oxford University Press, 2002).

4. Augustine

In my discussion of Augustine, I have drawn on two excellent biographies: Peter Brown, *Augustine of Hippo: A Biography* (London: Faber and Faber, 1967), and James J. O'Donnell, *Augustine Sinner and Saint: A New Biography* (London: Profile, 2005). For a useful brief account of Augustine's life and intellectual context, see O'Donnell, "Augustine: His Time and Lives," in Eleonore Stump and Norman Kretzmann, eds., *The Cambridge Companion to Augustine* (Cambridge: Cambridge University Press, 2001), 8–39.

Aquinas cites the passage from *De Ordine* on prostitution in Thomas Aquinas, *Summa Theologica,* 2a–2ae, 9.10.a, 11c. For an interesting discussion of the context of Augustine's views on the innocence of children, with regard to the doctrine of original sin and the practice of infant baptism, see O'Donnell, "Augustine and the Invention of Christianity," chap. 7 in *Augustine Sinner and Saint.* On Pelagius and Pelagianism, see O'Donnell, *Augustine Sinner and Saint,* 271–277; and Brown, *Augustine of Hippo,* chap. 29. There is an interesting discussion of the role of an exaggerated "hyper-Augustinianism" in Christian approaches to evil in Charles Taylor, *A Secular Age* (Cambridge: Harvard University Press, 2007), chap. 17, 642–656.

For useful further reading on Augustine's concept of the will, see Charles H. Kahn, "Discovering the Will: From Aristotle to Augustine," in John M. Dillon and A. A. Long, eds., *The Question of "Eclecticism": Studies in Later Greek Philosophy* (Berkeley: University of California Press, 1988), 235–259; A. Dihle, *The Theory of Will in Classical Antiquity* (Berkeley: University of California Press, 1982); John Rist, "Faith and Reason," in Stump and Kretzmann, *The Cambridge Companion to Augustine,* 26–39; Eleonore Stump, "Augustine on Free Will," in Stump and Kretzmann, *The Cambridge Companion to Augustine,* 124–147; and Simon Harrison, "Do We Have a Will? Augustine's Way in to the Will," in Gareth B. Matthews, ed., *The Augustinian Tradition* (Berkeley: University of California Press, 1999), 195–205.

For more detail on Augustine's *liberum arbitrium voluntatis* and its differences from modern free will, see the essay by J. B. Korolec, "Free Will and Free Choice," in Norman Kretzmann, Anthony Kenny, and Jan Pinborg, eds., *The Cambridge History of Later Medieval Philosophy* (Cambridge: Cambridge University Press), 627–644. For a comprehensive discussion of medieval debates on the relations between time, truth, and necessity, see Calvin Normore, "Future Contingents," in Kretzman, Kenny, and Pinborg, *The Cambridge History of Later Mediaeval Philosophy,* 358–382. On ancient versions of the debates, see R. J. Hankinson, "Determinism and Indeterminism," in Algra, Barnes,

Mansfeld, and Schofield, *The Cambridge History of Hellenistic Philosophy,* 513–541. The "master argument" of Diodorus is also discussed in part 2 of Susanne Bobzien, "Logic," in Algra, Barnes, Mansfeld, and Schofield, *The Cambridge History of Hellenistic Philosophy,* 83–92; and in the commentary on section 3 ("Modality"), in A. A. Long and D. N. Sedley, in *The Hellenistic Philosophers,* 234–236.

My brief discussion of Renaissance treatments of freedom has benefited from insights in the excellent Antonino Poppi, "Fate, Fortune, Providence and Human Freedom," chap. 17 of Charles B. Schmitt and Quentin Skinner, eds., *The Cambridge History of Renaissance Philosophy* (Cambridge: Cambridge University Press, 1988), 641–667.

5. The Philosopher and the Princess

For details of the lives of Princess Elisabeth and her mother, Elizabeth of Bohemia, I am indebted to Carola Oman's excellent biography, *Elizabeth of Bohemia* (London: Hodder and Stoughton, 1938); and also to L. M. Baker, ed., *The Letters of Elizabeth, Queen of Bohemia* (London: The Bodley Head, 1953). Several biographies of Descartes contain material about his relationship with Princess Elisabeth. Particularly useful are Desmond M. Clarke, *Descartes: A Biography* (Cambridge: Cambridge University Press, 2006), chap. 9, 248–275; Geneviève Rodis-Lewis, *Descartes: His Life and Thought,* trans. Jane Marie Todd (Ithaca, N.Y.: Cornell University Press, 1998), chap. 6, 143–187; Jack Rochford Vrooman, *René Descartes: A Biography* (New York: Putnam, 1970), chap. 6, 167–211; Richard Watson, *Cogito, Ergo Sum: The Life of René Descartes* (Boston: Godine, 2002), chap. 10, 205–220. On the possibility that Princess Elisabeth may have visited Descartes during his residence at the château at The Hague, see Vrooman, *René Descartes,* 171–172.

Another useful discussion of the biographical and philosophical background to the correspondence can be found in the introduction to Lisa Shapiro, ed. and trans., *The Correspondence between Princess Elisabeth of Bohemia and René Descartes* (Chicago: University of Chicago Press, 2007). Unfortunately, timing did not permit me to take into account this welcome translation and annotated edition of the entire correspondence.

Charles Taylor discusses Descartes's relations with Stoic and neo-Stoic accounts of the passions and of detachment in *A Secular Age,* chap. 2, sec. 4, pp. 130–136.

An interesting discussion of Elisabeth's influence on Descartes appears in Deborah Brown, *Descartes and the Passionate Mind* (Cambridge: Cambridge University Press, 2006), 13–23. Also of interest is Brown's discussion of fate and fortune, ibid., 171–176. For a useful discussion of the philosophical issues raised by Elisabeth's challenge to Descartes's treatment of mind-body interaction, and by Descartes's responses, see Daniel Garber, "What Descartes Should Have Told Elisabeth," chap. 8 in *Descartes Embodied: Reading Cartesian Philosophy through Cartesian Science* (Cambridge: Cambridge University Press, 2001), 168–188; and Lisa Shapiro, "Princess Elisabeth and Descartes: The Union of Soul and Body and the Practice of Philosophy," *British Journal for the History of Philosophy* 7, no. 3 (1999): 503–520.

6. Living with Necessity

For biographical details on the *cherem* pronounced on Spinoza, I have drawn on Asa Kasher and Shlomo Biderman, "Why Was Baruch de Spinoza Excommunicated?" in David S. Katz and Jonathan Israel, eds., *Sceptics, Millenarians and Jews* (Leiden: Brill, 1990), 98–141, reprinted in Genevieve Lloyd, ed., *Spinoza: Critical Assessments of Leading Philosophers* (London: Routledge, 2001), 59–99. I have also drawn on Steven Nadler's excellent biography, *Spinoza: A Life* (Cambridge: Cambridge University Press, 1999), esp. chap. 6. The Lucas biography mentioned is the one known as *The Oldest Biography of Spinoza,* ed. Jean Maximilien Lucas and trans. A. Wolf (London: Allen and Unwin, 1927). Also of interest is another old biography of Spinoza, written by John Colerus in 1705. It is translated as "The Life of Benedictus de Spinoza," in Frederick Pollock, ed., *Spinoza: His Life and Philosophy* (London: Duckworth, 1899), 386–418. A useful recent biography is Margaret Gullan-Whur, *Within Reason: A Life of Spinoza* (London: Jonathan Cape, 1998). The question where Spinoza lived after the *cherem*—and in particular whether the Jews prevailed on the Amsterdam authorities to have him exiled from the city—is discussed in Nadler, *Spinoza,* chap. 7. Nadler takes issue with claims made by Spinoza's early biographers, Lucas and Colerus, that he was forced to leave Amsterdam.

The Spinoza portrait described* is in the Herzog August Bibliothek Wolfenbüttel, ref. B117. It appears on the dust jacket of Steven Nadler's biography, as well as in several other books on Spinoza. There are of course hazards in reading into portraits judgments about the supposed character of their subjects. This portrait was long thought to have been painted from life but is now thought to be a copy from an older copper engraving, in which Spinoza looks less confident, less ironic, and more disgruntled. The history of visual representations of Spinoza—including the Wolfenbüttel portrait—is the subject of a fascinating pamphlet by Rudi Ekkart, *Spinoza in Beeld/Spinoza in Portrait: The Unknown Face* (Voorschoten, The Netherlands: Vereniging Het Spinozahuis, 1999).

Steven Nadler's excellent discussions of Spinoza's versions of providence, eternity, and immortality can be found in his book *Spinoza's Heresy: Immortality and the Jewish Mind* (Oxford: Clarendon, 2001), and in the pamphlet *Spinoza's Theory of Divine Providence: Rationalist Solutions, Jewish Sources,* Medelingen Vanwege Het Spinozahuis 87 (Budel, The Netherlands: Damon, 2005).

For fuller discussion of Spinoza's treatment of minds, bodies, emotion, and freedom see Genevieve Lloyd, *Part of Nature: Self-Knowledge in Spinoza's Ethics* (London: Routledge, 1994); and Lloyd, *Spinoza's Ethics* (London: Routledge, 1996); and also Susan James, *Passion and Action: The Emotions in Seventeenth-Century Philosophy* (Oxford: Oxford University Press, 1997). Spinoza's treatment of freedom and responsibility—and the contemporary relevance of his version of the imagination—are discussed in Moira Gatens and Genevieve Lloyd, *Collective Imaginings: Spinoza, Past and Present* (London: Routledge, 1999).

7. Designer Worlds

For an excellent discussion of the significance of the Lisbon earthquake in relation to the history of ideas of evil, see Susan Neiman, *Evil in Modern Thought: An Alternative History of Philosophy* (Princeton, N.J.: Princeton University Press, 2002). For biographical background on Voltaire, Theodore Besterman, *Voltaire* (Oxford: Basil Blackwell, 1976), is very useful. He discusses Voltaire's views on the Deists, and more generally his views on God, in chap. 7. Peter Gay offers a brief but fascinating analysis of *Candide* in relation to the Enlightenment in *The Enlightenment: An Interpretation,* vol. 1, *The Rise of Modern Paganism* (London: Weidenfeld and Nicolson, 1966), 197–203. See also the section on Voltaire in Gay's excellent bibliographical essay, ibid., 487–488.

Biographical details on Hume's life are drawn especially from an excellent biography, E. C. Mossner, *The Life of David Hume,* 2nd ed. (Oxford: Clarendon, 1980). I have also drawn on *The Letters of David Hume,* ed. J. Y. T. Grieg, 2 vols. (Oxford: Oxford University Press, 1932), and *New Letters of David Hume,* ed. Raymond Klibansky and Ernest Mossner (Oxford: Oxford University Press, 1954). See also the useful discussion on Hume in Gay, *The Enlightenment,* 1:401–419, and the section on Hume in the bibliographical essay, ibid., 551–552.

Hume's critique of ideas of natural design is still relevant to issues currently under debate about alleged incompatibilities between evolutionary theory and religious belief. Useful contemporary discussions of the more philosophical dimensions of the issues are three books by Daniel Dennett: *Darwin's Dangerous Idea: Evolution and the Meaning of Life* (New York: Simon & Schuster, 1995); *Freedom Evolves* (New York: Viking, 2003); and *Breaking the Spell: Religion as a Natural Phenomenon* (New York: Viking, 2006); and Philip Kitcher, *Living with Darwin: Evolution, Design and the Future of Faith* (Oxford: Oxford University Press, 2007).

8. Providence as Progress

Victor Gourevitch has offered a comprehensive and illuminating treatment of Rousseau's views on providence, including a very helpful discussion of his relations with Voltaire, in two interrelated essays: "The Religious Thought," in Patrick Riley, ed., *The Cambridge Companion to Rousseau* (Cambridge: Cambridge University Press, 2001), 123–146; and "Rousseau on Providence," *Review of Metaphysics* 53 (March 2000): 500–546. See also the useful introductions to his editions of Rousseau, *The Discourses and Other Early Political Writings* (Cambridge: Cambridge University Press, 1997); and *The Social Contract and Other Later Political Writings* (Cambridge: Cambridge University Press, 1997).

For an entertaining—and moving—account of Hume's relationship with Rousseau, see Mossner, *The Life of David Hume,* chap. 35, 507–532.

For further reading on Kant's concept of enlightenment and its significance for contemporary issues, see the extensive collection of eighteenth-century sources and recent interpretations in James Schmidt, ed., *What Is Enlightenment? Eighteenth-Century Answers and Twentieth-Century Questions* (Berkeley: University of California Press, 1996). On the related issue of the relations between reason, imagination, and emotion in Kant's treatment of the unity of the mind—and its ramifications for the interpretation of Kantian ethical theory—see Nancy Sherman, *Making a Necessity of Virtue: Aristotle and Kant on Virtue* (Cambridge: Cambridge University Press, 1997). Sherman also discusses Stoicism there in relation to Aristotelian and Kantian approaches to virtue. For a good discussion of the place of Kant's treatment of the "politics of reason" in the wider context of his philosophy, see Onora O'Neil, *Constructions of Reason: Explorations of Kant's Practical Philosophy* (Cambridge: Cambridge University Press, 1989), 3–50.

Kant's insertion of providence into human history represents a significant transitional moment, not only in the history of ideas of providence, but in the process of the "secularization" of time. Charles Taylor, in *A Secular Age,* has given a fascinating account of a rich set of interrelated and changing contrasts and tensions between "ordinary time, the time which is measured in ages" and "higher time, God's time, or eternity" (265). See chap. 9, "The Dark Abyss of Time," 322–351, on the modern "cosmic imaginary"; and especially chap. 19, "Unquiet Frontiers of Modernity," 711–727, where Taylor sums up the processes through which the sense of a "higher time" has receded, leaving room for new—and potentially unsettling—ways of experiencing time and memory. "In virtually all pre-modern outlooks," Taylor says, "the meaning of the repeated cycles of time was found outside of time, or in higher time or eternity. What is peculiar to the modern world is the rise of an outlook where the single reality giving meaning to the repeatable cycles is a narrative of human self-realization, variously understood as the story of Progress, or Reason and Freedom, or Civilization or Decency or Human Rights; or as the coming to maturity of a nation or culture" (716). In the context of Taylor's illuminating discussion, I want to suggest that Kant's temporalizing of providence in the *Idea for a Universal History* can be seen in retrospect as a significant point of transition in the emergence of the modern version of "secular" time. For Kant, human time could be suffused with the sacred power of providence. But his rapprochement of providence and progress can nonetheless be seen as helping to make possible an emerging sense of time as exclusively "secular."

9. Providence Lost

For an illuminating account of the origins and history of the modern concept of risk, see Peter L. Bernstein, *Against the Gods: The Remarkable Story of Risk* (New York: Wiley, 1996). In the introduction to his fascinating, though not always persuasive, study, Bernstein offers the following observation on the close connection between the concept of risk and the understanding of modernity: "The revolutionary idea that defines the boundary between modern times and the past is the mastery of risk: the notion that the future is more than a whim of the gods and that men and women are not passive before nature. Until human beings discovered a way across that boundary, the future was a mirror of the past or of the murky domain of oracles and soothsayers who hold a monopoly over knowledge of anticipated events" (1).

I discuss the implications of Spinoza's philosophy for our contemporary understanding of responsibility in more detail in Gatens and Lloyd, *Collective Imaginings*.

The account of judgment sketched by Hannah Arendt in her *Lectures on the History of Philosophy* follows her fuller treatment of thinking and willing in *The Life of the Mind* (New York: Harcourt Brace, 1971). An interesting discussion of her treatment of the relations between thinking, willing, and judging appears in Max Deutscher, *Judgement after Arendt* (Aldershot, U.K.: Ashgate, 2007).

Derrida discusses the paradoxes of futurity and the "perhaps" especially in Jacques Derrida, *The Politics of Friendship*, trans. George Collins (London: Verso, 1997). See esp. chap. 2, "Loving in Friendship: Perhaps—the Noun and the Adverb," 26–48. I discuss Derrida's treatment of futurity in relation to the concept of risk more fully in Genevieve Lloyd, "Fate and Fortune: Derrida on

Facing the Future," in *Philosophy Today,* SPEP supplement, 1999, 27–36. For an excellent treatment of these and related aspects of Derrida's philosophy, see Caputo, *The Prayers and Tears of Jacques Derrida.* Derrida returns to issues of futurity—with special reference to the contemporary relevance of Kant's philosophy—in his contribution to Borradori, *Philosophy in a Time of Terror.* I discuss the views he expresses there in my paper "Providence Lost: 'September 11' and the History of Evil," 23–43. See also my related discussion of Derrida on hospitality in Chapter 1 of this book.

Barry Unsworth has retold the story of Iphigenia's sacrifice in his excellent novel *The Songs of the Kings* (London: Hamish Hamilton, 2002).

Index

Absolute Spirit, in Hegel, 298–299
Acceptance, 20–21, 94, 96–97, 200. *See also* Appropriation
Action, human, in Euripides, 19, 38–56
Aeschylus, 15, 42
Affective reason, 191
Afterlife, Marcus Aurelius and the, 128; in correspondence between Descartes and Elisabeth, 184
Alcestis. *See* Euripides, *Alcestis*
Alexander of Aphrodisias, *On Fate*, 74–75
Altruism, 180–182
Anaximander, 15–16
Anselm of Canterbury, 156
Apollo, 21–25, 35, 69
Apollonius, 124
Appropriation: Stoic concept of, 92–94; in Spinoza, 195–196, 306; in Euripides, 324–331. *See also* Necessity
Aquinas, Saint Thomas, 156; *Summa Theologica*, 140
Arendt, Hannah: *Lectures on Kant's Political Philosophy*, 319; *The Life of the Mind*, 321–322
Aristotle, 73; *On Interpretation*, 153
Arnauld, Antoine, 246
Arrian (Flavius Arrianus), 109–110. *See also* Epictetus
Artemis, 69
Asceticism, 120
Atheism: Spinoza and, 230–231; Hume and, 258–261, 277
Athena, 69
Atlantis, 59
Attachment, 122–123

Aubrey, John, *Brief Lives*, 230
Augustine, Saint, 8–9, 129–159, 244; conversion, 129–131; *Confessions*, 129–131, 146; *City of God*, 130, 148–150; *De Ordine*, 131, 136–140; and Neoplatonism, 135–136; *De Libero Arbitrio Voluntatis*, 140–149; and divine justice, 141–147; *Retractions*, 144
Autonomy, 2, 151, 201

Balance: between good and evil, 2, 16; between opposites, 136; in modernity, 314–315
Bayle, Pierre, 238, 248, 250; *Pensées diverses sur la comète*, 277
Beauty, 126, 166–167
Beckett, Samuel, *Waiting for Godot*, 331
Belief, Hume on, 261–267
Best possible world: in Leibniz, 240, 244–245, 249–250, 311–312; in Voltaire's *Candide*, 252–257
Bodily awareness, in Descartes, 171–179
Boethius, Anicius Manlius Severinus, *The Consolation of Philosophy*, 153–156
Boswell, James, *Life of Johnson*, 276
Brown, Peter, 130–131

Calasso, Roberto, 62
Calcidius, 91
Carneades, 20
Cartesians, 182, 188, 201, 210–214, 225, 227, 308–310
Casearius, 196–197
Chance: in Plato's *Timaeus*, 61–63; Zeus

Chance (continued)
    and, 69; in Cicero's On the Nature of the
    Gods, 80, 86. See also Contingency
Christianity: Leibniz and, 138–148;
    Descartes and, 183–184; Spinoza and,
    226–227; Hegel and, 300. See also
    Religion, issues of
Christina, queen of Sweden, 186–189
Chrysippus, 20, 75–76, 91–93, 96–97,
    117–118, 141, 202; On Providence, 73–74
Cicero, M. Tullius, 7, 20, 52, 77–89,
    148–150; On the Nature of the Gods, 65,
    75–76, 80–89, 136, 251, 257–258, 265,
    267, 274; On Divination, 74; On Ends, 95;
    On Fate, 201–202
City of God, 129, 250. See also Cosmic
    city
Cleanthes, 96–97; "Hymn to Zeus,"
    71–73
Colerus, John, 277
"Collateral damage," 143, 313, 316
Communal life, in relation to Augus-
    tine's De Ordine, 136–137
Community of faith, in Augustine,
    145–146
Conatus (striving), in Spinoza, 203
Conflict: in Heraclitus, 16; in myths of
    Zeus, 69
Consolation: Boethius and, 153–156; in
    Hegel, 299–300
Constellations, as record of gods' acts,
    68
Contentment, Stoic ideal of, 111–114. See
    also Acceptance; Appropriation
Contingency, 23–25; and hospitality,
    29–33; openness to, 46–47; future,
    153; in Leibniz, 245–246
Control, modern attitude toward,
    307–310, 316
Cosmic city, 6–7, 129, 280, 296; Stoic
    ideal of, 18, 86–87, 91, 94–95
Cosmic justice, in Euripides, 14–19, 56
Cosmopolitanism, 18, 90–91, 287–297
Creation story, Plato's Timaeus as, 58–65
Cronus, 67–68
Cynics, influence of, 110, 118–120

Death, 27, 116–117; interconnections
    with life, 16, 22, 27; in Euripides' Alces-
    tis, 35–36; of Descartes, 189–190; of
    Hume, 274–278; of Spinoza, 277; and
    modernity, 307–308; in Euripides'
    Iphigenia at Aulis, 327–331. See also Fear
    of death; Mortality in Euripides'
    Alcestis
Debates, in Euripides, 19
Debt to nature: Stoic concept of,
    116–117; in Augustine, 141
Deception, in Euripides, 26–27, 36–37
Deism, 253
Democritus, 219
Derrida, Jacques, 320; Politics of Friendship,
    30
Descartes, René, 1–2, 9–10, 111, 149,
    157, 159–191, 201, 236, 249; letter to
    Pollot, 163–165; The Passions of the Soul,
    165–166, 185, 201, 210, 302–305;
    correspondence with Princess Elisa-
    beth, 165–186, 189–190; Principles of
    Philosophy, 166; Discourse on Method, 168;
    letter to Chanut, 185–189, 310; letter
    to Queen Christina, 186; death of,
    189–190; and Spinoza, 210–214. See
    also Will, human
Design: in Plato's Timaeus, 61–63;
    Epicurean rejection of, 77; Stoics and,
    86–87; Hume's rejection of, 264–
    265
Detachment, 94; Stoic ideal of, 8, 93,
    115–117, 122–126, 168, 174; in Des-
    cartes, 179–181. See also Acceptance
De Witt, Johan, 223–225, 231–232
Didion, Joan, The Year of Magical Thinking,
    307–308
Diodorus Cronus, 153
Diogenes Laertius, 17, 75, 92, 97–98
Dionysus, 46–56, 69
Divination, in Plato's Timaeus, 64
Divine foreknowledge, 149, 156
Divine freedom. See Freedom and neces-
    sity; Will, divine
Divine-human relations, in Euripides,
    36–37, 42–56

Divine punishment, in Augustine, 142–147
Division, as source of evil, 133–135
Dostoyevsky, Fyodor, *Brothers Karamazov*, 147
Duns Scotus, John, 156
Dutch-English War, 218–219
Dutch Republic, 218, 222–225
Dying, as lifelong process, 105. *See also* Death; Fear of death

Education, in Rousseau's *Emile*, 283–284
Eliot, George, *Middlemarch*, 31–32
Elisabeth of Bohemia, Princess, 10, 162–163, 190–191, 201; correspondence with Descartes, 165–186, 189–190
Elizabeth, Queen of Bohemia (the Winter Queen). *See* Frederick and Elizabeth of Bohemia
Embodiment, in Descartes, 166–179, 186–187
Emotion, 3–4; in Euripides' *Bacchae*, 46, 50–54; in Plato, 65–66. *See also* Passions
Enlightenment, 2, 233–238; Hume and, 258–259, 275
Epaphroditus, 109
Epictetus, 96, 109–124, 198; and practical Stoicism, 109–114, 120–124; on the master argument of Diodorus Cronus, 153
Epicureans, 7, 28, 52, 76–80, 94, 206; in Cicero's *On the Nature of the Gods*, 81–89
Epicurus, 104, 110, 264; *Letter to Menoeceus*, 79
Eternal verities, in Leibniz, 242–245
Euripides, 6–7, 12, 14–56, 121, 323–331; *Women of Troy*, 17–18; *Alcestis*, 19–36; *Hypsipile*, 20; *Electra*, 36, 42–44; *Helen*, 36–42; *Orestes*, 42, 44–45; *Bacchae*, 42, 45–56; *Iphigenia at Aulis*, 323–331
Event, in Derrida, 320–321
Evidence, and belief, 261–267
Evil, problem of, 8–9; in Augustine, 131–135, 137–140; in Boethius, 155–156; in Leibniz, 240–245, 247, 250, 313–314; in Rousseau, 285; in Kant's *Idea for a Universal History*, 290–291; in Spinoza, 313–314. *See also* Theodicy

Fallibility, human, in Leibniz, 312–313
Fatalism, 246
Fate: Stoic concept of, 74–75, 91, 149; in Boethius, 155; Christian, in Leibniz's *Theodicy*, 238–248. *See also* Necessity
Fates, 69
Fear, release from, 77
Fear of death: in Euripides' *Alcestis*, 21–26; Stoics and, 103–107, 125–128; Epictetus and, 114–124; Descartes and, 310
Feeling, in Rousseau, 283–284
Fittingness: in Leibniz, 240, 251; in Kant's *Idea for a Universal History*, 292–295
Flow of life, smooth, 97–109
Form, Platonic concept of, 140
Fortune: Zeus and, 69; in Machiavelli's *Prince*, 159; in Descartes, 303–304
Frederick and Elizabeth of Bohemia, 160–163
Freedom, human, 9; Stoics and, 96–97, 123–124; Epictetus and, 111, 113; in Plotinus, 133; in Augustine, 151; in medieval and Renaissance thought, 152–159; in Spinoza, 208–210; in Leibniz, 245–246. *See also* Freedom and necessity; Necessity
Freedom and necessity: in Augustine, 147–149; Spinoza and, 200–210, 227–234; Stoic view of, 201–202; Descartes and, 202; in Leibniz's *Theodicy*, 238–239; in Leibniz, 240–241, 249
Free will. *See* Will, divine; Will, human
French Revolution, 297
Friendship. *See* Intellectual friendship
Future contingents, debate over, 153
Future history, in Kant's *Idea for a Universal History*, 295–297

Gellius, Aulus, 96, 202
Gender: and embodiment, 171–179; and
    Cartesian detachment, 179–181; and
    superstition, 230
Gender roles, in Euripides' *Iphigenia at
    Aulis,* 328–329
Generosity, in Descartes, 304–305
Gesonides, 206–207
Gibbon, Edward, *Decline and Fall of the Ro-
    man Empire,* 124
Gods, ancient, 36–37; in Euripides,
    17–19, 21–22, 26–29, 36–44; in
    Plato's *Timaeus,* 64; Epicureans and,
    77–79, 82–83; Stoics and, 82, 84–85,
    89; Epictetus and, 118–119. *See also
    names of deities*
Good life: Stoic ideal of, 98–109; Des-
    cartes on, 168–170
Grace, divine, in Augustine, 144–145
Graves, Robert, 69–70
Greek comedy, 46–47
Greek tragedy, 14–19, 36, 46. *See also*
    Euripides
Grief, 307–308; in Euripides' *Alcestis,*
    22–24, 26–27, 33–34; Epictetus and,
    121–123; Descartes on, 163–165,
    177–179, 189

Happiness, Stoic concept of, 97–98. *See
    also* Joy
Hegel, G. W. F., 2, 11, 13, 298–301;
    Encyclopaedia of the Philosophical Sciences,
    299
Helen of Troy. *See* Euripides, *Helen*
Hera, 69
Heracles, in Euripides' *Alcestis,* 26–30
Heraclitus, 16–18, 45, 53, 56, 72
Hermes, 69
History: Rousseau's conception of,
    279–287; in Kant's *Idea for a Universal
    History,* 287–297
Homer, 99
Hospitality, in Euripides' *Alcestis,* 26–27,
    29–31
Hughes, Ted, version of Euripides' *Alces-
    tis,* 29–30, 32, 34–36

Human body, Lucretius's view of, 78. *See
    also* Bodily awareness, in Descartes;
    Embodiment, in Descartes
Human imperfection, 140; Augustine
    and, 130–131; in Spinoza, 228; in
    Leibniz, 244–245
Hume, David, 10–11, 230, 257–278,
    286; *Dialogues concerning Natural Religion,*
    65, 257–261, 265–274; letter to
    Hutcheson, 259; *A Treatise of Human Na-
    ture,* 259–261; *My Own Life,* 259–261;
    *An Inquiry concerning Human Understand-
    ing,* 261, 263–264; *Political Discourses,*
    266; death of, 274–278; "On Suicide,"
    277–278
Hypothetical necessity, 245–246

Illusion: in Euripides' *Helen,* 37–39; in
    Euripides' *Bacchae,* 49–51
Imagination, 3–4; in Spinoza, 232;
    in Kant's *Idea for a Universal History,*
    292–296. *See also* Social imaginary
Imitation, in Plato's *Timaeus,* 66
Impressions, right use of, 112–113
Impulse, Stoic concept of, 91–94, 96
Indifferents, Stoic concept of, 95,
    115–116
Individual, in Kant, 318–319
Intellectual friendship, 196–198; of
    Descartes and Princess Elisabeth,
    165–185; of Spinoza and Oldenburg,
    215–234
Intelligentia extramundana (Leibniz), 247
Interconnection, Leibniz's concept of,
    242, 244, 246–248. *See also* Part-whole
    relation
Invitation, hospitality of, 30
Israel, Jonathan, 223, 237

Jesuits, 260–261
Jewish tradition, Spinoza and, 206–
    207
Joy: Stoic concept of, 112–113; Spinoza's
    concept of, 212, 214
Judaism, Spinoza and, 192–200. *See also*
    Religion, issues of

Judgment, human, in living with uncertainty, 39–42
Justice, divine, 138–147

Kant, Immanuel, 2, 11, 287–298; *Idea for a Universal History with a Cosmopolitan Purpose*, 287–297, 318; and Rousseau, 287–288; and Leibniz, 289, 291; *What Is Enlightenment?* 291; *The Contest of Faculties*, 297; *Critique of Judgement*, 318

Leibniz, Gottfried, 2, 9–11, 62, 224, 235–252, 310–315; *Theodicy*, 238–252; and Spinoza, 241, 248–252; *Discourse on Metaphysics*, 245; and Descartes, 249; and Kant, 289, 291; and Hegel, 299
Light, Augustine's treatment of, 130
Lisbon earthquake of 1755, 252–255
Long, A. A., 97
Loss. *See* Grief
Love: in Augustine's *City of God*, 150–151; Descartes on, 185–189
Lucas, Jean Maximilien, 193
Lucretius, *De Rerum Natura*, 77–79
Lust, in myths of Zeus, 69

Machiavelli, Niccolò, 157–159
Madness, in Euripides' *Bacchae*, 47–51, 53–54
Maimonides, 206–207
Manicheism, 131–132
Marcus Aurelius, *Meditations*, 124–128, 247
Mathematical order, in Leibniz, 241–242
Medea, 121
Medicine: and changing human expectations, 24; philosophy as, 168
Metaphors: Heraclitean, 16–17; Platonic, 63, 134; wheel of Fortune, 70; dog tied to cart (Stoic), 96, 104; smooth flow (Stoic), 97–109; concentric circles (Stoic), 100, 103; water flow (Stoic), 107; visitors at the fair (Stoic), 109–114; runaway slave (Stoic), 114–115; leaving the festival (Stoic), 116, 123; Captain's call (Stoic),

122; mosaic pavement (Augustine), 137, 139; river of fortune (Machiavelli), 158–159; domestic enemies (Descartes), 174–177; theater as practice for detachment (Descartes), 175; moving stone (Spinoza), 208–209; wind of thought (Arendt), 322
Metaphysical evil, in Leibniz, 243
Metis, 68
Mind-body separation, in Descartes, 167–168
Mind-body union, in Descartes, 169–170
Miracles, Hume's treatment of, 260–263
Modernity, in Hegel, 300
Moral certainty: in Euripides' *Bacchae*, 48–51; in correspondence between Descartes and Elisabeth, 180–181
Moral evil, in Leibniz, 243
Moral luck, 315–317
Moral purpose, in Epictetus, 110–111, 113. *See also* Purpose of Nature, in Kant's *Idea for a Universal History*
Moral split, between divine and human realms, 42–45
Mortality in Euripides' *Alcestis*, 19–36. *See also* Death
Multiple voices: in Euripides' *Helen*, 41–42; in Euripides' *Orestes*, 44; in Euripides' *Bacchae*, 55–56

Nadler, Steven, 206–207, 224
Nagel, Thomas, 315–317
Nature: Rousseauian state of, 279, 281–282; Kantian purpose of, 289–292
Nature cycles, and myths of Zeus, 70
Necessity, 10, 20, 34–35, 55, 74, 306; acceptance of, 20–21, 96–97; in Euripides, 39, 324–331; in Plato's *Timaeus*, 61–63; as Ananke, 62; Zeus and, 69, 76; Epicurean rejection of, 77, 79–80; in Stoic thought, 90–98, 104–105, 107–109, 111–112, 117–119, 212; in Epictetus, 110; in Augustine, 147–149; in Descartes, 179–181, 302–305; in

Necessity (*continued*)
  Spinoza, 195–196, 306; in Hegel,
  299. *See also* Freedom and necessity;
  Mortality in Euripides' *Alcestis*
Nemesis (Leda), 70
Nemesius, 93
Neoplatonism, 131–134; Augustine and,
  130–131, 135–136, 140–141; Boethius
  and, 154
Neo-Stoicism, 168, 200, 211
Noble death, in Euripides' *Iphigenia at
  Aulis*, 327–331
Notion, in Hegel, 299

O'Donnell, James, 151–152
Oekeinosis, 92. *See also* Appropriation
Old age: in Euripides' *Alcestis*, 24–25; in
  Euripides' *Bacchae*, 46–47
Oldenburg, Henry, 10; correspondence
  with Spinoza, 215–234
Oman, Carola, 161–162, 190
Openness to the unexpected, 321
Opposites, transformation of, in Eurip-
  ides' *Bacchae*, 46–56
Opposition, in Plotinus, 135
Optimism: in Leibniz, 251–252, 314–315;
  Voltaire and, 252–257; in Rousseau,
  281–282; in Kant, 295–297, 317–320
Order: in Augustine, 136–138; in Leib-
  niz, 241–242
Orestes. *See* Euripides, *Electra*; Euripides,
  Orestes
Origin story: Plato's *Timaeus* as, 56–57;
  Rousseau's *Discourse on the Origins of
  Inequality* as, 278–285; Kant's *Idea for a
  Universal History* as, 292–296

Part-whole relation: in Augustine, 137,
  140; in Plotinus, 139–140; in Descartes, 185–189; in Spinoza, 204, 209,
  220–221
Passions: in Descartes, 9–10, 163–166,
  171–189, 302–335; in Spinoza, 9–10;
  in Euripides, 19. *See also* Emotion;
  Remedy for the passions
Pelagians, 144

Pentheus. *See* Euripides, *Bacchae*
Performance, in Plato's *Timaeus*, 58–60
"Perhaps," the, in Derrida, 320–321
Pessimism, Voltaire and, 257
Philodemus, 76
Philosophical writing, literary dimen-
  sions of, 3–4; in Plato's *Timaeus*, 57–58,
  65–66; in Seneca, 99; in Augustine's
  De Ordine, 136; in Spinoza, 194; in
  Voltaire, 257; in Hume's *Dialogues*,
  258–259, 265; in Kant's *Idea for a Uni-
  versal History*, 292–296
Philosophy, as figure in Boethius's *Conso-
  lation of Philosophy*, 154–156
Philosophy and theology, in Spinoza,
  219–221, 231–234
Physical evil, in Leibniz, 243. *See also* Evil,
  problem of
Physics, Epicurean, 77–78, 80
Pity, Voltaire and, 254, 257. *See also* Grief
Plato: *Republic*, 57–58; *Timaeus*, 57–67,
  72–73, 82, 88–89, 132–133, 155, 242,
  293; *Critias*, 58; *Theaetetus*, 100; *Laws*,
  132
Playfulness, and Stoic detachment, 117
Pleasure, 83, 106, Stoic concept of,
  97–98. *See also* Happiness; Joy
Plotinus, 140–141, 150, 155; *Enneads*,
  131–134, 137, 139
Plutarch, 75
Pollot, Alphonse, 163–165
Practical philosophy, Descartes and,
  168–189
Prayer, as acknowledgment of possibil-
  ity, 32–33
Probability: in Plato's *Timaeus*, 61, 64; in
  Hume, 262–265, 270–272
Progress, 2, 11; in Rousseau, 282,
  285–286; in Kant, 317–320
Prophecy, 37–38, 40
Proportion: in Plato's *Timaeus*, 65–66; in
  Hume, 263–264, 266–267
Providence: imaginative and emotional
  dimensions, 3–4; in Euripides, 56;
  in Plato's *Timaeus*, 63–67; Stoic
  conception of, 67–77, 87–88, 94–97;

Epicurean rejection of, 77–80; and divine justice, 138–140, 142–147; as Platonic Form, 141; Christianizing of, 148–150 (*see also* Augustine, Saint; Boethius, Anicius Manlius Severinus); and fortune, 152–159; in Descartes's remedy for the passions, 181–185; Spinoza's rejection of, 202–203, 206–207; particular and universal, 203–205; in Leibniz's *Theodicy,* 240–248; Hume's rejection of, 265; temporalization of, 280, 289–292; in Rousseau's *Emile,* 283–286; Kant's justification of, 296–297; modern absence of, 306–310

Purpose of Nature, in Kant's *Idea for a Universal History,* 289–292

Rational will, and detachment, 174–177

Reason, human: and impulse, 93; in Kant, 291–293, 317–318

Receiving principle (receptacle), in Plato's *Timaeus,* 61–63

Religion, issues of: Descartes and, 177–179; Spinoza's critique of, 214–234

Remedy for the passions: Descartes and, 163–166, 171–189, 302–305; Spinoza and, 210–214

Republic of Philosophers, 215–218, 231–232

Resemblance, in Euripides' *Alcestis,* 33–36

Reservation, Stoic concept of, 94–95

Responsibility, human, 7; in Euripides' *Bacchae,* 54–55; Epictetus on, 113; Spinoza on, 228; Voltaire on, 253–257; in absence of providence, 316–317

Rhea, 68

Rist, John, 150–151

Rousseau, Jean-Jacques, 253, 279–287; *Discourse on the Origins of Inequality,* 279–286, 288; *Emile,* 280, 283; *Julie, or the New Heloise,* 282; *The Social Contract,* 282; *Reveries of a Solitary Walker,* 286–287; and Kant, 287–288

Royal Society, 215–216

Rufus, Musonius, 109

Russell, Bertrand, 257

Secular, the, 5–6, 234

Sedley, D. N., 97

Seferis, 39

Self, modern, and ideas of providence, 6

Self-fulfillment, Descartes and, 180–182

Self-knowledge: and Stoic detachment, 117; and bodily awareness, 171; divine, 300

Self-preservation, in Plotinus, 135

Self-sacrifice, in Euripides' *Iphigenia at Aulis,* 324–331

Semblance, in Euripides' *Alcestis,* 33–36

Seneca, Lucius Annaeus, 92–93, 98–110; letters, 98–109; *On Providence,* 107–108; exile, 108–109; *De Vita Beata,* 168

Situated thinking, Augustine and, 145–146

Skepticism, 20; in Cicero's *On the Nature of the Gods,* 87–88; in Hume, 258–260, 265–274

Slavery, Epictetus and, 109, 111, 114–115

Smith, Adam, 275

Social contract, in Rousseau, 279

Social imaginary, 5–6

Socrates, 17; as figure in Plato's dilogues, 57–60

Socratic dialogue, 19

Sophists, 19

Sophocles, 15, 42

Soul's journey toward God, in Augustine, 141–142

Sphere, Stoics and, 82

Spinoza, Baruch de, 1, 9–10, 12, 150, 157, 159, 184, 192–234, 236–238, 306, 308; *Ethics,* 167, 194, 202, 204, 206, 209, 211–212, 214, 217, 220–222, 226, 232, 306, 313–314; and Cartesians, 182, 188, 210–214, 225, 227; expulsion from Jewish community, 192–200; correspondence, 197–200; *Commentary on Descartes's Principles,* 203; *Short Treatise on God, Man and His Well-Being,* 203;

Spinoza (*continued*)
　critique of religion, 214–234; *Theologi-*
　co-Political Treatise, 217, 221–
　227, 229, 231–233; letter to Boxel,
　230; and Leibniz, 241, 248–252;
　death of, 277
Spinozism, 308–310
Spontaneity, human: in Euripides' *Bac-*
　chae, 46–47, 53–55; in Leibniz, 246.
　See also Contingency; Hospitality, in
　Euripides' *Alcestis*
State of nature, in Rousseau, 279,
　281–282
Steadiness of purpose, as Stoic ideal,
　100–102
Stobaeus, 73
Stoicism, 7, 16, 18, 20, 44, 67–77,
　90–128; Epicureans and, 78–79,
　94; in Cicero's *On the Nature of the*
　Gods, 81–89; Augustine and, 135,
　146, 148–150; Descartes and, 168,
　185; Spinoza and, 200, 205–206,
　211–212, 220; Leibniz and, 239–240,
　242, 247–248; Hume and, 262, 266;
　Kant and, 292; Hegel and, 298. *See*
　also Chrysippus; Cleanthes; Epictetus;
　Marcus Aurelius; Seneca, Lucius An-
　naeus; Zeno
Stoicism, practical, 109–114, 120–124;
　Marcus Aurelius and, 124–128
Storytelling, in Plato's *Timaeus,* 58–61
Stranger's arrival (as appearance of
　divine), 46
Suffering, human: and divine justice,
　142–147; of children, 143–147; in
　Leibniz, 243–245, 251; in Voltaire's
　Candide, 252–257; in Hume, 270–271;
　in Kant's *Idea for a Universal History,*
　290–291; as "collateral damage," 313,
　316. *See also* Evil, problem of
Suicide: Seneca and, 108–109; Epictetus
　and, 123–124; Marcus Aurelius and,
　128
Superstition, Spinoza and, 230–231
Suspension of normal order, in Eurip-
　ides' *Alcestis,* 21–26

Swallowing/regurgitation, in myths of
　Zeus, 68–69
"Swerving" of atoms, 80
Synthesis: of classical and Christian
　thought, 152–159; Leibnizian,
　248–252

Taylor, Charles, 5–6; *Secular Age,* 322
Temporalization of providence, 280,
　289–292
Theater, Descartes and, 175
Theodicy: of Augustine, 132, 138–140;
　of Plotinus, 133–135; of Leibniz,
　235–252
Thirty Years' War, 160–163, 172
Thunderbolt as weapon of Zeus, 68,
　71
Time, flow of, 100, 102; in Augustine,
　146–147. *See also* History; Temporal-
　ization of providence
Time management, Descartes on,
　169–170
Titans, 68
Tolstoy, Leo, 31
Tranquillity, in Rousseau, 286–287
Transformation: in Euripides' *Bacchae,*
　51–54; of figure of Zeus, 67–77
Transience: in Marcus Aurelius,
　126–127; in Augustine, 146–147
Trojan War. *See under* Euripides
Truth: in Euripides' *Helen,* 37–42; in
　Euripides' *Bacchae,* 54–55; fiction in
　the service of, in Plato's *Timaeus,* 61;
　Spinoza's ideal of living for, 220–221;
　politics of, in Spinoza, 221–227
Tyche, 69–70

Uncertainty in divine-human relations,
　42–45
Universal reason, Stoic concept of,
　71–73, 84–85
Uranus, 68

Valla, Lorenzo, *De Libero Arbitrio,* 156
Van Blijenberg, William, 198–200
Visitation, hospitality of, 30

Voltaire (François-Marie Arouet), 10–11, 252–257; *Candide,* 252–257, 311; *Poem on the Disaster of Lisbon,* 253–254

Voluntas, Augustine's concept of, 147–148, 150–152. *See also* Will, human

War, futility of, 38–39
Wholeness, Seneca's emphasis on, 106. *See also* Part-whole relation
Will, divine, 20; in Spinoza, 204–206; in Leibniz, 240–241, 249. *See also* Freedom and necessity
Will, human, 11–12, 149; as locus of freedom, 8; Epicureans and, 80; Stoics and, 94, 104; in Augustine, 131; in Descartes, 179–181, 201–202, 209–210, 304–306; modern concept of, 316–317. *See also* Will, divine
William of Ockham, 156
Williams, Bernard, 2–3, 315–317; *Shame and Necessity,* 322
Wisdom, divine, in Leibniz, 240–241, 249
Wittgenstein, Ludwig, 209, 305
World-creature, in *Timaeus,* 64–65
World-soul, Platonic, 132–133

Zeno, 73, 96–97
Zeus, 7, 64, 67–77, 84, 111